Introduction to J++ (Version 6.0)

Applications and Applets

JDK 1.2 Compliant

Roy W. Goody
Mission College

Prentice Hall

Upper Saddle River, New Jersey   Columbus, Ohio

Library of Congress Cataloging-in-Publication Data

Goody, Roy W.
Introduction to Visual J++ version 6.0: applications and applets
/ Roy W. Goody.
p. cm.
ISBN 0-13-917899-6
1. Java (Computer program language) 2. Microsoft Visual J++.
I. Title.
QA76.73.J38G662 2000
005. 13 ' 3—DC21

Publisher: Charles E. Stewart, Jr
Copyeditor: Carol Mohr
Production Editor: Rachel Besen
Design Coordinator: Karrie Converse-Jones
Cover Designer: Mark Shumaker
Production Manager: Deidra M. Schwartz
Marketing Manager: Ben Leonard

This book was set in Times New Roman and was printed and bound by R.R. Donnelley & Sons Company. The cover was printed by Phoenix Color Corp.

Printed in the United States of America

10 9 8 7 6 5 4 3 2

ISBN: 0-13-917899-6

Prentice-Hall International (UK) Limited, *London*
Prentice-Hall of Australia Pty. Limited, *Sydney*
Prentice-Hall of Canada, Inc., *Toronto*
Prentice-Hall Hispanoamericana, S. A., *Mexico*
Prentice-Hall of India Private Limited, *New Delhi*
Prentice-Hall of Japan, Inc., *Tokyo*
Prentice-Hall (Singapore) Pte. Ltd., *Singapore*
Editora Prentice-Hall do Brasil, Ltda., *Rio de Janeiro*

To my parents, George and June, who continue to inspire me, even thought they are no longer with me.

Contents

Section II

GUI (Applet) Applications

Preface

The beautiful souls are they that are
universal, open, and ready for all things.
MONTAIGNE, 1580

Who should use this text?

Is this the right text for you? Any preface worth its salt should answer this question quickly. So here goes. This text is based on Microsoft's Visual J++, Version 6.0, with all demonstration programs compliant with the latest version of portable Java from Sun Microsystems (JDK 1.2). It is introductory in nature, aimed at those with little or no experience in object-oriented programming, but it does contain early chapters that are both an introduction to J++ and a review of the C language. It covers both conventional (*console*) and GUI (*Graphical User Interface*) applications, with all GUI applications based on Web-based applets. It is targeted at the college-level technology student, but offers enough "gentle" material for the technician and enough challenging material for the computer science, engineering, and advanced business student. Topics run the gamut from simple text output to file I/O to applet multithreading and animation. *However, what really sets this text apart from most is its laboratory-oriented approach. That is, it is both a theory text and a laboratory manual rolled into one.*

Interested? Then let's delve a little deeper into what this text is all about and who it is aimed at. First and foremost, this text takes dead aim at those with little or no previous programming experience, or whose programming experience is limited to the C language. To help the beginner, the writing style is conversational, and visual aids are used liberally. Furthermore, every chapter focuses on a specific, enjoyable, real-world project—each to be performed hands-on in a laboratory setting. The projects start simply and add new material in carefully measured incremental steps, always asking you to master one subject before advancing to the next and always building on what came before.

To help streamline the whole process, the two enclosed disks contain the source code and images for all the projects developed in this text. Although the text is aimed at J++/Explorer, all source programs will run under JDK/Netscape as well. After performing and analyzing each chapter's major project, you are invited to hone your skills from the list of exercises included with each chapter.

If all this sounds like you, then welcome aboard, for this text was written with you in mind. Even if your background includes a wealth of C programming experience, you will be at home within these pages—you will simply skim through the introductory chapters of Part 1.

What will you learn?

This text is based on Microsoft's Visual J++, Version 6.0 (known as VJ6). Using Version 6.0, we can satisfy a variety of programming needs: *console* applications with simple text output, *components* programs for Windows 98, *database* projects for Excel, and *browser applets* for the Internet. Will Java become *the* general-purpose programming language for today and tomorrow and a long time to come? Only time will tell.

Despite Java's broad-based appeal, this beginning text can't follow it into every nook and cranny of the vast programming landscape. We can't be all things to all people. Instead, we have singled out two areas for concentration: *console applications* and *browser applets*.

Non-GUI console applications were chosen because they give us the purest form of Java programming, without the distractions and special techniques required of fancier and more elaborate environments. Browser applets were chosen because...they are applets, and just about the hottest topic around. Besides, they give us a relatively painless entry into the wondrous world of the GUI—the basis of all modern windows-oriented programming.

Therefore, it should come as no surprise that this text is also divided into these two major sections: the console applications of Section I and the Java applets of Section II. Don't expect any dazzling displays and impressive interaction with the console projects of Section I; just expect to learn the fundamentals of Java...and isn't that enough? Then, once you have achieved a certain comfort level, it's time for your reward: applet GUIs, in Section II, with their breathtaking array of color, sound, text, interaction, and motion.

Web page design

Although Section II of this text includes a great deal of Web page design, its major purpose is to teach Java in a GUI environment. Those whose primary interest is Web page design might want to check out the many rapid development tools on the market, such as Microsoft's *Front Page* or Macromedia's *Dream Weaver*. With such design aids it's possible to create professional-looking Web pages without writing a single line of code. Again, the emphasis of this text is on the Java programming language in both GUI and non-GUI environments.

What is Java?

On May 23, 1995, Java was announced to the world. Now, just a few years later, the Java language has become a true phenomenon. Why? What is so special about Java? In a word: the *Internet*! What the Internet desperately needed was an *object-oriented* programming language that could reliably and safely send executable files (called *applets*) to the four corners of the world. Quite simply, Java was at the right place at the right time. If the Internet is the Gutenberg press of our time, then Java is the paper and ink.

By most accounts, J++ is considered just as powerful as its big brother, the venerable C++ language—but it is much easier to write and to maintain. Add to this its much touted ability as an *interpreted*, *portable* language to run on any machine that implements the *Java Virtual Machine* (JVM) software, and its ability to pass bite-size chunks of Java code about the Internet with the greatest of ease, and you have a winning combination.

Oh, and did I mention that Java is also *reusable* (classes will work anywhere), *maintainable* (easily modified), *robust* (resists errors), *scaleable* (easily expanded), *multithreaded* (simultaneous tasks), *dynamic* (classes loaded at run time), *distributed* (network supporting), and *secure* (resists viruses)?

Finally, Java offers a number of more technical improvements, such as the use of *references* over *pointers* and the removal of the *struct* data type. References in particular exemplify its "keep-the-good and throw-out-the-bad" philosophy. Why? Because pointers are notorious for planting intractable bugs in a program. Of course, Java has room for improvement (such as I/O), but it is still an infant language. As it matures and adapts, will it live up to its promises and expectations? Only time will tell.

Prerequisites

This text has no prerequisites. However, your background should include at least a cursory knowledge of C or C++. If you are completely new to programming, Chapters 2, 3, and 4 include a great deal of background material on C. Because we can't repeat an entire C text here, it might be helpful for some to have an introductory text on C close at hand.

The software

Visual J++ 6.0 (VJ6) comes in two editions: Standard and Professional. The scaled-down Standard version offers all the power needed by this text. However, if your future plans include database client/server applications for Windows and the Web, perhaps you should opt for the Professional version. Microsoft Corporation shows every intention of making their J++ software available at an attractive and competitive price. Be sure to watch for special academic versions and site licenses.

When writing the GUI applications of Section II, VJ6 gives us the choice of the original AWT (*Abstract Windows ToolKit*) package or the newer WFC (*Windows Foundation Classes*) package. This text uses the simpler AWT because this package of classes is ideally suited for the beginning student, and its use results in fully portable code that runs on any *Java Virtual Machine* (JVM). The WFC, on the other hand, is optimized for Windows applications and won't produce portable code.

To install the software, simply activate the CD-ROM and follow the directions. After installation, you may wish to install the shortcut J++ icon on the desktop:

To place such an icon on the desktop, bring up the *Exploring* window (**CLICKR** on *Start*, **Explore**). Expand the *Windows*, *Start Menu*, and *Programs* folders. Open (**CLICKL**) the *Microsoft Visual J++ 6.0* folder. Click and drag the icon to the exposed desktop.

That's it; the rest is up to you. Good luck and good programming.

Roy W. Goody

As this text goes to press, the future of Visual J++ rests in part on contract disputes with Sun Microsystems and a possible antitrust case with the Justice Department. Will there be one universal ("pure") form of Java patterned after Sun's JDK (*Java Development Kit*), or will Microsoft have its own version?

Until the dust settles, we feel it is best to be compliant with the latest release of JDK (Version 1.2). To achieve this, we have based all the demonstration programs of this text on the standard Java Core API; we have avoided all Microsoft extensions (WFC, J/Direct, etc); and we have made several JDK 1.2 modifications. *Therefore, all the demonstration programs of this text are fully JDK 1.2 compliant.*

Explorer Version 4.0 comes packaged with J++ version 6.0. Recently Microsoft released Explorer Version 5.0. Either Version 4.0 or 5.0 will fully support the applets of Section II.

Introduction

A Few Things You Should Know Before We Begin

You should know:

- *The development sequence*
- *The top-down structured design philosophy*
- *The meaning of the word "object"*

What is: The *Development Sequence*?

All the projects developed within this text will follow a conventional five-step development process:

1. Define the project
2. Develop the project
3. Write the code
4. Execute the program
5. Debug and modify the project

Step one (*project definition*) will give a short, concise overview statement about the purpose and goal of the project.

Step two (*project development*) will consist of a structure chart, showing the hierarchy of modules chosen for the project. Parameters may be included to show the flow of information between the modules. Sometimes, *pseudocode* is written within each module to show the program flow. (Pseudocode is an informal solution to a programming segment that is similar to a high-level language, but without the rules of syntax.)

Step three (*writing the code*) will turn to the computer for the first time and enter the formal program code for each module. Usually, each code module is compiled to check for and correct syntax errors.

Step four (*program execution*) will build and run the program, checking for proper operation. If simple and obvious logic errors occur, we return to step 3 and modify the program. If the logic errors are more involved and deep-routed, we move on to step five.

Step five (*debug and modify*) uses special techniques such as singlestepping and breakpointing to examine the program in detail in order to uncover and correct deeply hidden bugs. Also during step five, we have an opportunity to change and improve the program.

What is:
Top-down structured design?

Conventional programming languages (such as C), as well as the newer object-oriented languages (such as Java), follow to various degrees the *top-down structured design* paradigm. As diagrammed by Figure I.1, this widely accepted design philosophy is broken down into the *Structure Theorem* and *Modularization*.

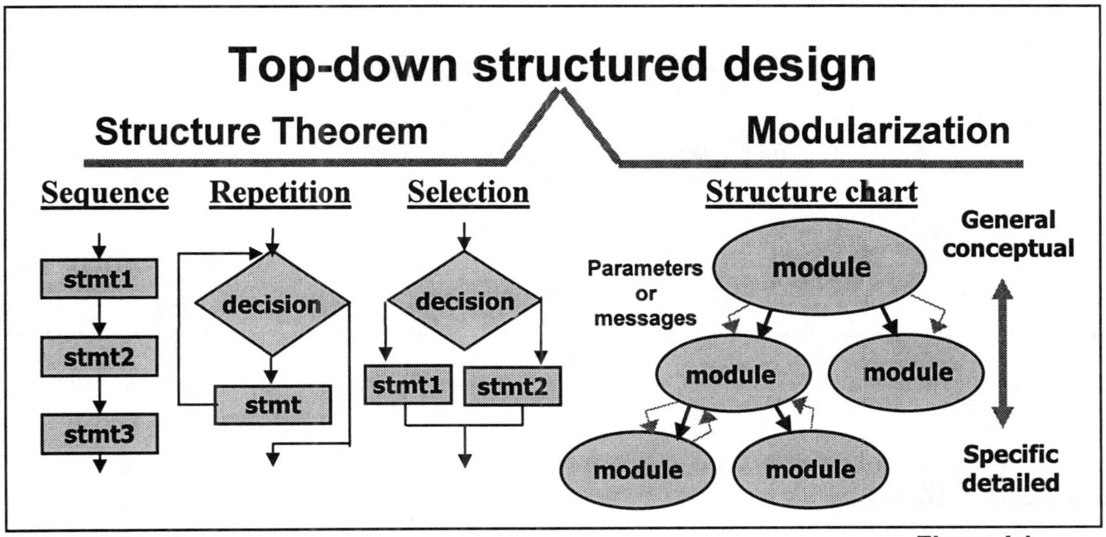

Figure I.1
Top-down structured design

The structure theorem

The structure theorem was formulated in the 1960s. It tells us that all programs, no matter now complex, can be constructed of single-entry, single-exit nested combinations of the three basic patterns of structured programming: *sequence*, *repetition*, and *selection*.

- *Sequence* means one statement after the other in order.
- *Repetition* means one or more statements placed in a loop and processed over and over a certain number of times.
- *Selection* means to choose one path among several possibilities (a fork in the road).

An example of the structure theorem is diagrammed by Figure I.2. Such a diagram might represent a typical Saturday morning activity. If I have money, I take the left-hand pathway and go to the mall. Within the mall, I spend money until I run out. If I do not have money, I take the right-hand pathway and simply eat breakfast and go for a walk. Note that all modules, regardless of their nesting level, have a single entry path and a single exit path.

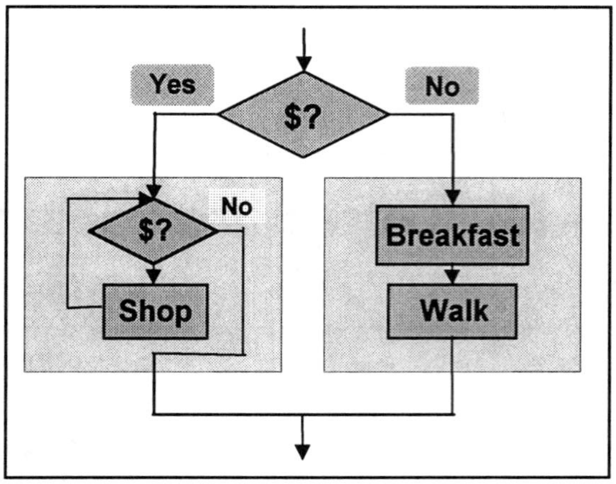

Figure I.2
Top-down structured design

Modularization

Modularization is the second major part of top-down structured design. It is the process of breaking down a large complex project into a hierarchy of modules, with the general and conceptual modules at the top and the specific and detailed modules at the bottom. The goal is for these modules to be relatively independent in order to support *parallel programming* (several programmers working on separate modules at the same time).

When diagrammed as in Figure I.1, this hierarchy of modules is known as a *structure chart.*

With the older, procedure-based programming languages (such as C), these modules hold the program code and are called *functions*. These functions are separate from the data, and are where the emphasis is placed. The data plays a secondary role. The bottom line? Maintenance and troubleshooting can be very difficult. A change or an error in one data structure can ripple though the entire program, affecting many functions.

With the newer OOP (object-oriented programming) languages (such as Java) these modules are called *classes*, with each class a self-contained structure that includes both functions (called *methods*) and their associated data (called *member variables*). In fact, with Java's classes, the emphasis resides with the data instead of the methods. The classic picture of Figure I.3 is a data bulls-eye, surrounded by methods that receive *messages* and operate upon the data. Since each class represents an independent, self-contained, "black box," a change or error within one class module will not influence or affect any other class module. With an OOP, our parallel programming goal is achieved.

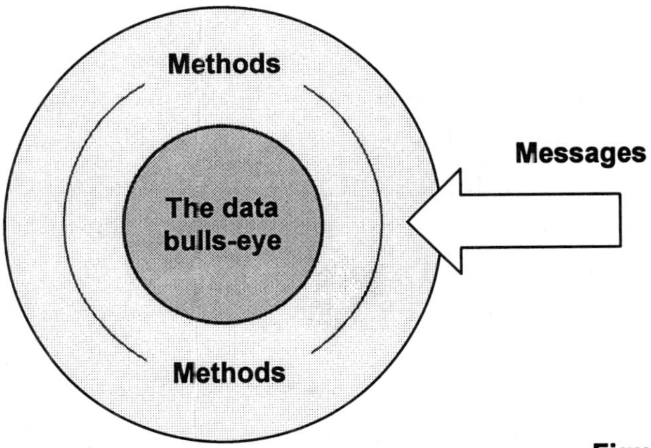

Figure I.3
The class structure

It is common practice to store both *built-in* modules (those available with the programming language) and *user-defined* modules (those created by the designer) in a library of modules until they are needed.

However, the biggest difference between C's procedures and Java's classes is that classes can produce (instantiate) *objects*.

What is: An *object*?

To mention a loved object...
is to invest that object with reality.
ANNE LINDBERGH, 1935

The purpose of object-oriented programming is to bring the familiarities of the real world into cyberspace.

Look around you. I mean, really look around you! What makes up this space where we live—this real world? The answer is, it is made up of *things* and *types of things*. There are things such as *my poodle*, *my shepherd*, or *my terrier*—all types of *dogs*. There are things such as *Venus* and *Mars* and *Jupiter*—all types of *planets*. And there are things such *my Ford*, *my Mercedes*, or *my Toyota*—all types of *cars*. And on and on it goes, everywhere we look. This is our world.

Clearly, *things* (like my poodle and my Ford) are real. Just as clearly, *types of things* (like dogs and cars) are not real; they are just generic representations that categorize things. It is only the *things* of our world that we can pet on the forehead, view through telescopes, or drive around the block.

Since things and types of things make up the world in which we live, is it also not completely natural that we should bring this same paradigm into cyberspace? This is the motivation behind object-oriented programming. In cyberspace, types of things are known as *classes* and things are known as *objects*.

Cars and cyberspace

As a case in point, consider type of thing (class) *car*. When we hear the word *car*, it instantly brings to mind a number of characteristics common to all cars. These characteristics fall into two categories: *attributes* and *behaviors*. Attributes are the passive nouns, and behaviors are the active verbs. For example, all cars have such attributes as *color*, *engine rpm*, and *odometer reading*; and such behaviors as *start*, *accelerate*, and *turn*. However, at the generic class level none of these attributes or behaviors can be specified in any way. There is nothing real about the abstract term *car*.

Now consider Sam's *Mercedes*. Sam's Mercedes is in fact a specific instance of a car (an *object*), with exact and well-known attributes and behaviors. It has a specific color (silver), a specific engine rpm (5,020), and a specific odometer reading (45,672). Furthermore, it most certainly starts, accelerates, and turns. The same is true of Mary's Mustang: It also has unique and specific characteristics. As shown in Figure I.4, think of class *car* as a generic representation of all cars, and think of Sam's *Mercedes* and Mary's *Mustang* as real objects—something you can touch and hold...and drive.

Figure I.4
Classes and objects

It is useful to think of class *car* as a template—like a cookie cutter. Of course the template itself is not real. But, when it is used to stamp out unique copies of itself (Sam's *Mercedes* and Mary's *Mustang*), these named copies then become real objects, with specific attributes and behaviors.

In the classic case, think of objects *Mercedes* and *Mustang* as a self-contained "black box" entities, with their *behavior* receiving *messages* from the outside, which in turn operate upon their *attributes* and set, change, or return their *state*.

Objects in cyberspace

Okay, it's one thing to visualize a real touchable object like Sam's *Mercedes*, and to distinguish it from the abstract, generic term *car*. Now you're telling me to make the same distinction between various kinds of data stored in memory. How can anything stored in memory be a real object?

It can…with a little imagination. This is the one big philosophical hurdle associated with object-oriented programming (OOP). Yes indeed, from this point on, we must learn to think of certain types of data stored in memory as real objects—like my poodle, the planet Venus, and Mary's Mustang.

So, the question is, under what conditions do we take out our class "cookie cutter" and stamp out an object?

Objects are created in cyberspace when the logic and nature of the problem demands multiple instances of a class, each one unique, separate, and distinct.

Shared attributes and behaviors

Color, *odometer reading*, and *engine rpm* are clearly attributes (*member variables*) that are unique, separate, and distinct for each car object. However, what about attributes *time* and *date*?

There is certainly not a Sam time and a separate Mary time; there is only one time and it is shared by all. The same is true of today's date. To handle such generic shared items, Java gives us key word *static*. When an attribute or behavior is tagged static, there exists only one copy—shared by all classes and objects. When the time or date is changed (daylight savings time or leap year), it is changed for all.

In Chapters 1 though 5, we deal exclusively with the conventional programming world of generic shared (*static*) attributes and behavior. Beginning with Chapter 6, specific and unique objects will be added to the mix—and our view of programming will never again be the same.

Inheritance

Can you list all the attributes and behavior that might belong to class *car*? The problem is, the list could easily be thousands of items long. Furthermore, if we created a class called *bicycle*, many of these attributes and behavior would be common to both—giving us a complex and redundant system. The solution is to arrange the classes in the *inheritance hierarchy* of Figure I.5.

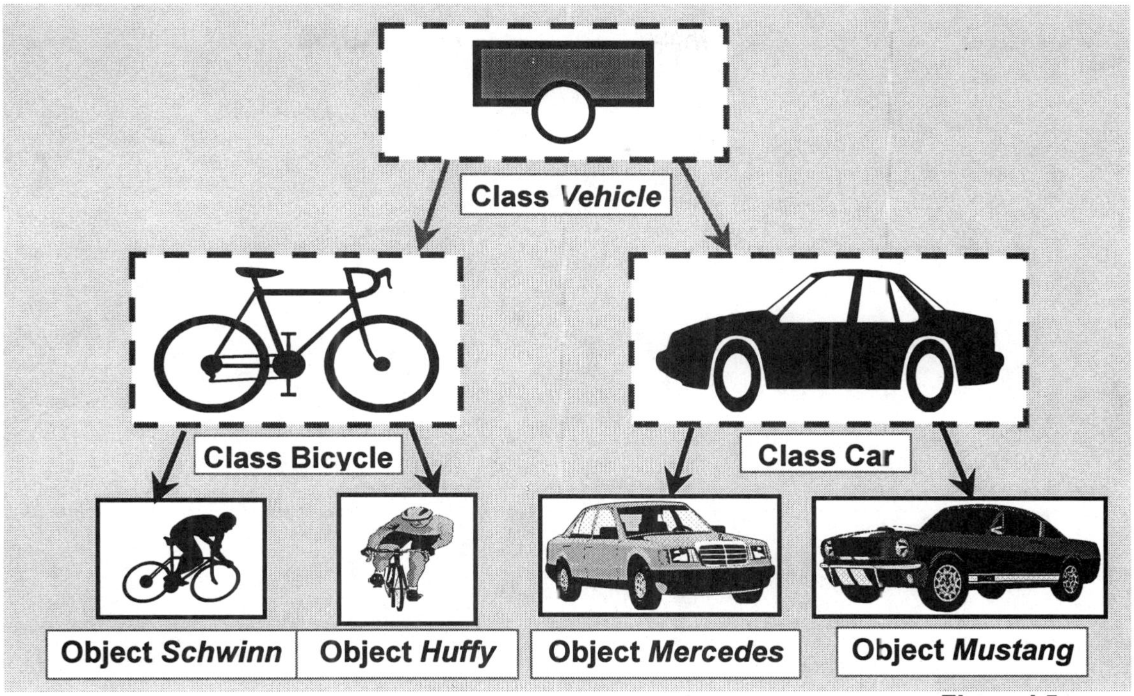

Figure I.5
Inheritance hierarchy

That is, all the attributes and behaviors that are common to both bicycles and cars are moved up into class *vehicle*. This includes such items as *color*, *odometer reading*, *accelerate*, and *turn*. The only attributes and behaviors that remain in class *car* are those specific to motor vehicles (*engine rpm* and *start*). The net result: Class *car* is greatly simplified.

In OOP terms, we say that both classes *bicycle* and *car* inherit the common attributes and behaviors belonging to class *vehicle*. Carrying the whole arrangement one step further, many of the attributes and behaviors of class *vehicle* can in turn be moved into a still higher level class (*transportation*?) that includes all forms of travel. *Sub*class *car* would then inherit all the attributes and behavior of both *super*classes *vehicle* and *transportation*. If you extend this idea to all the dozens of built-in classes, then it becomes clear that the entire Java Core API is one vast inheritance hierarchy.

We could say a lot more about classes, objects, data members, methods, static tags, messages, and inheritance here, but that would not be in keeping with the stated "hands-on" philosophy of this text.

So…let's get started.

Section I

Stand-Alone (Console) Applications

Section I of this text introduces stand-alone programs called *console applications* and concentrates on J++ fundamentals.

The lessons are pure unfettered Java: Output is simple ASCII characters in the text mode, and all input is by way of the keyboard. No windows, mouse or other GUI (*Graphical User Interface*) techniques are used.

Part 1
The Fundamental Structures of J++

The four chapters of Part 1 are presented primarily as an introduction to the development environment (*Visual Studio 6.0*) and the most basic J++ structures. Because Java's syntax is derived from the C language, a review of C is naturally included.

To help us focus on the basic structures of the J++/C language, no class objects are created in Part 1. This means that all Part 1 programs are built of one-copy-only things that are shared.

If you are quite familiar with the C language, you may wish to skim these early chapters. But don't skip them entirely, because some very important J++ and Visual Studio concepts are introduced.

CHAPTER

1

Project Hello World

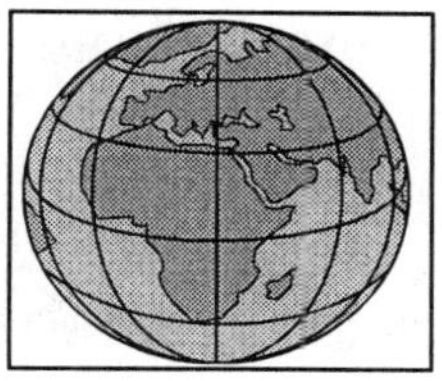

The *Main* Method and Visual Studio 6.0

Objectives

- *To use the Development Environment (Visual Studio 6.0)*
- *To execute the "Hello World" stand-alone application*
- *To introduce the debugging feature of J++*

Discussion

In keeping with time-honored tradition, our very first project is the classic "Hello World" routine, in which the simple greeting *Hello World* is written to the screen. By keeping the code simple, we are better able to concentrate on the step-by-step processes that we will follow in this and all future chapters.

The primary purpose of this chapter is to introduce Microsoft's powerful *Visual Studio 6.0.* It's the same development package used by other Microsoft programming languages, such as C and C++. It's promoted as an *Integrated Development Environment* (IDE) that will run under any present or future version of Windows or Windows NT. This latest 6.0 version goes a long way towards giving us the ability to design, write, execute, and troubleshoot our Java programs with an ease and efficiency never before possible. As future versions of J++ are released, the IDE is sure to be improved and updated.

A gentle start

A typical J++ program consists of a hierarchy of multiple built-in and user-defined classes, each with multiple data members and methods, with certain select classes generating objects. In other words, a large and complex program. The opposite, however, is true of this first chapter. Project *HelloWorld* scales things down to the bare minimum. We use only two classes: a single static user-defined class and a single built-in class—objects are not part of the picture.

Solutions and projects

When using Java we don't just write *programs*, or even create *projects*—we develop *solutions*. As shown by the diagram of Figure 1.1, a solution is at the top of the hierarchy and consists of one or more *projects*. A project in turn contains one or more *packages*, each containing one or more *classes*, which hold one or more *methods*. This solution hierarchy is simply another sign of the times in which we live: We no longer write tiny little programs, we now create vast solutions involving multiple projects!

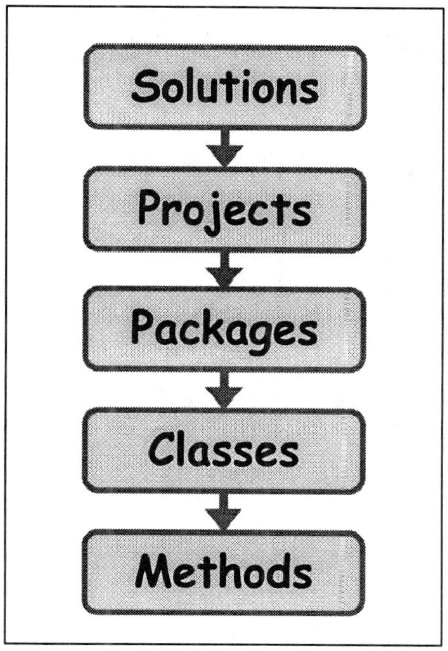

Figure 1.1
Java development hierarchy

In this text, each chapter will correspond to a solution, with each solution holding one or more projects.

Hands-On Procedure

1. Create a folder called *Java* on the C drive to hold all the solutions of this text. (Or, create a folder and pathway of your choice.)

To create pathway *C:\Java*: **CLICKR** on *Start*, **CLICKL** on *Explore* to bring up the *Exploring* dialog box. Select C:, **File**, **New**, **Folder**, enter *Java* in the *new folder* box, **CLICKL** anywhere else to accept the change, and exit the *Exploring* box when done.

CLICKL = click left
CLICKR = click right
DCLICKL = double click left.
BOLD TYPE = click left.

Step one—Project definition

2. Following the five-step process given in the introduction, our first step is to define the primary project within solution *Chapter1*.

> **Project *HelloWorld* will write "*Hello World*" to the console screen.**

Step two—Structure chart

3. After project definition, we next create the structure chart of Figure 1.2. Note that all five layers in the hierarchy are shown: *solution*, *project*, *package*, *class*, and *method*.

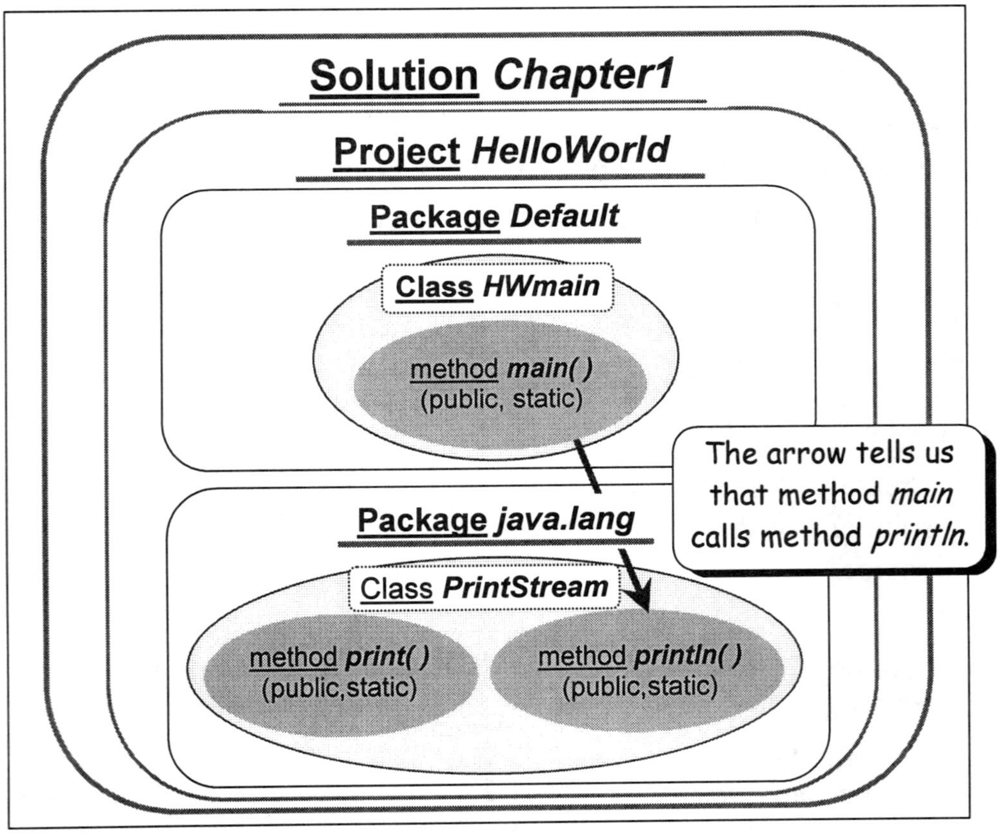

Figure 1.2
Full-layered structure chart

4. However, to avoid such unnecessary clutter, in the future our structure charts will show only the class and method layers of Figure 1.3—the layers of primary interest to the programmer.

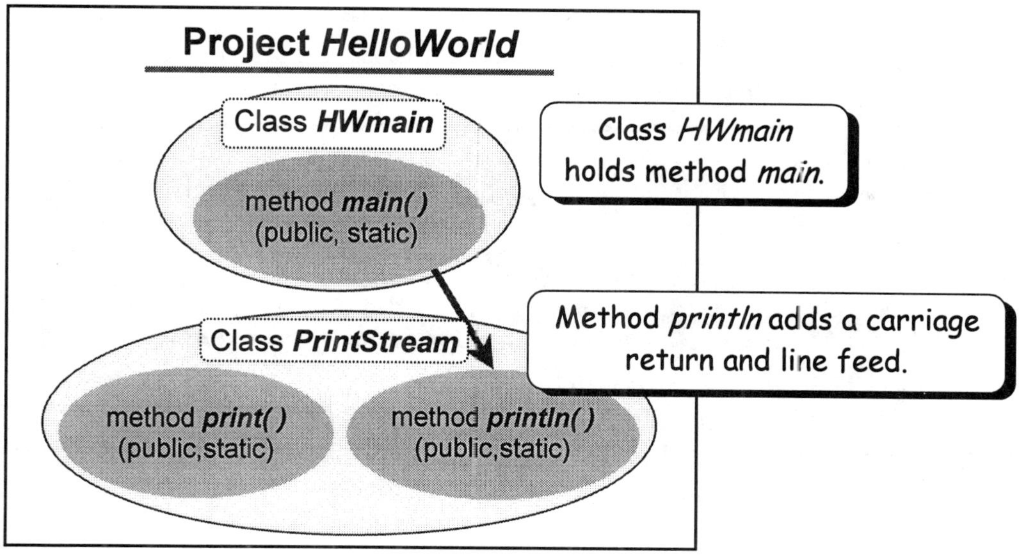

Figure 1.3
Simplified structure chart

Step three—Write the program

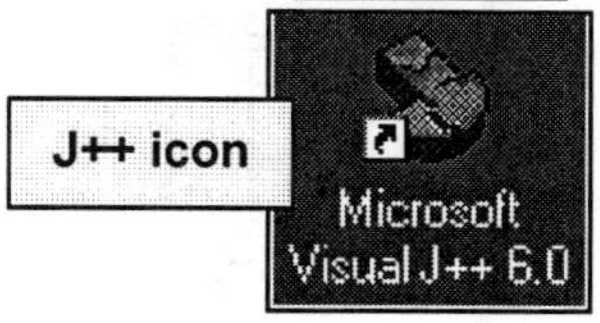

5. If the *Visual Studio 6.0* window (Figure 1.5) is already open, click the *Open Project* toolbar button and select the *New* tab (or **File, New Project**).

   If the *Visual Studio 6.0* window is not open, **DCLICKL** the J++ icon on the desktop. Or, if the icon is not present: **Start**, drag to *Programs*, drag to *Microsoft Visual J++ 6.0*, **Microsoft Visual J++ 6.0**. The *Visual Studio* window will open, overlaid by the *New Project* dialog box of Figure 1.4.

CLICKL = click left
CLICKR = click right
DCLICKL = double click left.
BOLD TYPE = click left.

6. Fill in the *New Project* dialog box as shown in Figure 1.4. (Selecting *Console Application* puts us in the stand-alone mode.)

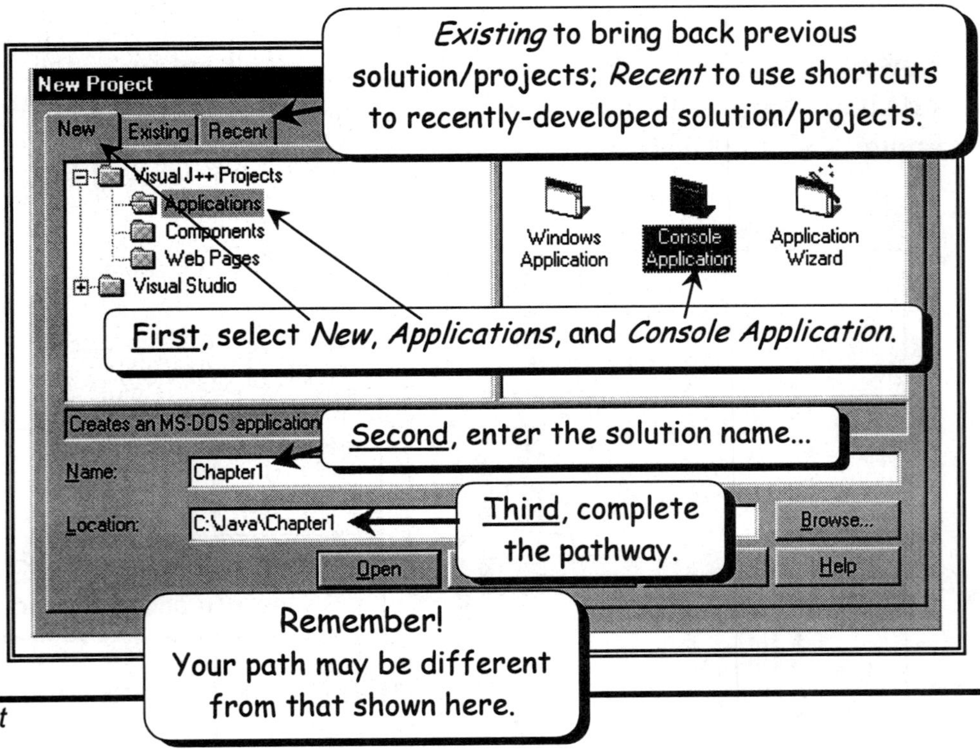

Figure 1.4
New Project dialog box

Solution or project?

When we create a brand new solution/project for the first time, should we enter the solution name (*Chapter1?*) or the project name (*HelloWorld*) in the *Name* field of the *New Project* dialog box?

The bottom line is this: When the process is over we should have created a folder with the solution name, and when that folder is opened, all the associated projects should be automatically available. The only way to accomplish this is to enter the solution name (as shown in Figure 1.4).

7. Click **Open** to bring up the *Visual Studio* window. Depending on past history (has anyone else used the software?), the initial window should resemble Figure 1.5.

8. Perhaps the most striking feature of the Visual Studio development environment is the rather imposing number of available windows and toolbars. In fact, as listed in Table 1.1, there are an amazing 19 windows and 14 toolbars that can be displayed at any given time.

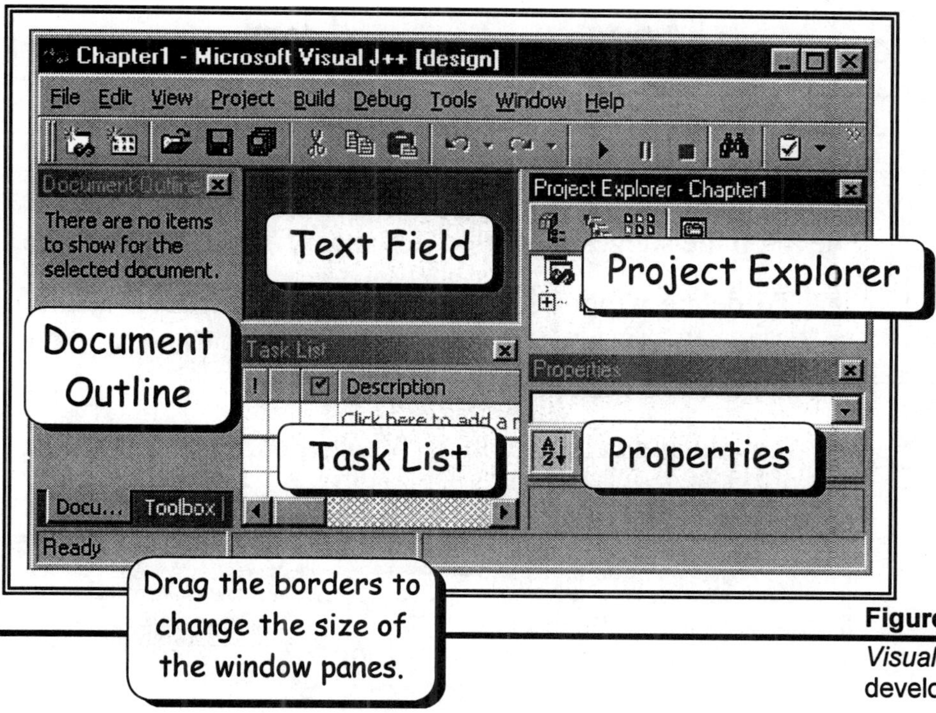

Figure 1.5
Visual Studio 6.0
development window

Windows: Regular	Windows: Debug	Toolbars
Project Explorer	Immediate	Build
Properties	Auto	Database Diagram
Toolbox	Locals	Debug
Task List	Watch	Design
Comp. Manager	Threads	Full Screen
Deployment Mgr.	Call Stack	HTML
Object Browser	Running Documents	Link View
Document Outline		Query
Output		Site Diagram
Data View		Source Control
Script Outline		Standard
J/Direct Call Builder		Table
		View
		Window UI

Some windows offer tabs, giving even more selections.

In this text, we will use only a select few of these windows and toolbars.

Table 1.1
Visual Studio 6.0
windows/toolbar table

Clearly, to avoid unnecessary clutter, we must display only those windows and toolbars of immediate interest.

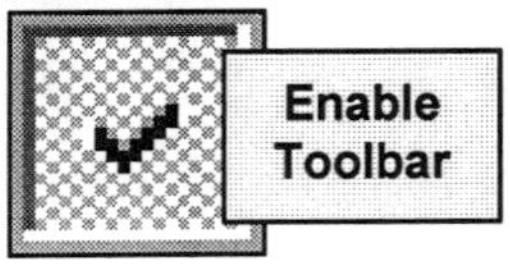

9. By adding and removing windows and toolbars as necessary, develop the suggested scaled-down configuration of Figure 1.6.
   - To delete windows, **CLICKL** on the *Exit* icon at the upper right of each window. To add windows, **View**, **CLICKL** on the desired window.
   - To add and delete toolbars, **View**, **Toolbars**, **CLICKL**.

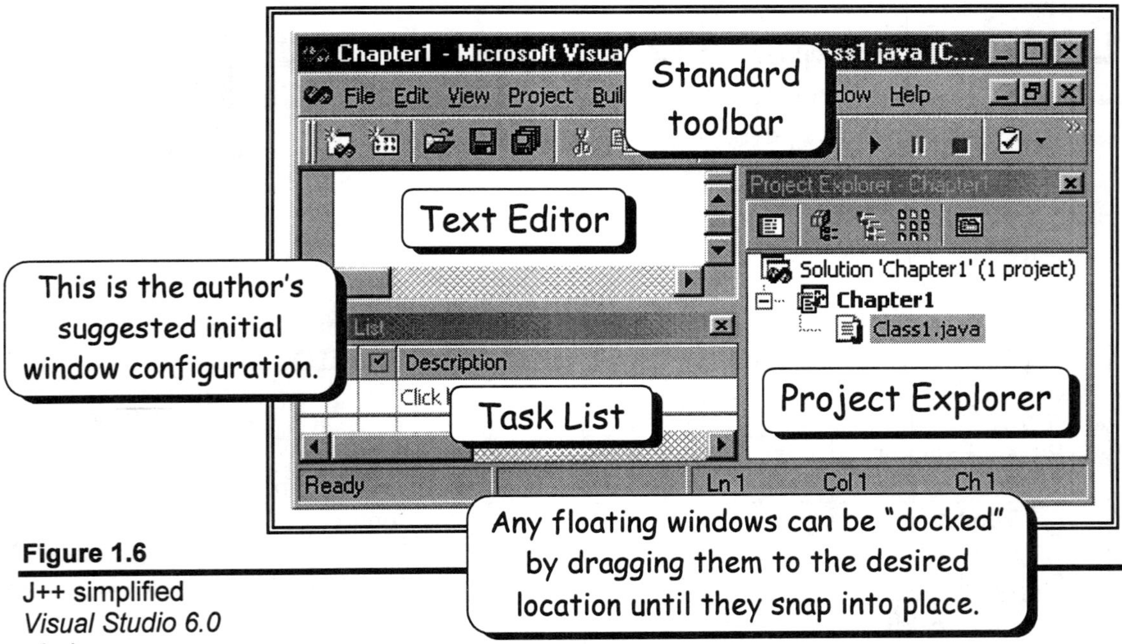

Figure 1.6
J++ simplified *Visual Studio 6.0* window

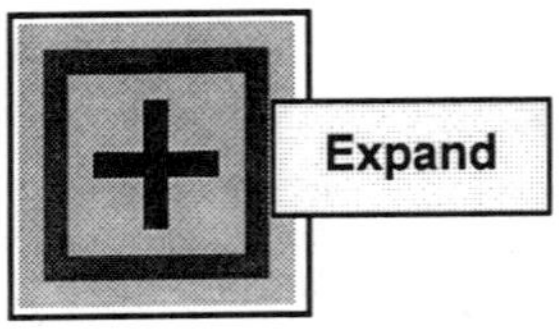

10. Look at the *Visual Studio* window and locate the *Project Explorer* windowpane of Figure 1.7. Be sure to fully expand the project tree by clicking on the "+" sign. As shown, the system has automatically generated a default class (*Class1.java*), within a default project (*Chapter1*), within the selected solution (*Chapter1*).

> To view the entire directory structure going back to the root directory, use the *Windows Explorer*.

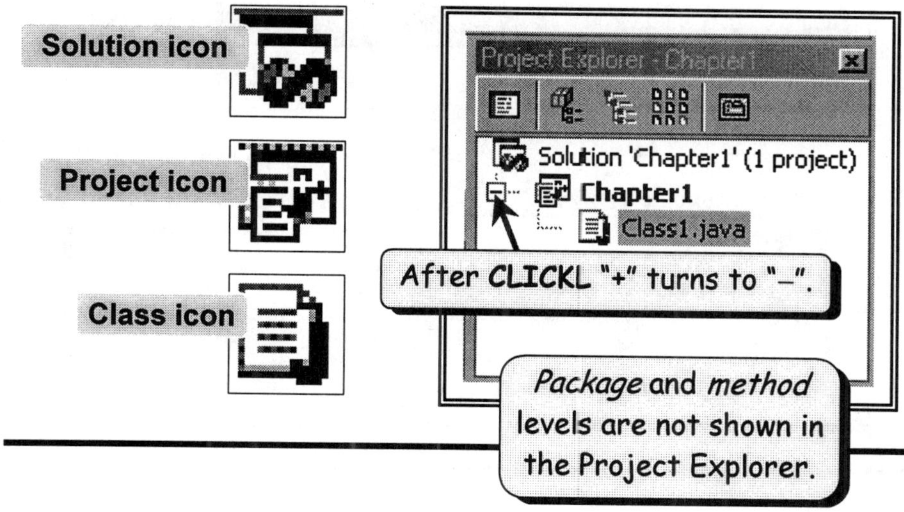

Figure 1.7
Project Explorer window pane

11. To make our programs more descriptive and readable, we will change the default names of both the project and the class. You are free to choose any names you wish, but to be consistent we recommend project name *HelloWorld* and class name *HWmain*.

> Be aware that class *Class1* can not be directly renamed. Instead, we must remove class *Class1* from the project and add new class *HWmain*.

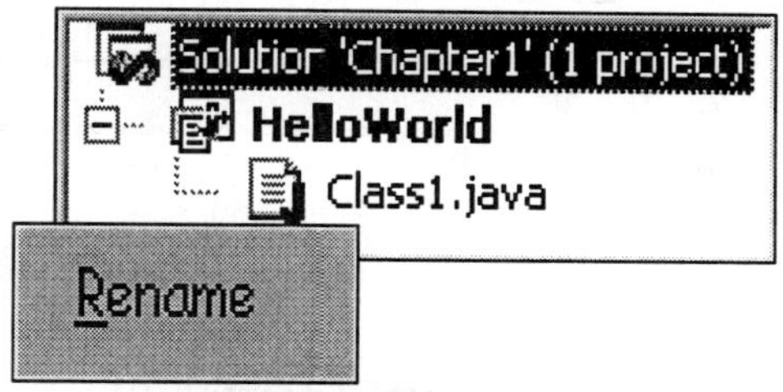

- To rename the project, **CLICKR** on project *Chapter1*, **Rename**, enter new name (*HelloWorld*), **CLICKL** anywhere within the *Project Explorer* window to accept the change.

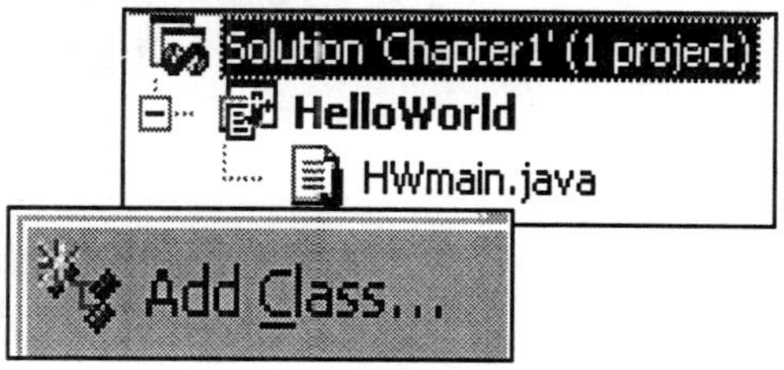

- To change the name of *Class1*: **CLICKR** on *Class1*, **Remove From Project**, **CLICKR** on project *HelloWorld*, **Add**, **AddClass**, **ClassMain**, enter *HWmain*, **Open**.

12. Whenever *Class1's* name is changed, we must also check the project's properties. This is accomplished by: **CLICKR** on project *HelloWorld*, **HelloWorld Properties** to bring up the *Properties* dialog box of Figure 1.8. If the class name (*HWmain*) is properly listed (and it should be), **OK**.

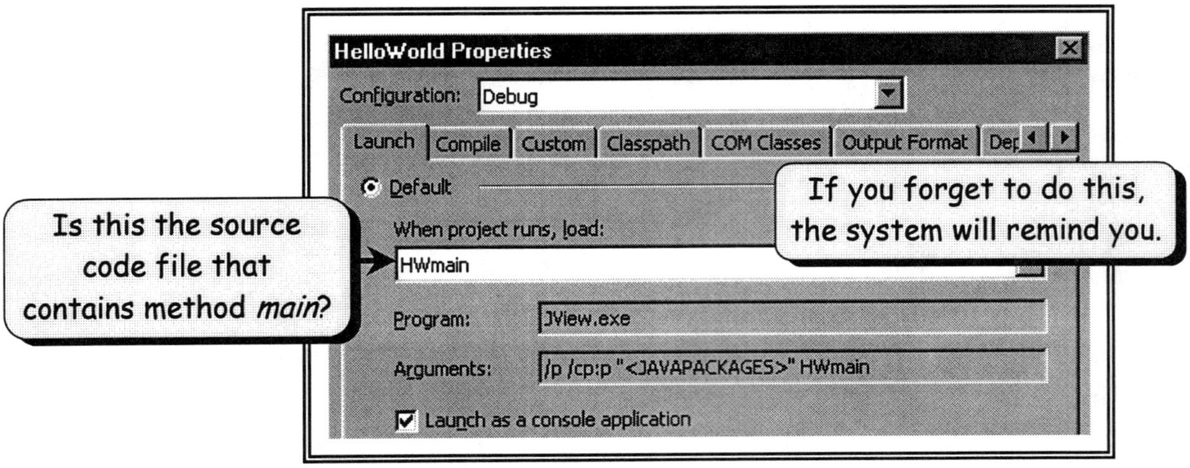

Figure 1.8
Properties Dialog box

Enter code

13. **DCLICKL** on *HWmain.java* (if necessary) to bring up the default code template of Figure 1.9 in the *Text Editor* window.

```
public class HWmain
{
      public static void main (String[ ] args){
      }
}
```

Moving the opening bracket here saves a line.

Placing "main" within the class name reminds us that this class holds method *main*.

Figure 1.9
HWmain default code template

14. To complete the final step, add the necessary "HelloWorld" code to method *main*—as shown in Figure 1.10.

```
// Class HWmain holds the main method.
public class HWmain
{
      public static void main (String[ ] args){
            System.out.println("Hello World");
      }
}
```

All text after "//" on any line is ignored by the compiler.

Spaces, tabs, and new lines are ignored by the compiler.

Figure 1.10
Completed program

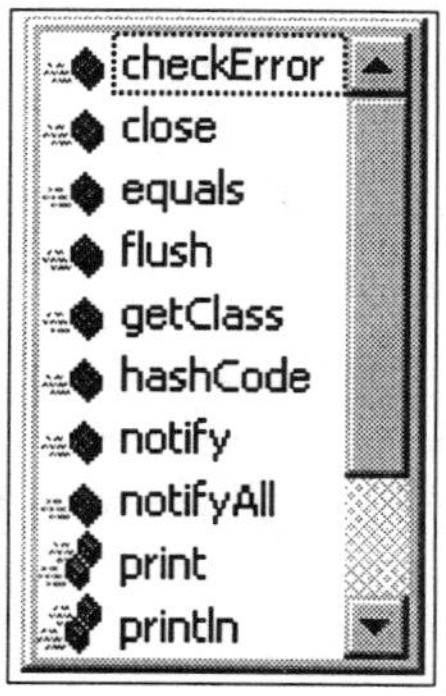

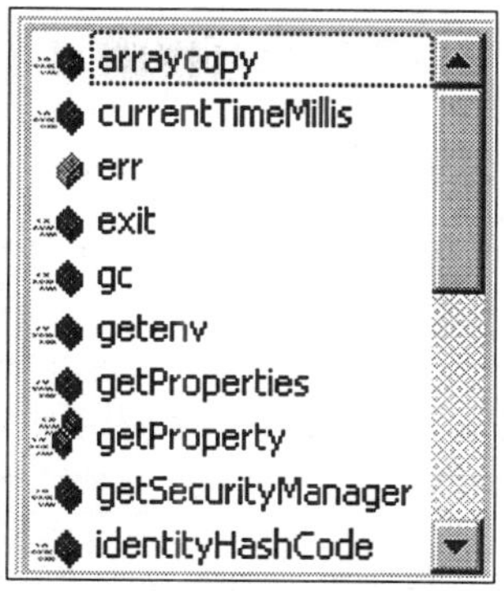

At various times during code entry, the "intelliSense" system automatically presents menu choices. To take advantage of this optional shortcut way of adding code, **DCLICKL** on any item.

ESPRESSO

This is our first "coffee break." They are titled "espresso" because they give a deeper, stronger, and more robust explanation of various topics. Since they are based on the hypertext concept, they can be skipped or skimmed as needed.

Can you explain all the terms of method *main*?

First of all, method *main* is always present for stand-alone applications and is the starting point for program execution. As with all methods, method *main* must be defined within a class.

Modifier *public* means that method *main* can be called from any program code that is outside the class. Modifier *static* means there is only one main method, it is shared, and it is accessible without first creating an object. Modifier *void* means the method does not return a value as a parameter.

String args[ ] defines an array of strings and provides a means for method *main* to receive input parameters from the command line.

System.out.println( ) writes a line of code to the output screen. *Out* (a field of class *System*) represents the "standard" output stream and is already open and ready to accept output data. Method *println* (a method of class *PrintStream*) sends its argument to the open stream.

Step four—Execute the program

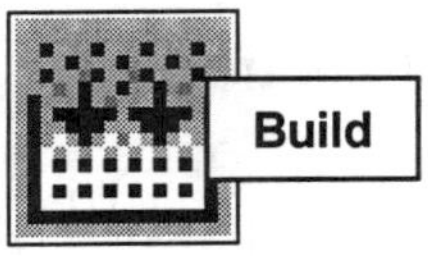

15. **Build**, **Build** to compile the files and check for syntax errors. (If errors are listed in the *Task List* window, make the necessary corrections.)

> **Build** complies the code and combines all necessary classes.

16. **CLICKL** on the *Start* toolbar button to execute the program. Did the following three events occur in sequence?

    a) The system enters the debug mode, and the output window (*JVIEW*) is created.

    b) String *Hello World* is printed (briefly!) to the screen, as shown in Figure 1.11. (If you are irritated by how quickly the screen output came and went, read on.)

    c) The output window is automatically closed, and the system exits the debug mode.

Figure 1.11
Output file (jview.exe)

17. Modify the code as shown below and predict what will be printed to the screen. (Were your predictions correct?)

```
System.out.print("Hello");
System.out.println(" World");
```

> Reminder: *print* leaves the cursor at the end of the line.

ESPRESSO

Why do mice have two buttons?

Did you notice that your mouse has a right button? If you like shortcuts, you'll like that right button. Here's what you should do to help develop its magic powers:

First, **CLICKR** (click right) anywhere within the toolbar area and note that we have a shortcut way of bringing up the toolbar menu. If you wish, **CLICKL** to enable/disable each toolbar until you are generally familiar with its overall function and appearance. (When done, enable only the **Standard** toolbar.)

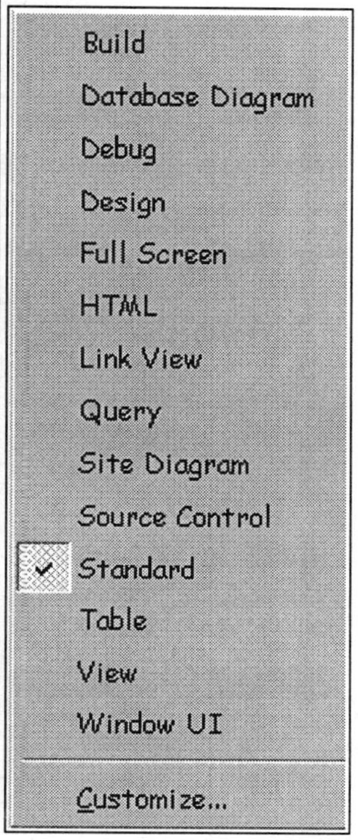

Next, **CLICKR** within any window (such as the *Project Explorer* window) and note the small "docking" menu that comes up. As shown, all windows are docked (locked in place and move in unison with surrounding windows) by default. **DCLICKL** on the colored title bar at the top of the Project Explorer window and note that the window "floats," and can be then dragged to anywhere on the Environment window. Drag the window to the far right of the screen until in snaps back in place. If you *Hide* a window, it can be brought back via the **View** menu selection.

Suggestion

Select any block of code and move the cursor over the selected code. **CLICKR** and note the "mini-menu" that comes up. Experiment with *Cut*, *Copy*, *Delete*, and *Paste* until you can quickly and easily erase, copy, and relocate code.

Syntax error checking

> A program contains two kinds of errors: *syntax* and *logic*. Syntax errors are formal code violations such as spelling and punctuation. Logic errors are those made by the programmer which prevent the system from acting as expected. The compiler automatically checks for syntax errors, but can not help out with logic errors.

18. To see how the system reacts to a syntax error, remove the semicolon from the end of any *println* or *print* statement and re-build the program.

a) Did the *Task List* window strongly suggest that a semicolon was missing from a *println* statement?

Yes **No**

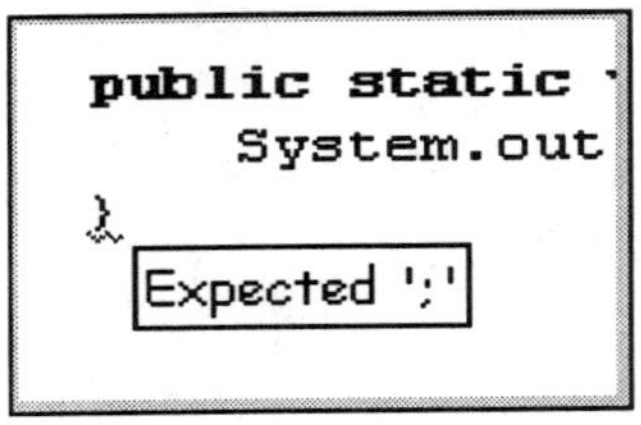

b) Did small "squiggles" appear on the screen at the expected locations of the errors. When we move the cursor over the red squiggle, were we given a hint?

Yes **No**

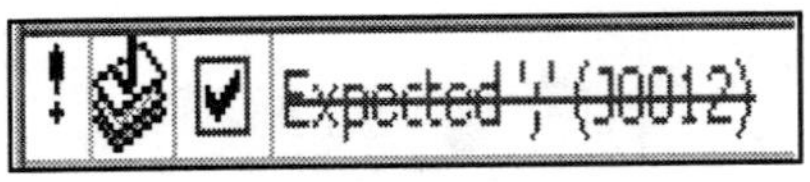

c) Correct the error by adding back the semicolon. As each item is corrected, can we click the check box and have the item crossed out?

Yes **No**

19. Re-build the program. This time, was the *Task List* empty?

Yes **No**

Step five—Debug and modify

Logic error checking

> All syntax errors have been eliminated. However, if the program does not execute as expected, then you have one or more logic errors.

The J++ Visual Studio offers two basic modes of operation: *Edit* (to enter the source program) and *Debug* (to execute and troubleshoot the program). To root out logic errors we enter the debug mode and make use of the *singlestep*, *breakpoint*, and *access variables* features.

In this chapter, we will concentrate on the singlestep feature. Singlestepping is controlled by way of the menu, the keyboard, or toolbar buttons.

- To enter the debug mode for singlestepping, press **F10**.
- To exit the debug mode, press **Shift/F5**.

20. Press F10 (*step over*) to enter the debug mode and bring up the debug window format of Figure 1.12. (Be sure to select the *Locals* tab of the *Variables* window.)

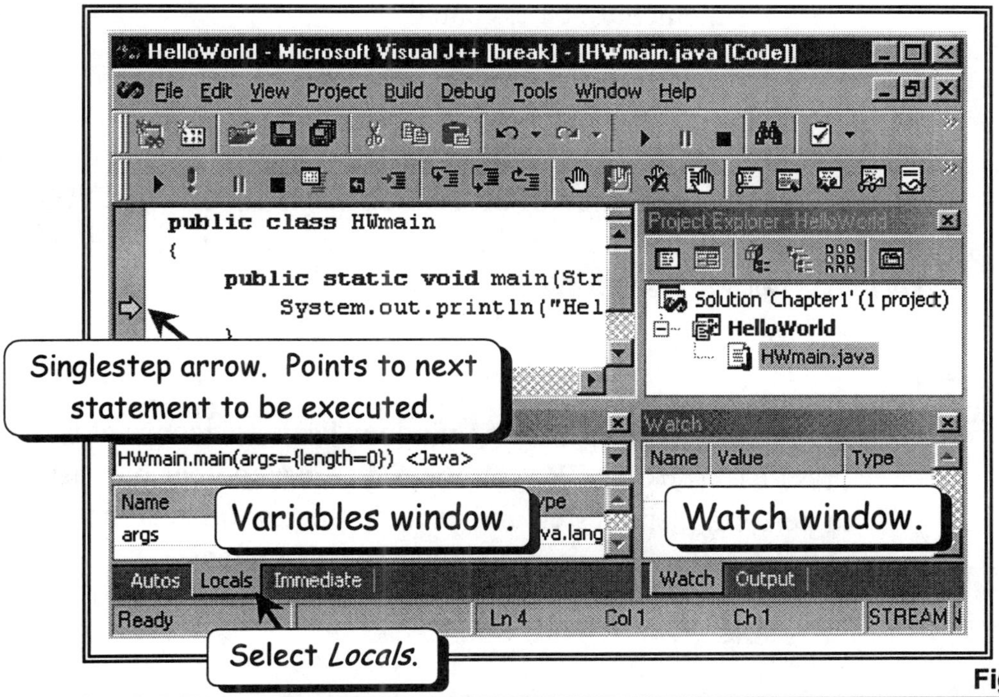

Figure 1.12
Singlestepping within the J++ *Debug* mode

Note that the debug toolbar shown below is automatically added to the toolbar array. (If not, **CLICKR** anywhere on the toolbar and enable *Debug*.) These debug toolbar buttons are an alternative to the menu or keyboard options.

21. When we enter the debug mode, are the following five windows automatically created? *Immediate*, *Autos*, *Locals*, *Watch*, *Output*. (Hint: Be sure to also count windows that can be selected by tabs.)

    Yes **No**

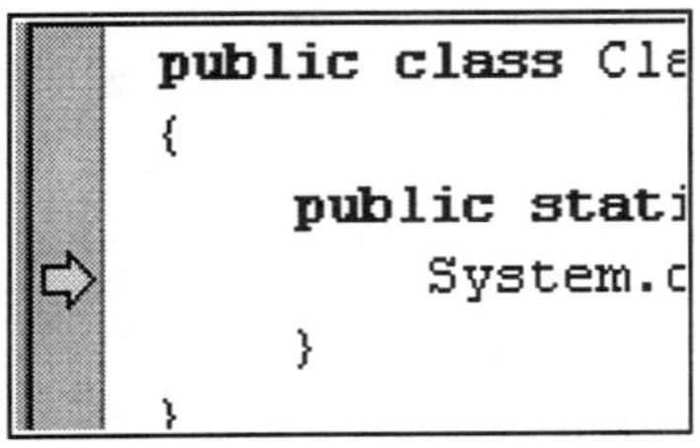

22. Note the yellow singlestep arrow. Does it initially point to the start of the program, and does it indicate that *System.out.println* is the next statement to be executed?

    Yes **No**

23. Bring up the *JVIEW* output window by **CLICKL** on the *JVIEW HWmain* icon at the bottom of the screen. Does it show that the *println* statement has not yet been executed and string *Hello World* has not yet been printed?

    Yes **No**

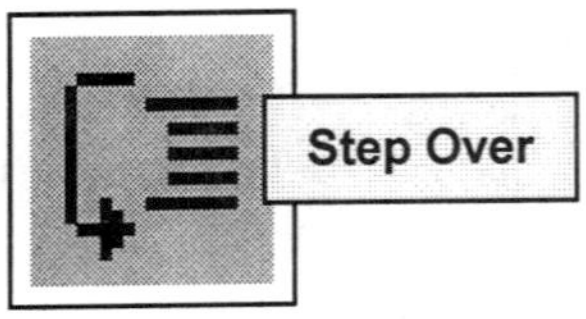

24. Shrink the JVIEW output window back to icon status. Press F10 (or **CLICKL** on the *Step Over* toolbar button) to perform a singlestep and execute the *println* statement. Did the yellow arrow move down one statement?

    Yes **No**

25. Again bring back the *JVIEW* window. Does it now display *Hello World*, indicating that the print statement was executed?

    Yes **No**

26. During the singlestep process was the only activity noticed within the *Watch* and *Variables* (*Locals* tab) windows a reference to *args*? Since our program contained no variables, is this reasonable?

    Yes **No**

27. Continue singlestepping with F10 through the end of the program. Did we automatically exit the debug mode?

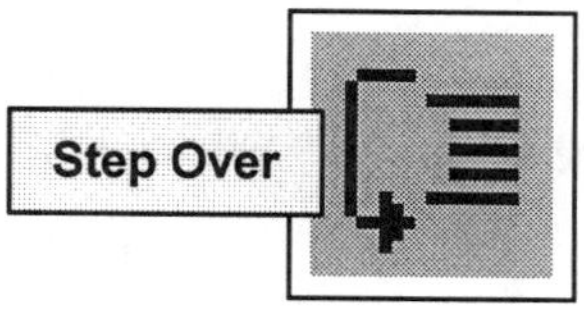

    Yes **No**

> To exit the debug mode at any time, press *Shift+F5*, or **Debug, End**. **File, Close All**, if you are shutting down the computer.

Exercises

> These suggested exercises appear at the end of all chapters, and are primarily the reader's responsibility.
>
> For now, to perform each new exercise, we suggest that you simply erase the old code from within method *main* and add the new code. (In the next chapter, we will have the option of making each exercise a new *project* to be added to the chapter *solution*.)

a) Print out your name and address, as you would on an envelope.

b) Print "7\7" to the screen and explain what happened and why it happened. (Hint: A backslash indicates that the character to follow is to be interpreted as ASCII code.)

> Note: Some computers may require a sound card, speakers, and special settings when using ASCII '\7' to sound a beep.

c) Use the *newline* escape character ("\n") to write "Hello" and "World" on two lines with a single *println* statement.

d) Use one or more *indent* escape characters ("\t") to write *HelloWorld* to the center of the screen.

e) Print the following to the screen, beeping after each line:

```
Roses are red
violets are blue
Java is great
and so are you!
```

f) Repeat exercise e) above, but double-space the lines.

g) After executing the following, explain what \u0041 stands for.

```
System.out.println("I got an \u0041");
```

ESPRESSO

What are *byte codes*?

When J++ translated our *HelloWorld* program, it did not generate machine-language code—instead it generated *Java byte codes*. Best described as "partially-digested" code, these byte codes are universal in nature and completely independent of the computer that produced them. When the program is run (*Start*), a byte code interpreter on any *Java virtual machine* (JVM) finishes the compilation process down to machine-specific code.

Why use byte codes? Because they are universal, secure, and small in size. About the only drawback is execution speed. It takes a long time to fully digest those byte codes into machine language. Today, however, many systems include a *just-in-time* compiler. They work by compiling the byte code into machine code and saving the results. Then, when any program segment is repeated, this compiled code is run.

Questions and Problems

1. *Methods* consist of a collection of *classes*.

   True **False**

2. *System.out.println* outputs data to the standard output device. What is the standard output device?

3. What do you think "ln" stands for in "println"?

4. *Methods* in J++ are equivalent to what in C?

5. Write "methods" or "classes" in each of the fill-in spaces below:

   In Java, all executable code must reside within ________________, which in turn must reside within ________________.

6. Show two ways of adding comments to a source program.

7. A *public* method is available to all other methods in the program.

   True **False**

ESPRESSO

What files are generated during program development?

Using the *Explorer* to examine the *Chapter1* solution folder, here are the types of files we find inside:

- *Chapter1.sln* holds the solution source code.
- *Chapter1.suo* holds the solution byte code.
- *HelloWorld.exe* holds the executable code.
- *HelloWorld.vjp* holds the project code.
- *HWmain.class* holds the compiled byte code.
- *HWmain.java* holds the original source code.

Only generated for Win32 machines running *Internet Explorer*.

When the project is run, *jview.exe* starts the Java VM (virtual machine). Using the information set in the *Properties* dialog box, the Java VM finds *Hwmain.java*, which holds the source code. The VM loads the corresponding class (*HWmain.class*), and executes the *main* method.

8. What does it mean to *dock* a window?

9. What two windows are automatically created when we enter the debug mode?

10. Why are identifiers such as *class*, *int*, and *static* called *reserved words*?

11. What is the difference between a *solution* and a *project*?

12. File *HWmain.java* holds "partially digested" Java byte code.

    True **False**

13. What does it mean to "call" a method?

CHAPTER

2

Project Amazing Facts

Constants, Variables, and Operators

Objectives

- *To introduce and review the basic data types of J++/C*
- *To use the J++/C built-in operators*
- *To solve a number of problems, many with surprising results*

Discussion

The English language is a hierarchical top-down system—from *book* to *chapter* to *paragraph* to *sentence*, with each sentence composed of *words* and *punctuation*. A programming language follows the same pattern—from *project* to *program* to *module* to *statement*, with each statement composed of *constants*, *variables*, and *operators*. This chapter covers these programming *statements*.

We continue the reduced programming format of Chapter 1. All user-defined code is found within method *main*, and the only built-in methods are the familiar *print* and *println*.

Variables

A *variable* is a specific location in memory that holds changeable data. As shown in the example below, a variable is created by a *declaration* statement and initialized by an *assignment* statement.

```
int speed;
speed = 80;
```

As an option, both the declaration and assignment statements can be combined into a single *initialization* statement:

```
int speed = 80;
```

As diagrammed below, *int* (integer) is the type of data the memory location can hold, *speed* is the symbolic address of the 32-bit memory location, and *= 80* is the optional assignment of an initial constant value.

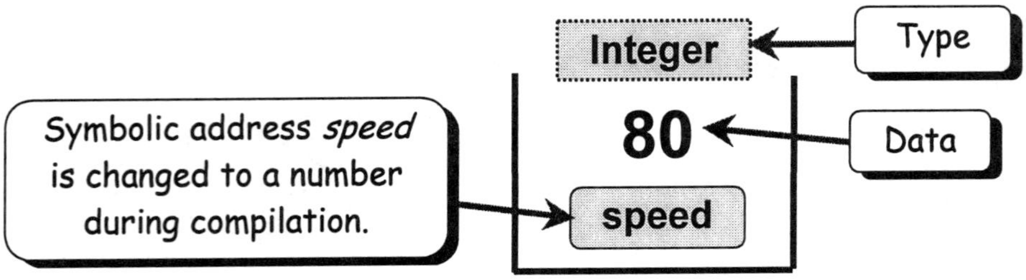

The Java basic types

Variables can hold a variety of values, from the age of your dog, to the distance to the nearest star, to the letter grade you received on your last quiz. To accommodate this wide range of values and types, J++ offers the eight *basic* (intrinsic) *types* of Table 2.1.

Basic data type	Size (bits)	Range	Default value
byte	8	±127	0
short	16	±32,768	0
int	32	±2,147,483,648	0
long	64	±9,223,372,036,854,775,808	0
float	32	±1.4E–45 to ±3.4E38	0.0
double	64	±4.9E–324 to ±1.8E308	0.0
boolean	8	true, false	false
char	16	'\u0000' to '\uffff'	'\u0000'

These *unicode* values are a superset of ASCII.

Table 2.1
The eight basic data types

These eight basic types are divided into four categories:

- **Integer**. Type *integer* includes data types *byte*, *short*, *int*, and *long*, and is probably the most commonly used. All integer types hold whole, signed values, differing only in their size—as shown by the table. Integer *literals* (numeric values) are usually written in decimal or hexadecimal (where prefix *0x* means hexadecimal).

```
127    0x45    322457899234
```

Hexadecimal

- **Floating point**. Type *floating point* includes data types *float* and *double*. Based on scientific notation, they hold the widest range of values. Typical floating point literals are listed below.

```
34.55        3.0E–4        –0.334e45
```

- **Character**. Type *character* includes data type *char* and is used to store a single ASCII character code. The standard way of extracting ASCII character codes is by enclosing them in single quotes and letting the compiler look up the corresponding code:

```
'A'      't'      '7'
```

However, we can always look up the codes ourselves and enter them directly in decimal or hexadecimal.

```
65      0x74      0x37
```

For those codes that don't have direct keyboard counterparts, we can enter their ASCII codes in decimal or hexadecimal:

```
0xA (new line)      0xD (carriage return)
0x9 (tab)           0x8 (backspace)          0x7 (bell)
```

However, what do we do when such characters are to be included in *strings* (a sequence of characters enclosed by quotes)? For this, we use special symbols and *escape codes*.

```
\n (new line)       \r (carriage return)
\t (tab)            \b (backspace)
\7 (bell)
```

When using escape codes as individual characters, just remember to enclose them in single quotes.

- **Boolean.** Only a single basic data type (*boolean*) belongs to this category. It holds only two values: *true* and *false*.

True **False**

Operators

The operators of Table 2.2 perform a variety of operations on the data types and their literals. They are ranked in order of priority, with the highest priority at the top and the lowest at the bottom.

When analyzing a statement with multiple operators, the system scans the statement from left to right looking for and executing the highest priority operators. The process is repeated for each priority level. The standard rule is: If there is any doubt about priority, use parenthesis to force the issue.

Operators	Description
. [] ()	The dot operator, brackets, and parenthesis
++ -- ! ~ instanceof	Increment, decrement, NOT, 1's complement, reference comparison
* / %	Multiply, divide, modulus
+ –	Add, subtract
<< >> >>>	Left shift, right shift, unsigned right shift
< > <= >=	Less than, greater than, less than or equal, greater than or equal
== !=	equal to, not equal to
& | && || ^	Bit-wise AND, bit-wise OR, logical AND, logical OR, EXCLUSIVE OR
?: = op=	ternary, assignment, combinational
,	Separation operator

Table 2.2
The operators, listed in priority

A few examples

Operators will be used throughout the text, so a few brief examples here of the more commonly-used operators should suffice. (The *relational* operators such as "less than" and "equal to" will be introduced in the next chapter.)

- Either of the statements listed below increments (adds one to) variable *speed*. The third option is identical to the second, but uses the shortcut *combinational* operator (+=).

```
speed++;
speed = speed + 1;
speed += 1;
```

- The first statement listed below uses the shorthand *combinational* operator (<<=) to shift variable *number* to the left two places. The second shifts variable *number* to the left two places and assigns the result to variable *answer*. In both cases, zeros are walked in on the right.

```
number <<= 2;
answer = number << 2;
```

Combinational operator (<<=)

- The *bit-wise* operators (|, &, and ~) are used for individual bit manipulation. In the two statements below, each bit of byte variable *hand* is ANDed with each like bit of binary 00000001. Since all the resulting bits from D1 to D7 are guaranteed to be zero, this is also known as a *masking* operation.

```
hand = (byte)(hand & 1);
hand &= 1;
```

What is *(byte)*? (See the next page.)

- The following statement uses the *boolean* operators (||, &&, and !) to simulate the action of a NAND gate. Each *boolean* variable (*result*, *in1*, *in2*) holds *true* or *false*. Note the use of parenthesis to force the AND operation before the NOT operation.

```
result = !(in1 && in2);
```

Promotion and demotion

When an operation is performed on variables and constants of the same type, there is no problem. But what if the data types are mixed? In this case, C and J++ use a rather involved set of rules based on data type ranking. Look back at Table 2.1 and you'll see how the *integer* and *floating point* data types are ranked (from the low-level *byte* at the top to the high-level *double* at the bottom).

- Any lower-ranking type can be directly assigned to any higher-ranking type. However, the opposite does not hold. Any higher ranking type can only be assigned to a lower ranking type if a *cast* operator is used. (A cast operator is a data type in parenthesis that forces the conversion to be done.)

  In the following example, the higher-ranking *double* variable (*cash*) is cast down to the lower-ranking *integer* variable (*dollars*). In the process, double value 3.34 is rounded off to integer value 3.

```
double cash = 3.34;
int dollars;
dollars = (int)cash;
```

When *cash* is demoted, all overflows are lost and all decimals are rounded off.

- When any operation is performed on variables of mixed type, the lowest ranking is promoted to the higher ranking and the operation is performed. The result remains at the higher ranking.

```
double distance, speed = 55.7;
byte time = 4;
distance = speed*time;
```

Byte variable *time* (4) is automatically promoted to type *double* (4.0).

- All constants (literals) are automatically of type *integer* (if they are whole numbers) and of type *double* (if they are floating point numbers). Therefore, the result of any operation that includes a constant is automatically of type *int* or *double*.

```
hand = (byte)(hand & 1);
hand &= 1;
```

Literal "1" is of type *int*.

We are now ready to put our knowledge to the test. This chapter's solution consists of three small programming *vignettes*. Don't be surprised if some of the results are rather unexpected.

Vignette 1: Project *Temperature*
Vignette 2: Project *RainDrop*
Vignette 3: Project *Sherlock*

Hands-On Procedure

Step one—Project definition

1. Our first project explores an interesting fact related to temperature scales.

Vignette #1: Write project *Temperature*, which converts –40° Celsius (Centigrade) to Fahrenheit and displays the result.

Step two—Structure chart

2. All the programming vignettes of this chapter follow the same structure chart (Figure 2.1) as project *HelloWorld* of Chapter 1.

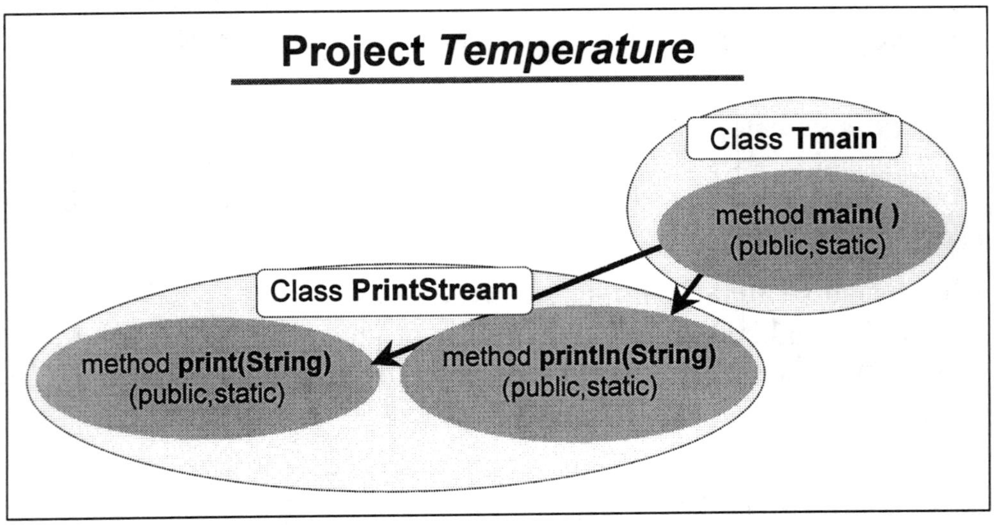

Figure 2.1
Project *Temperature* structure chart

Step three—Write the program

> **CLICKL** = click left
> **CLICKR** = click right
> **DCLICKL** = double click left.
> **BOLD TYPE** = click left.

3. If not already open, bring up the *Visual Studio* window as outlined in Chapter 1: **DCLICKL** the desktop icon (or, **Start**, drag to *Programs*, drag to *Microsoft Visual J++ 6.0*, etc).

   If the *Visual Studio* window is already open, be sure to close any existing projects by **File**, **Close All**.

J++ icon

4. If not already open, bring up the *New Project* dialog box as outlined in Chapter 1: Click the *Open Project* toolbar button, *New* tab (or **File**, **New Project**).

Open Project

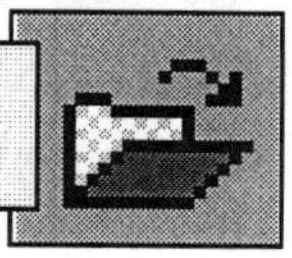

5. Fill in the New Project dialog box by: **Applications**, **Console Application**, enter solution Name (*Chapter2*) and Location (such as *C:\JAVA\Chapter2*), **Open**.
6. Rename the project and class names as shown by following the steps outlined in Chapter 1:

   - Rename the project by **CLICKR** on *Chapter2*, **Rename,** enter ***Temperature***.
   - Rename *Class1* by **CLICKR** or *Class1*, **Remove From Project**, **CLICKR** on project *Temperature*, **Add**, **Add Class**, **ClassMain**, enter *Tmain*, **Open**. **CLICKR** on *Temperature*, **Temperature Properties**, **OK**.

7. If necessary, **DCLICKL** on *Tmain* to bring up the default code of Figure 2.2.

```
public class Tmain
{
      public static void main (String[ ] args){
      }
}
```

Figure 2.2
The starting point

8. Add all necessary code to method *main*, as shown by Figure 2.3. (First we'll run the program, then we'll analyze it.)

```
// What is so special about -40 degrees?
public class Tmain
{
    public static void main (String[ ] args){
        byte C,F;
        C = -40;
        F = 9*C/5 + 32;
        System.out.println(C+"C = "+F+"F.");
    }
}
```

?

There is only one copy of static method *main*.

String concatenation operators.

Figure 2.3
Source program

Step four—Execute the program

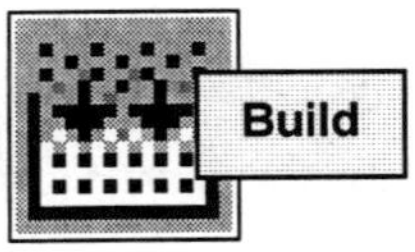

9. **Build**, **Build** (or **CLICKL** on the *Build* toolbar button) to compile and combine all classes, and to check for syntax and compiler errors.

10. We have a syntax error! Note the following error message in the *Task List* window:

Cannot implicitly convert 'int' to 'byte' (J0068)

a) To show the location of the error, **DCLICKL** on the error message. Did the cursor move to the error location?

Yes **No**

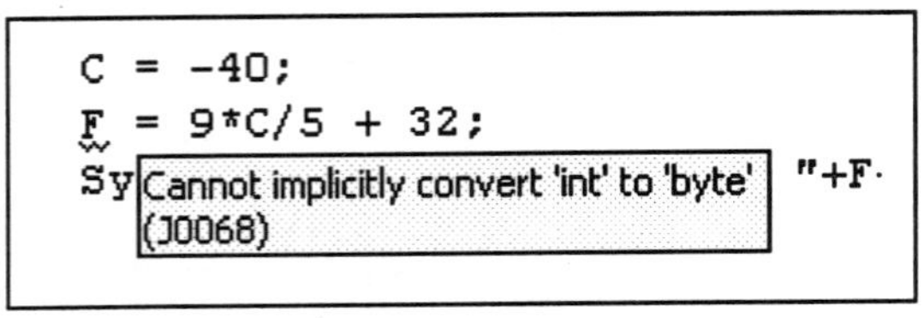

b) Note the error-location "squiggle" under variable *F*. When we move the cursor to this location, is the error message repeated within a box?

Yes **No**

> Error J0068 occurred because *byte* variable *C* was converted to *int* prior to the calculation, and the resulting *int* value can not be assigned to the lower-ranking *byte* variable *F*. As shown below, one solution is to use the (byte) *cast* operator to force the assignment.
>
> **F = (byte)(9*C/5 + 32);**
>
> For a more detailed explanation of the error: **CLICKR** on the selected error in the *Task List* window, **Show Task Help**. (Note: a *Library* CD-ROM may have to be in place to complete this step.)

11. Add the (*byte*) cast operator as shown in the previous step and *rebuild*. Was the error eliminated?

    Yes **No**

12. Execute (*Start*) the program and note (quickly!) the result of the calculation. (Remember: To freeze the output screen, we will singlestep the code shortly.)

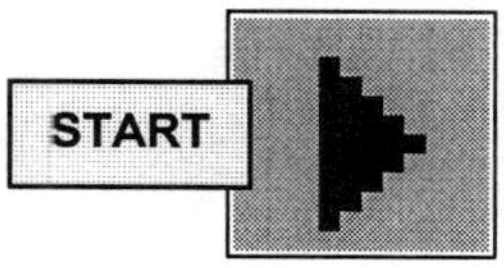

    Did you know that –40°C equals –40°F? It's an amazing fact. (Are there any other temperatures for which this is true?)

    Yes **No**

13. Enter other values of C between –89 and +53. Were the results correct?

    Yes **No**

14. Enter values of C outside the –89 to +53 range. What happened and how can you correct the problem? (Hint: Promote the data type.)

Analyzing the program

15. Looking at Figure 2.3 (with the cast operator added), here is how the program progresses.

```
F = (byte) (9*C/5 + 32);
```

Suggestion: Use F10 to singlestep through the program as you review each line. After each step, simply move the cursor over any initialized variable to see its contents.

- We define (declare) byte variables *C* and *F*. We choose type *byte* because we are sure that the answer lies within the ±127 range for variables of this type. (Although not as important as in the past when memory was limited, choosing the lowest-ranking type that will do the job will conserve memory and speed up execution.)

```
byte C,F;
```

- We use the assignment operator (=) to load –40 into byte variable C.

```
C = –40;
```

- We make use of the *add*, *multiply*, and *divide* operators (+, *, /) to convert the centigrade temperature to Fahrenheit. The result is cast and assigned to byte variable *F*.

```
F = (byte)(9*C/5 + 32);
```

- We print the result to the screen. As used here, the "+" operator means *string concatenation*, and not add. That is, the "+" operator converts a variable to a string, and combines the string segments.

If at least one of its two operands is a string, "+" means *concatenation.*

```
System.out.println(C+"C = "+F+"F.");
```

Vignette #2: Write project *RainDrop*, which will determine the number of atoms in a single rain drop.

In *Chapter 1*, we added new project code by first erasing old code from the previous project's *main* method. In this chapter, we will create a new project for each new vignette.

16. Add new project *RainDrop* to solution *Chapter2*.

> To add the new project to the existing solution: **CLICKR** on solution *Chapter2*, **Add Project**, **Console Applications**, enter *RainDrop* in the Name field, **Open**.

17. Following the sequence for project *Temperature* (step 6), rename the project and class names, and set the *RainDrop* properties.

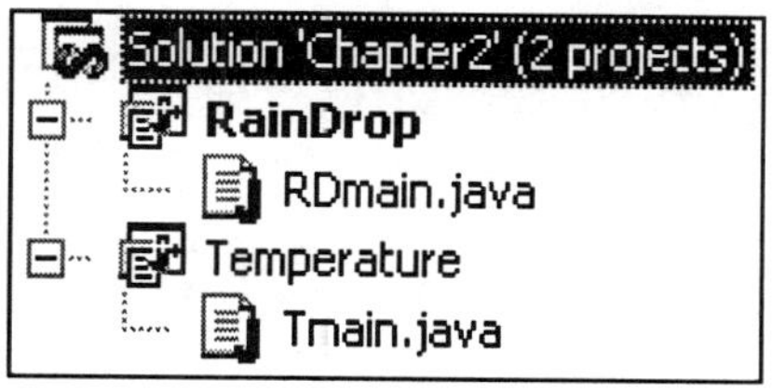

18. Make project *RainDrop* the present (active) project by **CLICKR** on *RainDrop*, **Set as Start Up Project**. (Did *RainDrop* turn **bold**?)

19. To determine the number of atoms in a raindrop we divide the volume of a raindrop (of radius *R*) by the volume of an atom (of radius *r*):

$$\frac{4/3\pi R^3}{4/3\pi r^3} = \frac{R^3}{r^3}$$

> **R = 1cm**
> **r = 1angstrom**

20. Bring up class *RDmain* (**DCLICKL**) of project *RainDrop* and enter the "raindrop" code of Figure 2.5.

```
// A raindrop has a radius of 1cm.
// An atom has a radius of 1A (angstrom).
// There are 1.0e8A in a cm.
public class RDmain
{
      public static void main (String[ ] args){
            byte r;
            float R,atoms;
            r = 1; // Radius of atom in angstroms.
            R = (float)1.0e8; // Radius of raindrop in angstroms.
            atoms = (R*R*R)/(r*r*r);
            System.out.println("A raindrop contains "+atoms+" atoms.");
      }
}
```

> Type *float* is required to hold the large expected numbers.

> The cast operator (*float*) is required because the constant (1.0e8) is automatically of type *double*.

Figure 2.5
Vignette *Raindrop* source program

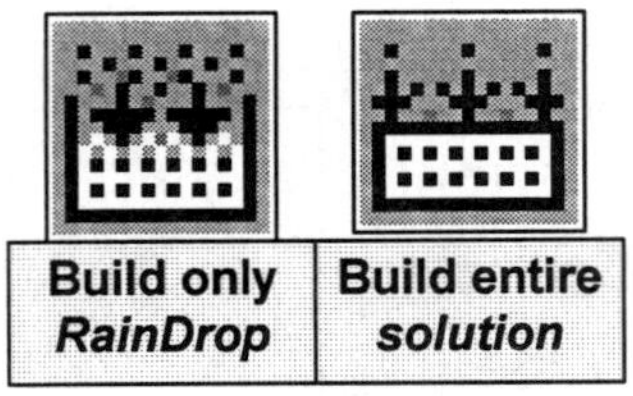

21. Build the program (**Build, Build RainDrop**) to check for syntax errors. Correct any errors that occur.

22. Execute (*Start*) the program and note the results.

    a) Did the answer appear in floating point format?

    Yes **No**

    b) Were you surprised that there are a million billion billion (10^{24}) atoms in a raindrop? It's an amazing fact!

    Yes **No**

Vignette #3: Write project *Sherlock*, based on a famous problem in deductive logic from the Sherlock Holmes episode *Silver Blaze*. It involves a logical analysis of "*The dog that did not bark*" clue.

23. The scene is as follows: Holmes is on the grounds of an old mansion at night and needs to determine if the suspect is nearby. Here is the logic of the situation, as Holmes saw it:

If the moon is out, OR lightning is flashing, AND the dog is NOT barking, then the suspect is nearby.

Our task is to solve this problem for the following logical state and determine if the suspect is nearby.

Moon (M) is not out
Lightning (L) is flashing
Dog is not barking (B)
Suspect (S) = ?

If a dog is NOT barking at lightning, the suspect must be nearby quieting the dog.

24. Using previous techniques (step 16), add project *Sherlock* to solution *Chapter2*, rename the project and class names, set the properties, and make *Sherlock* the current project.

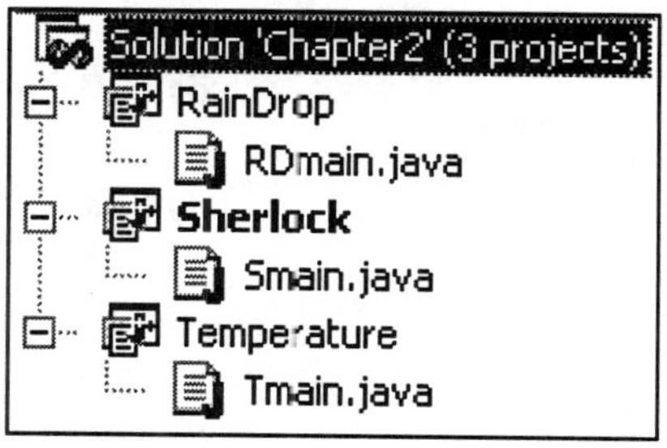

25. Add the code of Figure 2.6 to class *Smain*. As expected, the solution makes use of Boolean variables and logical operators to solve the problem.

```
// Can a dog that does not bark be a clue to a mystery?
public class Smain
{
    public static void main (String[ ] args){
        boolean Moon,Lightning,Bark,Suspect;
        Moon = false;
        Lightning = true;
        Bark = false;
        Suspect = (Moon || Lightning) && (!Bark);
        System.out.println("True means the suspect is present.");
        System.out.println("Suspect = "+Suspect);
    }
}
```

Use parenthesis to force the issue if there is any doubt about precedence.

Figure 2.6
Vignette *Sherlock* source code

26. In this third vignette, there are several new items to explore:

- For the first time we declared and initialized *boolean* variables:

```
boolean Moon,Lightning,Bark,Suspect;
Moon = false;
Lightning = true;
Bark = false;
```

- We then used the *boolean* operators to evaluate the logic of the situation:

```
Suspect = (Moon || Lightning) && (!Bark);
```

27. Run the program and note the result. (Be sure to set **Sherlock** as the *StartUp Project* by **CLICKR**, *Set as StartUp Project*)

    a) Is it **true** that the suspect is nearby (quieting the dog)?

    Yes **No**

    b) Are you surprised by the fact that an event that did NOT happen (the dog did NOT bark) can be a clue to a mystery? It's an amazing fact!

    Yes **No**

28. For a complete and thorough test of the software, you should enter other logical combinations of *moon*, *lightning*, and *bark* into the program and note the results. Did the program work for other combinations?

    Yes **No**

---

29. As a second solution to our *Sherlock* problem, we can use integer variables and bit-wise operators (see Table 2.2).

    We start with the same three variables (*M*, *L*, and *B*), but this time each is represented by a single bit within a byte variable.

30. By modifying the present project (or creating a new project), write the second *Sherlock* version of Figure 2.7.

31. Run the program and note the results. Does it also correctly predict that the suspect is present (*suspect = 01*)?

    Yes **No**

32. As always, test your program for as many input combinations as you can. Did the program give the correct result for all tested combinations?

    Yes **No**

```
// 1=true; 0=false.
public class Smain
{
    public static void main (String[ ] args){
        byte logicState,moon,lightning,bark,suspect;
        logicState=0x02;
        moon = logicState;
        lightning = (byte)(logicState>>1);
        bark = (byte)(logicState>>2);
        suspect = (byte)((moon | lightning)&(~bark));
        System.out.println("Suspect = "+(suspect & 01));
    }
}
```

Again, suggest use of parenthesis to force priority.

Figure 2.7
Second version of Vignette *Sherlock*

33. Briefly, here is now the program works:

a) All variables are declared as *bytes*, and the logic of the crime scene is assigned to variable *logicState*. (Moon is not out, lightning is striking, and the dog is not barking.)

						B	L	M
logicState						0	1	0

b) Because bit-wise operations can not be done on different bit positions, the next step is to line up all three variables in the same bit position (D0), but in different variables. This is done using the assignment and shift operators.

```
moon = logicState;
lightning = (byte)(logicState >> 1);
bark = (byte)(logicState >> 2);
```

For example, *logicState* >> 2 means that all the bits of variable *logicState* are rotated right two positions and zeros are "walked" into the left positions.

> The (*byte*) cast operator is needed because the shift operations promote the resulting values to type *integer*.

After all three instructions have been executed, we have:

moon								0
lightning								1
bark								0

c) The next step is to logically combine the byte variables using bit-wise operators. (Note: The "~" operator is the 1's complement.)

```
suspect = (byte)((moon | lightning) & (~bark));
```

First, variables *moon* and *lightning* are ORed together, giving a logic "1" in the crucial D0 bit position. Next, all the bits of variable *bark* are inverted, giving a "1" in the D0 position. Finally, when the results of each of these operations are ANDed together, we have a "1" in the D0 position—which is assigned to *suspect.*

d) The final print step includes a *mask* operation (*suspect & 01*), so only bit D0 can ever be active. The result (*suspect* = 1) is printed to the screen.

```
System.out.println("Suspect = "+(suspect & 01));
```

The bit-wise operators make good use of the basic Boolean axioms listed below:

A + 0 = A	A * 0 = 0
A + 1 = 1	A * 1 = A

Where "+" is the OR operator and "*" is the AND operator. As shown, the OR operator ("+") can drive individual bits high (while leaving others alone). The AND operator ("*") can drive individual bits low (while leaving others alone).

ESPRESSO

What about keyboard input?

It would sure to easier to test the programs of this chapter if we could input values from the keyboard. The problem is, keyboard entry in the stand-alone mode is quite difficult under Java. In fact, it's so tricky we have delayed its introduction all the way until Chapter 10.

However, if you or your instructor would like to add in this feature before Chapter 10, you are free to try. Just be aware, keyboard entry involves arrays, strings, exceptions, and wrappers.

Step five—Debug the program

Variable access by cursor

The easiest way to view the contents of a variable is to move the cursor over the variable in question. (In a future chapter, we'll examine the *Variables* window.)

34. Select project *Temperature*. (**CLICKR** on *Temperature*, **Set as Startup Project**.)

35. Press F10 to enter the debug mode. (Or **Debug, Step Over**.)

36. With the yellow singlestep arrow at the first executable instruction (*C = –40*), move the cursor over variables C and F anywhere in the program. Is it true that nothing is displayed?

```
byte C,F;
C = -40;
F = (byte) (9*C
```

Yes **No**

37. Press F10 once and execute the *C* = *–40* instruction.

    a) Now move the cursor over variable *C* (anywhere in the program). Is "*C* = *–40*" displayed?

    Yes **No**

    b) Move the cursor over variable *F*. Again, is nothing displayed for this variable?

    Yes **No**

    c) From steps a) and b) can we conclude that when using the cursor method, variable contents are displayed only after they have been initialized?

    Yes **No**

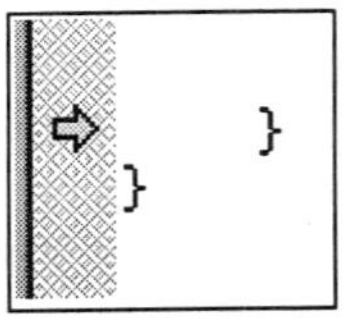

38. Using F10, singlestep all the way through the program, placing the yellow arrow on the next to the last bracket. Move the cursor over any of the variables anywhere in the program. Are the contents of all variables now displayed?

    Yes **No**

39. If necessary, Shift+F5 to exit the debugger.

Exercises

The exercises in this chapter range from very simple to challenging, and are offered to give added practice in the C/Java language basics. If you are well versed in the fundamentals of C, you may wish to skim or skip these exercises. For each exercise in this and all future chapters, you have the option of adding another project to each solution (**CLICKR** on solution name, **Add Project**).

To bring back a previous project: **File**, **Open Project** (or click *the Open Project* toolbar button), **Existing** (or **Recent**) tab, find and **DCLICKL** the desired folder, and **DCLICKL** the solution icon.

a) Write project *Add*, which adds the contents of *int* variables *checking* and *savings* and places the result into *int* variable *totalMoney*. The result is also printed to the screen.

b) Write project *MPG*, which divides variable *miles* by variable *gallons* and prints the mpg (miles-per-gallon) to the screen.

c) Write project *Speed* which determines the speed of rotation of the surface of the earth at the equator. (Hint: Circumference = $2\pi r$ and radius of earth ≈ 4,000 miles.)

d) Write project *Light* which determines how long it takes sunlight to reach the earth. (Hint: The earth is approximately 92 million miles from the sun, and light travels approximately 186,000 miles/second.)

e) Write project *Average*, which prints to the screen the average value of variables *profit* and *loss*.

f) Using the *modulo* ("%") operator, write project *Divide*, which divides two integers and prints both the quotient and the remainder to the screen.

g) Write project *F2C*, which takes Fahrenheit variable *F* and writes its Centigrade equivalent to variable *C*.

h) Write project *NAND*, which uses bit-wise Boolean operations to simulate a NAND gate. Assume that the two inputs to the NAND gate occupy bit positions D0 and D1 of byte variable *input* and that the output is printed to the screen as a 0 or 1.

i) Write project *TreasureMap*, which combines the lower four bits of variable *bottomMap* with the upper four bits of variable *topMap*. (Hint: Make use of the *bit-wise* operators.)

j) Run the following code, and report if there is any different in writing the *increment* and *decrement* (++ and --) operators before or after the variable. (Reminder: As used below, the "+" is the *concatenation* operator, and not *add*.)

```
int num1 = 8;
int num2 = 8;
System.out.println(++num1+" "+num2++);
```

k) Your weight varies inversely as the square of the distance from the center of the earth. If you weigh precisely 150lbs when exactly 4,000 miles from the center, write a program to determine exactly how much would you weigh after climbing only three flights of stairs (approximately 100 feet).

l) Using logical or bit-wise Boolean operators, solve the following:

I will go to the show if either Mary or Sue arrives, but not both.

Hint: Using Boolean operators: S = (M || S) && !(M && S);

m) The closest star to earth (other than our sun) is the very faint *Proxima Centauri*, "only" four light-years away. Traveling at 50,000 mph, at what date in our past would a space ship have had to depart in order to arrive at the star today? (Was it before the last ice age?)

n) Write project *Calendar*, that takes the number of days and reports its corresponding month, week, and day. (Assume that each month = 30 days.) For example, if the number of days is 69, it reports 2 months, 1 week, and 2 days. (Hint: Suggest use of *divide* and *modulo* operators.)

Questions and Problems

1. When declaring a simple integer, is initialization optional?

   Yes **No**

2. What is the lowest-ranking data type required to hold the national debt? (Hint: The national debt is over five trillion.)

3. A maximum *double* type number is how many times bigger than a maximum *float* type?

ESPRESSO

When is a variable changed?

Below, assume that variable *number* holds 0xC:

```
answer = number >>2;
```

We can reasonably conclude that the contents of variable number is shifted to right two times (zeros shifted into the left), and the result (0x3) assigned to variable *answer*. The question is, what about variable *number*? Did it also change to 0x3?

The answer is no—it remained the same. To change variable *number*—as shown by either statement below—the result must be assigned back to *number*.

```
number = number >> 2;
number >>= 2;
```

The only exceptions to this rule are the *unary* operators. In each case below, the contents of variable *number* is changed.

```
number++;
number--
~number;
```

4. Using binary math (powers of two), how do we calculate the range of values held by type *short*?

5. What is the difference (if any) between 'A,' 65, 0x41, '\0x41', and '\u0041'?

6. If the ASCII code for A is 65, what is printed to the screen by the following sequence?

```
int ch1 = 65;
System.out.println(ch1);
char ch2 = 65;
System.out.println(ch2);
```

7. Consider the statement: *Thomas Jefferson* lived in the *White House* at *1600 Pennsylvania Ave.*

   a) Which item is a *symbolic address*?

   b) Which item represents *data* (the contents of an addressed location)?

   c) Which item represents the specific numerical address of the symbolic address?

   d) What type of "data" would you say resides at this location?

8. Why would the following code generate an error?

```
int a = 40000;
byte b;
b = a;
```

9. Continuing with question 8, what would be stored in variable *b* after the following?

```
int a = 40100;
byte b;
b = (byte)a;
```

10. What is printed to the screen (and sounded from the speaker) when the following statement is executed?

```
System.out.println("Four score\rand\b7\7years\tago.");
```

11. The largest prime number known to exist is $2^{859,433} - 1$. Can this number be stored in any J++ data type? (A prime number is one that can be divided evenly only by itself and one.)

    Yes **No**

12. Which of the following are floating point numbers? (Circle your selections.)

    0.5 3.0E–45 112 –300.1

13. A *cast* operator is required to promote a variable type.

    True **False**

14. What is the *scope* and *lifetime* of a *local* variable?

15. When performing operations on variables of type *byte*, they are first converted to type *int*.

    True **False**

16. In each case, use priority rules to determine the contents of variable *number*:

```
number = 2 + 3*4 + 5;
number = (2+3)*4 + 5;
number = (2+3)*(4+5);
```

17. The two statements below are equivalent. The second statement uses the "op=" combinational operator as a shorthand notation.

```
apples = apples + 5;
apples += 5;
```

Using this as a guide, rewrite each of the following in combination form:

a) grapes = grapes*40;

b) peaches = peaches >> 4;

18. After each of the following operations, determine the contents of variable *number*. (Hint: Looking at Table 2.2, do math operations have priority over logical operations?)

```
number = 0x44 | ~0xF0;
number = ~0x34 & ~0x86;
```

19. Why do you think operators such as – (negation), ~ (bit-wise complement), ++ (increment), and – – (decrement) are called *unary* operators? Why are the + (add), – (subtract), * (multiply), and / (divide) operators called binary operators?

CHAPTER

3

Project Fever

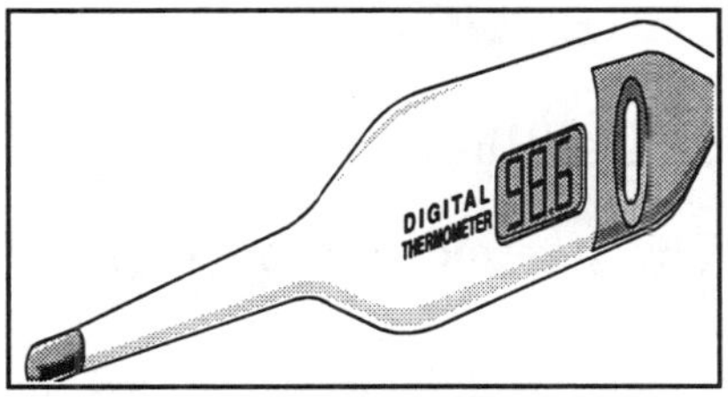

The Structure Theorem and Control Flow

Objectives

- *To introduce and review the elements of the structure theorem*
- *To review the basic flow control statements of J++/C*
- *To sound an alarm for abnormal body temperatures*

Discussion

This chapter continues our discussion of the basic structures of the J++/C language. The next step beyond simple variables and operators is the *structure theorem*, in which all programs can be constructed of nested combinations of the three basic patterns: *sequence*, *repetition*, and *selection*.

- *Sequence* is the sequential listing of statements—the only pattern used by the programs of the previous two chapters.
- *Selection* is the process of choosing among alternatives, and is the job of the *if/else* and *switch* control flow statements.
- *Repetition* forms a loop and is carried out with the *while*, *do/while*, and *for* control flow statements.

Selection

The simple *if*

The statement below demonstrates the simplest form of selection:

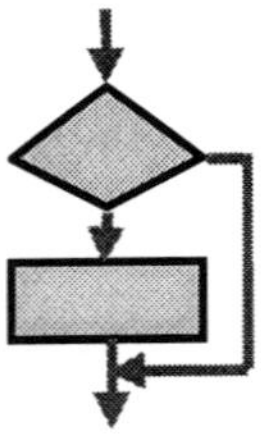

```
If(number = = 7)
    payoff = 100;
```

"==" is the *equals* operator.
"=" is the *assignment* operator.

The expression in parenthesis is called a *conditional expression* and always reduces to *true* or *false*. If the contents of variable *number* is indeed equal to (= =) 7, then the expression is *true* and the assignment statement that follows (*payoff = 100*) is executed. Otherwise, the statement is skipped.

The *if/else* expression

The *if/else* selection statement shown below demonstrates the full selection process (one that offers an alternative).

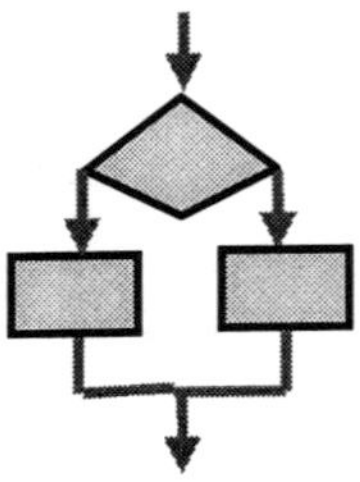

```
If(number = = 7)
    payoff = 100;
else
    payoff = 10;
```

Equals (= =) is called a *relational* operator.

If variable *number* does indeed hold 7 (true), we win $100; if it does not hold 7, the else condition, (false) we win only $10.

The ternary operator

For simple, straightforward *if/else* statements, the following *ternary* (three-argument) shorthand alternative to the previous example can be very attractive.

```
payoff = (number == 7? 100:10);
```

> The expression in parenthesis is either 100 or 10.

The compound conditional expression

A *compound conditional expression* introduces Boolean logic into the mix. In the case below, we win $100 if variable *number* holds either 7 or 11.

```
If((number == 7)||(number == 11))
    payoff = 100;
else
    payoff = 10;
```

> If you test any of these in the laboratory, make sure all variables (such as *number*) are initialized before they are used.

The compound statement

If more than one statement follows an *if* or an *else*, then it is compound and must be set off with brackets. (Brackets are optional when a statement is not compound.)

```
If((number == 7)||(number == 11)){
    tai = 100;
    mary = 100;
}
else{
    sam = 10;
}
```

> A compound statement: brackets required.

> A single statement: brackets optional.

The cascaded *if/else*

If the selection process involves a multi-pronged "fork in the road," we have the *cascaded* if/else chain:

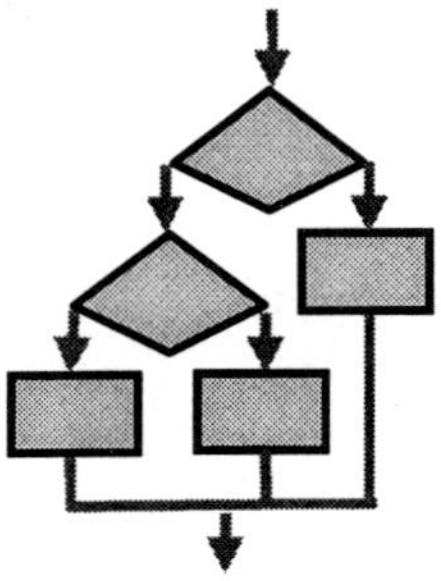

```
If(score > 90)
    grade = 'A';
else if (score > 80)
        grade = 'B';
    else
        grade = 'C';
```

The chain can continue for as long as we wish.

The *switch* statement

And finally, for certain kinds of multi-pronged fork-in-the-road problems, the *switch* statement presents an attractive alternative.

```
switch(grade){
    case 'A':
    case 'B':
    case 'C': System.out.println("Good grade");
              break;
    case 'D':
    case 'F':  System.out.println("Could be better");
              break;
     default:  System.out.println("No such grade");
}
```

Variable must be integer or char.

'A' or 'B' or 'C' results in "Good grade."

In our example, the *switch* statement looks at the contents of char variable *grade* and scans down the list of cases. When a match is found, the corresponding statement is executed, and we *break from* (exit) the switch statement. If no match if found, the *default* statement is executed.

Repetition

The *while* statement

The *while* statement is the simplest way to implement a loop. The following program segment displays the count from 1 to 10.

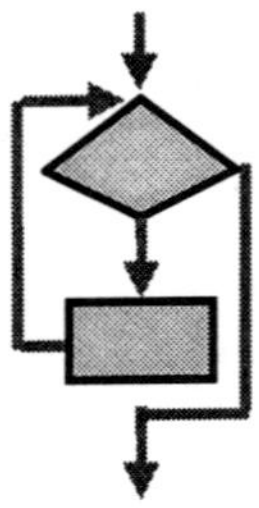

```
int i = 1;
while(i < 11){
    System.out.println(i);
    i++;
}
```

Statement is compound, so brackets are required.

First, variable *i* is initialized to 1. When the action moves to the *while* statement, it checks the conditional expression ($i < 11$) to see if *i* is less than 11. If *true*, it enters the body of the loop, prints *i* to the screen, and increments *i*. Action then automatically returns to the conditional expression. The process continues until the condition turns *false*.

ESPRESSO

What is *terse*?

For more compact and concise code, Java allows us to string together operators. The following is equivalent to the earlier example, but requires fewer lines of code. That's terse.

```
int i = 0;
while(++i < 11)
   System.out.println(i);
```

Some programmers prefer the earlier method (++ and < separate).

However, how did we know that the system would increment variable *i* first, then check the condition? The answer is, by the placement of the increment operator (++) before the variable.

Had we placed the ++ operator after the variable, then the condition would have been checked first.

```
int i = 0;
while(i++ < 11)
   System.out.println(i);
```

In the first case, 1 through 10 was printed to the screen. Can you determine in this last case what will be printed to the screen? Try it! (Answer is given below.)

(1 through 11 is printed to the screen.)

The *do/while* statement

The *do/while* statement is a useful alternative when the exit condition is emphasized, and we know that the loop must be processed at least once. The best examples will come later, so we'll just settle here for our familiar *count* program.

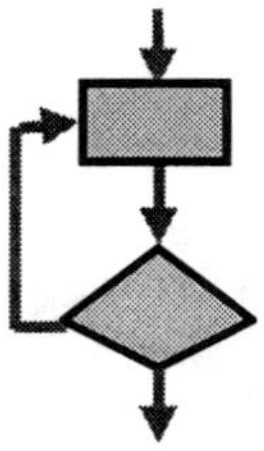

```
int i = 1;
do{
     System.out.println(i);
}while(++i < 11);
```

> Does it count from 1 to 10?

The *for* statement

We have saved the best for last. The *for* statement is often preferred for most loops because of its compactness and versatility. Consider our count program segment again:

```
for(i = 1;i < 11;i++){
     System.out.println(i);
}
```

> The brackets here are optional, but must be used for two or more statements.

There are three fields within the expression, set off by semicolons. The first (*i* = *1*) is the initialization field. It is processed just once upon first entering the *for* loop. Action then moves to the conditional field (*i* < *11*). If the condition is *true*, we process the body of the loop (*System.out.println(i)*), then automatically move to the iterative field (*i*++). We complete the loop by moving back to the conditional field. The process continues until the condition turns *false*.

The nested loop

A *nested* loop (a loop within a loop) makes for very compact and powerful code. As a case in point, the following double-nested loop prints the times tables from zero to nine to the screen.

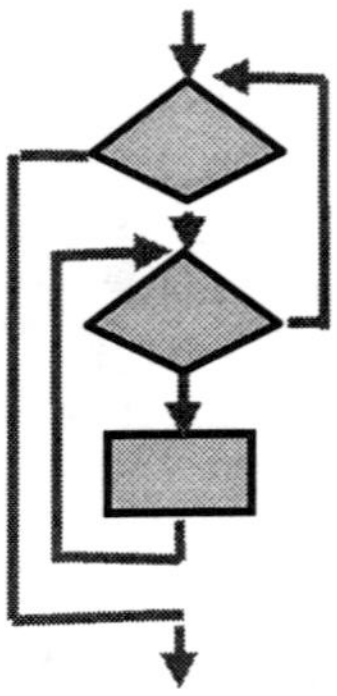

```
for(i = 0;i < 10;i++)
     for(j=0;j < 10;j++)
          System.out.println(i+" times "+j+" equals "+(i*j));
```

We enter the outer *for* loop, initialize *i* to zero, and drop down into the body of the loop (since the test condition is true). However, the body of the outer loop is another loop. We spin around this inner loop ten times and print the first round of times tables. We then return to the outer loop, update *i* to 1 and repeat. The process continues until *i* = 10 and we finally drop out of the outer loop.

Break and *Continue*

The *break* and *continue* statements provide a way to exit or repeat loop statements from within the loop.

- When *break* is executed, execution immediately leaves the loop.
- When *continue* is executed, execution immediately passes to the loop's conditional expression.

The program segment below is both an example and a brain teaser. Can you determine how many times "HI" is written to the screen? Try it!

```
int i = 0;
while(true){
   if(++i%2 == 0 )
      continue;
   System.out.println("HI");
   if(i > 10)
      break;
}
```

Determines if *i* is odd or even.

(The answer is 6.)

As a word of caution, be aware that many programmers frown upon the use of *break* and *continue* within a loop. They can be used very effectively, but it requires careful judgment and experience to do so.

However, the founders of Java thought enough of break and continue to retain their use. They even included a new *labeled break*, to allow exit to any nesting level. Nevertheless, break and continue will be used very sparingly within this text.

Hands-On Procedure

Step one—Project Definition

This chapter also continues the reduced programming format of Chapter 1. No objects are created, and all program code is within method *main*.

1. Project *Fever* is based on our body temperature.

Project *Fever* will print *Danger, temperature of _____* to the screen and sound a beep for every degree above 99°F. Otherwise *Temperature OK* is printed to the screen. As an added challenge, our fever thermometer was purchased in Europe and only reads in Celsius (Centigrade).

Step two—Structure chart

2. The structure chart of Figure 3.1 is the same as used for the two previous chapters.

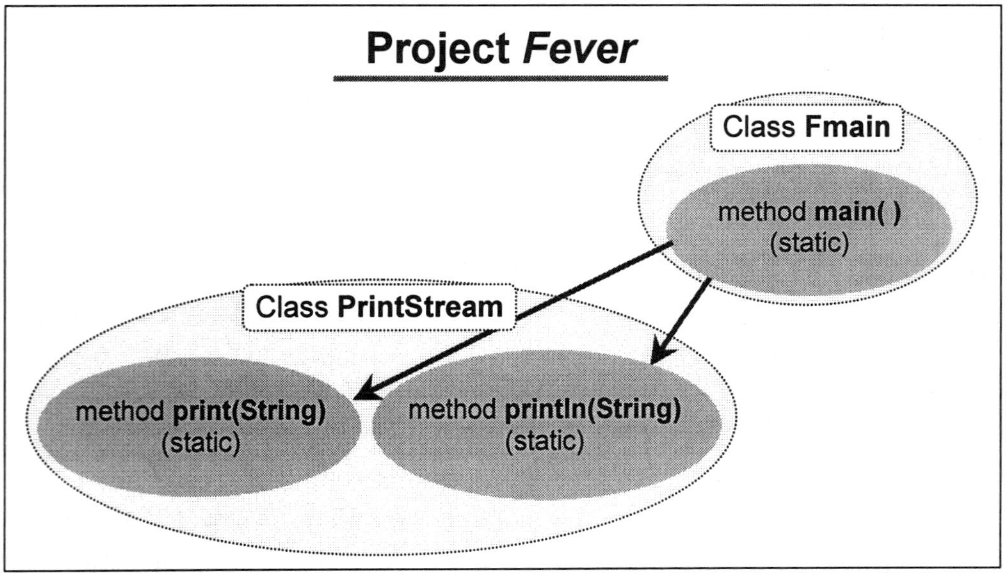

Figure 3.1
Project *Fever* structure chart

Step three—Write the program

3. Following the same steps as in Chapters 1 and 2, create project *Fever* within solution *Chapter3*, rename the project and class files, and complete class *Fmain* of Figure 3.2.

Reminders:

- To create project *Fever* within solution *Chapter3*, bring up the *New Project* dialog box. **Console Application**, enter Name *Chapter3*, check Location (such as *C:\Java\Chapter3*), **Open**.
- To change the project name from *Chapter3* to *Fever*: **CLICKR** on project *Chapter3*, **Rename**, enter *Fever*, **CLICKL** anywhere on window.
- To change the class name from *Class1* to *Fmain*: **CLICKR** on *Class1*, **Remove From Project**, **CLICKR** on project *Fever*, **Add**, **Add Class**, **ClassMain**, enter *Fmain*, **Open**. **CLICKR** on *Fever*, **Fever Properties**, **OK**.

```
public class Fmain
{
    public static void main (String[ ] args){
        int tempC,tempF,i;
        tempC = 40;
        tempF = 9*tempC/5 + 32;
        if(tempF > 99){
            System.out.println("Caution! Your temperature is "+tempF);
            for(i=0;i<(tempF – 99);i++)
                System.out.print('\7');
        }
        else
            System.out.println("Temperature OK.");
    }
}
```

We have nested a *for* within an *if*.

Figure 3.2

Project *Fever* final design

4. Looking at Figure 3.2, let's review the program code.

- We start with the first statement within method *main*.

```
int tempC,tempF,i;
```

This statement declares local variables *tempC*, *tempF* and *i* as integers. (All variables of the same type can be listed together.)

- This first executable statement is called an *assignment* statement. Integer 40 is assigned to variable *tempC*.

```
tempC = 40;
```

- Next, we convert the Celsius reading to Fahrenheit and assign the result to variable *tempF*.

```
tempF = 9*tempC/5 + 32;
```

- We then check for dangerous temperatures. If the contents of variable *temp* is greater than 99, all the statements within the brackets are executed; otherwise "Temperature OK" is printed.

Since the *if* statement is *compound*, brackets are required.

```
if(temp > 99){
     ...
}
else
     System.out.println("Temperature OK.");
```

- Having determined that the temperature is dangerous (above 99), we give a written warning.

```
System.out.println("Caution! Your temperature is "+temp);
```

Remember that the "+" sign in this context is the *concatenation* operator. The contents of variable *temp* is converted to a string and appended to the "caution" string.

- Next comes the audio warning. We enter a *for* loop and spin around the body *tempF – 99* times, beeping each cycle.

```
for(i=0;i<(tempF – 99);i++)
    System.out.print('\7');
```

Substitute "beep" for '\7' if your computer is beepless.

For example, if *tempF* is 104°F, then *tempF–99 = 5*. We then beep five times as *i* goes from 0 to 4.

Step four—Execute the program

5. Build the program and check for syntax errors. Make any necessary corrections.

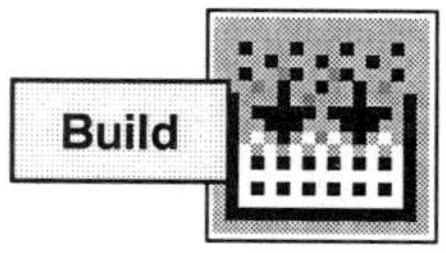

6. Start the program and note the results. Did the system beep five times, and was "*Caution! You have a temperature of 104°.*" printed to the output screen? (If not, check for obvious errors, or go on to the debug section.)

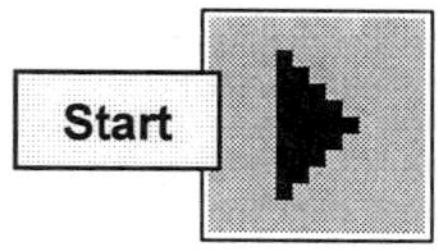

Yes **No**

ESPRESSO

Sound card?

In most computers, sending a series of ASCII 7's to the output system sounds a series of beeps. If this did not happen, perhaps your computer relies on a sound card and external speakers. The problem is that the sound card runs in parallel with the program and successive beeps may be lost. To correct the problem, we use an "empty loop" to place an appropriate delay between the beeps:

```
for(j=0;j < 100000000;j++)
    ;
```

In the debug mode, F10 processes empty loops in one step.

Adjust this delay number as required.

7. Repeat for a temperature of 35°C. Was "*Temperature OK.*" printed to the screen? (When done, return the temperature back to 40°C.)

   Yes **No**

Step five—Debug the program

Stepping through selection and repetition

> Singlestepping and accessing variables is an excellent way of studying and troubleshooting the *selection* and *repetition* patterns.
>
> When singlestepping, be sure to remove or comment out (using "//") any delay you may have added to accommodate a sound card and external speaker.

8. Press F10 to enter the debug mode.

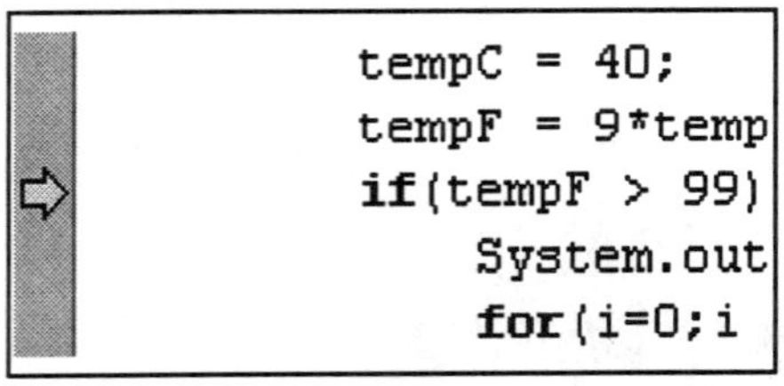

9. Using F10, step to the *if* statement. Move the cursor over variable *tempF*. Since 104 > 99, is it reasonable that the next singlestep will move us to the "Caution" statement?

   Yes **No**

10. Press F10 and note the singlestep arrow. Did it move to the "Caution" statement?

    Yes **No**

11. Using F10, step to the *for* statement. Since 104 – 99 is greater than variable *i* (0), is it reasonable that the next singlestep will enter the loop and move to the *print* statement?

    Yes **No**

12. Press F10 and verify your predictions.

13. Press F10 again and again. Do we step through the *for* loop five times and exit to the *else* statement? Does variable *i* increase by one each complete loop?

    Yes **No**

14. Press F10 several times. Do we skip the *else* statement, move to the closing bracket of method *main*, and exit the program?

    Yes **No**

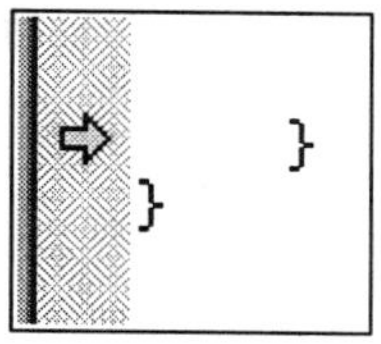

15. Using the editor, assign 35 to variable *tempC* and step through the program. Do we skip the *if* statement and process the *else* statement?

    Yes **No**

16. If necessary, Shift+F5 to exit the debugger.

Exercises

Reminders:

- To perform an exercise, you may modify an existing project or add a new project. (Even if associated with different solutions, do not use the same project name twice.)
- If variable types are not specified, the choice is yours.

a) Write project *Larger*, which places the largest of variables *first* and *second* into variable *theLargest*. The largest variable is also displayed. (Choose any *int* or *float* type.)

b) Write project *Lucky*, which beeps if variable *mynumber* holds a 7 or an 11 or a 13.

c) Write project *Tempwarning*, which accepts an int parameter and return 'H' (for "hot") if above 100 and 'C' (for "cold") if below 100.

d) Write project *Temperature*, which prints a table showing the *Centigrade* and equivalent *Fahrenheit* temperatures from –100C to +100C in units of 10. (Hint: Use the *\t* tab operator to position the columns.)

ESPRESSO

What is *pseudocode*?

Pseudocode is an informal anything-goes program solution that bridges the gap between the structure chart and the final code. Pseudocode for project *Fever* might look like the following:

```
Load C
Convert to F
 If F > 99
    Print caution
    Beep F – 99 times
 else
    Print OK
```

Pseudocode helps the programmer get the main ideas down on paper quickly without the burden of obeying all the formal rules of syntax and without confronting every minor detail. If you are writing program code and find yourself stalled, it might be time to consider pseudocode.

e) Modify project *Temperature* to beep when printing the line in which the Centigrade and Fahrenheit temperatures are equal.

f) Write project *Blastoff* which displays the numbers from 10 to 1, with each value spaced one second apart, and then prints "BLASTOFF." (Hint: Use a nested loop to delay one second.)

g) Modify project *Count* to count up and display from 0 to 50 by threes (0, 3, 6, 9, etc.). (Hint: To display the numbers horizontally and separated by commas, use *print(number+ ", ").*)

h) Program *Updown* checks char variable *direction*. If 'U', it displays the numbers from 1 to 100. If 'D', it displays 100 to 1.

i) Program *Circuit* uses char variable *SP* and int variables *R1* and *R2* (initialized to values of your choice). If *SP* holds 'S' we print the equivalent series resistance; If 'P', we print the parallel equivalent. (R_S=R1+R2, R_P=R1*R2/(R1+R2)).

j) Write program *Count3or7* which prints all the numbers from 1 to 100 that are evenly divisible by 3 or 7. (Hint: A%B returns the remainder of A divided by B.)

k) Write a program that prints all numbers from 1 to 100 to the screen, except those evenly divisible by 7.

l) Write program *Stop* which prints increasing integers to the screen at the rate of 10 per second. The printing stops as soon as the product of the last two numbers printed is greater than 27,414,333. (Be sure to use an IF in your program.)

m) Write project *Freefall*, which prints a table of the distance an object falls in free fall every second from 0 to 100 seconds. (Hint: Distance = $16t^2$.)

n) Modify project *Freefall* so the distance values will be printed in real time (one second apart). Also, a beep is sounded for each printed value.

o) Using a nested loop, write project *Times*, which prints the times table for all numbers from 5 to 11.

p) Write project *Multiply* which multiplies variables *width* and *height* and gives the answer in beeps. (For example, 4 x 7 = 28 beeps.)

q) Write project *OddEven* which examines variable *number* and writes EVEN to the screen if it's even, and ODD if it's odd. (Hint: Look at the LSB.)

r) Write project *Ones*, which examines int variable *mynumber* and prints the number of 1's.

s) Modify project *Ones* to beep when any three consecutive 1's are found.

t) Write project *Alphabet*, which prints the alphabet (A through Z to the screen at the rate of two characters/sec., with each letter on a different line.)

u) Modify project *Alphabet* to also beep whenever a vowel (A, E, I, O, and U) is printed.

v) Write project *Digit*, which scans all the numbers of type byte from 1 to 100 and sounds a beep whenever it finds a number with a "1" in bit position D3.

w) Write project *Remainder*, which scans all the numbers from 1 to 1000, and beeps every time it finds a number that has a remainder of 3 or 4. (Hint: Use the *modulo* operator.)

x) Write project *PrimeNumber*, which generates and displays all numbers from 0 to 100 at the rate of one/sec. A beep is heard whenever it finds a prime number (a number than can only be divided evenly by 1 and itself).

y) Modify project *PrimeNumber* so the computer searches for and displays the largest prime number integer. (Hint: Start with the highest positive integer and work backwards.)

z) Modify project *Fever* of Figure 3.2 so the system will also sound an alarm and print an appropriate message for body temperatures below 95°.

aa) Using the *switch* operator, write project *Football*, which looks at variable *score* and prints "Point after" if it's 1, "Safety" if it's 2, "Field goal" if it's 3, "Touchdown" if it's 6, and "That's an illegal score" if anything else.

bb) Modify project *Football* so a beep is heard whenever a touchdown is scored.

cc) Using nested if/else statements, rewrite project *Fever* of this chapter (Figure 3.2) to print "Much too low" if temp is lower than 90, "Too low" if between 90 and 97, "Just fine" if 98, "A little high" if 99 or 100, "Too high" if between 101 and 104, and "Danger, much too high" if higher than 104.

dd) Write project *Wage* which adds $2 or 10% (whichever is greatest) to variable *wageRate* and then prints, "You just got a _____% raise."

ee) Using nested *if/else* statements, write project *Vowel*, which examines variable *letter* and writes, "That's a capital letter," "That's a lower-case letter," or "That's not a letter." (Hint: Carefully examine the ASCII code patterns.)

Questions and Problems

1. What are the three basic patterns of the *structure theorem*?

2. Rewrite the loop portion of the fever program of Figure 3.2 using the *while* statement instead of the *for* loop.

3. Repeat question 2, but using the *do/while* statement.

4. Show how to print out the following arithmetic progression using all three types of the repetition flow control statements. (Hint: What is added to each number to give the next number?)

   2, 5, 10, 17, 26, 37, 50, 65, 82

5. If decimal 42 is equal to 0x2A, what does this say about the designator "0x"?

6. Variables *num1* and *num2* hold integers. Using the *println* statement, show how the "+" operator performs two completely separate functions by printing the following:

   "The sum of ______ and ______ = ____________."

   (num1) (num2) (num1 + num2)

7. Rewrite the *for* statement of Figure 3.2 using the "<=" (less-than-or-equal-to) relational operator.

8. Using an *if* statement, write a program segment that beeps if variable *number* is between 4 and 25, but not 13.

9. Using the *switch* statement, write a program that looks at variable *craps* and responds:

    "You loose" (If craps = 7 or 11.)
    "You win" (If craps = any other number between 2 and 12.)
    "That's not a legal number" (If any other number.)

10. Can the switch statement handle "greater than" or "less than" situations? (Why not?)

11. Write the flow chart that corresponds to project *Fever* of Figure 3.2.

12. Show two different ways to code the following statement. (Hint: One way uses two *if*s; the other way uses a compound conditional statement.)

    If variable *number* holds a 7 or an 11, print "You win!"

CHAPTER

4

Project Fever 2

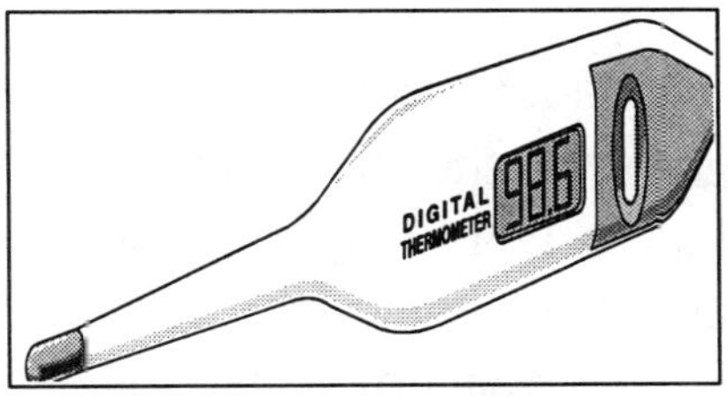

Modularization and Methods

Objectives

- *To introduce and review methods and parameters*
- *To break up the main method of Chapter 3 into modules*
- *To again sound an alarm for abnormal body temperatures*

Discussion

In this final chapter of J++ and its C origins, we apply the techniques of modularization to project *Fever* of the last chapter.

As we learned from the introduction, *modularization* is the process of breaking down a large complex project into a hierarchy of bite-size modules from the top down. In the C language, these modules are called *functions*, and in Java they are known as *methods*. The methods at the top are conceptual and general in nature, while those at the bottom are specific and detailed. Communication between methods is accomplished by way of *parameters* and *global variables*.

Methods can be *built-in* (provided by the software) or *user-defined* (generated by the programmer). In both cases, the programming language software makes sure they can be easily stored and retrieved.

Modularization is a truly universal technique—whether you are going to the moon or building a home…or writing a program. In fact, given today's large-scale programs, it is downright vital. How could we ever bring to market next year a project that requires 100 person-years of work if we can't break up the program and parcel out the modules to 100 programmers.

The *println* method

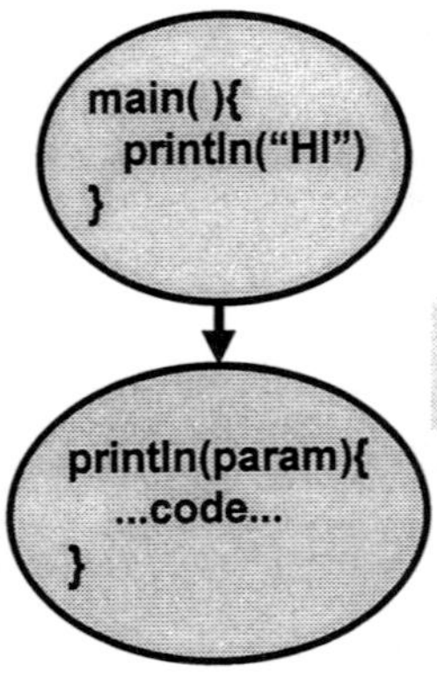

Actually, all of our programs so far have used modularization—we just didn't point it out. *Println* is a built-in method from class *PrintStream*. We call method *println* by writing its full name. (*References*, such as *System.out*, will be introduced in Chapter 6).

```
System.out.println("HI");
```

When called, we jump to method *println*, process the code, and automatically return to the next statement of the calling routine. The data item inside the parenthesis (string "HI") is called a *parameter* (or *argument*). When *println* is called, parameter "HI" is passed to method *println* for screen display.

User-defined methods

Println is a built-in method. What's new to this chapter are user-defined methods. A user-defined method can be as simple as that given below—a method that returns the average value of two integers.

```
public static void main(String args[ ]){
    System.out.println(average(12,34));
}

static int average(int n1, int n2){
    return (n1 + n2)/2;
}
```

Calling routine: Call *average* and pass parameters.

Called routine: Accept parameters and return result.

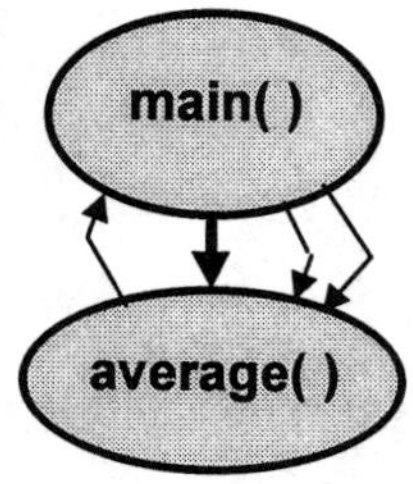

Let's follow the action, just as it would be executed.

Step 1: Processing action begins with the first statement of method *main*.

```
System.out.println(average(12,34));
```

Right away, we are confronted with *nested* method calls (method *average* is nested within method *println*). In such a case, the innermost method (*average*) is called first.

Method *average* is called and integer parameters 12 and 34 are passed.

> *Parameters* 12 and 34 are literal constants. In general, parameters can be any expression that reduces to a number. Often, they are simple variables.

Step 2: Method *average* receives the parameters by way of two local integer variables (*n1* and *n2*). The return type to the left of *average* (*int*) specifies the type of data that will be returned back to the calling routine.

```
int average(int n1,int n2)
```

Step 3: Within the body of method *average*, we generate the average value and return the result back to the calling routine.

```
return (n1 + n2)/2;
```

Step 4: We jump back to *main*, execute the next operation (call *println*, the outer nested method), and print the result to the screen.

```
System.out.println(average(12,34));
```

Global versus local variables

We have two kinds of variables at our disposal: *global* and *local*.

- Global variables are defined outside of all methods and have a universal scope (everybody can access) and a permanent lifetime (always valid).
- Local variables are defined inside methods and have a limited scope (valid only within the method in which they were declared) and a temporary lifetime (created upon method entry and destroyed upon method exit). So far, all of our variables have been local.

Global variables are used for inter-modular communication and are an alternative to parameters (which are local). Listed below is the same *average* program we looked at a moment ago, but with all parameters replaced by global variables.

```
static int n1,n2,answer;

public static void main(String args[ ]){
      n1 = 12;
      n2 = 34;
      average( );
      System.out.println(answer);
}
static void average( ){
      answer = (n1 + n2)/2;
}
```

Global variables.

Void functions do not return a value and can not use the *return* statement.

No parameters are passed.

Action automatically returns upon reaching the closing bracket.

So, it seems we have our choice: Inter-modular communication by way of parameters or by way of global variables?

- Global variables are very handy when a large number of modules need access to the same variable. However, these "cookie-jar" variables pose a severe security problem: If everybody has access, how long will your data remain valid?
- Parameters, on the other hand, are very secure. Even more important, the programmer is free to use any names at all for the parameter variables (the sending and receiving parameter variables can be different).

In most cases, inter-modular communication by way of parameters is the preferable choice. For the built-in functions, it is really the only choice; otherwise, the programmer would have the burden of remembering specific global variable names.

With OOP languages such as Java, global variables are limited to the scope of a class, and therefore the security problem is all but eliminated. As we will see in Chapter 6, global variables form the very heart of that elusive *object.*

Hands-On Procedure

Step one—Project definition

1. At the definition stage, projects *Fever* and *Fever2* are identical.

Project *Fever* will print *Danger, temperature of ___* to the screen and sound a beep for every degree above 99°F. Otherwise *Temperature OK* is printed to the screen. As before, our fever thermometer was purchased in Europe and only reads in Celsius.

Step two—Structure chart

2. At the structure chart level of Figure 4.1, however, the two programs are quite different.

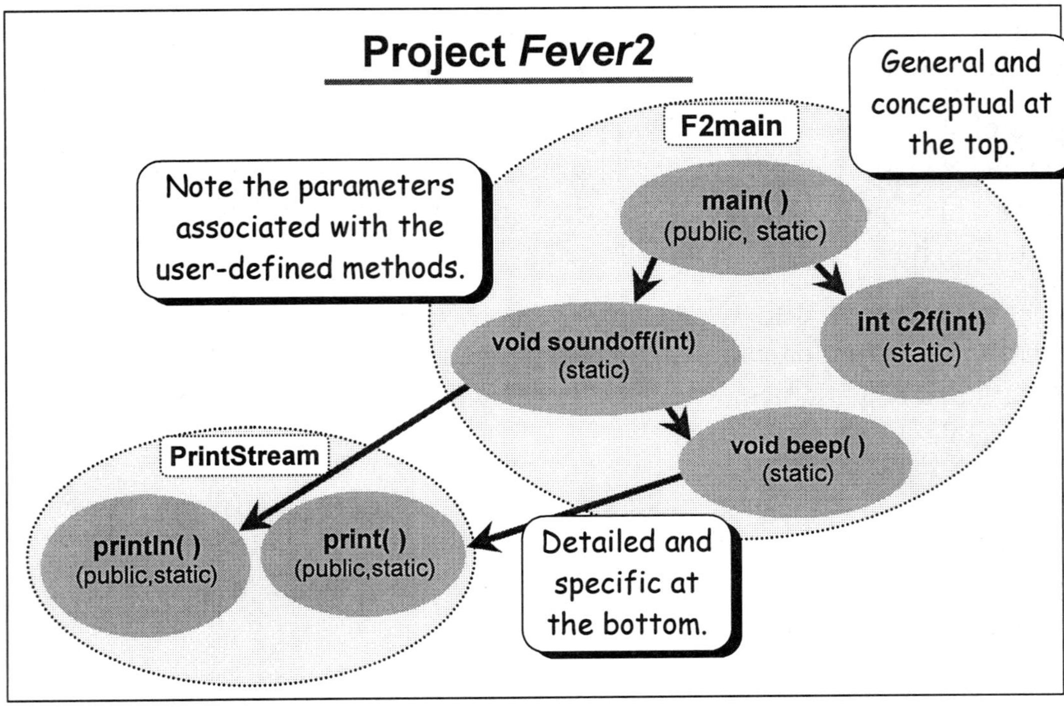

Figure 4.1
Project *Fever2* structure chart

Looking to Figure 4.1, the major difference is the modularization of user-defined class *F2main* into a hierarchy of four methods—all *static*.

Modularization is more an art than a science. Why did we break up the program into the modules shown in Figure 4.1? Because these blocks of code form logical entities that fit together in a hierarchy.

Low-level method *c2f* is a classic case in point. It encompasses one clear and discernible task—neither too simple nor too complex. When we hear the name of the method, it brings the intent of the code (temperature conversion) immediately to mind.

What this block design accomplishes is nothing short of a miracle: We take a complex multifaceted program of many lines of code and break it up into a few bite-size modules arranged in a hierarchy.

Step three—Write the program

3. Create project *Fever2* within solution *Chapter4*, and rename the files as shown.

4. **DCLICKL** on *F2main* to bring up the default outline, and enter the program code of Figure 4.2. (You may wish to save time by copying code from *Fever* to *Fever2*.)

```
// Main calls c2f and soundoff. Soundoff calls beep.
public class F2main
{
    public static void main (String[ ] args){
        soundoff(c2f(40));
    }

    static int c2f(int tempC){
        return(9*tempC/5 + 32);
    }

    static void soundoff(int temp){
        int i;
        if(temp > 99){
            System.out.println("Caution! Your temperature is "+temp);
            for(i=0;i<(temp – 99);i++)
                beep( );
        }
        else
            System.out.println("Temperature OK.");
    }

    static void beep( ){
        System.out.println('\7');
    }
}
```

High-level method.

Mid-level methods.

All methods are static; all variables are local.

Low-level method.

Reminder: Add delay if using sound card. If sound is not available, change '\7' to "beep."

Figure 4.2
Class *Fever2* final design

> As a reminder, note that all methods are one-copy-only (shared) and therefore all are tagged *static*. If any method was not declared static, then it could only be accessed by way of objects...and we won't be doing that until Chapter 6.

Step four—Execute the program

BOLD TYPE = click left.

5. **Build**, **Build** to check for syntax errors. Make any necessary corrections.

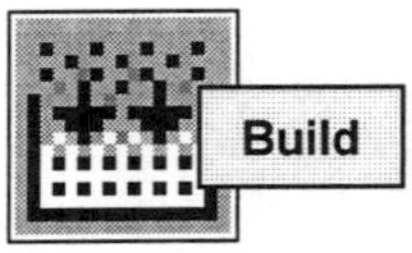

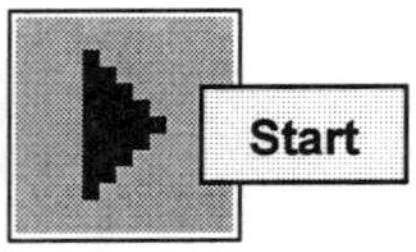

6. Start the program. Did it operate as expected? (Suggestion: Try several different temperatures.)

Yes **No**

Step five—Debug (study) the program

Singlestepping into a Method

> When we arrive at a user-defined method (such as *soundoff*) during singlestepping, we have an option. We can step *over* the method by pressing F10, or we can step *into* the method by pressing F11.
>
> When we step *over* the method (F10), we execute the entire method in one step and move on to the next statement. When we step *into* the method (F11), we enter the new method and automatically move to its first statement.

7. Press F10 to enter the debug mode. Is *the present position marker* (yellow arrow) pointing to the first executable statement (method *soundoff*)?

Yes **No**

> At this time, we have the option of pressing F10 again and stepping *over* method *soundoff*, or pressing F11 and stepping *into* method *soundoff*. For comparison purposes, let's do both.

8. Press F10 (step *over*) again. Was method *soundoff* (and therefore the complete program) executed and did the yellow arrow move to the closing bracket of *main*?

   Yes **No**

9. Press F10 again. Did we exit the program and the debug mode?

   Yes **No**

At this time, be sure to remove or comment out the delay that may have been added to method *beep* in order to accommodate a sound card.

10. Press F10 to re-enter the debug mode and again move to the first statement (method *soundoff*).

11. This time, press F11 (step *into*). Did we move to the first (and only) statement of method *c2f*?

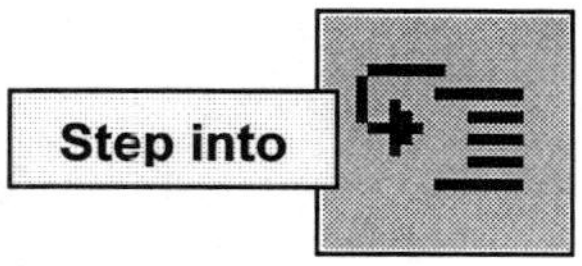

    Yes **No**

12. Press F10. Did we execute the conversion (*9*tempC/5+32*) and return to *soundoff*?

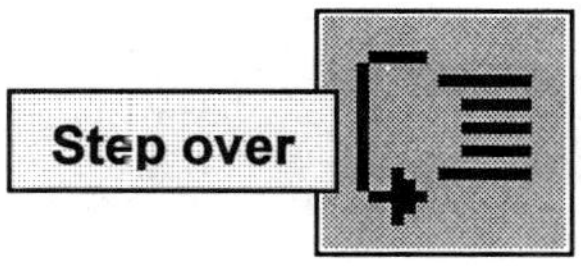

    Yes **No**

13. Press F11. Did we step *into* function *soundoff*, and does the yellow arrow now point to the first executable statement within method *soundoff*?

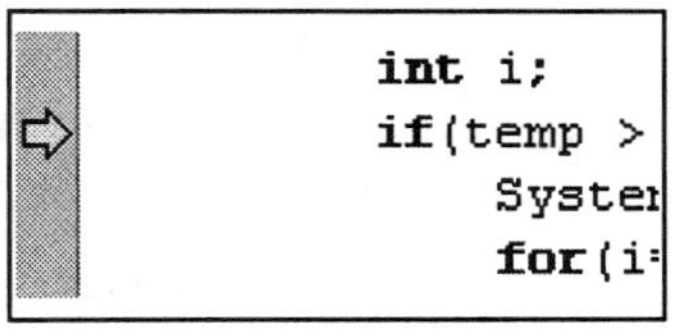

    Yes **No**

14. Once inside method *soundoff*, press F10 several times until the yellow arrow points to the next decision point (method *beep*). Press F11 once and step into method *beep* (yellow arrow pointing to *beep*). Press F10. Did you hear the beep?

    Yes **No**

    Press F10. Did we automatically return to the *for* loop?

    Yes **No**

15. Continue using F10 and F11 as you wish to step through the program until you fully understand its operation. Do we eventually return to *main* and exit the program?

    Yes **No**

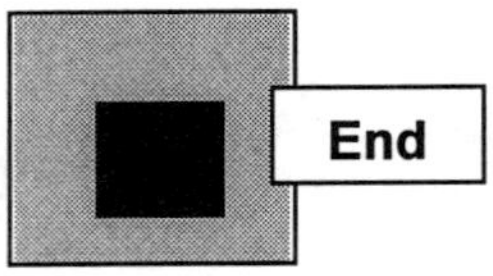

Shift+F5 to exit (end) the debug mode at any time. **File, Close All** if you are done with this project.

Exercises

To bring back a previous project: **File, Open** (or click *the Open Project* toolbar button), **Existing** (or **Recent**) tab, **DCLICKL** the *Solution* folder, **DCLICKL** the *Solution* icon.

a) Rewrite project *Fever2* of Figure 4.2 using global variables for all inter-modular communication. (In this case, why is the use of global variables to be discouraged?)

b) Write method *largest*, which receives two integer parameters and returns the larger one. Method *main* tests method *largest* by sending two integer parameters and displaying the return value.

c) Write method *craps*, which receives two integer parameters, each in the range of 1 to 6. If their sum is 7 or 11, a beep is heard and char '$' is returned. Otherwise, char '0' is returned. Method *main* tests method *craps* by sending parameters and displaying the return character.

d) Write method *parity*, which receives a byte parameter and returns 'E' if the parity is even and 'O' if the parity is odd. *Main* tests *parity*. (Even parity means an even number of 1s; odd parity means an odd number of 1s.)

e) Write method *salary*, which receives parameters *hours*, *wageRate*, and *bonus* and returns the total *earnings* that week. If the total is greater than $1,000, a beep is heard. *Main* tests *salary*.

ESPRESSO

How can I trap a return value?

If a function uses the *return* statement to return a value, then that value must be picked up and used by the calling routine; Otherwise it will just wither away on the vine.

A function (method) that returns a value can be used anywhere a variable can be used. The return value is treated just like the contents of a variable.

Here are three common ways that the elusive return value is accepted and used by the calling function:

- Assign the return value to a variable.

```
answer = average(12,34);
```

- Nest the method within another method which passes a parameter of the same type.

```
System.out.println(average(12,34));
```

- Use the method within a conditional expression:

```
if(average(12,34) > 20)
```

Incidentally, if a function returns a value, we aren't required to make use of it. We can simply ignore it if we wish.

Also, be aware that the *return* statement can be placed anywhere within a method and (if executed) will cause the action to immediately jump back to the calling routine. However, J++ checks to make sure that the *return* statement can always be reached. (For example, a *return* statement inside a *for* loop may never be executed if action never enters the loop.)

f) Write method *msec*, which accepts an integer parameter and delays that many milliseconds. Test and calibrate your method by passing parameter 10000 from *main*.

g) Write method *count*, which receives two integer parameters and displays the count from lowest to the highest at the rate of two characters/sec. (Method *main* calls method *count*, which in turn calls method *msec*.)

h) Write method *TimesTable*, which receives an integer parameter and creates a multiplication table. The example shown below is for *parameter* = 2, but you should use a larger value. *Main* calls method *TimesTable*.

```
0 x 0 = 0
0 x 1 = 0
0 x 2 = 0
1 x 0 = 0
1 x 1 = 1
1 x 2 = 2
2 x 0 = 0
2 x 1 = 2
2 x 2 = 4
```

i) Modify method *count* to sound a beep whenever it prints an integer that is evenly divided by seven. (Hint: Use the *modulo* operator.)

j) Write method *CountFaster*, which receives a parameter and counts down from the parameter value to zero at a faster and faster rate. (The time in seconds between counts equals the count value.) *Main* tests *CountFaster*.

k) Write method *printNumbers*, which receives an int parameter and prints it to the screen parameter number of times. (That is, if it receives a 4 it prints 4444.) *Main* tests *printNumbers*.

l) Write method *binary*, which receives a byte and prints its binary equivalent to the screen as a series of 1s and 0s at the rate of 1/sec. *Main* tests *binary*. (Hint: Use the bit-wise AND operator (&) to test each bit and print "0" or "1".)

m) Write method *divide*, which receives two integers (*dividend* and *devisor*) and returns their quotient. However, if the devisor is 0, the system beeps, prints "Can't divide by 0," does not attempt to perform the division, and returns 0. *Main* tests *divide*.

n) Write method *FreeFall*, which accepts an integer parameter and prints to the screen in real time the distance traveled in free fall from 0 to parameter seconds. ($D = 16t^2$.) Method *FreeFall* calls method *msec*. *Main* tests *FreeFall*. For example, for parameter = 3 seconds:

```
You fall 0 feet in 0 seconds.
You fall 16 feet in 1 seconds.
You fall 64 feet in 2 seconds.
You fall 144 feet in 3 seconds.
```

o) Using the switch operator, write method *football*, which receives an integer parameter and prints "Extra point," "Safety," "Fieldgoal," "Touchdown," or "Illegal score" to the screen. To simulate the computer thinking, a one second delay is placed between execution and display. A beep sounds for every illegal score. *Main* tests *football*.

p) Write method *progression*, which receives four integers and prints "Arithmetic progression" if each number in order equals the sum of all the previous numbers. Otherwise it prints, "Random progression." *Main* tests *progression*.

q) Modify project *Fever* by adding method *extremeDanger*. Method *extremeDanger* sounds 10 beeps for each degree above 107° (42°C).

r) Write method *stocks*, which receives three integer parameters representing three consecutive closing Dow averages. If the Dow always went up, "Bull" is printed and a beep sounds; if the Dow always went down, "Bear" is printed. Otherwise, "Neutral" is printed. *Main* tests *stocks*.

s) Write method *alphabet*, which receives a char parameter. If the parameter is 'U', it prints the upper case alphabet to the screen at the rate of two characters/sec. If the parameter is 'L', it prints the lower case alphabet. *Main* calls alphabet. ('A' = 65 and 'a' = 97.)

t) Write project *Lottery*, in which method *process* looks at three integers (parameters). If all numbers are equal, you win the jackpot and 10 beeps are sounded. Otherwise, no beeps are sounded. Method *main* calls method *process*.

u) Modify project *Lottery* (method *process*) so a single beep is sounded if any two integers are the same.

v) Write project *GradeAverage*, which sends three grade characters to method *GPA*, which returns the grade point average (A = 4.0, B = 3.0, etc.). During the calculation, method *GPA* sends the grades to method *bonus* for further evaluation. Method *bonus* returns an extra .2 grade points if the first grade is the lowest.

w) Write project *Resistor*, which determines the series or parallel equivalent of two resistor values. Method *main* calls method *seriesParallel*, which in turn calls methods *series* and *parallel*. Inter-modular communication is by way of two float parameters (the resistor values) and a char parameter (ASCII 'S' or 'P'). A beep is heard whenever the equivalent value is greater than 1MΩ or less than 100Ω.

x) Write project *PrimeNumber*, which sends two integers (the first always smaller than the second) and a character (L or H) to method *prime*. If the character is 'L', method *prime* calls method *lowest*, that returns the lowest prime number in the range of integers sent. Otherwise, method *highest* returns the highest prime number found.

y) When a method calls itself, it's known as *recursion*. By calling method *power* (shown below), determine 5^3. Be sure to singlestep through the program and explain its operation.

```
static int power(int x, int n){
    if(n > 1)
        return x*power(x,n–1);
    else
        return x;
}
```

Method *power* is valid only for positive values of x and n.

Questions and Problems

1. What is the difference (if any) between a *function* and a *method*?

2. How is a function called?

3. Regarding *top-down design*, what kinds of modules are at the top, and what kinds are at the bottom?

4. For real-world project *moon-landing*, create a three-layered structure chart and list as least one activity at each level.

5. What is a *parameter* (or *argument*)?

6. Referring to Figure 4.2, what is the one (and only) *compound* statement?

7. When singlestepping, what is the difference between F10 and F11?

8. Referring to the structure chart of Figure 4.1, why does method *beep* call method *print*?

Part 2

J++ Classes and Objects

The six chapters of Part 2 cover the essentials of an object-oriented programming (OOP) language, and all the material should be covered in detail. We'll start with simple J++ classes and objects and finish with keyboard input. Along the way we'll cover such essential topics as *arrays*, *strings*, and *constructors*.

After Chapter 5, get ready for objects!

CHAPTER

5

Project DrawTree

Class Modularization and Overloading Methods

Objectives

- *To modularize our project at the class level*
- *To control access to methods and member variables*
- *To draw an image of a tree*

Discussion

Why do biologists classify all living things in a top-down hierarchy—from *kingdom* to *phylum* to *class* to *order* to *family* to *species*? One reason is that it helps them organize, group, and classify the amazing diversity of life found in nature.

The same is true in the world of programming. When Pascal and C were king and programs were simpler, only the venerable *function* was needed to modularize the code. As programs grew in size and complexity, the designers of C++ and J++ saw a clear-cut need for additional layers.

The Java hierarchy

As first introduced in Chapter 1, there are five distinct layers to the J++ hierarchy (Figure 5.1). In the previous chapter, we modularized our programs at the *method* level; in this chapter we move up the hierarchical ladder and modularize our programs at the *class* level. From this chapter on, we can expect our structure chart layout to resemble the top-down hierarchy of Figure 5.2.

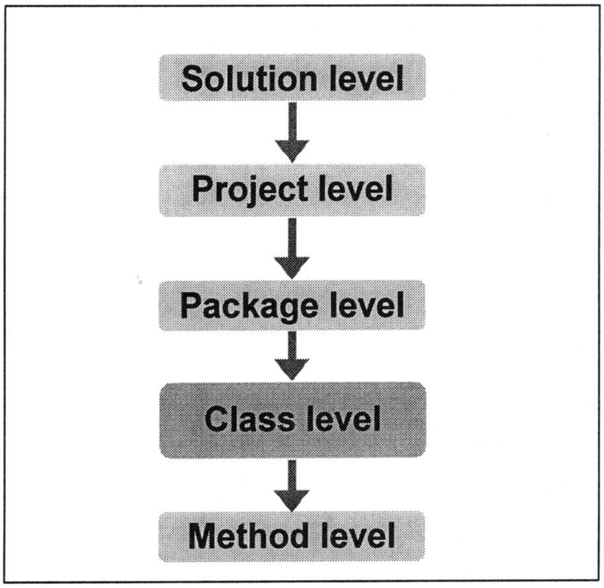

Figure 5.1
The five J++ layers

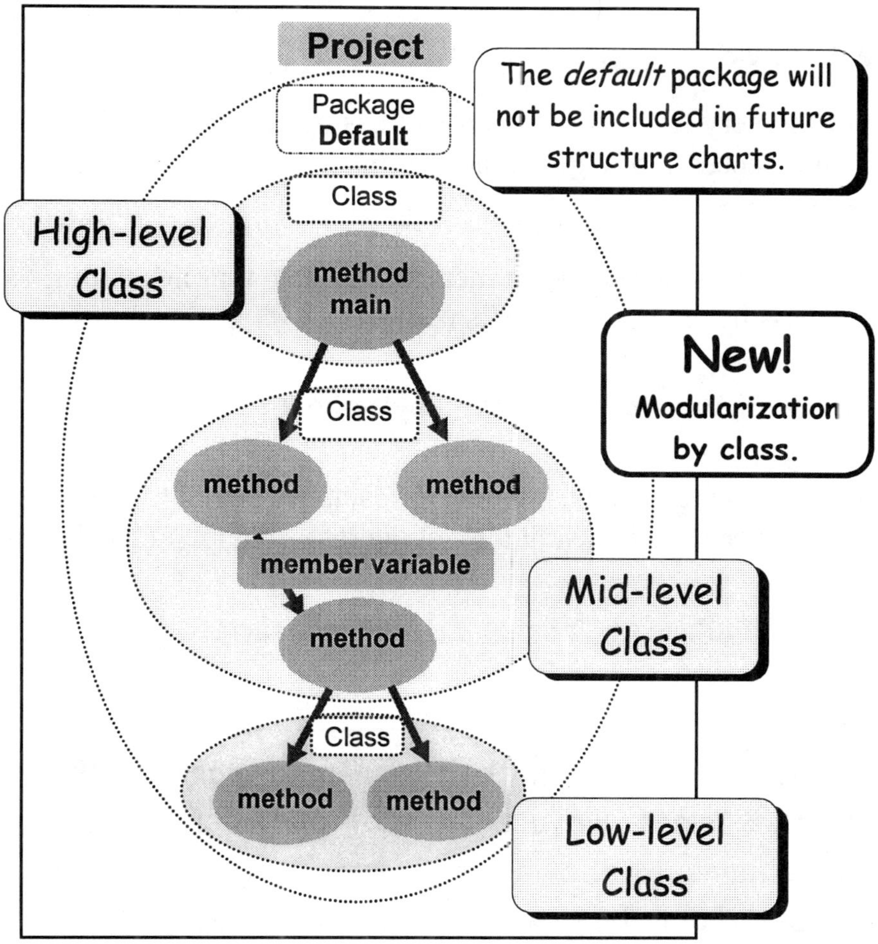

Figure 5.2
Modularization by class

As we will see throughout this text, the *class* is the centerpiece of Java programs. Why? Because it is from the venerable class that we will derive those elusive objects...starting in Chapter 6.

The member variable

Reviewing Figure 5.2, note the *member variable* within the mid-level class. For now, member variables (also known as *data members*) are simply variables that are global *within a given class*. They are not to be confused with local variables, which are valid *only within a method*. Member variables are not used by project *DrawTree* of this chapter; in the next chapter, they will form the very heart of that long-anticipated object.

Access

For the very first time, our project has more than one class. Because of this, accessing methods and member variables takes on an added dimension.

- We access a method or member variable that lies within the same class by simply writing its name.

```
myVariable          myMethod( )
```

- We access a static method or member variable that lies within another class by using the dot operator to append its class name.

```
MyClass.myVariable      MyClass.myMethod( )
```

To access a static method or member variable that lies in another class, we use the dot operator to append the class name to the member name! (Local variables are accessed only from within methods as always.)

Access control

With multiple classes, another equally important consideration is access control (*scope* and *visibility*). To see how important access control really is, lets look closely at a common item found in every living room—your television set.

- Despite the complexity of modern-day television, the only controls readily available are the on/off switch, volume control, and channel select. These limited controls, accessible to all, we call *public*.

- A few other more detailed controls, such as tint and horizontal lock, are partially hidden. Such controls, accessible only to a knowledgeable user, we call *friendly*.

- The rest of the controls are used for fine-tuning and are permanently sealed within the casing. These controls, accessible only to a trained service technician, we call *private*.

Because objects in cyberspace are patterned after the physical objects around us, is it any surprise that classes and objects in J++ follow the same pattern?

- **Public** is the least restrictive. *Public* member variables and methods are accessible to all methods in all packages. A well-written class offers a limited number of carefully chosen public member variables and methods.

- **Friendly** is the default case. *Friendly* members are accessible only to other members of the same package.

- **Private** is the most restrictive. *Private* data members and methods are only accessible to other members of the same class. Within a complex, well-modularized class, most of the member variables will be private.

> From here on, we must decide if each and every method and member variable best falls into the *private*, *friendly*, or *public* category. (Local variables are not involved.)

Tools

Because the classes and methods found at the lower levels of the hierarchy often perform basic and fundamental operations of the kind required by most programs, they are often called *tools*. It is common practice for *tool-building* to be among the first tasks accomplished.

In this chapter, we will create a special user-defined class called *BasicTools*. Initially, this class will hold several key methods related to time and sound. We certainly can expect to add to these basic tools many times throughout the remainder of this text. In future chapters, other tools classes will be developed to hold low-level behavior.

ESPRESSO

What about packages?

If modularization is useful at the *class* level, why not the *package* level? The answer is, our projects are simply too small to split them into a hierarchy of packages. Instead, we will let all of our user-defined classes fall automatically into the *default* package.

However, suppose *myMethod* is a built-in method that lies in a class belonging to another package? In this case, to access *myMethod*, shouldn't we do the following?

```
myPackage.MyClass.myMethod( )
```

We certainly could, but you'll never see it done in actual practice. That's because of the two alternatives listed below:

- Package *java.lang* is available by default. (This is how we have enjoyed automatic access to class *PrintStream*.)
- We can use the keyword **import** to enable access to packages.

Overloading methods

Suppose we wish to add to class *BasicTools* a special version of method *beep* that receives an int parameter and beeps that many times. Java has made just such a process easier than ever. It's called *method overloading* and its illustrated by Table 5.1.

Simple beep	Multiple beep

static void beep( ){
    System.out.println('\7');
}
	static void beep(int num){
	    while(num–– > 0)
	        System.out.println('\7');
	}

Return types are not counted as part of the name.

Table 5.1
Overloaded versions of method *beep*

Although methods *beep( )* and *beep(int)* appear to have the same name (*beep*), they really don't when we include the parameters as part of the method name. That is, *beep( )* and *beep(int)* are two completely separate and distinct methods. We will find that many of Java's built-in methods are overloaded.

You should be aware that overloading only applies within the same class. In other words, it's possible for two methods to have the same full name, but perform entirely different functions—if they are defined in separate classes. (This is because the complete name now includes the unique class name.)

Character-mapped graphics

In the stand-alone mode, we lack anything like a *set-cursor* method. Therefore, the ability to draw graphics is extremely limited. Making good use of methods *print* and *println*, however, we can draw just about any pattern of ASCII characters line by line as we move down the page.

```
      *
     ***
    *****
   *******
  *********
 ***********
*************
```

A simple drawing of a tree, shown at the right, will be our first project. (Additional features will be added during the exercises.)

Hands-On Procedure

Step one—Project definition

1. In this chapter, we will use a crude form of character-mapped graphics to draw a familiar item.

> **This chapter's project will use asterisks to draw a seven-branch image of a tree at the top center of the screen—a branch at a time.**

Step two—Structure chart

2. The structure chart of Figure 5.3 shows a hierarchy of three user-defined class layers. (Class *PrintStream* will no longer be included.)

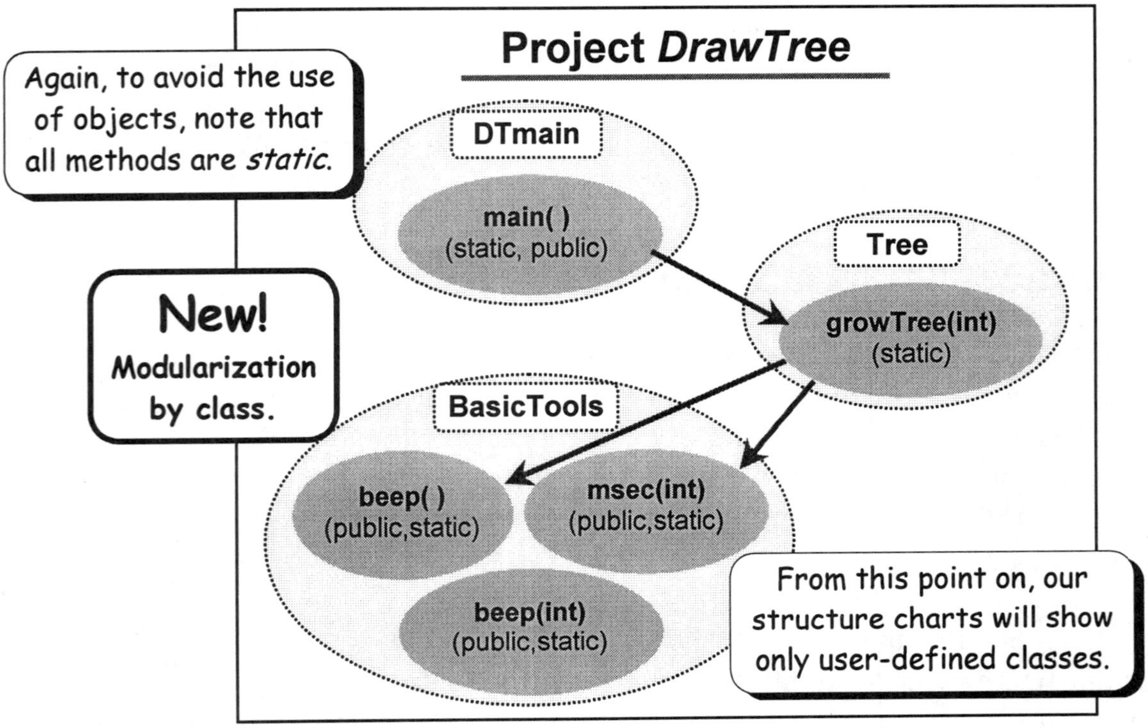

Figure 5.3
Project *DrawTree* structure chart

Because of their universal nature, all the methods of class *BasicTools* have been tagged *public*. Because we wish to limit the access of class *Tree* to package *default*, it is tagged *friendly* (by default). Class *DTmain* must be tagged *public* so the Development Environment can gain access.

Step three—Writing the program

3. Following the guidelines of Chapters 1–4, create project *DrawTree* within solution *Chapter5*, rename the project and *Class1* files as shown, and set the *DrawTree* properties.

> Which class? Which of the three classes (*DTmain*, *Tree*, and *BasicTools*) do we complete first? Because the upper classes depend on the lower classes, it often makes sense to complete the lower-level classes first.

4. To create user-defined class *BasicTools*: **CLICKR** on project *DrawTree* within the *Project Explorer* window, **Add**, **Add Class** to bring up the *Add Item* dialog box of Figure 5.4, **CLICKL** on *Class*, enter class name (*BasicTools*), **Open**.

> **BOLD TYPE** = click left.

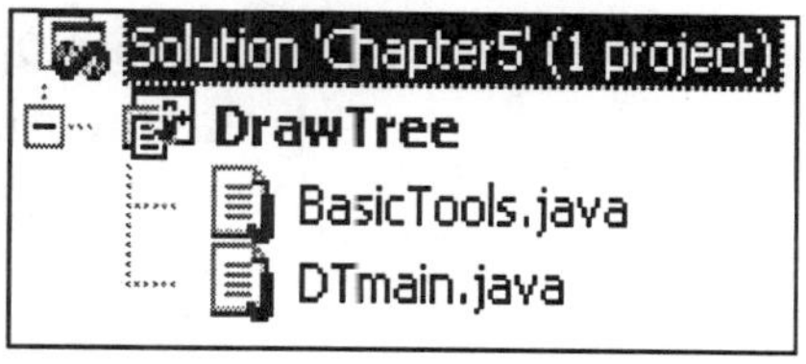

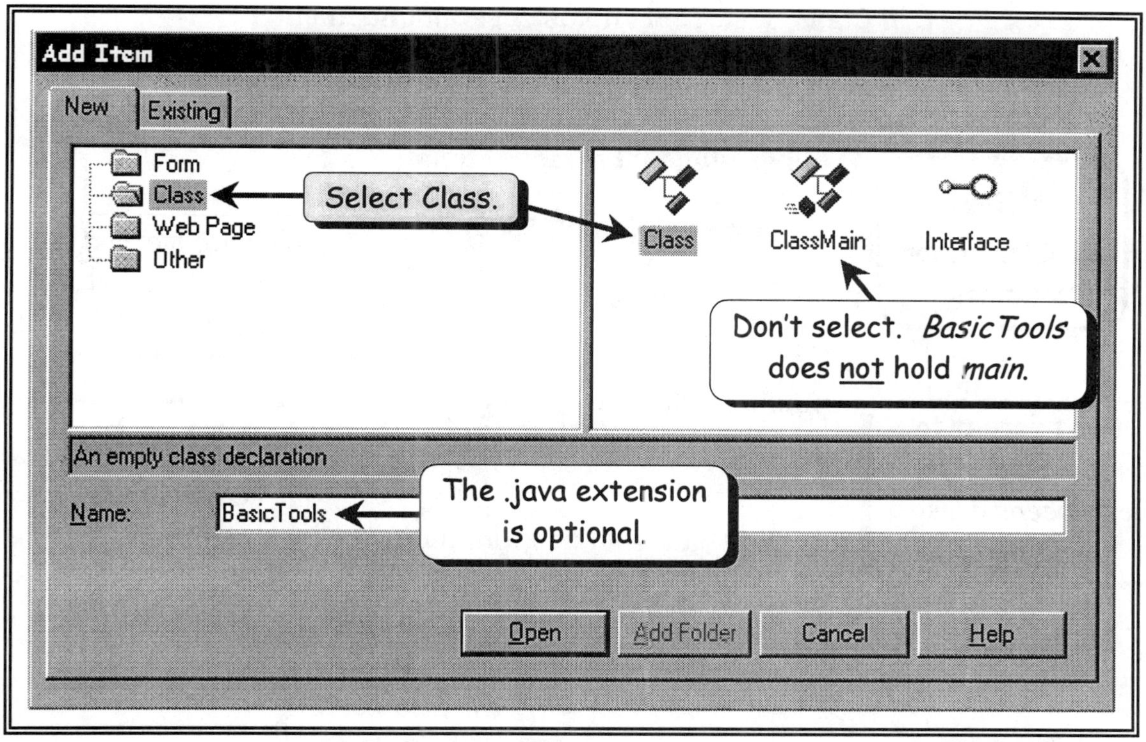

Figure 5.4
Add Item dialog box

5. **DCLICKL** on *BasicTools* in the *Project Explorer* window. Did the default class outline appear on the screen?

   Yes **No**

```
public class BasicTools
{
}
```

6. Following Figure 5.5, enter the three methods shown into class *BasicTools*. As with most tools, all the methods fall into the "everybody-can-use" and "share-and-share-alike" categories and are therefore tagged *public* and *static*.

> **Reminders**: A method or member variable tagged *public* is accessible from any other class. If tagged *static*, only one shared copy is created and it is directly accessible by way of its class name (without first generating an object).

```
// Class BasicTools holds several fundamental
// methods related to time and sound.
class BasicTools
{
    public static int msec(int time){
        int i;
        for(i=0;i<(time*25000);i++)
            ;
        return time;
    }

    public static void beep( ){
        System.out.print('\7');
    }

    public static void beep(int num){
        while(num-->0)
            System.out.print('\7');
    }
}
```

import java.lang is listed by default.

New! Modularization by class.

To calibrate method *msec*, we will adjust this value.

Don't forget to add a delay to both *beeps* if using a sound card.

New! Overloaded methods.

"\7" will also work.

Figure 5.5
Class *BasicTools*

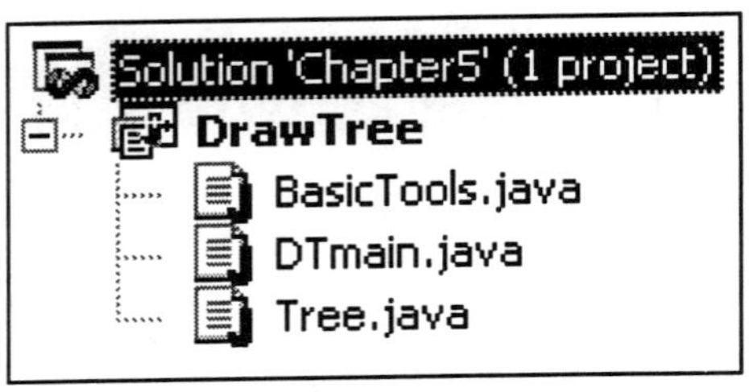

7. Using the same techniques, add and complete mid-level class *Tree* of Figure 5.6. (**CLICKR** on project *DrawTree*, **Add**, **Add Class**, etc.)

```
public class Tree
{
    static void growTree(int height){
        int i,j,spaces,leaves;
        for(i=0,spaces=40,leaves=1;i<height;i++){
            for(j=0;j<spaces;j++)
                System.out.print(' ');
            for(j=0;j<leaves;j++)
                System.out.print('*');
            System.out.println( );
            spaces--;
            leaves+=2;
            BasicTools.beep( );
            BasicTools.msec(500);
        }
    }
}
```

Class *Tree* uses only local variables. (No global member variables.)

New! Accessing a method in another class.

Methods *beep* and *msec* add sound and visual effects.

Figure 5.6
Class *Tree*

Although a detailed analysis is left as an exercise, we should point out the following:

- Of all the possible parameters that we could send to method *growTree*, we have chosen only the tree *height*.
- The outer loop controls the number of branches. The two inner loops control the number of spaces to each branch and the number of leaves making up each branch.
- To widen each branch as they are drawn from the top down, we decrease the number of spaces and increase the number of leaves.
- To call *beep* and *msec*—which lie in another class—we append the class name (*BasicTools*).

8. Next we complete class *DTmain*, the third and final class. Select (**CLICKL**) *DTmain* to bring up the familiar class outline, and add the code of Figure 5.7. Because most of the work is done by the lower-level classes, the code for *main* is very brief (call method *growTree* and send seven branches.)

New!
Accessing a method in another class.

```
// Each time growTree is called, a single tree
// of parameter height is drawn.
public class DTmain
{
      public static void main (String[ ] args){
            Tree.growTree(7);
      }
}
```

Pass the number of branches as a parameter.

Figure 5.7
Class *DTmain*, holding the *main* method

ESPRESSO

Why?

Why did we create class *Tree*; why did we design method *growTree*; and why did we send parameter *height*?

The answers are always the same: To the designer, these decisions seemed the most logical and reasonable at the time. We chose class *Tree* as a handy descriptive "container" to place all tree-related behaviors. We chose to place most of the code in method *growTree* in order to leave *main* as clean as possible. We chose parameter *height* because that is the only attribute we wish to vary.

In Chapter 6 we will have another important reason for creating class *Tree*: To produce tree *objects*.

```
*
**
***
****
*****
******
*******
```

Step four—Execute the program

9. Build and run the program, noting the output screen. Was the tree drawn as expected, were beeps sounded according to our specifications, and were the branches drawn one-half second apart?

    Yes **No**

10. The chances are good that the branches were not drawn one-half second apart because method *msec* is not properly calibrated.

    To calibrate method *msec*, pass it a large parameter (such as 10000) and time the delay with your watch. Using ratios, make any necessary adjustments to the constant (presently shown as 25000). (Those using sound cards be aware of the delay built into method *beep*.)

```
for(i=0;i<(time*25000);i++)
 ;
```

What value did you use?

ESPRESSO

Are there any naming conventions?

Programs consist of *keywords* and *identifiers*. Keywords are built-in elements that come with the software and can't be changed by the programmer (*new*, *public*, *static*, etc.).

Identifiers include names of variables, classes, methods, and objects, and are selected by the programmer. Some naming conventions are required, while others are merely suggested.

Identifier rules required by Java:

- They can't be keywords
- They consist of any combination of letters, numbers, and characters, but must start with a letter. They can not include white spaces.
- They are case sensitive.

Identifier rules suggested by Microsoft:

- Start class names with capital letters, and capitalize words within the name. (Such as *BasicTools*.)
- Start member variable and method names with lowercase letters and capitalize words within the name. Variables should be nouns and methods should be verbs. (Such as *myCash* and *growTree*.)
- Avoid the use of the underscore ("_").

11. Repeat the program using trees of various heights. Were they drawn properly?

Yes **No**

Step five—Debug and modify

The *Locals* window

In Chapter 2, we used the cursor method to view variables. In this chapter we introduce the *Locals* window. It allows us to view any variable in real time during singlestepping or execution.

12. Press F10 to enter the debug mode, and note that the *Locals* window of Figure 5.9 automatically appears.

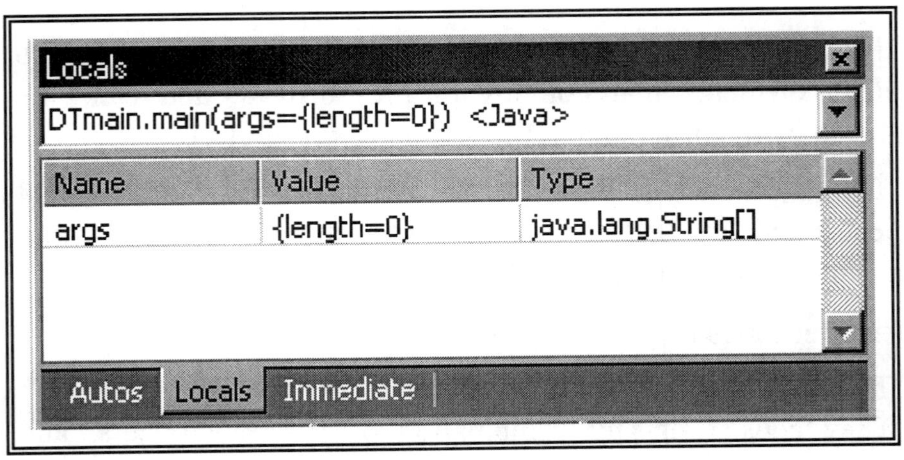

Figure 5.9
The *Locals* window

The *Locals* window offers three tab options: *Autos*, *Locals*, and *Immediate*.

- *Autos* only displays local variables used in the current and previous statements.
- *Locals* displays all local variables.
- *Immediate* accepts expressions to be evaluated or executed.

13. Select the *Locals* option, which causes all local variables to be listed.

14. Using F10 and F11 as necessary, step to the first executable instruction within method *growTree*. Are all variables but parameter *height* listed as "not in scope" (not yet initialized) in the *Locals* window?

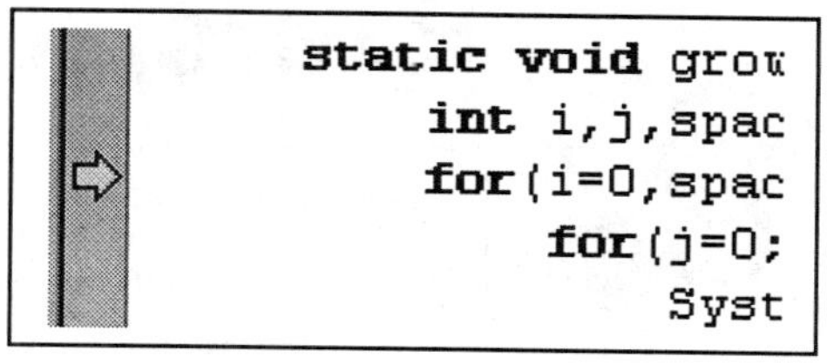

Yes **No**

15. Using F10, step to the *System.out.println* statement.

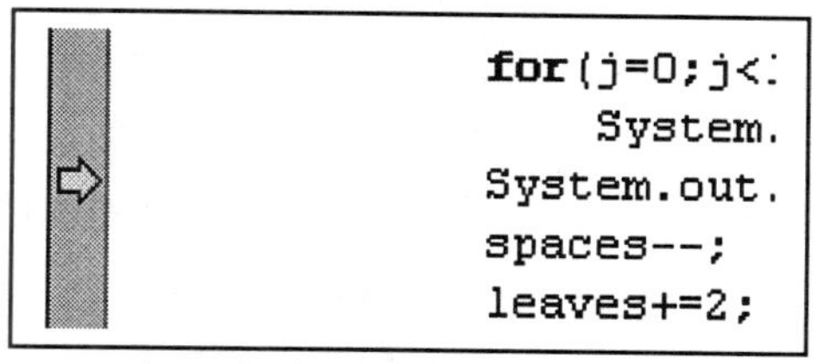

a) Are all five variables now "in scope" and holding expected values?

Yes **No**

b) Can we conclude that variables must be initialized before they can appear as "in scope" in the *Locals* window?

Yes **No**

16. Continue stepping through the program using F10 and F11. Be sure to bring back the output screen periodically to view the output. As each variable is initialized or changed, was the *Locals* window automatically updated to show the correct values?

Yes **No**

> If you are using a sound card, and you wish to step into method *beep*, be sure to comment out the added delay.

17. If you wish, repeat the singlestep process, but with the *Autos* tab selected. This time, were only the previous and present line variables listed?

Yes **No**

> Also, don't forget that once a variable has been initialized within the debugger, we can view its contents at any time by simply moving the cursor over the variable.

18. To exit the debugger at any time, press *Shift+F5*.

Exercises

Reminder: You are free to add new projects to solution *Chapter5* (**CLICKR** on solution *Chapter5*, etc.), or to modify old projects. For the new projects, we recommend the usual three classes: *ClassMain* at the top, a new user-defined class in the middle, and class *BasicTools* at the bottom. *Divide up the new code between the top two classes in any way you wish.*

a) Modify method *growTree* so any or all of the following are passed by way of parameters: The horizontal placement, the vertical placement, the shape of the tree, and the ASCII character (leaf) used to draw the tree.

b) Add method *trunk* to class *Tree*. Method *growTree* will call method *trunk*, which draws in a tree trunk. Be sure to send all appropriate parameters to method *trunk* (*position*, *thickness*, *length*, etc.)

c) Use either of the following to provide the ability to draw trees upside-down (as if reflected in water):

- Create a second method for upside-down trees.
- Pass an "upside-down" parameter to *growTree*.

Use your new methods to draw a "lake" scene (A tree and its reflection in water).

d) Make use of the new upside-down method of the previous exercise to draw a diamond (tree and its reflection).

e) Add overloaded method *beep(int num,int time)* to class *BasicTools*. This new method accepts *num* and *time* parameters, and beeps *num* times spaced *time* msec apart. Using three levels of classes (and the new *beep* method), write project *countdown* in which numbers 1 to 10 are printed to the screen and the corresponding number of beeps is sounded for each number. However, the beep rate is adjusted so the total time between numbers is a constant.

f) Using three layers of classes (application, mid-level, and tools), and passing the appropriate parameters, create project FOREST, which draws a number of trees of various locations and size. (Of course each tree will occupy a separate range of rows.)

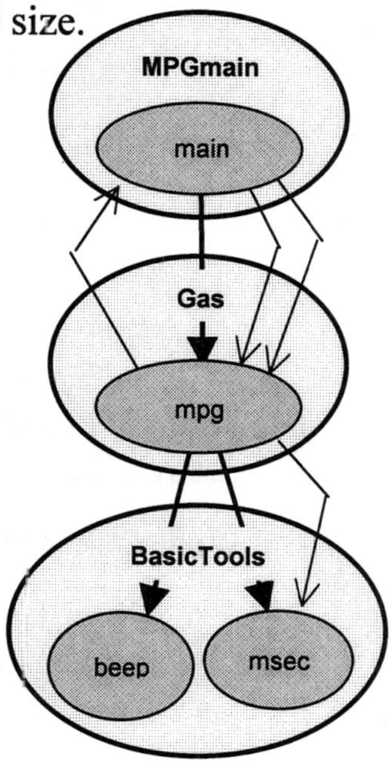

g) Using three levels of classes (*MPGmain*, *Gas*, and *BasicTools*), write project *MPG*, which takes variables *miles* and *gallons* and prints mpg (miles-per-gallon) to the screen. If the mpg is greater than 30, five beeps are sounded one second apart.

h) Using three levels of classes, write project *Alphabet*, which prints a sequential list of letters to the screen on a diagonal (as shown below). The beginning and ending letter (such as C and G) are determined by parameters. The letters would be printed one-half second apart and a beep would be heard after each letter appears. (Hint: The ASCII code for A is 65, B is 66, etc.)

```
C
 D
  E
   F
    G
```

i) Modify project *Alphabet* so the case (upper or lower) of the letters is determined by another parameter.

j) Using three levels of classes, write project *Marquee*, which shows the name of a movie moving continuously across the screen from left to right. The scanning speed is passed as a parameter. (Hint: The escape code for carriage return is '\r'.)

k) Using three levels of classes, write project *FreeFall*, which shows a "rock" (asterisk) moving down the screen as it would under gravity. (Hint: The increase in distance = $16(t+1)^2 - 16t^2$. Calibrate your system so each vertical space equals approximately 20 feet.)

l) Modify project *FreeFall* to show the trajectory for a rock with an initial horizontal velocity. (Hint: Place the following code at the appropriate place in method *FreeFall*, which assumes a time from zero to six seconds.)

```
for(i=0;i<t*12;i++)
      System.out.print(' ');
```

Questions and Problems

1. What makes any given method a *tool*?

2. A *package* is a collection of *classes*.

   True **False**

3. A *friendly* method can be accessed by other methods outside its present package.

   True **False**

4. Does method *beep(1)* perform the same operation as method *beep()*?

   Yes **No**

5. Regarding the *Variables* window, what is the difference between tabs *Auto* and *Locals*?

6. Write *method*, *class*, or *variable* beside each of the following:

Item	method, class, or variable?
Tree	
msec	
main	
length	
DTmain	
i	

7. Regarding your automobile, tag each of the following *public*, *friendly*, or *private* depending on the ease of access.

Item	Tag
The dip stick	
The steering wheel	
The timing chain	

8. If method *myMethod* below were tagged private, why would the following statement make no sense?

```
MyClass.myMethod( );
```

9. Why would we require fewer layers to classify all the animals on earth a billion years ago when life first appeared?

10. Classes provide a convenient way to cluster related methods, thus reducing the number of modules required by a complex project.

True **False**

11. Why is overloading sometimes called *simple polymorphism*? (Hint: When a man turns into a werewolf, it is known as *morphing*.)

CHAPTER

6

Project CyberBank

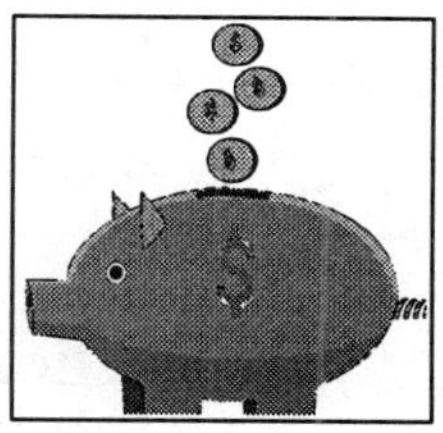

Classes and Objects

Objectives

- *To contrast classes and objects*
- *To create multiple objects from a single class*
- *To build a CyberBank*

Discussion

To use objects, or not to use objects—that is the question. In Part I we wrote many useful projects without ever creating an object. It was easy; we simply tagged every method as shared (*static*). So, who needs objects? In this pivotal chapter we have a very good reason for using them: Its called *security*.

Things anyone?

As we learned in the introduction, the real world in which we live consists of *things* and *types of things*. There are planets in general, and there are Mars, Venus, and Earth—all instances of type *planet*. There are cars in general, and there are Mary's Mustang, Sam's Mercedes, and Tai's Toyota—all instances of type *car*.

In object-oriented programming (OOP), a type of thing is known as a *class* and a thing (or specific instance of the class) is known as an *object*.

The question is, when will our programs require the use of objects? Why can't we continue to use nothing but one-copy-only, shared (*static*) attributes and behaviors? We are about to have all of our questions answered.

Class *BankAccount*

An ordinary bank account is often used to demonstrate the need for objects. In this case, individual objects play an especially crucial role, for the last thing on earth we expect is for the bank to mix up its customer's accounts.

First, we create class *BankAccount*. Into class *BankAccount* we place the same appropriate *attributes* and *behaviors* that are found in real-world bank accounts. Recall from the introduction that attributes are the nouns, or *member variables*, of the class; and behaviors are the verbs, or *methods*, of the class.

To hold the total cash on hand, we include member variable *myCash*. To carry out typical operations on *myCash*, we include methods *getBalance*, *makeDeposit,* and *withDraw*.

So far all this seems quite standard; so what's different and special about class *BankAccount*?

> What's different about class *BankAccount* is that member variable *myCash* and methods *getBalance, makeDeposit*, and *withDraw* can not be shared, and therefore can not be tagged *static!*

Okay, since shared, common accounts are hardly the stuff of which secure and reliable bank accounts are built, we dutifully remove the *static* tag from all methods and member variables—giving us the initial design of Figure 6.1.

```
public class BankAccount
{
    int myCash;

    int getBalance( ){
        return myCash;
    }

    void makeDeposit(int amount){
        myCash += amount;
    }

    void withDraw(int amount){
        myCash – = amount;
    }
}
```

New! Non-static *member variables* and *methods.*

myCash is a global (member) variable; *amount* is a local variable.

All methods and member variables must be defined within a class.

Figure 6.1
Class *BankAccount* initial design

Now, is our cyberbank ready to open? Not at all. For starters, there is only one *BankAccount* class (Figure 6.1), but two early customers have just lined up to apply for accounts. As it stands now, class *BankAccount* is just a generic design outline (a blueprint) for all bank accounts—its not a real cyber-object able to hold real cyber-cash for each customer. But the stage is set.

Objects at last!

Here is the key:

> Class *BankAccount*, with its non-static members, is a generic *template* (a *type* of thing).

When the two customers arrive to open up accounts, the bank takes out its *BankAccount* class template (Figure 6.1) and stamps out two new instances of itself—like a cookie cutter. Each instance becomes a completely separate and unique *object*, and is assigned a distinct object name (such as *a1* and *a2*).

These newly created BankAccount *objects* are now very real, in the sense that each occupies a new and separate area of memory, and each *myCash* member variable can now be assigned a unique and specific amount of cash for each customer. These important ideas are summarized in Figure 6.2.

Object creation

Exactly how will individual real *BankAccount* objects be created (*instantiated*) from the generic class template? (Certainly not with cookie cutters!) The answer is, they are created with *genesis statements*—a term coined by the author to highlight their central role in the creation of objects.

Without further ado, let's use the amazing genesis statement to create two new bank account objects from class *BankAccount*:

```
BankAccount a1 = new BankAccount( );
BankAccount a2 = new BankAccount( );
```

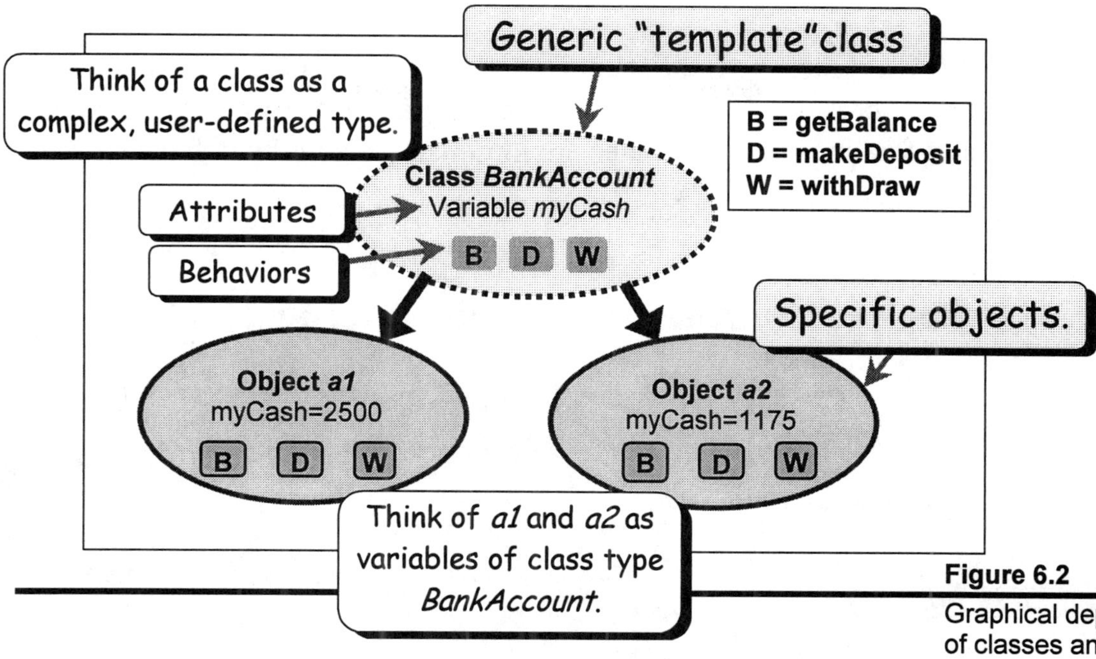

Figure 6.2
Graphical depiction of classes and objects

Looking more closely at the Genesis statements, we see that each is made up of five parts:

```
      1        2 3  4       5
BankAccount a1 = new BankAccount( );
BankAccount a2 = new BankAccount( );
```

- Item 1 (*BankAccount*) is the class type.
- Item 2 (*a1* and *a2*) are variables that hold references (pointers) to specific objects of type *BankAccount*.
- Item 3 (=) assigns an object pointer to a reference *variable*.
- Item 4 (*new*) sets aside a separate block of memory to hold each object.
- Item 5 (*BankAccount()*) is the constructor method that creates the objects.

As shown below, think of the genesis statement as a special form of a standard integer initialization statement:

```
        int   speed  =  80;
BankAccount a1       =  new BankAccount( );
```

After each genesis statement, it is very helpful to visualize the newly created object and reference in graphical form: (All integer and floating-point attributes are initialized to zero by default.)

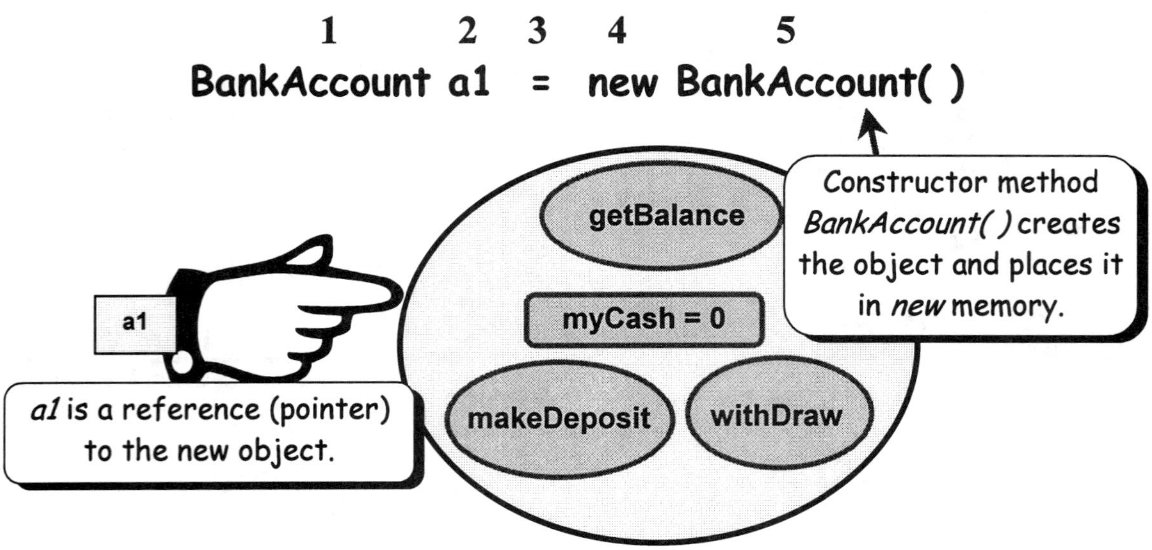

To summarize, the left half of the genesis statement (1 and 2) declares a null reference (pointer) to objects of type *BankAccount*. The right half (4 and 5) takes new memory from the *heap* (a special memory pool) and calls the constructor method (*BankAccount( )*) to create a real object of type *BankAccount*. The assignment operator (3) then updates reference *a1* to point to (refer to) the new object.

Objects are here to stay

Can you now answer the question we posed at the beginning of the chapter: Why do we need objects? Why don't we just make every method and global variable static, as we've done so far? The answer is deceptively simple:

Objects are required when the logic and nature of the problem demands multiple instances of a class, each one unique, separate, different...and "real".

Object variables—the bulls-eye

As stated in the introduction, the *member variables*—such as *myCash*—are the central feature of an object (the bulls-eye). Why? Because member variables (also known as *fields*) hold individual and distinct values for each object and can not be shared.

> Member variables make up the visible attributes of an object. They are the means by which one object differs from another. They are the "personality" of an object.

To qualify for *member variable* (attribute) status, a variable should be permanent or global (or both). Here are two quick tests:

- Permanent: When we leave the object and return later, must the variable data still be valid?
- Global: Is the variable accessed by more than one method?

> Time out for some quick definitions
>
> Variable *myCash* is defined outside of any method and is therefore a *member* (global) *variable*.
>
> - If static, they are further classified as *class* variables.
> - If non-static, they are *object* (or *instance*) variables. ←

Variable *myCash* is an object variable.

Ready?

Using two genesis statements we have now created two very real cyber bank accounts for our two new customers. Are we now ready to open the doors and let them in? The answer is, not quite. First, we must take care of *access* and *security*. (After all, are we not dealing with a "real" cyberbank?)

Access

You see, we don't presently have any way of accessing each customer's object variable (*myCash*) and its related methods. We can't append a class name (such as *BankAccount*) as we did in the previous chapter because there is only one class but two objects. (Besides, none of the object variables or methods are *static*.)

Here is the answer: We use the dot operator and append the reference name. The example below shows how each customer gains access to its own unique version of method *getBalance*.

```
a1.getBalance( )
a2.getBalance( )
```

It's a hierarchical process: First use a reference to point to the desired object, and then specify the desired attribute or behavior within the selected object.

A final comparison

- To access a member variable or method within the same class or object, just write the name of the member variable or method.

```
msec(1000)
```
Same class (static)

```
myCash     getBalance( )
```
Same object (non-static)

- To access a member variable or method within another class or object, append the class or reference name.

```
BasicTools.msec(1000)
```
Another class (static)

```
a1.myCash     a1.getBalance( )
```
Another object (non-static)

Global variables revisited

In Chapter 4 we cautioned against the casual use of global variables. However, member variable *myCash* is defined outside of any method and is clearly global. The difference is, *myCash* is only global within each *BankAccount* object. When outside the object, access must be qualified by the object reference name. The bottom line: member variables are only *quasi*-global. This eliminates most of the security considerations that argue against the use of global variables.

Security

Suppose you put a large "public" jar of cookies out on the kitchen table. How long would they last? The same is true of member variable *myCash*. If such a variable is tagged *friendly* or *public*, then other classes have direct access to your cash—and you might just as well wave goodbye to all of it.

For this reason, any member variable that holds vital information should be tagged *private*, and should be accessible only from within the class in which it is declared. But, in the case of *myCash*, how then do I get at my money? The answer is, by way of *friendly* or *public* methods. The difference is that active methods, unlike passive member variables, can screen and filter any requests for access to your cash. This technique of hiding data within a class is known as *encapsulation*; and when we use methods to access the data, it is known as sending a *message*.

ESPRESSO

What are *constructor* methods?

Did you notice the *constructor* method (*BankAccount( )*) at the end of all genesis statements?

```
BankAccount a1 = new BankAccount( );
```

This is the king of all the methods. It is the master enzyme that replicates objects from the original strand of class DNA. Without the constructor method, there would be no objects in cyberspace—only useless class templates.

The constructor method is easy to identify: its name is always the same as the class name (*BankAccount* in our case) and it never returns a value. We will revisit constructors in Chapter 9 in a big way.

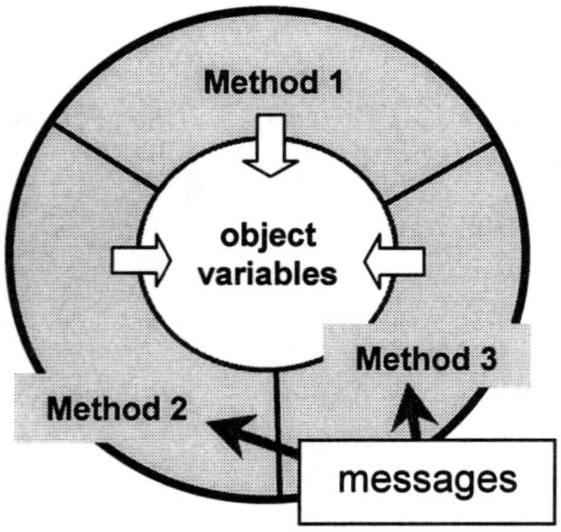

In summary

In the classic case, think of an object as a living cell, with an outside membrane interfacing other objects and classes. At the center of the cell is a nucleus of private object variables (or *fields*), that hold the DNA *state* of the object. Surrounding and protecting the nucleus are methods we can call—representing *messages* the cell can accept to operate upon the private data and change, show, or return its state.

Ready?

Is our cyberbank now ready to open and serve its two patiently waiting clients? At long last, yes it is! The bank manager will now write the class, create two class objects, open up the doors, and watch proudly as the customers safely access their individual accounts.

Hands-On Procedure

Step one—Project definition

1. In this chapter, we will perform a typical bank account operation—the transfer of money from one account to another.

We create two bank account objects, deposit $2,500 into each private account, and verify the balance. We transfer $700 from one account to the other, and show the new balance of each. A beep is heard whenever a balance is shown. At the end of the day, the bank manager prints the total deposits.

Step two—Structure chart

2. The structure chart of Figure 6.3 reveals the many new features that appear when objects are part of the design.

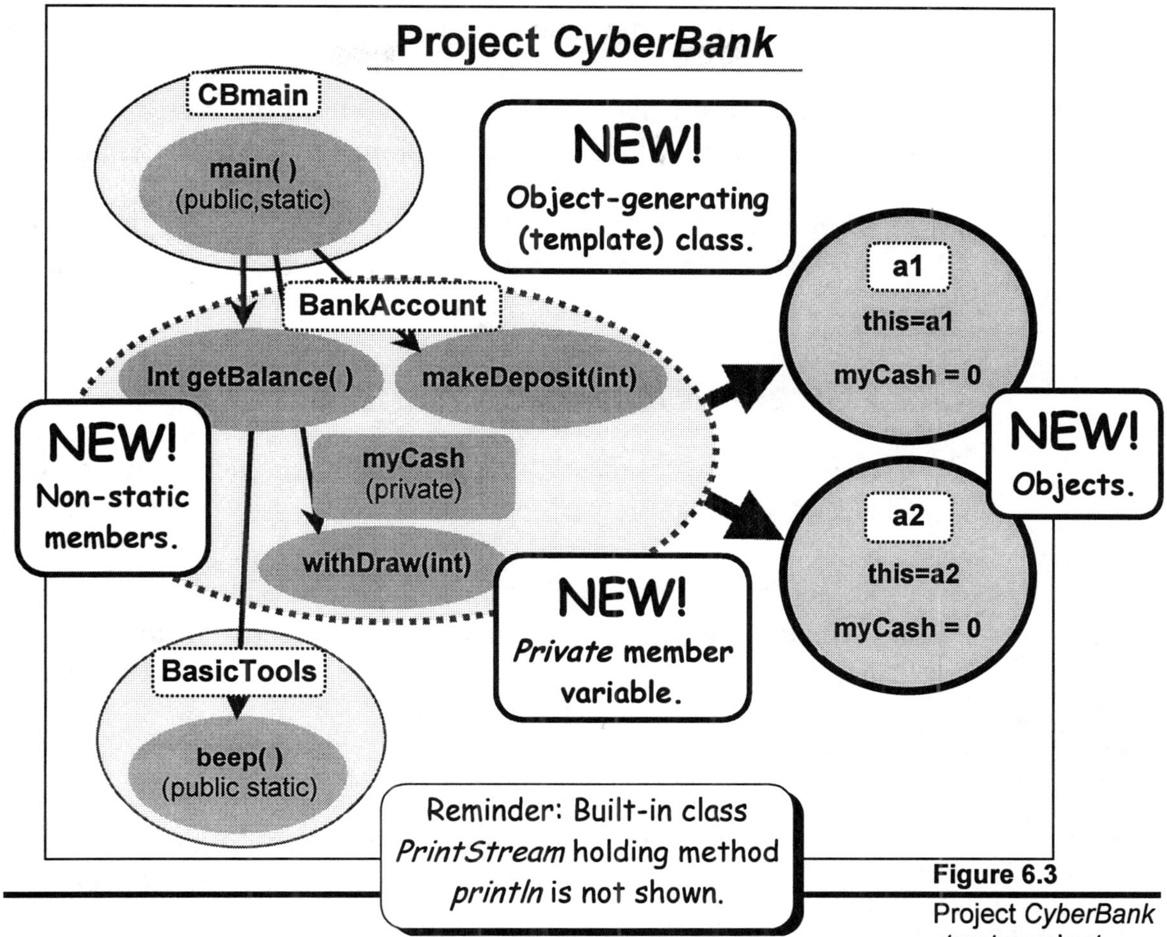

Figure 6.3
Project *CyberBank* structure chart

- Objects (*a1* and *a2*) are not normally shown on a structure chart because they are created during execution.

> When objects are created, new memory is set aside only for the member variables. The methods are individualized by passing into each a copy of the reference—which is placed into variable *this*. *This* is used to access *myCash* (*this.myCash*), where *this* is normally invisible.

- To indicate the special status of class *BankAccount*, it is assigned a broken border and is called a *template* class. It is special because all of its behaviors and attributes are non-static, and therefore it is destined for object-hood.

- For the first time, one of our classes (*BankAccount*) has a member variable (*myCash*). It most definitely can not be static, since instances of itself must hold the current account balance for each of our bank customers. No sharing allowed!

- For security reasons, member variable *myCash* is tagged *private*. (The only way to access a private member variable is by way of friendly or public methods.)

Step three—Write the program

3. Create project *CyberBank* within solution *Chapter6*, rename the files, and set the project properties.

4. First, add and complete class *BasicTools*. To avoid reinventing the wheel, we copy class *BasicTools* directly from solution Chapter5:

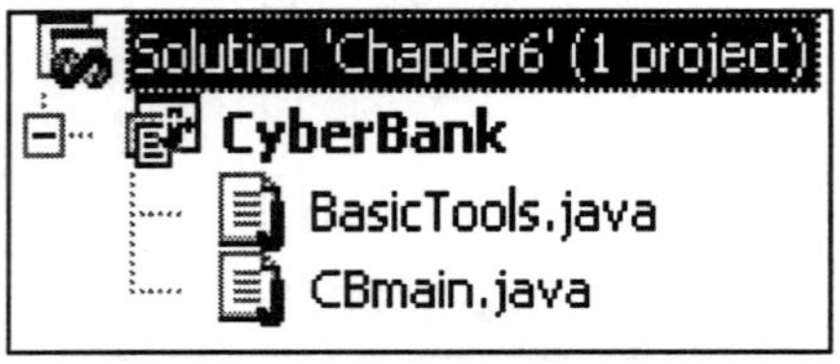

BOLD TYPE = click left

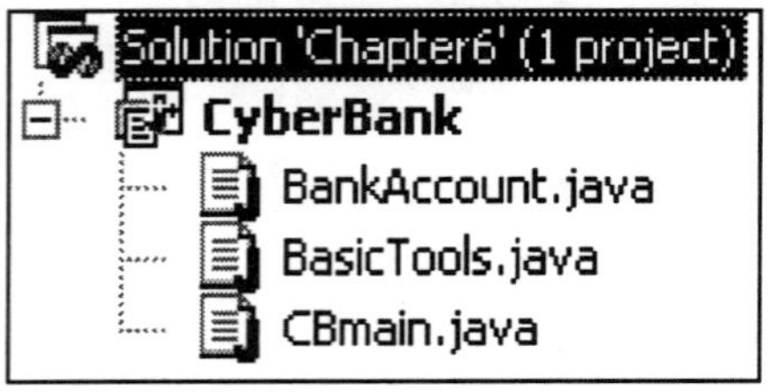

- Within the *Project Explorer* window, **CLICKR** on *CyberBank*.

- **Add**, **Add Class**, *existing* tab, find and open solution *Chapter5*, **DCLICKL** on *BasicTools.java*. And just that simple, class *BasicTools* from project *DrawTree* is now a genuine part of project *CyberBank*.

5. Next, add and complete special object-producing class *BankAccount* of Figure 6.4.

6. Finally, complete class *CBmain* of Figure 6.5.

7. By way of review, contrast the two "external" method calls shown below. Object *a1* is a genesis-created object reference for a unique non-static method (*makeDeposit(2500)*); *BasicTools* is a class pointer for a shared, single-copy static method *(beep())*.

```
a1.makeDeposit(2500);
BasicTools.beep( );
```

```
// Class BankAccount will spin off bank account objects.
public class BankAccount
{
        private int myCash;

        public int getBalance( ){
                return myCash;
        }

        public void makeDeposit(int amount){
                myCash += amount;
        }

        public void withDraw(int amount){
                myCash -= amount;
        }
}
```

> **New!** *Private* member variable.

> **New!** Non-static methods.

> Friendly methods are also okay here.

Figure 6.4
Class *BankAccount*

```
public class CBmain
{
        public static void main (String[ ] args){
                BankAccount a1 = new BankAccount( );
                BankAccount a2 = new BankAccount( );
                a1.makeDeposit(2500);
                a2.makeDeposit(2500);
                System.out.println("A1 = $"+a1.getBalance( ));
                System.out.println("A2 = $"+a2.getBalance( ));
                a1.withDraw(700);
                a2.makeDeposit(700);
                System.out.println("A1 = $"+a1.getBalance( ));
                System.out.println("A2 = $"+a2.getBalance( ));
                System.out.println("Total = $"+(a1.getBalance( )+a2.getBalance( )));
                BasicTools.msec(5000);
        }
}
```

> **New!** Object creation.

> **New!** Accessing methods within objects.

> In Chapter 9 we'll find a more suitable way to personalize each bank account.

Figure 6.5
Class *CBmain*

ESPRESSO

More personality?

Wouldn't it be better to include more attributes within class *BankAccount*, in addition to the single *myCash*? How about the customer's name and account number, and perhaps even the customer's transaction history?

Yes it would; and we'll be doing exactly that in Chapter 9, after we learn how to handle *arrays* and *strings*.

Step four—Execute the program

An analysis of the program will be saved for the debug section.

8. Build project *CyberBank* and check for syntax errors.

9. Execute (*Start*) project *CyberBank*.

   a) Did the system find class *BasicTools*?

      Yes **No**

   b) Did the screen display the proper results (Figure 6.7)?

      Yes **No**

   c) Did you hear a beep when each balance was displayed?

      Yes **No**

   d) Were the total deposits correct?

      Yes **No**

Figure 6.7
Screen output

Step five—Debug and analyze

During this debug/analysis session, special attention is paid to the display of objects.

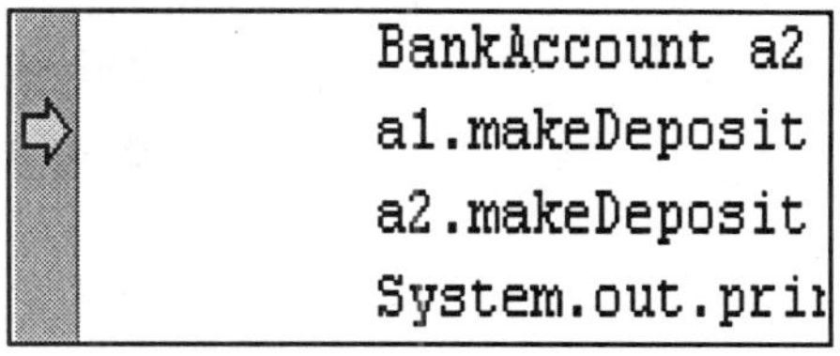

10. Using F10, singlestep through the two genesis statements (yellow arrow pointing to *a1.makeDeposit(2500);*). Fully expand the object tree in the *Locals* window, as shown by Figure 6.8.

    a) Does it tell us that references *a1* and *a2* also automatically reference class *java.lang.Object*? (This *inheritance* property is the subject of Chapter 12.)

    Yes **No**

    b) Is object variable *myCash* a private integer and was it initialized to zero?

    Yes **No**

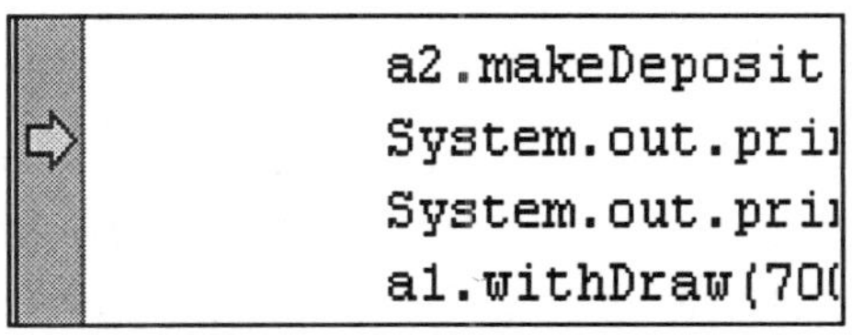

11. Using F10, execute the next two statements. Referring to the *Locals* window, were both object variables assigned $2,500?

    Yes **No**

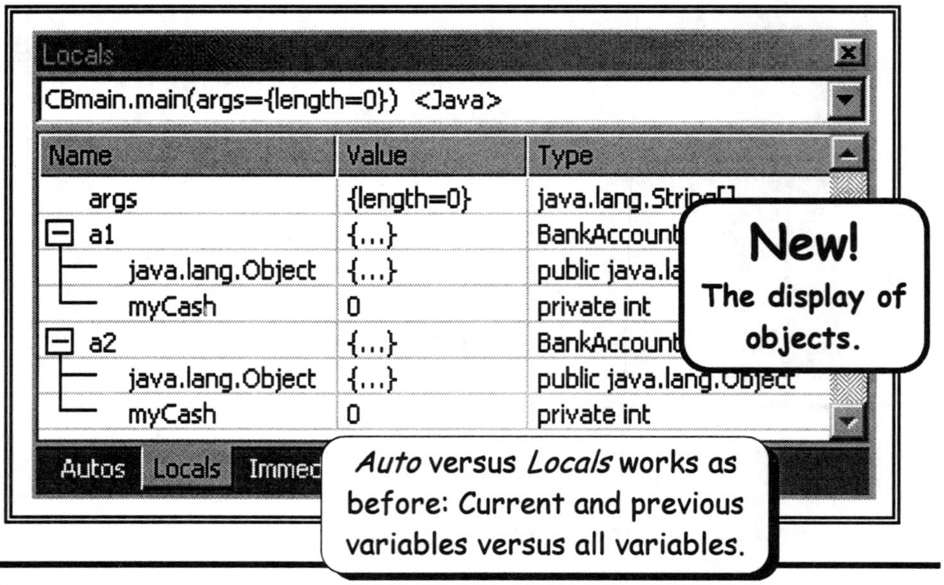

Figure 6.8
Displaying objects

12. Using F10, step through the next two statements (*getBalance*). Were the correct balances displayed in the JVIEW window and were beeps sounded?

    Yes **No**

13. Using F10, step through the next two statements (the exchange of $700). Were object variables *myCash* correctly updated for each object?

    Yes **No**

14. Using F10, step through the remainder of the program. Were the balances and total correctly shown in the JVIEW window and held for five seconds?

    Yes **No**

15. Re-enter the debug mode and repeat the singlestep process. However, this time make use of F11 to step into the first *makeDeposit* statement. (Genesis statements can not be stepped into.) Fully expand the *Locals* window of Figure 6.9.

a) Is local variable *amount* now visible and is it properly initialized to $2,500?

Yes **No**

b) After pressing F10, is object variable *myCash* updated to $2,500?

Yes **No**

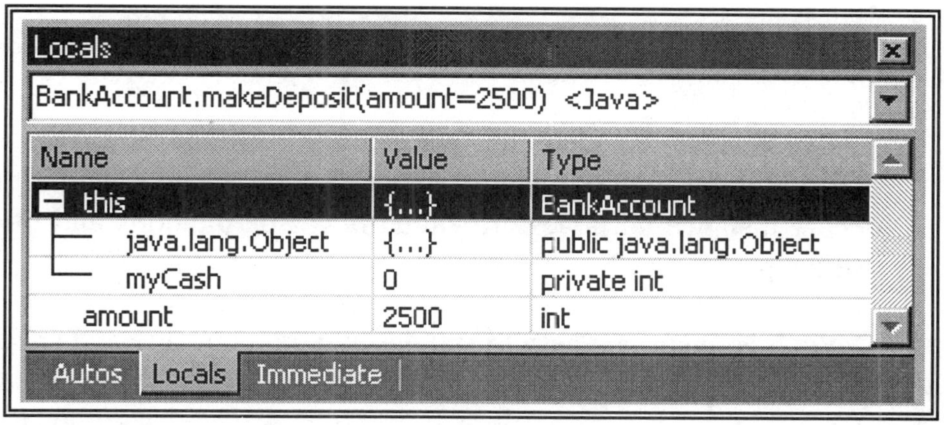

Figure 6.9
Inside *makeDeposit*

Referring to Figure 6.9, notice identifier *this*. As previously stated, *this* is an invisible local variable automatically created by the system. The use of *this* distinguishes *a1's* methods from *a2's*.

It works as follows: When we call method *makeDeposit*, the pointer held in reference *a1* is passed to *this* as an invisible parameter. Using *this* (still invisible), method *makeDeposit* is able to access a1's unique copy of *myCash*.

```
public void makeDeposit(int amount){
        this.myCash += amount;
}
```

This is normally invisible, but can be appended as shown.

The bottom line is this: When an object is created, new memory must be allocated only for the object variables. The object methods are individualized by the unique reference value passed to parameter *this*. (Static methods do not receive the *this* parameter.)

16. Continue stepping through the program in like manner, using F11 to step into each unique method at least once. (If necessary, press Shift+F5 to exit the debugger.)

ESPRESSO

Mutators and accessors?

By convention, methods that *change* instance variables are called *mutator* methods and often use the prefix "*set*." Those that *access* instance variables are called *accessor* methods and often use the prefix "*get*."

Such conventions help to standardize the language and should be used whenever possible. However, for us this is not a hard and fast rule. For example, we prefer *makeDeposit* rather than *setDeposit*.

Exercises

a) Modify method *withDraw* so the balance can never be negative.

b) Modify method *makeDeposit* to warn the user if the new current amount is greater than $100,000 (and therefore not fully projected by FDIC insurance).

c) Modify project *BankAccount* of this chapter to hold dollars and cents. (Hint: Use type double.)

d) By assigning another *BankAccount* reference to an existing account object, create a joint account.

When developing an original project:

1. Draw a structure chart showing the three classes (main, template, and tools).
2. Look for multiple things, and label the template class with the type of thing.
3. Add the permanent or global *member variables* ("bull's eye") to the template class. Append *private* where appropriate.
4. Using *public* or *friendly* methods of your design, add the supporting behavior to the template class.
5. Complete the *main* class and the rest of the program.

e) Project *Camping* creates three campsite objects—two of them occupied. The program scans the campsites at the rate of one/second and beeps for each occupied site found. The percentage that are occupied is displayed.

Suggest template class *CampSite*, which includes member variable *occupied* (boolean) and methods *void setSite(boolean)* and *int getSite()* (return 1 if occupied, 0 if not).

f) Write project *Sports* in which two football teams score as follows: touchdown (Giants), touchdown (Vikings), field goal (Giants), touchdown (Vikings). Each score is displayed and each touchdown sounds a beep. The final scores are displayed and the winner is announced.

Suggest template class *FootballTeam* to hold private attribute *score* and methods *void addPoints(int)* and *int getScore( ).* (Method *addPoints* displays each score and beeps for touchdowns.)

g) Within project *Television* we create two TV objects, turn them both on, tune the first to channel 7 and the second to channel 44, display the channel settings, and turn them both off. Be sure to include code to make sure that a TV set is on before it is tuned, and to beep and prevent tuning to the R-rated channel 44.

For this exercise, use behaviors and attributes of your own choosing.

h) Modify project *Television* so a password (secret number) can be sent that then allows access to channel 44.

i) Within project *Olympic* three skater objects perform the compulsory round followed by the free skate round. Scores from 0.0 to 6.0 are assigned and displayed for each of the six performances. The scores are tabulated and the winner declared. (The compulsory score counts 25% and the free skate counts 75%.)

> Suggest template class *Skater* that holds *double* attributes *compulsoryScore* and *freeSkateScore*, and behavior *void setScore(double,char)* (that also displays the score) and *double getTotalScore( )* (that also displays the total score).

j) Within project *School*, Sam, Mary, and Tai are given grades of B, C, and B. Your program will show all grades, increase the grade of each one level, and again show each. It will finish with, "________ students got A's."

> Suggest template class *Student* to include private char member variable *myGrade* and methods *void setGrade(char)*, *void changeGrade(int)*, *char getGrade( )*, and *void showGrade( )*. (Method *changeGrade(int)* will change a grade up or down parameter number of grade levels.)

k) Modify method *changeGrade* of project *School* to automatically assign an A and print "Can't raise an A" if you try to increase a grade above the level of A.

l) Write project *Company*, which includes three employee objects, each assigned an initial salary of $25,000. They are given raises of 10%, 15%, and 25% respectively—however no employee can earn more than $28,000. The resulting salaries are printed, along with the total payroll.

> Suggest template class *Employee*, holding private attribute *salary* and methods *int getSalary( )*, *void showSalary( )*, *void setSalary(int)*, and *void raiseSalary(int)*. (*raiseSalary* also limits the maximum to $28,000.)

m) Project *IRS* involves a small country with just three taxpayer objects. John makes $2,400/month, Anne makes $3,080/month, and Jose makes $3,900/month. Based on a rate of 28%, taxes are paid, and both the cumulative wages and taxes are displayed each month for a year. When done, "The government took ______ in total taxes from _______ in total wages." is printed.

> For this exercise, use behaviors and attributes of your own choosing.

> As fully explained in Chapter 12, the expression below (using static method *random* from class *Math*) returns a random integer in the range of *a* to *b* each time it is called:
>
> **(int)(a+Math.random( )*(b–a+1));**
>
> Each of the remaining projects uses random numbers.

Cast *char* to create random letters.

n) Within project *Mall*, two shopper objects are created and given credit limits of $100 and $120. Round robin random purchases are made in the range of $1 to $10 until both cards are "maxed out" (reduced to zero).

- If a shopper successfully purchases an item, the remaining credit is printed.
- If a shopper tries to purchase an item above the remaining credit limit, "Not enough credit" is printed.
- If a shopper has no credit left, "Out of credit" is printed.

> Suggest template class *Shopper* that includes private attribute *credit*. Methods *void setCreditLimit(int), void spendCredit( )*, and *int getCredit( )* access the variables.

o) Write project *Grandprix* in which two object racecars alternately increase their distance in random segments from 10 to 50 miles at the rate of one segment per second. The cumulative distances are displayed. The first to reach 500 miles is the winner.

> Suggest template class *RaceCar* to include private member variable *milesDriven* and supporting methods *void addRandomMiles( )* and *int getMiles( )*.

p) Write project *Lottery* in which two object players alternately draw and display random numbers from one to ten at the rate of two per second. The first to draw a seven is the winner. (Ties don't count!)

> Suggest template class *Player* to include attribute *myNumber* and supporting behaviors *void drawNumber( )*, *void showNumber( )*, and *int getNumber( )*.

> Note: Because no score is maintained by project *Lottery*, no permanent data need to be stored. Variable *myNumber* qualifies for *member variable* status because it is global—not permanent. It is possible (but not desirable) for all behavior to be placed into one method (*drawNumber*), and therefore no member variables would be needed at all.

q) Write project *Stockmarket* in which two object investors each hold a different stock. Each stock is initialized to $200, and their value is randomly increased or decreased by an amount within the range of –20 to +20 each day for a month. The value of each stock is displayed each day. (One month happens in one second.)

> Suggest template class *Stocks* to hold private member variable *myStock*, and methods *void setValue(int)*, *int getValue( )*, and *void changeValue( )*.

r) Within project *MPG*, objects *ford* and *chevy* and given 10 and 12 gallons respectively. Each car drives continuously in random mileage segments from five to ten miles. When either car runs out of gas they both stop. After each segment, print the increasing odometer reading and the decreasing gas-level reading as integers. (The Ford gets 12mpg and the Chevy gets 15mpg.)

> Suggest template class *Car* to hold attributes *gasLevel*, *odometer*, and *mpg*, supported by behaviors *void setMPG(int)*, *void pumpGas(int)*, and *void driveSegment( )*, and *int getGasLevel( )*. (Caution: miles per gallon must be a type *double* operation.)

s) Project *TallestTree* increases the height of three trees randomly from two to eight feet each year (starting from zero). Tree height is displayed continuously (where each year happens in 500ms) until one of the trees exceeds 384 feet (the world's tallest). A beep sounds, and the number of years passed is displayed.

> Suggest template class *Tree* to hold member variable *height* and behavior *void growYearly()* and *int getHeight()*.

t) Project *HighCard* deals and displays ten rounds of single cards (with values of two through nine) to two player objects at the rate of one round/second. The highest card wins. The final scores are displayed.

> Suggest template class *CardPlayer* to hold member variables *myCard* (permanent) and *score* (global), and behaviors *void dealRandomCard()*, *void incrementScore()*, *int getCard()*, and *int getScore()*.

u) Write project *Craps* in which two player objects roll dice at the rate of one round of play per second until *both* players simultaneously roll a seven (and "crap out"). Each rolled eleven pays $10. All dice values are shown as the game is played. The final winnings are displayed.

> Suggest template *Player* to hold attribute *winnings* and behavior *void rollDice()* and *int getWinnings()*.)

v) Write project *CoinToss*, in which three player objects toss coins in round robin fashion at the rate of one round per second. The "heads" or "tails" value of each toss is displayed. The first player to toss four heads in a row is the winner.

> Suggest template *Player* to hold attribute *numberOfHeads* and behaviors *int getNOH()* and *void tossCoin()*.

w) Write project *SlotMachine*, in which two player objects starting with $500 each pull a slot machine handle in round robin fashion for 50 rounds. Each pull costs $1 and displays three random numbers (each from 5 to 10). Three sevens pays the jackpot of $200, two sevens pays $8, and one seven pays $1. The cumulative cash holdings of each are continuously displayed.

Suggest template *Player* to hold attribute *myCash* and behaviors *void setCash(int), int getCash( )*, and *void pullHandle( )*.

x) Write a random number project of your choosing.

ESPRESSO

What is a *black box*?

To the typical user, a television set is a *black box*. That is, all of the components and circuitry are hidden behind the casing. Only the public controls (channel select and volume control) are accessible. The user doesn't care what's inside the casing as long as the public controls work as expected. In fact, it's possible to completely redesign the internal circuitry, and the user may not even notice.

Objects are also *black boxes*. The user of the object sees only the public and friendly behaviors and attributes. All the private members are hidden from view (encapsulated). As long as the public interface remains unchanged, the internal members can be completely redesigned and the user will not even notice.

Questions and Problems

1. The greater the number of instances of a class (objects) and the greater the number of attributes within each object, the greater the need for object oriented programming (over conventional C programming). Nevertheless, is it possible to create a single object from a template class? Is this desirable?

2. A J++ program consists of user-defined or built-in classes filled with attributes and behaviors (data members and methods). These attributes and behaviors can only be accessed if they are "real." To turn a data member or method real we can append *static* or we can create an object.

    True **False**

3. Consider the following two statements:

```
int myVariable = 80;
BankAccount a1 = new BankAccount( );
```

   a) Is a genesis statement similar to a simple variable definition and initialization?

      Yes **No**

   b) Can we call reference *a1* a pointer variable of type *BankAccount*?

      Yes **No**

   c) Does *myVariable* hold integer 80, and does *a1* hold an address (pointer to an object)?

      Yes **No**

   d) Is it legal to split a variable initialization into the *declaration* and *assignment* parts shown below?

      Yes **No**

```
int myVariable;
myVariable = 80;
```

   e) Following on d) above, show how to legally split the genesis statement into two parts.

4. Within one project, there is only a single copy of any attribute tagged *static*.

    True **False**

5. What two major types of items are contained in a *class*?

6. An *instance of a class* and an *object* are the same.

   True **False**

7. What does it mean to say that member variables live as long as the associated object lives?

8. Show how to create object *myToys* from class *Toys*.

9. Why is object-oriented programming of particular importance to banks?

10. Objects are required whenever we create multiple instances of a class, each one specific and unique.

    True **False**

11. Why are the member variables and methods of class *BankAccount* not tagged static?

12. Why is an *object* called a *high-level* representation of data?

13. *This* holds the present object reference, and is only valid when program action is within an object.

    True **False**

14. All static members are stored in a single location, separate from all objects.

    True **False**

15. Why is it likely (but not required) that every object will have at least one member variable? (Hint: Is at least one variable likely to be permanent or global?)

16. Consider the following analogy. When we use a genesis statement to create an object of class *Car*, the word *new* creates the garage.

    True **False**

17. Why is it possible for an object to be composed of nothing but member variables (no methods)?

18. A variable tagged *static* is a *class* variable and is allocated once when the class is loaded; if not static, the variable is an object variable and is allocated each time a genesis statement creates a new object.

    True **False**

CHAPTER

7

Project GradeSort

Array Objects

Objectives

- *To write projects that use arrays*
- *To sort a sequence of grades from lowest to highest*
- *To introduce two-dimensional arrays*

Discussion

You are a busy teacher. You are confronted with the daunting task of sorting quiz grades from lowest to highest. You would like to use the computer, but the mere thought of creating separate variables for every quiz score makes you think twice...until you realize that modern-day programming languages offer a very useful data type: the *array*.

An *array* is an ordered collection of memory locations, identified by *element* numbers starting from zero. It's perfect for holding and processing our many quiz scores.

An array is an object—or is it!

In Java, arrays seem to have a split personality. They easily pass the Chapter 6 test (Can a project have more than one?), but then simple integers pass the test as well—and instances of integer variables are not usually classified as true blue objects.

Here then is the problem: In most texts, arrays are described as objects, yet they seem to have more in common with the basic (intrinsic) data types (such as *int*). So let's start off by clearing the air on this subject.

If an array is really an object, then it should be created by a genesis statement. And it is! As shown below, and diagrammed by Figure 7.1, an array object of four quiz scores is created by either of the following genesis-like statements:

```
int[ ] scores = new int[4];
int[ ] scores = {77,66,59,89};  <-- Direct initialization.
```

Further supporting its object credentials, an array contains a member variable (*length*). Finally, an array object inherits all the methods of class *Object*, and can be cast as type *Object*. (*Inheritance* gives a class access to methods of related classes—an important concept covered in Chapter 12.)

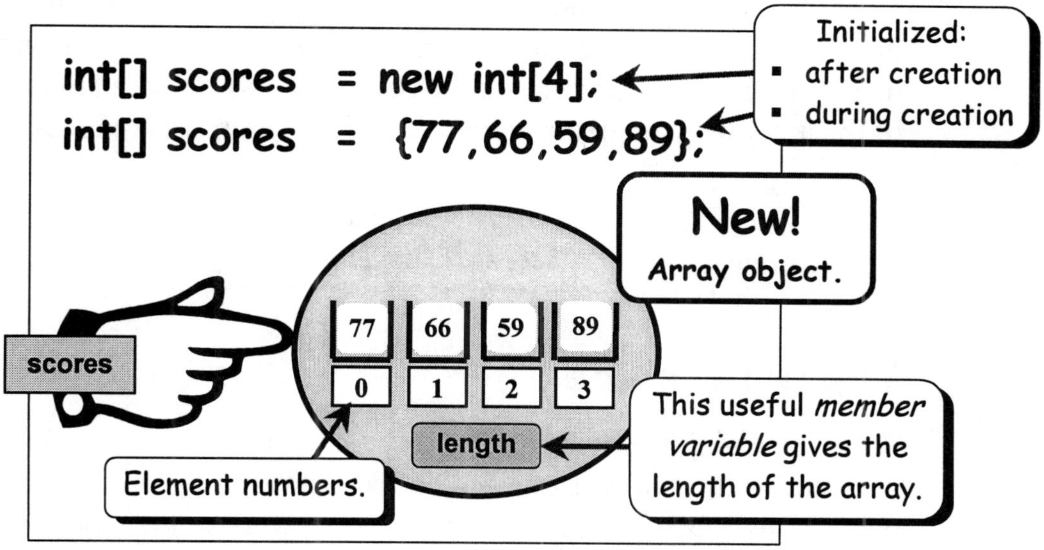

Figure 7.1
The array as an object

Arguing against the array as an object, no constructor methods are called when an array object is created. Furthermore, if you examined the Core API (*Application Programming Interface*) hierarchy chart of built-in classes you would not find any class called "Array." To top it off, no dot operator is required to access the array, and the array "class" offers only a single data member (*length*). So what's going on?

Here is one way of looking at the array data type. Whenever any variable or class is created, J++ automatically creates what can best be described as a "shadow" array class in the background. This means we can immediately create an array object of any data type—including object references!

```
int[ ] scores = new int[4];

BankAccount[ ] customer = new BankAccount[1000];
```

If the array type is a basic type (such as *int*), then the elements of the array hold simple whole numbers; if the array type is a class (such as *BankAccount*), then the elements hold references to objects.

To access an array, no dot operator is required. Instead, as shown below, we access the entire array as a single unit by using the array's name (reference). In the second case, we access individual elements of the array by placing the element number within square brackets.

```
scores
scores[7];
```

Scores holds an address; scores[7] holds data.

The bottom line

After reviewing the evidence, here is what we will do. For the most part, arrays in Java will be handled like arrays in C—as a basic data type. Only when we create an array, access its single data member (*length*), or make use of the inherited methods of class *Object* will an array take on the characteristics of an object.

Array objects in action

Let's wrap up our discussion of arrays with a simple example. The program segment of Figure 7.2 creates array *scores* and passes the array reference to method *display*—which prints it to the screen.

- *Scores* holds the address of the first element (points to 77).
- *QuizValues[0]* holds the data of the first element (77 itself).

```
public static void main(String args[ ]){
    int[ ] scores = {77,66,59,89};
    display(scores);
}

static void display(int[ ] quizValues){
    int i;
    for(i=0;i< quizValues.length;i++)
        System.out.println(quizValues[i]);
}
```

The array's address (reference) is passed to method *display*.

QuizValues.length = 4.

Figure 7.2
An array demonstration program

ESPRESSO

Why do we pass a reference?

When we pass a simple integer as a parameter, we *pass by value*. That is, we pass the data itself. However, if our array has 10,000 elements, this won't do at all. We certainly can't pass thousands of separate values—it would take too long and use up too much memory.

Instead, we *pass by reference*. That is, the array stays right where it is and we pass its *address* (the address of the first element). Since all addresses are sequential, we can easily locate any of its values by referring to their element numbers (0 to 9,999).

In Java, such an address is called a *reference*, and in C it's called a *pointer*. In Figure 7.2, reference *scores* passes the four elements of the array by reference.

Multi-dimensional arrays

Suppose our class of five students takes three quizzes over the course of a semester. The 15 quiz scores are conveniently stored in a two-dimensional array, as shown in Figure 7.3.

	Student 1	2	3	4	5
Quiz 1	93	74	77	55	81
Quiz 2	78	77	72	75	80
Quiz 3	92	88	82	83	69

Figure 7.3
Two-dimensional array

Such multi-dimensional array objects are easily created using either of our previous genesis formats.

```
int[ ][ ] scores = new int[3][5]

int[ ][ ] scores = {{93,74,77,55,81},
                    {78,77,72,75,80},
                    {92,88,82,83,69}};
```

The entire array is passed by reference…

```
scores
```

…and they are processed within nested loops using variables of the type:

```
scores[i][j];
```

Toolbox

In this chapter, we will be adding yet another class of static methods to our toolbox. By way of review, recall what makes a method a programming "tool":

> To qualify for "tool" status, a method should have such a basic and universal nature that it stands a good chance of being used in many future projects.

In this chapter, we will create a new tools class called *ArrayTools*. Class *ArrayTools* will make a good companion to class *BasicTools*—although its behavior is not nearly as fundamental.

BOLD TYPE = click left

Of course, the vast majority of *built-in* methods (such as *println*) naturally fall into the *tools* category since they are designed by definition to be useful to any number of projects. These built-in classes can be viewed at any time by **Help (Contents, Index** or **Search**).

Hands-On Procedure

Step one—Project definition

1. In this chapter, we will perform a number of operations on an array of grades.

> **Project *GradeSort* will sort an array of ten grades from lowest to highest.**

Step two—Structure chart

2. Our structure chart design is shown in Figure 7.4.

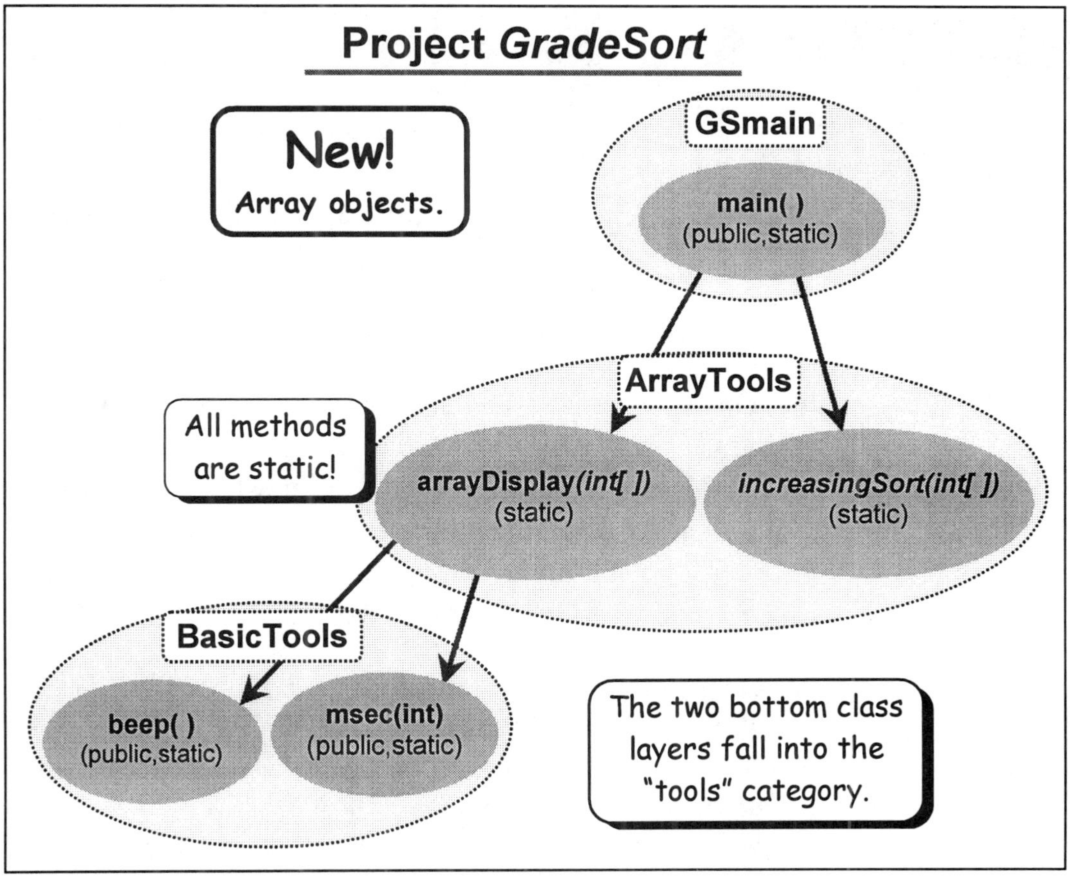

Figure 7.4
Project *GradeSort* structure chart

Surprise! No user-defined object-producing (template) classes are needed! Once again, this is due to the logic and nature of the problem: We don't need user-defined objects because we don't need multiple instances of any user-defined class.

- Low-level class *ArrayTools* holds two methods. Method *increasingSort(int[])* will accept a reference to a one-dimensional integer array and sort the array. Method *arrayDisplay(int[])* will accept the same reference and print the array to the screen.

- Low-level class *BasicTools* was created in project *DrawTree* of Chapter 5 and will be added to this project.

Step three—Write the program

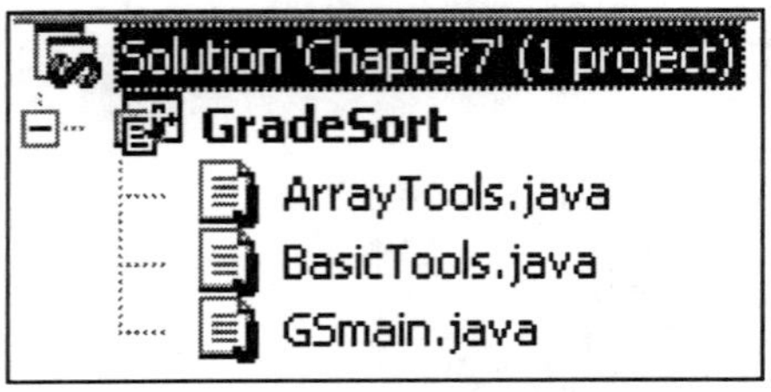

3. Create project *GradeSort* within solution *Chapter7*, add previous class *BasicTools* from *Chapter5* or *Chapter6*, rename appropriate files, and set the directory.

4. Add and complete new class *ArrayTools* of Figure 7.5.

5. Let's briefly review each of the methods of class *ArrayTools*:

   - **increasingSort(int[ ]).** This method accepts a reference to an integer array. It makes use of the "bubble sort" technique to sort the integers from lowest to highest. That is, we make a number of scans through the array, comparing and if necessary switching adjoining pairs of numbers. During the process, the small numbers "bubble up" to the top of the list.

   - **arrayDisplay(int[ ]).** This method also accepts a reference to an integer array object and beeps (to indicate display underway). Within the *for* loop, we use an array variable (*numbers[i]*) to print each element to the screen one at a time as variable (*i*) ranges from 0 to *numbers.length.* A half second delay between each printing gives a more dramatic effect. The *println* method moves the cursor to the next line.

```
// Class ArrayTools holds several basic
// methods that process arrays.
public class ArrayTools
{
      static void increasingSort(int[ ] numbers){
            int temp,i,j;
            for(i=0;i<numbers.length;i++)
                  for(j=0;j<numbers.length-1;j++){
                        if(numbers[j] > numbers[j+1]){
                              temp = numbers[j];
                              numbers[j] = numbers[j+1];
                              numbers[j+1] = temp;
                        }
                  }
      }

      static void arrayDisplay(int[ ] numbers){
            int i;
            BasicTools.beep( );
            for(i=0;i<numbers.length;i++){
                  System.out.print(numbers[i]+",");
                  BasicTools.msec(500);
            }
            System.out.println( );
      }
}
```

Length is a data member of shadow class *Array*.

New! Passing array objects.

Bubble sort is not the most efficient sorting technique—just the simplest.

Display numbers slowly, for more dramatic effect.

Figure 7.5
Methods added to class *ArrayTools*

6. Complete class *GSmain*. Because most of the work is done by the tools classes, the *main* method of Figure 7.6 is the essence of brevity. We display the array object before the sort process, perform the sort process, and display the array object after the sort process.

Step four—Execute the program

7. Start (execute) the program. Did the screen display the proper before-and-after results (Figure 7.7)?

    Yes **No**

```
// Class GSmain holds the main method.
// The program is "all tools."
public class GSmain
{
      public static void main (String[ ] args){
            int[ ] scores = {90,70,82,75,98,64,88,59,77,91};
            ArrayTools.arrayDisplay(scores);
            ArrayTools.increasingSort(scores);
            ArrayTools.arrayDisplay(scores);
            BasicTools.msec(4000);
      }
}
```

New! Creating array objects.

All class names point to static behaviors.

Hold the output for viewing.

Figure 7.6
Class *GSmain*

Figure 7.7
Screen output

Step five—Debug and modify

In this brief debug session, we will see how arrays are displayed during singlestepping.

8. Press F10 twice, to enter the debug mode and execute the array *genesis* statement. Are the elements of the array now displayed in the *Locals* window (as in Figure 7.8)?

   Yes **No**

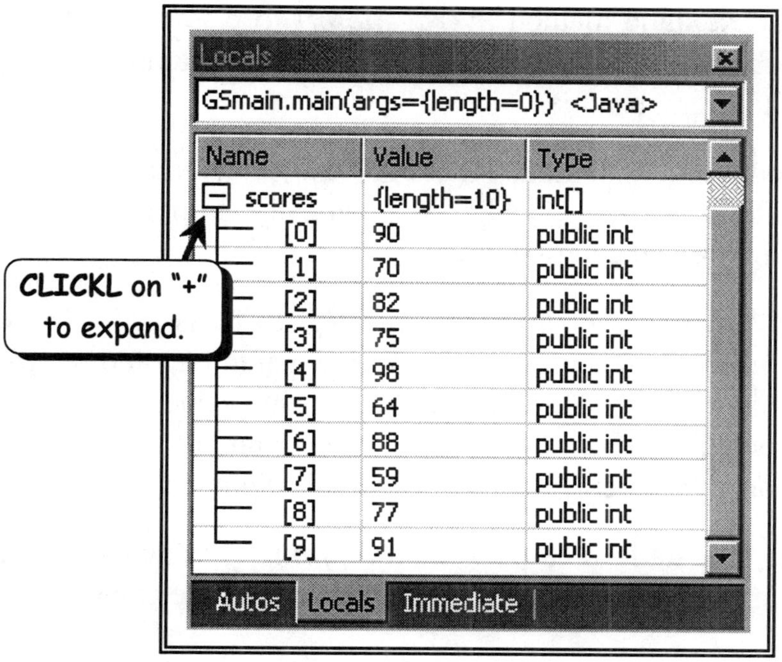

Figure 7.8
Expanded view of array

9. If you wish, use F11 to step into either of the methods of *ArrayTools* and follow the processing of the array. Be sure to track the various variables by way of the *Locals* window.

10. Exit the debug mode with Shift+F5.

Exercises

a) By making a small modification to method *increasingSort(int[])*, add static method *decreasingSort(int[])* to class *ArrayTools*. Test your method on an integer array.

b) By overloading method *increasingSort(int[])*, add static method *increasingSort(char[])* to class *ArrayTools*. Test the new method by sorting an array of ASCII grades.

c) Modify method *arrayDisplay* so the final comma is not printed. (Hint: "\b" is the backspace escape character.)

d) Add and test static method *average(int[])* to class *ArrayTools*. Method *average(int[])* accepts an int array parameter and returns the average value.

e) By modifying method *average(int[])*, create method *averageDropLow(int[])*, which automatically drops the lowest score and returns the new average.

f) Add and test static method *median(int[])* to class *ArrayTools*. Method *median(int[])* accepts an int array parameter and returns the median value. (There are just as many values above the median as below. For arrays with an even number of elements, the median is the average of the two middle elements.)

g) Add and test static method *match(int[],int[])*, which receives two int arrays and returns the number of like elements that match.

> As first introduced in Chapter 6 the following static method from class *Math* will return a random integer in the range of *a* to *b* each time it is called:
>
> **(int)(a+Math.random( )*(b–a+1));**

h) Using method *random*, fill up array *scores* (Figure 7.6) with random numbers in the range of 30 to 100. Sort and display the array as usual.

i) Using method *random*, fill up ten-element integer array *stocks* with random numbers in the range of 9,000 to 10,000. Using method *upDow*, analyze the array and report the number of days that the stock market went up (higher than the previous day).

j) Integer array *wages* holds the hourly wage-rates for eight people. Analyze the array and increase all wages by either $2 or 10%, whichever is highest.

k) Six temperatures are taken every day for three days. Using a two-dimensional array, analyze the temperatures and report the day with the highest average. Also report the time and day of the highest temperature recorded. (Use method *random* to create the temperatures if you wish.)

l) Nine-element integer arrays *round1* and *round2* hold the random golf scores (one to five) for two rounds of golf. Write to array *best* the best (lowest) score at each hole.

m) Analyze arrays *round1* and *round2* of the previous exercise and plot a table that shows how many times scores of one, two, three, four, and five were shot.

n) Using method *random*, deal seven cards from two to nine. Analyze the hand and beep if the hand holds any two-of-a-kind.

o) Write method *getGPA(char[])*, which accepts an array of ASCII character grades (A, B, C, D, F) and returns the GPA as a floating point number from 0.0 to 4.0.

p) Write method *countGrades(char[],char)*, which accepts an array parameter and a grade parameter (char from A to D), and returns the number of times that grade is found in the array.

q) Write method *displayGradeTable(int[])* to accept a parameter to an array of grades (0 to 100) and print a table that lists how many As, Bs, Cs, and Ds are found in the array. (Assume that scores 90–100 are an A, 80–89 a B, 70–79 a C, and below 70 a D.)

r) Write method *CorBetter(char[])*, which receives an array of char grades and raises all Ds and Fs to Cs.

s) Using the cast operator, write method *floatToInt*, which transfers (copies) the elements of float array *num1* to int array *num2*.

t) Using the *arraycopy* method shown below (from class *System*), copy the last five elements of ten-element array *herNumbers* to the first five elements of ten-element array *hisNumbers*. Be sure to display both arrays before and after.

> ***arraycopy*(source reference, int source position, destination reference, int destination position, int length).**

u) Fill arrays *die1* and *die2* with random die values from one to six. Add like array elements and display the frequency of each sum (2 to 12) in a table. (Did seven occur more frequently?)

v) Using class *BankAccount* from Chapter 6, what is printed to the screen when the following program is executed?

```
public class CBmain
{
  public static void main (String[ ] args){
       BankAccount[ ] customer = new BankAccount[1000];
       customer[300] = new BankAccount( );
       customer[400] = new BankAccount( );
       customer[300].makeDeposit(1000);
       customer[400].makeDeposit(2000);
       System.out.println(customer[300].getBalance( )+customer[400].getBalance( ));
  }
}
```

Questions and Problems

1. Show two ways of creating six-element char array *letters*.

2. To call a static method, it is not necessary to create an object.

   True **False**

3. An array is created from class *Array*.

   True **False**

4. Show how a 100-element array of object *ages* is created and referenced by *myAges*.

5. How do you determine the length of array *temperature*?

6. When using the following genesis statement, what are the initial values of all the array elements?

```
int[ ] days = new int[365];
```

7. Does an array object hold any methods? (If not, where is method *arraycopy*?)

8. Is it possible to pass array *scores* as a global variable rather than a conventional parameter? Why are conventional parameters usually preferred over global variables?

9. A reference is closely related to which of the following? (Circle all that apply.)

   a) Data.
   b) Address.
   c) Pointer.

10. What does the following program segment accomplish?

```
for(i=0;i<100;i+=5)
   answer +=numbers[i];
```

CHAPTER

8

Project Word Processor

Class *String*

Objectives

- *To write projects that use strings*
- *To find a word in a string*
- *To introduce the String class*

Discussion

A *string* is a sequence of ASCII characters treated as a single entity. In Java, as well as most languages, strings are defined within double quotation marks as follows:

```
"San Francisco"
"(408) 555-1212"
"Four score and seven years ago."
```

Since the processing of words and sentences is what this project is all about, the *string* data type is the perfect solution.

Strings are objects!

Is it likely that a project will contain more than one unique string? Of course it is…and therefore, strings are full-fledged objects (with none of that wimpy "shadow" stuff that we encountered with arrays). Class *String* is listed in the *API Hierarchy Chart* and comes with 42 very useful and well-documented static and non-static constructors and methods.

As shown below, the string genesis statements offer the same two options as their array counterparts. However, the first option uses a conventional constructor, which provides for direct initialization.

"New" is implied.

```
String speech = new String("Four score and seven years ago");
String speech = "Four score and seven years ago.";
```

String speech = "Four score and seven years ago."

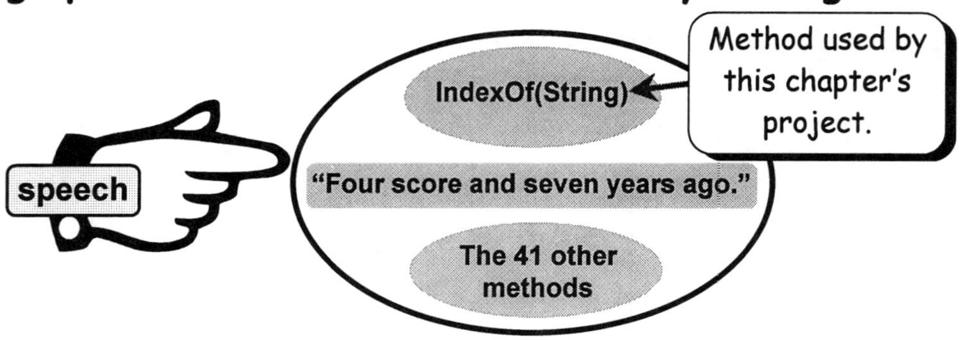

To access a string, we simply use the string's reference. To show how easy it is, the following example creates string object *speech* and prints it to the screen.

```
String speech = "Four score and seven years ago.";
System.out.println("Lincoln said: "+speech);
```

Remember, if *speech* were an array object reference, the array's address would be printed.

However, when accessing individual characters of a string (required for this chapter's project), we don't use anything like the array's square brackets. Instead, we make use of built-in methods.

The methods of class *String*

For a complete listing of all the 42 constructors and methods of class *String*, use the Help facilities. A sampling of those available are listed in Table 8.1. As is often the case with the built-in classes, many of the methods are overloaded (accept a variety of parameters).

Method	Description
charAt(int)	Locates a character within a string.
indexOf(String)	Searches for sub-strings and returns their position.
startsWith(String) and *endsWith(String)*	Checks for a string prefix and suffix

Table 8.1
A few useful methods of class *String*

In this chapter, we will make good use of method *indexOf*, which returns the location of a sub-string within a larger string. To prepare us, the simple example on the following page prints the location of the word "years" within Lincoln's very famous speech. (What number will be printed to the screen?)

```
String speech = "Four score and seven years ago.";
System.out.println("Years, is at position: "+speech.indexOf("years"));
```

Arrays of strings

Incidentally, in case you're wondering, "class" array also "shadows" class *String*—as it does every class. What does this mean? It means that we can create arrays of strings.

To illustrate the process, the code below creates and displays an array of names (an array of *String* objects).

```
String[ ] names = {"Mary","Tai","Sam"};
for(i=0;i<names.length;i++)
    System.out.println(names[i]);
```

As shown below, the genesis statement that creates the array of strings looks quite interesting in graphical form. How many objects did this one statement create?

Number of objects created = ____________

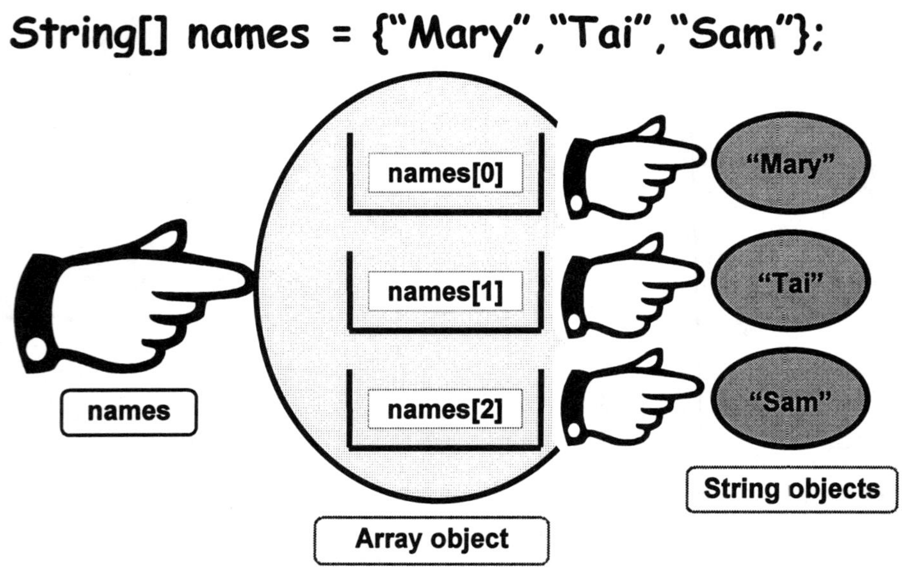

The StringBuffer class

Standard Java Strings are treated as constants, just like literal numbers. In other words, once they are created, strings can't be changed.

If this seems terribly limiting, there is a way out. It's called the *StringBuffer* class. Objects of the *StringBuffer* class can be changed. All we have to do is apply the correct built-in methods. A brief sampling of the 30 available constructors and methods of the *StringBuffer* class is listed in Table 8.2.

Method	Description
StringBuffer(String)	Constructs a string buffer object from a string object.
append(String)	Appends the specified value.
Insert(int,int)	Inserts an integer in a string.
setLengt(int)	Changes the length of the string.

Table 8.2
Sample methods of the *StringBuffer* class

The first item is worth pointing out because it is a constructor method that changes a *String* object into a *StringBuffer* object. The statement below is a case in point.

```
StringBuffer speech2 = StringBuffer(speech);
```

In other words, our original six-word Gettysberg Address was incomplete. By converting the speech to an object of class *StringBuffer* (reference *speech2*), we can *append* the rest of the speech and history can be made.

```
speech2.append("our forefathers brought forth...");
```

Hands-On Procedure

Step one—Project definition

1. This chapter's project will involve a common word processor function.

> **By performing a "find" operation, locate a specific word within a sentence, and mark the location of the word.**

Step two—Structure chart

2. Our structure chart design of Figure 8.1 is typical of those with a single purpose in mind.

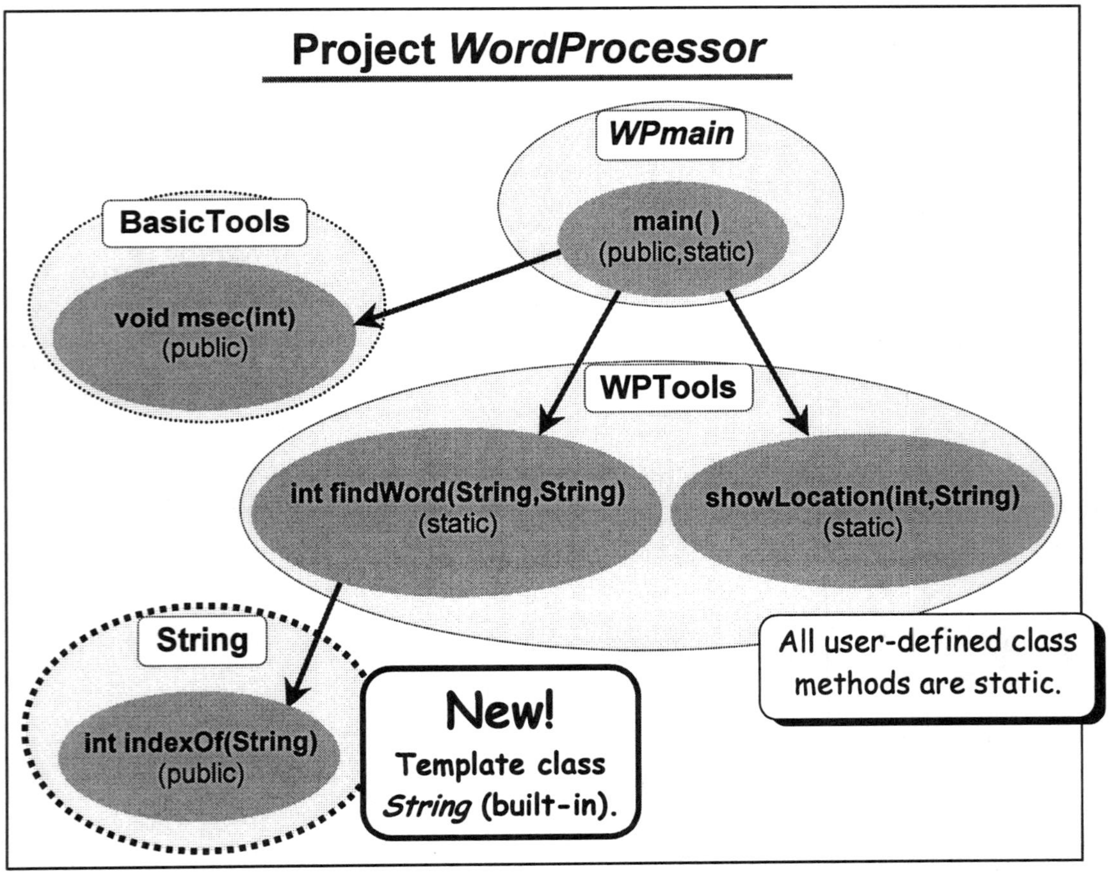

Figure 8.1
Project *WordProcessor* structure chart

> Because this is the first time we have used a full-fledged built-in class, we have violated our general rule and included built-in class *String* in our structure chart. To avoid clutter, this will seldom be the case in the future.

- Because of the nature of the project, no user-defined objects are needed. To solve project *WordProcessor*, all we need are low-level "tools" classes (*BasicTools*, *WPTools* and *String*) and the ever-present high-level *main* class (*WPmain*).

- In keeping with the nature of the project (no user-defined objects), all user-defined methods are static. However, since class *String* always generates objects, most of its methods (including *indexOf*) are not static.

Step three—Write the program

3. Create project *WordProcessor* within solution *Chapter8* and add class *BasicTools*.

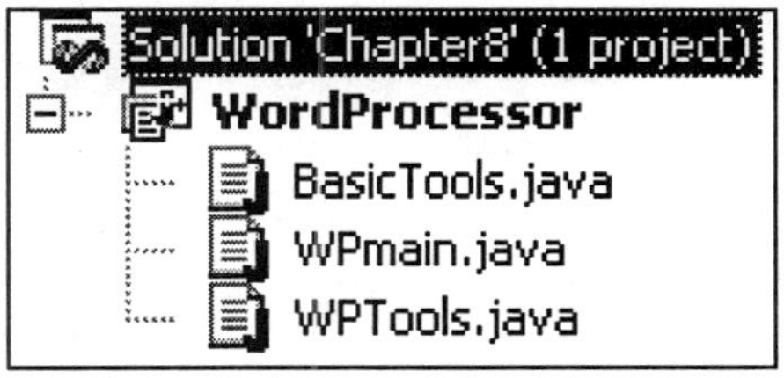

4. Add and complete new class *WPTools* of Figure 8.2 (**CLICKR** on *WordProcessor*, **Add**, etc.)

5. Let's briefly review each of the methods of class *WPTools*.

   - Method *findWord* accepts two string references: The string to search (*toSearch*) and the word we are looking for (*toFind*). These references are passed to built-in method *indexOf*, which returns the searched-for string location to variable *index*. If the word was found, its position is printed to the screen. If not (–1 is returned), the user is so notified. The index value is returned.

   - Method *showLocation* receives an index value and a string. It first prints the string to the screen. It then positions the cursor by using the *print* method to write a series of spaces equal to the index value. Finally, an asterisk is printed at the index location by the *println* statement and a beep is sounded.

```
// Class WPTools holds basic string processing methods.
public class WPTools
{
    static int findWord(String toSearch,String toFind){
        int index;
        index = toSearch.indexOf(toFind);
        if(index == -1)
            System.out.println("Did not find "+toFind);
        return(index);
    }

    static void showLocation(int index,String s){
        if(index != -1){
            System.out.println(s);
            while(index-->0)
                System.out.print(" ");
            System.out.println("*\7");
        }
    }
}
```

New! Methods of class *String*.

If the string is not found, -1 is returned.

Return the location of the word (or -1).

"*\7"

Figure 8.2
Methods added to class *WPTools*

6. Finally, finish class *WPmain* of Figure 8.3. Once again, modularization pays off handsomely, as method *main* is short and sweet.

> We will use our newly designed word processor utilities to locate the word "dark" in the string: "It was a dark and stormy night."

- First, we create two string objects: The string to search ("It was a dark and stormy night") and the string to find ("dark").
- The two step "find" process follows: We call method *findWord* to locate string "dark," and we send the returned integer location to method *showLocation*.

- Note the use of nested methods in line four to produce more compact code. If you prefer, the following unnested solution can be easier to code and to document.

```
indexValue = WPTools.findWord(novel,word);
WPTools.showLocation(indexValue,novel);
```

```
// Search for the word "dark".
public class WPmain
{
    public static void main (String[ ] args){
        int indexValue;
        String novel = "It was a dark and stormy night";
        String word = "dark";
        WPTools.showLocation(WPTools.findWord(novel,word),novel);
        BasicTools.msec(5000);
    }
}
```

New! Creating string objects.

We are searching for "dark".

Method *findWord* is nested within method *showLocation*.

Figure 8.3
Class *WPmain*

Step four—Execute the program

7. Execute (*Start*) the program. Did the screen display the proper results (Figure 8.4)?

   Yes **No**

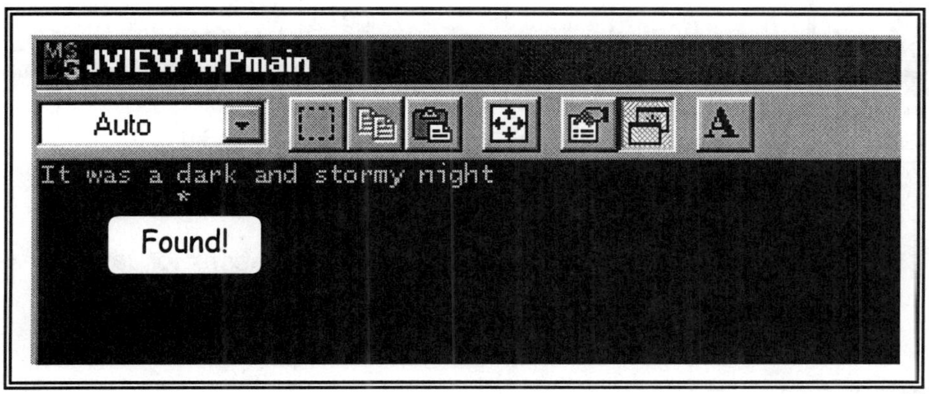

Figure 8.4
Screen output

8. Repeat using another word to search for (such as “stormy”). Also repeat using a word that is not in the string. In both cases, did the system properly respond?

   Yes **No**

Viewing class *String*

9. Would you like to see for yourself all the members of built-in class *String*? There are several ways of doing this:

   - This first method is useful for obtaining an overview of all J++ documentation. Just perform **Help**, **Contents** and expand the “books” in the order shown in Figure 8.5. Open package *java.lang* and **DCLICKL** on Class *String*. To see all the members of class *String*, “surf” to *String Members*.

   BOLD TYPE = click left.

   - This second method is useful when you are interested only in class *String*. **Help**, **Index**, enter *String*, **Display**, **DCLICKL** on class *String*, **Class Members**.

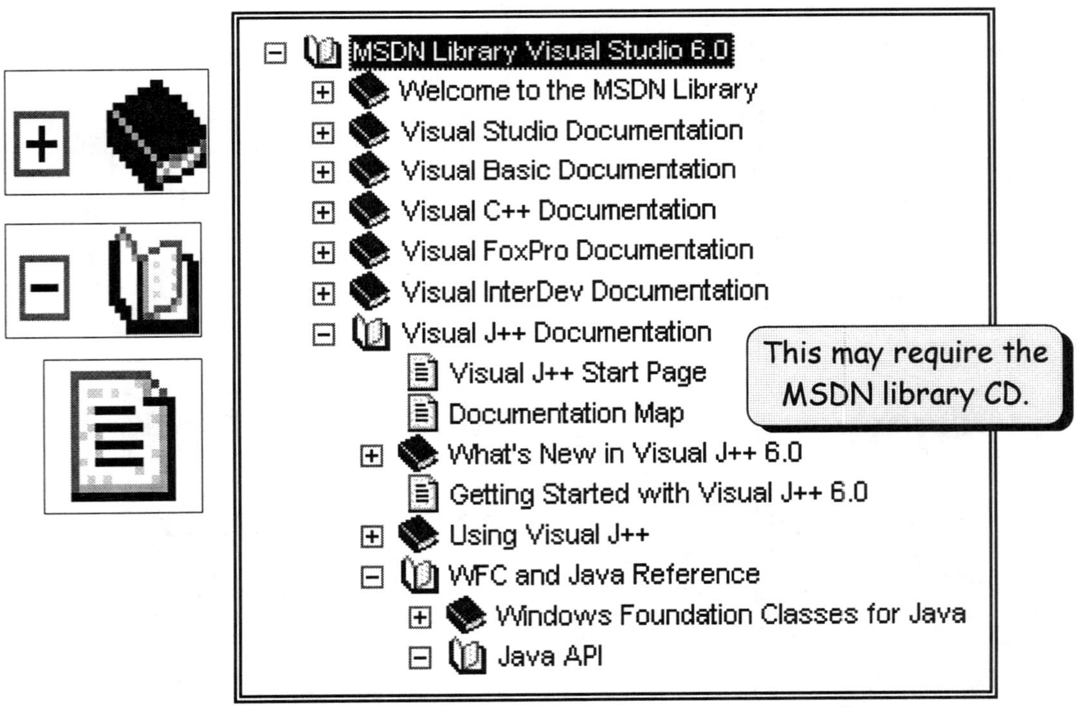

Figure 8.5
The *Contents* window

10. Within class *String*, scroll to method *String.indexOf*, the method used in the project of this chapter.

```
public int indexOf(String  str);
```

Is a detailed description of this method given?

Yes **No**

11. **CLICKL** on the "go back" arrow. Do you find yourself retracing your steps?

Yes **No**

12. Exit the window when done.

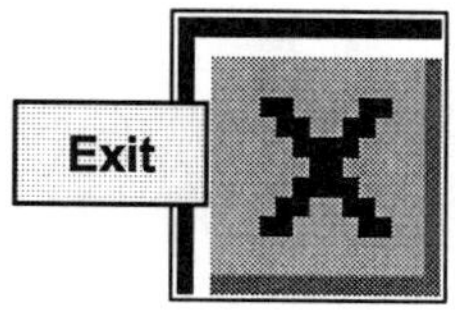

Step five–Debug and modify

This time, we will take a break from our study of debug techniques and concentrate on several project modifications.

Multiple instances of the search word

13. Suppose our text string contains two or more of the same word:

```
"It was a dark, dark, oh so very dark, and stormy night."
```

If we search for the word "dark," it is only reasonable that all three locations be marked. To accomplish this, we must modify both methods *findWord(String,String)* and *showLocation(int,String)*. The results are shown in Figure 8.6.

The testing and analysis of these modified methods is left largely as an exercise. However, we should at least point out that we are taking advantage of a special overloaded version of the *indexOf* method. The example below searches string *toSearch* for string *toFind*, starting from *indexValue*.

```
toSearch.indexOf(toFind,indexValue)
```

```
class WPTools
{
     static int[ ] findWord(String toSearch,String toFind){
          int i=0,indexValue=0;
          int[ ] index = new int[10];
          while(true){
               index[i]=toSearch.indexOf(toFind,indexValue);
               if(index[i]==-1)
                    break;
               indexValue=index[i]+1;
               i++;
          }
          return index ;
     }

     static void showLocation(int[ ] index,String s){
          int oldindex=0,offset=0,i=0;
          System.out.println(s);
          while(true){
               if(index[i]==-1)
                    break;
               offset=index[i] - oldindex;
               while(offset-->0)
                    System.out.print(" ");
               System.out.print("*");
               BasicTools.beep( );
               oldindex=index[i]+1;
               i++;
          }
          System.out.println( );
     }
}
```

We assume 10 or fewer instances of the search word.

Figure 8.6
Modified methods *findWord* and *showLocation*

The StringBuffer class

Our task in this section is to expand String *novel* by appending and inserting string segments where necessary. Because *String* objects are constants and can't be changed, we must first convert *novel* to a *StringBuffer* object.

14. By adding the code shown below to method *main*, write and display the following expanded novel.

    It was a dark, oh so very dark, and stormy night.
    Lightning was flashing against the dark sky.

```
StringBuffer novel2 = new StringBuffer(novel);
novel2.insert(13,", oh so very dark");
novel2.append("\nLightning was flashing against the dark sky.");
```

15. Using either the regular version (Figure 8.3) or the modified version of method *findWord* (Figure 8.6) on your new novel (*novel2*). Did it properly locate the "dark" words?

Exercises

a) Explain the operation of the modified methods of Figure 8.6.

b) For each of the statements below, what is printed to the screen? Be sure to explain your answer. Try it! (Hint: Statements are processed from left to right.)

```
System.out.println(1 + 2 + "is a nice number");
System.out.println("A nice number is "+ 1 + 2);
```

c) Modify and test method *showLocation* to beep at the placement of each asterisk.

d) Write project *LetterFrequency*, which determines the number of *e*s in a string. Suggestion: Add method *countLetters* to class *WPTools*, which accepts a text string and a char parameter, and returns the number of times that letter appears in the text. Method *countLetters* will use method *charAt* from class *String*.

e) Develop and test project *WordFrequency*, which determines how many words are in a string. Suggestion: Add method *countWords* (making use of method *charAt*) to class *WPTools*. (Hint: Count the number of spaces and add one.)

f) Modify project *LetterFrequency* to print out a table of letter frequencies—as shown below:

```
a: 2
b: 0
c: 1
        etc.
```

g) Create an array of five words (strings). Write project *FindWord*, which scans the array looking for the word "Gold." When found, it prints the location of the word in the array (or it prints, "Gold not found.") Hint: Your program may use a statement of the form:

```
if(words[i] .equals("Gold"))
```

h) Add method *repeatedWord* to class *WPTools*, which accepts a text string and marks any words that appear twice in a row. Test your new method on a string of your choice.

i) Using a design of your choice, write project *Match*, which compares two strings and reports the percentage of characters that are the same. (Hint: Make use of method *equals* from class *String*.)

j) Add method *spellChecker* to class *WPTools*, which accepts a text string and marks any misspelled words. (Hint: create a dictionary as an array of strings. Then, make use of built-in method *regionMatches* to compare each word of the text to each entry of the dictionary.)

k) Add method *censored* to class *WPTools*, which scans a String and blanks out all four-letter words.

l) Create an array of 10 strings that hold the first names of 10 people. Making use of method *compareTo*, write a program to determine the number of people whose first name is "Bob."

m) Design a string program of your own choosing.

Questions and Problems

1. Does class *String* contain both static and non-static methods?

   Yes **No**

2. Is method *indexOf* overloaded?

   Yes **No**

3. Using genesis statements, show two ways of creating string object *theater* and initializing it with "To be or not to be, that is the question."

4. What is the primary difference between the *String* class and the *StringBuffer* class?

5. When we create an array of strings, are the following formats equivalent?

   String[ ] names = {"Sam", "Bob", "Tam"};

   String names[ ] = {"Sam", "Bob", "Tam"};

6. How many data members (*object variables*) does a string object contain? (Hint: Examine class *String* for data members.)

7. Do the following two statements perform the same function?

   Yes **No**

```
string1.equals(string2);
string2.equals(string1);
```

8. Consider the following program segment, which returns "yes" if the string parameter holds four aces, and returns "no" otherwise:

```
public class Class1
{
    public static void main (String[ ] args){
        System.out.println(PokerTools.fourAces("4AA7AJA"));
    }
}

public class PokerTools
{
    static String fourAces(String hand){
        int i,count=0;
            for(i=0;i<hand.length( );i++)
                if(hand.charAt(i) == 'A')
                    count++;
            if(count == 4)
                return "Yes";
            else
                return "No";
    }
}
```

   When strings are listed directly as parameters ("4AA7AJA," "Yes," and "No."), the system creates string objects and passes invisible references.

   True **False**

CHAPTER

9

Project CyberBank2

Constructors

Objectives

- *To use constructor methods to add "personality" to objects*
- *To create String objects*
- *To improve project BankAccount by adding names and account numbers*

Discussion

One of the hallmarks of the high-tech business is that you never rest or your laurels. Even before one product is shipped, work is well underway on the next, improved version. So it is with project *CyberBank* of Chapter 6. The following four major improvements will be included in this second product release. Don't be surprised if these "simple" changes add considerable complexity to the project.

- Personalize each bank account.
- Require a PIN (personal identification number) before access is allowed.
- Pay each customer interest.
- Store each customer's transaction history (performed as an exercise).

Constructors

Looking back at project *CyberBank* of Chapter 6, and comparing our *BankAccount* objects with the real McCoy, one thing is clear: Objects *a1* and *a2* don't have enough individual "personality." A bare minimum would be the name and PIN of each individual customer. To accomplish this, we turn our attention to the *constructor* method.

The *constructor* method is anything but new; they are called when a genesis statement is executed—such as those from Chapter 6:

```
BankAccount a1 = new BankAccount( );
```

BankAccount( ) calls the constructor method.

The constructor method has the same name as the class, and it has the awesome responsibility of creating the object itself. So what's new with project *CyberBank2* of this chapter? In a nutshell, initialization of attributes. This is the long-awaited answer as to how each object will start off life with a unique and distinct personality.

The classic way of passing these character traits to the constructor method is by way of parameters. As a case in point, a typical genesis statement used within this chapter will be modified as follows:

```
BankAccount a1 = new BankAccount("Mary",4442);
```

That is, as each new *BankAccount* object is created, we pass each customer's name and PIN directly to the constructor method within each object.

When the parameters are received by the constructor method (newly added to class *BankAccount*), it promptly initializes the corresponding object variables.

```
Class BankAccount
{
      private String myName;
      private int myPIN;

      BankAccount(String name,int number){
            myName = name;
            myPIN = number;
      }
}
```

Constructor *BankAccount( )* is added to class *BankAccount.*

Parameter variables are local and temporary.

Object variables are global and permanent.

The above code is classic. To give each individual object a distinct and unique personality, we pass attributes to the constructor method by way of local parameters—which in turn are assigned to private object variables, which are global (within the class) and permanent.

By the way, did you notice that the constructor method does not (can not) have any return type (including *void*). That's because constructor methods have a clearly defined purpose: Create the object and initialize attributes—nothing else. Try to give a constructor method a return type and the compiler will scold you.

ESPRESSO

The missing constructor!

First question: In Chapter 6 each genesis statement called a corresponding constructor method. Okay, then where was the constructor method?

The answer is, it was hidden! When a genesis statement is executed, the compiler looks within class *BankAccount* for the constructor method. If it isn't there (as it wasn't in chapter 6), the compiler automatically creates and executes a default constructor. If the constructor method is there (as it will be in this chapter), it calls ours instead. The bottom line: We place a constructor method in our template class only if we wish to include additional code.

This is related to Java properties called *inheritance* and *overriding*, important concepts to be covered in future chapters.

Second question: Why didn't we just initialize attributes *myName* and *myNumber* directly, rather than the roundabout way of the constructor method?

Well, for starters, the two attributes are tagged *private* for increased security—so, we don't have direct access. But even if that were not the case, initialization of attributes at a later time is just too unreliable to leave up to the whim of the programmer.

Mixing static and non-static members

A customer's name, account number, and cash balance are never to be shared. However, the interest rate offered by the bank is the same for all—it is shared. Therefore, as shown below, the interest rate attribute is tagged static.

```
private int myCash, myPIN;
private String myName;
static int interestRate;
```

What does this mean?

- There is only one copy of variable *interestRate* and it is shared among all the objects of the class. (If a change is made by any, they all see the change.)
- We don't have to first create an object reference in order to access member variable *interestRate* from the outside. With static variables, access is by way of the *class* name.

To achieve these properties, the system places the static members of each class in a separate location in memory during compilation. When each new object is created during execution, it's just the non-static members that are copied into each new object location.

Following on the convention adopted in Chapter 6, we call non-static members object members, and static members class members.

An array member variable

Our final modification is left as an exercise. By adding an integer array member variable to class *BankAccount*, the bank manager can maintain a record of withdrawal transactions for each customer. As shown below, the array is updated each time the customer withdraws cash.

```
private int[ ] myRecord = new int[10];
int i;

void Withdraw(int withdrawAmount){
        ...
    myRecord[i++] = withdrawAmount;
        ...
}
```

This can't be shared, so don't make it static.

Why is array *myRecord* a member variable (defined outside all methods and therefore global)? Because it must be accessed by more than one method and it must be permanent.

All the bank manager has to do is add a special method to class *BankAccount* to access and display the customer's private withdrawal record.

Hands-On Procedure

Step one—Project definition

1. This chapter's project uses constructor parameters to give each bank customer a unique identity.

> **The bank manager sets the interest rate at 5%, and creates and initializes two accounts. Mary opens her account and deposits $900. The bank manager pays Mary interest due. Tai tries to withdraw $1,000 without first opening his account.**

Step two—Structure chart

2. The structure chart of Figure 9.2 shows the five new methods and four new data members added to template class *BankAccount*.

   - Method *BankAccount( )* is the constructor method, which receives name and PIN parameters and initializes member variables *myName* and *myPIN*.

   - Method *openAccount* accepts a PIN parameter and either allows or prevents access by setting Boolean attribute *accountState* to *true* or *false*. (*accountState* is initialized to *false* by default.)

   - Static method *setInterestRate* receives an integer interest rate parameter and places the rate in static class member *interestRate*.

   - Method *payInterest* takes the interest rate from static class member *interestRate* and calculates the interest due. This value is added to the customer's cash account (*myCash*), displayed on the screen, and returned (in case it is needed by the calling routine).

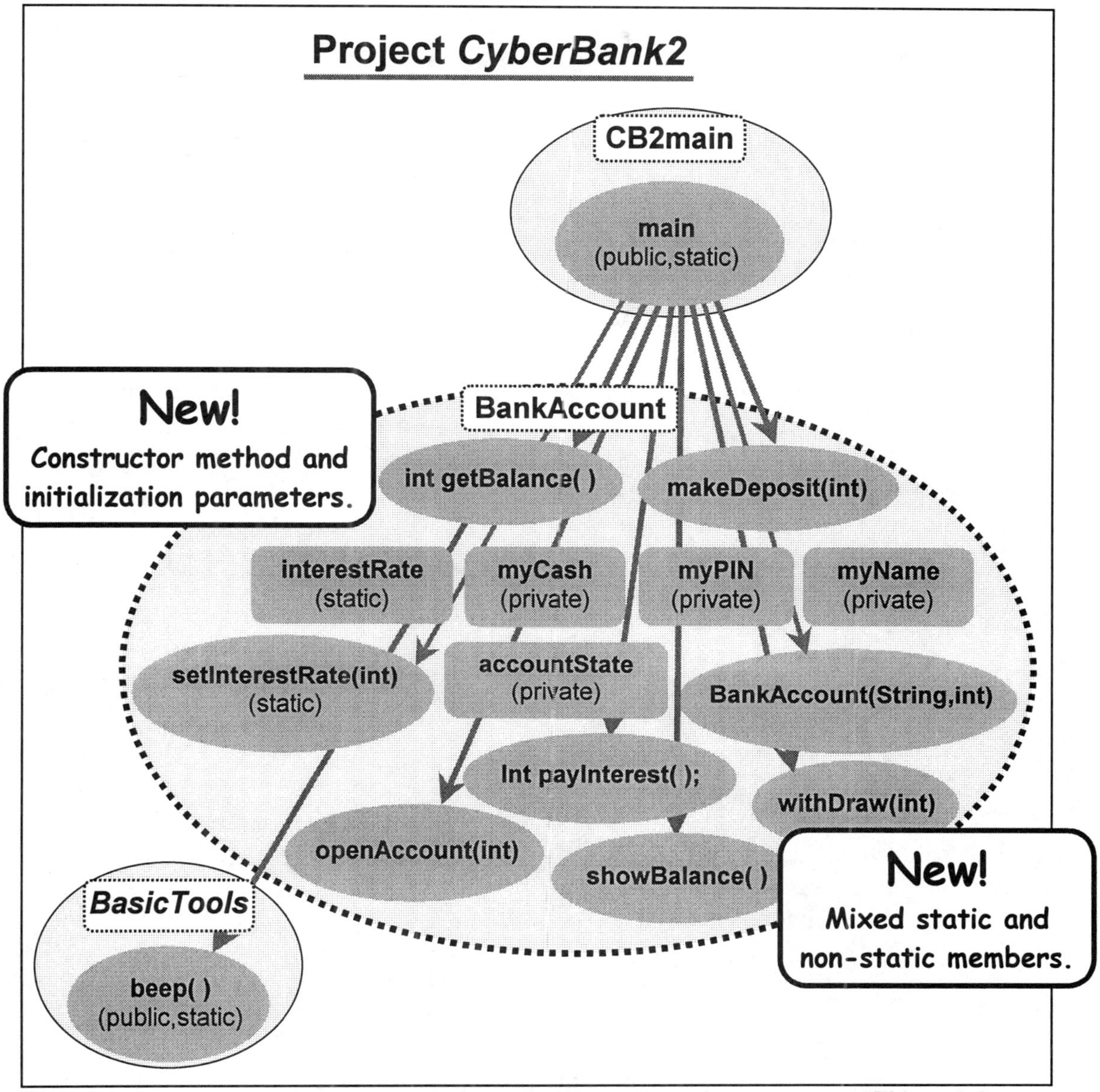

Figure 9.2
Project *CyberBank2* structure chart

Step three—Write the program

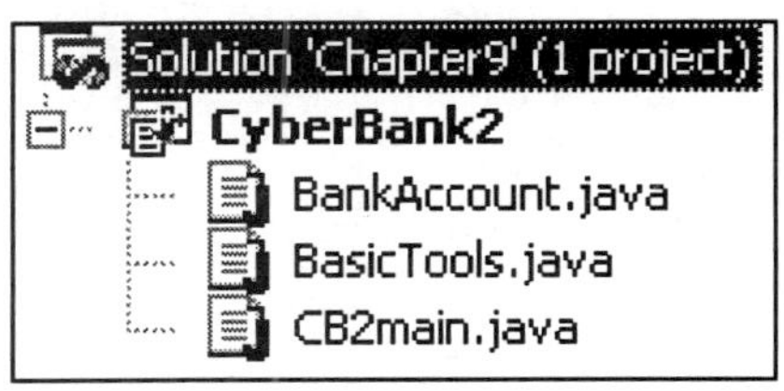

3. Create project *CyberBank2* within solution *Chapter9* and add previous class *BasicTools*.

4. Add and complete new class *BankAccount* of Figure 9.3.

```
// Class BankAccount is "personalized" with a constructor.
public class BankAccount
{
      private int myCash,myPIN;
      private String myName;
      private boolean accountState;
      private static int interestRate;

      BankAccount(String name,int number){
            myName = name;
            myPIN = number;
      }

      void openAccount(int number){
            if(number == myPIN){
                  System.out.println("Access granted to "+myName);
                  accountState = true;
            }
            else{
                  System.out.println("Access denied");
                  accountState = false;
            }
      }

      void withDraw(int withdrawAmount){
            if(accountState == true)
                  myCash -= withdrawAmount;
            else
                  System.out.println("Access denied to "+myName);
      }

      void makeDeposit(int depositAmount){
            if(accountState == true)
                  myCash += depositAmount;
            else
                  System.out.println("Access denied to "+myName);
      }
```

New!
Mixing object (non-static) and class (static) members.

New!
Constructor method and initialization parameters.

Method *openAccount* allows access if the received PIN equals the initialized PIN.

Continued on next page.

Figure 9.3

Class *BankAccount* modified (Continued on next page)

Continued from previous page.

```
    int getBalance( ){
        if(accountState == true){
            BasicTools.beep( );
            return myCash;
        }
        else
            System.out.println("Access denied to "+myName);
        return 0;
    }

    void showBalance( ){
        if(accountState == true)
            System.out.println(myName+", your balance is $"+myCash);
        else
            System.out.println("Access denied to "+myName);
    }

    static void setInterestRate(int rate){
        interestRate = rate;
    }

    void payInterest( ){
        int interest;
        myCash += (interest = myCash*interestRate/100);
        System.out.println(myName+", you earned $"+interest+" interest.");
    }
}
```

Boolean variable *accountState* controls access.

Method *setInterestRate* is shared (static).

Figure 9.3
Class *BankAccount* Modified (Continued From previous page)

5. Note the following special features of Class *BankAccount*:
   - For security reasons, all member variables are *private*.
   - Member variable *interestRate* and method *setInterestRate* are static. This means there exists only one copy of each and all BankAccount objects share them.
   - What happens if we attempt to access an account that has not been opened?
6. Complete class *CB2main* of Figure 9.4. (The statements in **bold** would be executed by the bank manager.)

```
public class CB2main
{
      public static void main (String[ ] args){
            int interest;
            BankAccount.setInterestRate(5);
            BankAccount a1 = new BankAccount("Mary",4442);
            BankAccount a2 = new BankAccount("Tai",6776);
            a1.openAccount(4442);
            a1.makeDeposit(900);
            a1.showBalance( );
            a1.payInterest( );
            a1.showBalance( );
            a2.withDraw(1000);
            BasicTools.msec(2000);
      }
}
```

Manager sets interest rate.

New! Constructor parameters.

Customer 2 (Tai) tries to withdraw $1,000.

Figure 9.4
Class *CB2main*

Step four—Execute the program

7. Execute the program. Did the screen display the proper results (Figure 9.5)?

   Yes **No**

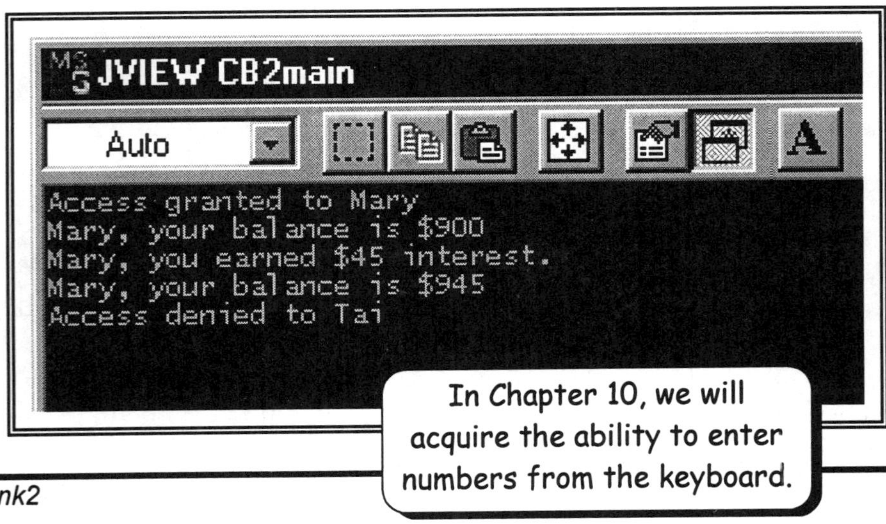

Figure 9.5
Project *CyberBank2* screen output

ESPRESSO

What about built-in constructors?

As an example of built-in constructors, we use the **Help** menu to list the following seven overloaded constructor methods from class *String*.

Default constructor.

```
String( );                          String(char[ ],int,int);
String(byte[ ],int);                String(String);
String(byte[ ],int,int,int);        String(StringBuffer);
String(char[ ]);
```

In general, most built-in classes offer one or more such constructor methods. Why are they there? Simple. Whenever we write a genesis statement for any built-in class, one of the listed constructors must be used to create the object.

8. Project *CyberBank2* of this chapter covers nearly every major concept of classes and objects. We strongly suggest that you carefully step through the entire program, making sure each and every step is thoroughly understood.

Step five—Debug and modify

The Watch window

The *Locals* window was highlighted in previous chapters. It displayed variables and objects either Automatically (current and previous statement) or Locally (all variables local to the current function.

In this chapter we highlight the *Watch* window. By way of a handy select and drag process, this window allows us to list and change only those variables of interest.

9. Using F10, step to *a1.openAccount(4442)*. Select (highlight) reference *a1* anywhere in the program and drag it to the first box of the *Watch* window (as shown in Figure 9.6). After expansion, are the initial values of all five member variables of object *a1* displayed?

   Yes **No**

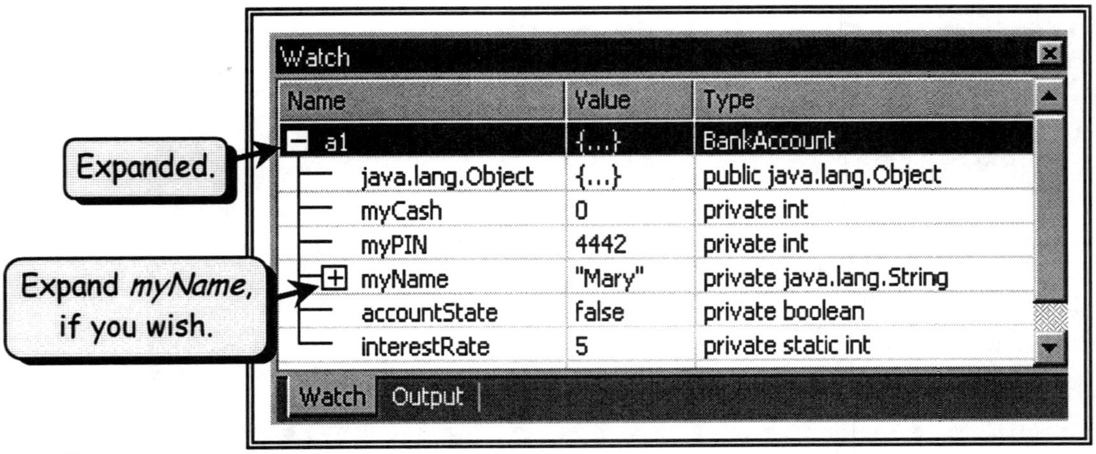

Figure 9.6

The *Watch* window

10. Press F11 to step into method *openAccount*. Did the *a1* watch value change to "not found" (indicating *a1* is local to class *CB2main*)?

    Yes **No**

11. Select and drag local variable *number* to the *Watch* window. Did it properly display PIN integer 4442?

    Yes **No**

12. From within the *Watch* window, change value 4442 to 4422 and click box *a1* to accept the change (turning 4422 red). Continue stepping with F10. After leaving the method, was "Access denied" displayed?

    Yes **No**

13. If you wish, continue stepping through the program, displaying and changing variables of your choice in the *Watch* window.

ESPRESSO

Is there another way to initialize static variables?

Yes, in a manner similar to the constructor for non-static data members, we can make use of the special *class initializer method* shown below:

```
static{
    interestRate = 5;
}
```

This *static* initializer method is run immediately after the class is loaded, before any objects have been created.

Exercises

a) As an incentive, the bank initializes all new accounts with $500. Modify the program of this chapter (especially constructor method *BankAccount*) to accomplish this.

b) Modify class *BankAccount* to print, "____'s account created." whenever a new bank account object is created.

c) Modify class *BankAccount* to print "*Access permanently denied*" if the incorrect account number is entered three times in a row for any customer.

d) Modify the program to accept type double for member variable *interestRate*. Test your program with an interest rate of 5.2%.

e) Provide a means to screen the assignment of the interest rate so it falls within allowed limits.

f) Modify the program so the account can not be overdrawn.

g) Modify the program so a warning is written if the account goes above $100,000 (the FDIC limit).

h) Following the suggestions in the discussion, add the **bold** code listed below to class *BankAccount* to allow the bank manager to print out the history of withdrawal transactions for any customer. (Be sure to include array *myRecord* in class *BankAccount* as a member variable.) Test your code by making several withdraws and calling *getAccountRecord*.

```
void withDraw(int withdrawAmount){
    if(accountState == true){
        myCash -= withdrawAmount;
        myRecord[i++] = withdrawAmount;
    }
    else
        System.out.println(myName+"'s account is not OPEN");
}
```

```
void getAccountRecord( ){
    System.out.println(myName+"'s withDraw record is:");
    for(i=0;i<10;i++)
        System.out.print(myRecord[i]+",");
    System.out.println( );
}
```

i) Modify the code of Exercise *h* so the transaction record printout stops upon reaching the first zero.

j) Develop project *MyComputer*. First, create class *PC*, which consists of attributes *pcName* and *pcRAM*, and methods *addRAM* and *showRAM*. Write a *main* method which creates computers "clone1" and "clone2," each initialized with 8Mbytes of RAM. The program adds another 8Mbytes of RAM to clone1 and 16Mbytes to clone2. Finally, it displays the total RAM of each.

k) Project *BigRace* gives the *Tortoise* a 100-foot head start over the *Hare*. Both move in random segments from 1 to 10 feet. The tortoise moves one segment per hour; the hare moves two segments per hour. Show the progress of the race during the first day.

> Hint: Develop template class *Racer*, to include attributes *hour* (static), *distance*, and *name*, and behaviors *showHour( )* (static), *showDistance( )*, *move( )*, and *Racer( )* (the constructor).

l) Project *GoForBroke* stakes gamblers *Sam* and *Mary* each to $2,000. Each round of bets changes the cash randomly by –100 to +90. Play continues until either player goes broke, or 25 rounds have been completed—whichever comes first. The cash holdings are continuously displayed.

> Hint: Develop template class *Gambler*, to include attributes *round* (static), *cash*, and *name*, and behaviors *getRound( )* (static), *getCash( )*, *makeBet( )*, and *Gambler( )* (the constructor).

m) Include additional attributes and behaviors into any of the Chapter 6 exercises, and be sure to initialize appropriate variables by way of the constructor.

Questions and Problems

1. A constructor method has the same name as the class it instantiates, and it is executed at the time of object creation.

   True **False**

2. Why don't constructor methods return values? (Hint: What is their sole purpose?)

3. Use constructors to perform the following:

   a) Using a genesis statement, create an object of class *House*, and send the object two stories and three bedrooms.

   b) Write the constructor that creates the house and initializes attributes my*Stories* and *myBedrooms*.

ESPRESSO

Do I see a pattern forming?

Yes you do. For all the stand-alone chapters of Section I, our projects will be divided into three distinct class layers:

- **Top-level class**: At the top level will be the application class holding method *main*. If needed, genesis statements create all required class objects.
- **Mid-level class**: At this intermediate level we will find most of the unique code that solves the specific problem at hand. If any class is to spawn objects and hold data members, it is most likely a mid-level class.
- **Low-level class**: At the lowest level we find the familiar tools classes, which have a good chance of supporting other future projects.

Of course, the larger projects found in the "real world" go way beyond this simple three-layered approach. For us, it is simply a way to avoid confusion during these early stages of learning.

4. Why are the constructors of class *String* called *overloaded*?

5. Why would objects created for the Pentagon generally have *private* attributes?

6. What will be printed by the following program segment?

```
String one = new String("Sam");
String two = new String("Mary");
String three = new String("Tai");
String[ ] names = {one,two,three};
for(i=0;i<names.length;i++)
     System.out.println(names[i]);
```

7. What is printed to the screen by the following program segment? (Hint: See Table 8.2 on page 159.)

```
StringBuffer samSays = new StringBuffer("I am  years old");
samSays.insert(5,14);
System.out.println(samSays);
```

8. What is printed to the screen by the following program segment?

```
int i;
StringBuffer samSays = new StringBuffer( );
for(i=1;i<=10;i++){
     samSays.setLength(i);
     samSays.insert(i,10-i);
     System.out.print("\r"+samSays);
     BasicTools.msec(1000);
}
samSays.append(" Blast off!");
System.out.println("\r"+samSays);
```

ESPRESSO

A Java program lives!

Here's one "lively" way of thinking about object-oriented programming (OOP).

Gather together all the user-defined and built-in classes that your project will need. Pretend, for starters, that all are "lifeless" (non-static attributes and behaviors). To gain access to the attributes and behaviors of a class, *they must be brought to life*.

- Place static in front of all attributes and behaviors (data members and methods) that are to be shared (only one copy will exist). These are brought to life during compilation. They are accessed externally by way of the class name.
- Write genesis statements for all the remaining classes that contain at least one non-static ("lifeless") attribute or behavior. When these genesis statements are executed, "living" objects will be created in the image of their corresponding template classes. Their attributes and behaviors are accessed externally by way of the reference names.

After compilation and genesis execution, imagine a project container filled with these living objects and static members. During program execution, these living members are accessed.

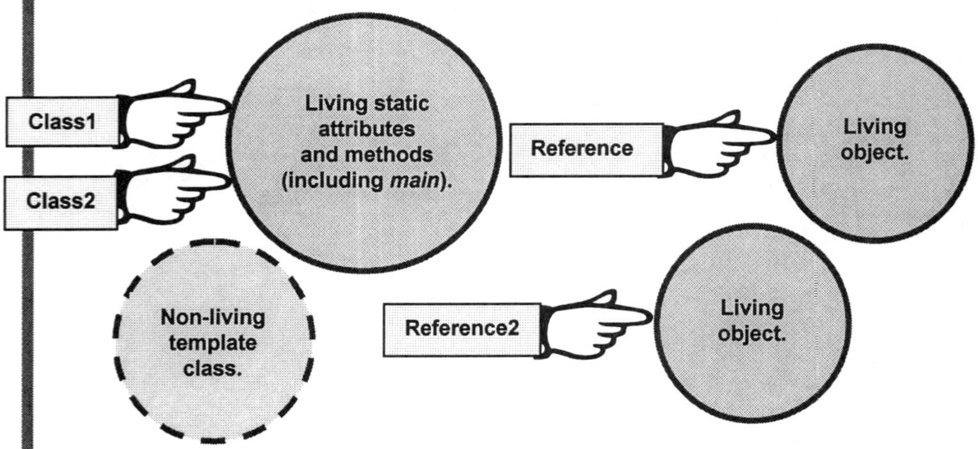

CHAPTER

10

Project MathQuiz

Keyboard Input, Exceptions, and Wrapper Classes

Objectives

- *To input data from the keyboard*
- *To process an exception*
- *To write a math assessment program*

Discussion

In the previous chapters we made good use of the *print* and *println* methods to output data to the standard output device: *the screen*. In this chapter, we will close the circle and introduce several ways of inputting data from the standard input device: *the keyboard*.

For keyboard input, J++ offers the *System.in.read( )* built-in method from class *InputStream*. Those of you familiar with C's *scanf* will find this method quite limiting, as it only inputs byte arrays of ASCII code. Our response will be to take this as a challenge. It will be our responsibility to convert these byte arrays into more useful data types, such as integer and string.

Another consideration with method *System.in.read( )* is that it "throws an exception." It's all part of the rather complex error-handling system of J++. This is the very first time we have been forced to consider exception handling, and it's one reason we waited so long before introducing keyboard input.

Exceptions

Ideally, every method should check for execution errors. The conventional method used by C functions is to return a single error indicator. For many reasons, this is not very effective. Therefore, Java has borrowed a new error reporting mechanism from the Ada programming language: *exceptions*.

Using baseball terms, the exception mechanism sounds quite simple. First we *throw* an error and then we *catch* the error. What's new is the ability to place the error catcher anywhere in the program code, no matter how many method layers are placed between the thrower and the catcher.

Divide by zero

Let's follow the exception process with a very simple case. Suppose method *main* sends parameters *dividend* and *divisor* to method *divide*, and displays the returned *quotient*. Figure 10.1 is a case in point.

```
// Method main sends two parameters to method divide,
// and displays the returned quotient.
class ExceptionTest
{
      public static void main(String args[ ]){
            System.out.println(divide(10,2));
      }

      static int divide(int dividend,int divisor){
            return(dividend / divisor);
      }
}
```

Why are both methods *static*?

Figure 10.1
A simple *divide* program

The *divide* program is very simple. Method *main* sends 10 and 2 to method *divide*, which returns the quotient (5) for display. However, suppose method *main* now sends 10 and 0 to method *divide*. Since dividing anything by zero is an illegal mathematical operation, the calling method (*main* in this case) should be notified so it can take appropriate action. Since an error message must be passed from one method to another, it qualifies for *exception* handling.

You *throw* and I'll *try* to *catch*

Now look at the new version of our *divide* program (Figure 10.2). This time we have added all the necessary trappings of exception handling. As shown, we are sending 10 and 0 to method *divide*. This should trigger the exception-handling process.

Let's follow the action from start to finish:

- Method *main* calls method *divide* and sends parameters 10 and 0. To notify method *main* that an exception might be forthcoming, we append "*throws Exception*" to method *divide*.
- Method *divide* checks the divisor and finds that it is zero. It uses a constructor method (*Exception("Shame! You divided by zero!")*) and the keyword *new* to create an exception object from class *Exception*—which it *throws*.

- The system immediately exits method *divide* (executes no further statements) and moves to the closing bracket of the *try* block.
- The system then searches for a *catch* block to process the error object. The catch block "catches" the error object and assigns reference *error* to point to the object.
- At this point, a number of actions are possible. We have chosen the simplest: To use the *println* method to display the string error object directly to the screen.

```
// Method main sends two parameters to method divide,
// and displays the returned quotient.
class DTmain
{
    public static void main(String args[ ]){
        try{
            System.out.println(divide(10,0));
        }
        catch(Exception error){
            System.out.println(error);
        }
    }

    static int divide(int dividend,int divisor) throws Exception{
        if(divisor == 0)
            throw new Exception("Shame!  You divided by zero!");
        return(dividend / divisor);
    }
}
```

New! Exception processing.

Catch the error.

error references the string object.

Throw the error.

Figure 10.2
Exception handling demonstration

Back to the keyboard

Armed with our newfound ability to process exceptions, we can return to the major task at hand: inputting data from the keyboard. Using the *read()* method, the sample program of Figure 10.3 shows how it is done.

```
byte[ ] bArray = new byte[10];
try{
     System.in.read(bArray);
}
catch(IOException error){
     System.out.println(error.toString( ));
}
```

Method *toString* (from class *Throwable*) converts the error message thrown by *read( )* to a string.

Figure 10.3
Keyboard input

Referring to Figure 10.3, we first create a 10-element byte array object (*bArray*). We then call method *read(bArray)*, which continuously inputs characters from the keyboard to the array until "Enter" is pressed. The rest of the code handles any exceptions that might be thrown our way by the *read* method. Part of our responsibility will be to convert the byte array to more useful data types.

Hands-On Procedure

Step one—Project definition

1. In this chapter, we will write a program to help young people master their times tables.

> **We ask a series of five math problems. For each problem, the system indicates if the response is right or wrong. When done, the total score is displayed.**

Step two—Structure chart

2. The structure chart of Figure 10.4 shows a system of three user-defined classes. (*KBTools* is the third tools class to be developed so far.)

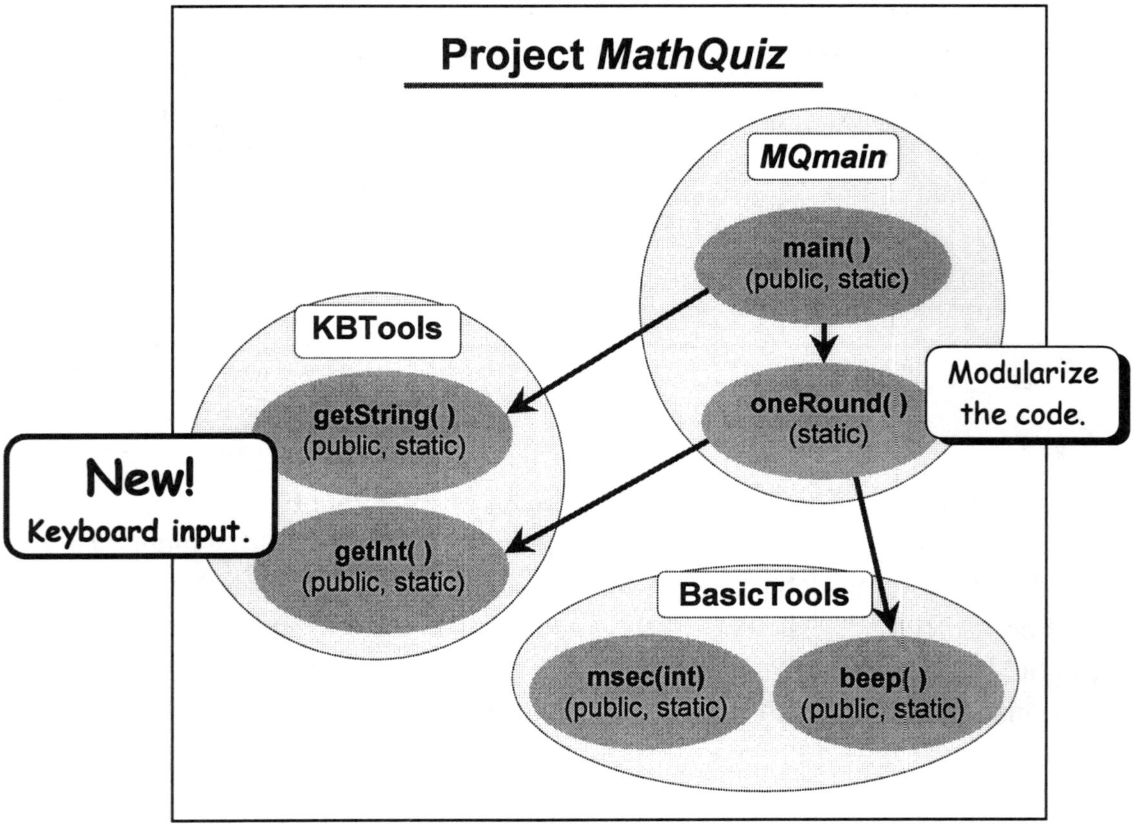

Figure 10.4
Project *MathQuiz* structure chart

- Back we go again to a project that requires no user-defined objects. The reason is always the same: The nature of the project. Our project is a math tutorial designed for only a single student. We have no need for multiple instances of any user-defined class.

- As we have done in the past, we opted to place all the static keyboard routines in a separate "tools" class (*KBTools*). Methods *getInt* and *getString* were chosen because integer and string input is the most common.

- Creating method *oneRound*, which performs one round of play (five questions), is purely for modularization reasons (to offload code from a higher-level module to a lower-level module).

Step three—Writing the program

3. Create project *MathQuiz* within solution *Chapter10*. Add previous class *BasicTools* and new class *KBTools* of Figure 10.5.

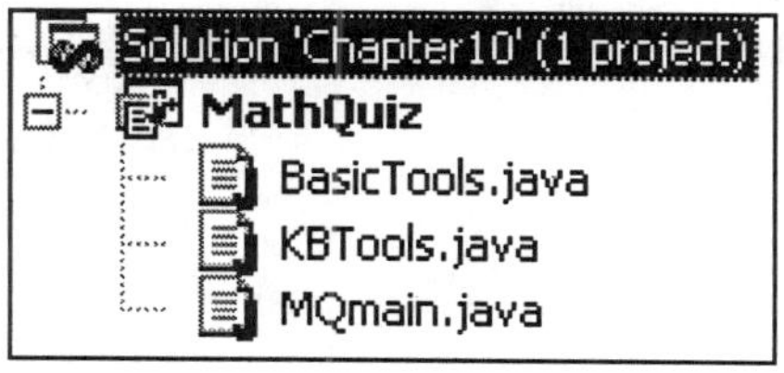


```
// Class KBTools holds several static methods
// for inputting data from the keyboard.
import java.io.*;
public class KBTools
{
      static int getInt( ){
            int i;
            byte[ ] bArray = new byte[11];
            try{
                  System.in.read(bArray);
            }
            catch(IOException error){
                  System.out.println(error.toString( ));
            }
            for(i=0;bArray[i]!=13;i++)
                  ;
            return Integer.parseInt(new String(bArray,0,i));
      }

      static String getString( ){
            int i;
            byte[ ] bArray = new byte[50];
            try{
                  System.in.read(bArray);
            }
            catch(IOException error){
                  System.out.println(error.toString( ));
            }
            for(i=0;bArray[i] != 13;i++)
                  ;
            return new String(bArray,0,i);
      }
}
```

We import package *java.io* so we can access class *IOException*.

New! Keyboard input.

New! Wrapper class.

"parse" means to convert (from a string to an integer).

New! Exceptions.

Return up to the carriage return (13).

Figure 10.5
Class *KBTools*

4. Class *KBTools* offers a wealth of interesting insights.

   - Beginning with method *getString( )*, we create a 50-byte array to hold input strings of up to 50 characters. Next, we input the byte array from the keyboard (*read(bArray)*) until *Enter* is pressed—making sure we catch any exceptions that might be thrown from the *read* method.

     Because we terminated data entry by pressing *Enter*, the end of the byte array contains a carriage return (ASCII 13) and a linefeed (ASCII 10). When we locate the end of the array (ASCII 13), we automatically generate the length of the array (*i*).

```
for(I = 0;bArray[i] != 13;i++)
    ;
```

     The final step is to use a constructor method from class *String* to create and return a string object from the byte array object. (*0,i* means we start at offset *0*, and convert a byte array of length *i*.)

```
return new String(bArray,0,i);
```

   - Method *getInt* follows a similar pattern. We create an array of up to nine characters (11 including the *linefeed* and *carriage return*) in order to hold integers from 0 to 999,999,999. We input the characters from the keyboard (*read*), determine the length of the string by locating the carriage return, and construct a string object from the byte array.

     This time, however, we need one additional step. We use the *parseInt* method from "wrapper" class *Integer* to convert the string to an integer value for return to the calling method.

```
return Integer.parseInt(new String(bArray,0,i));
```

parseInt is a static method from wrapper class *Integer.*

ESPRESSO

What is a "Wrapper" class?

Each of the intrinsic data types (*boolean*, *char*, *double*, *float*, *integer*, *long*) has a corresponding *wrapper class* (*Boolean*, *Character*, *Double*, *Float*, *Integer*, *Long*). Note that the wrapper class names begin with a capital letter.

The purpose of the wrapper classes is to "wrap" each of the intrinsic data types in a class. This provides two major features:

- First, a *reference* (pointer) to the data is created. This allows us to pass the data "by reference" rather than "by value." When we pass by reference, we can alter the original value rather than just a copy—that's one advantage.
- Second, within each wrapper class we have at our disposal a rich variety of *fields*, *constructors*, and *methods* (such as *parseInt* from wrapper class *Integer*).

Suggestion: Using *Help*, view the contents of the *Integer* wrapper class.

5. Finally, we add class *MQmain* of Figure 10.7. Briefly, here is what takes place.

    a) Using method *getString*, we input and respond to the student's name. We then call nested method *oneRound*.

    b) Within method *oneRound*, we define a five by two local array to hold the five test questions, and enter a five-iteration loop. With each pass we print the next problem to the screen and ask for the answer using the *getInt* method. If correct, we congratulate the student, increment the score, and sound a beep. If not correct, we say "Sorry, that's wrong."

    c) The total score is returned for printing to the screen.

```
// Class MQmain runs the math quiz tutorial.
public class MQmain
{
    public static void main (String[ ] args){
        System.out.println("What is your name?");
        System.out.println("Hi "+KBTools.getString( )+"\n");
        System.out.println("Your score is "+oneRound( )*20+"%");
        System.out.println("Press ENTER to exit program.");
        KBTools.getString( );
    }

    static int oneRound( ){
        int[ ][ ] factors = {{3,4},{5,7},{18,2},{50,10},{13,21}};
        int score,i,answer;
        for(i=0,score=0;i<factors.length;i++){
            System.out.println(factors[i][0]+" x "+factors[i][1]+" = ?");
            System.out.println("What is the product?");
            answer = KBTools.getInt( );
            if(answer == factors[i][0]*factors[i][1]){
                System.out.println("That's right!\n");
                score++;
                BasicTools.beep( );
            }
            else
                System.out.println("Sorry, that's wrong.\n");
        }
        return score;
    }
}
```

New! Keyboard input.

New! Two-dimensional array.

Figure 10.7
Class *MQmain*

Step four—Execute the program

6. Execute project *MathQuiz* and note the screen output of Figure 10.8.

   a) Did the program correctly evaluate both right and wrong answers?

      Yes **No**

   b) Was a beep heard for each correct answer?

      Yes **No**

Figure 10.8
Project *MathQuiz* partial screen output

ESPRESSO

Treasure without a map?

Look at the statement below, from method *getString*.

```
return new String(bArray,0,i);
```

What we seem to have is half a genesis statement—an object without a pointer! Don't we need to create a reference to point to the object (as shown below)? How can we locate treasure without a map?

```
String myReference = new String(bArray,0,i);
```

Actually, the reference is there; we can't see it because it's hidden. The rule is this: When constructors are listed as parameters (such as placed after *return* statements), the system automatically creates and assigns a temporary (invisible) reference, which is passed between the modules.

7. Return to class *MQmain* of Figure 10.7 and change the values listed in the two-dimensional array as desired. Rerun the tutorial and note the results. Did the system correctly handle the new set of values?

   Yes **No**

8. Will the system properly handle multiplication problems whose product is as large as one billion?

   Yes **No**

Step five—Debug the program

Exception: A case study

> The *parseInt* method converts a string of ASCII characters to an integer. However, if one or more of the string elements is not a number (0x30 to 0x39), it throws a *NumberFormatException* error. If no one is around to handle (catch) the error, the system crashes.

9. Execute program *MathQuiz* of this chapter and incorrectly enter one or more letters when asked for an answer to any of the five math problems.

   a) Did the program instantly crash, and did it display: "An exception of *java.lang.NumberFormatException* was not handled"?

      Yes **No**

   b) Did the error indicator (an arrow) point to the statement holding the *parseInt* method?

      Yes **No**

10. Surround the *parseInt* method with the exception-handling code on the next page and repeat. When a letter is incorrectly entered, does it properly respond (and not crash)?

    Yes **No**

```
try{
      return Integer.parseInt(new String(bArray,0,i));
}
catch(NumberFormatException error){
      System.out.println(error.toString( ));
      System.out.println("Oops! Enter numbers only!");
      BasicTools.beep( );
}
return 0;
```

Exercises

a) Write method *average*, which inputs two integers from the keyboard and returns their average value. Method *main* calls *average* and prints the average value to the screen.

b) Write program *Lottery*, which generates six random integers from one to ten and places them into an array. Six integers from one to ten are then entered from the keyboard. The number that matches (regardless of position) is reported.

c) Modify exercise b) for 25 plays, where each play costs $10. The cumulative winnings are reported. (Three matches pays $20, four matches pays $200, five matches pays $2,000, and all six matches pays a jackpot of $2,000,000.)

d) Using keyboard input, modify project *Resistor* from Chapter 4. (Strings *series* or *parallel* are input from the keyboard, along with two resistor values. The equivalent value is printed.)

e) Using keyboard input, modify project *DrawTree* from Chapter 5 to input the tree height. (If you wish, further modify the code to input tree position.)

f) Write a project that asks for your full name (first, middle, and last) and stores the three strings in an array. It then prints, "Hello Mr./Ms: ___________, your first name is ____________, and your middle name is ____________."

g) Add keyboard input to any of the other projects from previous chapters. (For example, any of the gambling games from Chapter 6 could be modified to accept numbers, cards, or bets.)

h) Modify method *oneRound* so it can automatically process quizzes that are of any arbitrary length.

i) Using a design of your choice, write project *PassWord.* During execution, the client is asked for a password—up to three times. The system responds with "Password correct," "Try again," or "You are locked out." (If locked out, program action stops.)

j) Use an array of strings with project *PassWord* to allow up to 10 possible passwords.

k) Add method *getCharArray* to class *KBTools.* Method *getCharArray* receives a reference to a char array, inputs characters from the keyboard, and prints them to the screen.

l) Modify project *MathQuiz* for two or more players. This means objects must be created from a new class (Player?). Each object will hold a minimum of the player's name and cumulative score. Constructors will initialize and personalize each player object. After each round of play, scores will be displayed and compared.

m) Using constructor *Double* and method *doubleValue* from class *Double*, create method *getDouble* and add to class *KBTools*. Test *getDouble* with *main*.

n) Write a quiz program that asks a series of questions, such as "Who was the ____ president of the United States?" The blank should be displayed as a 1, 2, or 3. The answers should be typed in by the user. When done, the total score is reported. (Hint: Store the correct answers as an array of strings, and use method *equalsIgnoreCase* from class String.)

o) Write a program that continuously inputs integers from the keyboard and adds them to a five-element integer array. What happens when the array overflows? Add an appropriate exception to respond to the problem.

p) Modify project *MathQuiz* so the numbers in the math problems are random.

Questions and Problems

1. After pressing 1, 2, and 3 from the keyboard, what exactly is in the first three elements of array *bArray*?

2. Why are the keyboard routines placed in a tools class?

3. Why is an object of class *Exception* like a baseball? (Hint: See Figure 10.2.)

4. Why didn't we create user-defined objects for this chapter's project?

5. What kind of parameter is received by the built-in *read* method?

Part 3

More Advanced Topics

The four chapters of Part 3 move us up a notch into more advanced material and slightly larger and more involved projects.

You can pick and choose the material somewhat, especially if you are anxious to get into Web browser design.

However, don't pass over these chapters entirely as you would be missing some very essential topics—not the least of which are random numbers, advanced math, inheritance, file I/O, and vectors.

CHAPTER

11

Project Eighth Wonder

Class *Math*

Objectives

- *To add methods to class KBTools*
- *To perform advanced math*
- *To study compound interest*

Discussion

Compound interest is often called the eighth wonder of the world—and for good reason. Amazing things happen when events are governed by exponential growth.

Suppose a distant ancestor of yours deposited one cent in the Bank of the Red Sea exactly 2,000 years ago, at the time of the birth of Christ. Fortunately for you, this venerable bank—the world's oldest—is still in operation. Over the years, the account paid a miserly 2% interest compounded yearly—not exactly a rousing return.

Yet you wonder, as you thumb through the passbook just found within a dusty chest in your attic: What could this be worth? Would it even pay to travel to the Middle East to claim your prize? We shall see!

Compound interest

The formula for compound interest is well known and is shown below.

$$E = P(1 + R)^T$$

E (Earnings)	dollars
P (Principal)	dollars
R (Rate)	0–1 (0–100%)
T (Time)	years

For example, 100 years after the original penny was deposited, the net earnings was still less than 10 cents! It sure didn't grow very fast…at least at first.

$$E = .01(1 + .02)^{100} = 7.2 \text{ cents}$$

Class *Math*

The Java language has access to hundreds of built-in classes, with more added all the time. Because they are used so often, some are worthy of special study—such as class *String* of Chapter 8 and class *Math* of this chapter.

Class *Math* is found in package *java.lang* and includes the two fields and 30 methods of Table 11.1.

- The methods of class *Math* operate only upon the simple intrinsic types (*int*, *long*, *float*, and *double*). Since multiple instances of these types are generated via the declaration process, there is no need to generate multiple instances of class *Math*.

> Therefore, all the methods of class *Math* are static.

- Note that most input parameters and return types are *double*. This 64 bit floating point standard works on numbers that vary over the enormous range of $\approx\pm 10^{308}$.
- All intrinsic types in Java are signed. To un-sign a value, we use method *abs* to take its absolute value.
- All data members and methods are tagged *public*.

Math vignettes

As with Chapter 2, this chapter is actually three smaller projects in one. The first is presented in detail; the last two are primarily the responsibility of the reader.

- Vignette #1 (project *EighthWonder*) uses the *pow* (power) method to determine compound interest.
- Vignette #2 (project *StripChart*) uses the *sin* (sine) method to generate a sinusoidal wave.
- Vignette #3 (project *DiodeCurve*) uses the *exp* (exponent) method to generate a diode trace.

Fields

Name	Description
E	The **double** value that is closer than any other to *e*, the base of the natural logarithms.
PI	The **double** value that is closer than any other to *pi*, the ratio of the circumference of a circle to its diameter.

Methods

Name	Description
double **abs**(double)	Returns the absolute value of a **double** value.
float **abs**(float)	Returns the absolute value of a **float** value.
int **abs**(int)	Returns the absolute value of an **int** value.
long **abs**(long)	Returns the absolute value of a **long** value.
double **acos**(double)	Returns the arccosine of an angle (0.0 through *pi*).
double **asin**(double)	Returns the arcsine of an angle (-*pi*/2 through *pi*/2).
double **atan**(double)	Returns the arctangent of an angle (-*pi*/2 through *pi*/2).
double **atan2**(double, double)	Converts rectangular coordinates (**b**, **a**) to polar (r, *theta*).
double **ceil**(double)	Returns the smallest (closest to negative infinity) **double** value that is not < the argument and == to an integer.
double **cos**(double)	Returns the trigonometric cosine of an angle.
double **exp**(double)	Returns the exponential number *e* (i.e., 2.718...) raised to the power of a **double** value.
double **floor**(double)	Returns the largest (closest to positive infinity) **double** value that is not > the argument and == an integer.
double **IEEEremainder** (double, double)	Computes the remainder operation on two arguments as prescribed by the IEEE 754 standard.
double **log**(double)	Returns the natural logarithm (base *e*) of a **double** value.
double **max**(double, double)	Returns the greater of two **double** values.
float **max**(float, float)	Returns the greater of two **float** values.
int **max**(int, int)	Returns the greater of two **int** values.
long **max**(long, long)	Returns the greater of two **long** values.
double **min**(double, double)	Returns the smaller of two **double** values.
float **min**(float, float)	Returns the smaller of two **float** values.
int **min**(int, int)	Returns the smaller of two **int** values.
long **min**(long, long)	Returns the smaller of two **long** values.
double **pow**(double, double)	Returns of value of the first argument raised to the power of the second argument.
double **random**()	Returns a random number between **0.0** and **1.0**.
double **rint**(double)	Returns the closest integer to the argument.
long **round**(double)	Returns the closest **long** to the argument.
int **round**(float)	Returns the closest **int** to the argument.
double **sin**(double)	Returns the trigonometric sine of an angle.
double **sqrt**(double)	Returns the square root of a **double** value.
double **tan**(double)	Returns the trigonometric tangent of an angle.

Table 11.1

The methods of class *Math*

ESPRESSO

Do you feel free?

Free, that is, to use objects if they are needed, and not to use them if they are not needed? Free to use 10 levels of class modularization…or three levels…or no levels at all, if that's what the problem calls for? Free to create some variables as data members, and others as local variables, as the situation dictates? Free to tag methods and data members as *static* if they are shared, and *private* or *public* if you want them hidden or totally accessible?

If we are truly free, then we know how to handle the simplest of projects: We might place all code in method *main* in a single class—as we did for Chapters 1–3. No objects, no data members, no modularization.

On the other end of the scale might be a huge project to revamp the entire IRS system. As a truly free, independent, and unrestrained programmer, the chances are good that we would create a vast, multilayered hierarchy of projects, packages, classes, and methods. One class might be called *TaxPayer*, and each of the 120 million taxpayers in the United States would constitute a separate object of this class. Certainly, class *TaxPayer* would have data members for our name, social security number, income and deductions, and a whole host of methods to operate upon them. It is reasonable to assume that modifiers such as *static* and *private* would be used where appropriate, and that the code would be liberally sprinkled with exception processing.

Most projects, of course, lie between these two extremes, and most of ours are decidedly on the simpler side of the ledger. Given this enormous range of complexity, our task is to match each solution to each problem, using all the techniques that are necessary and avoiding those that are not.

As we approach the projects of this and all future chapters, we should have these all-important ideas uppermost in our minds.

Hands-On Procedure

Step one—Project definition

1. Our first vignette will determine our earnings from the Bank of the Red Sea.

> **Vignette #1: Project *EighthWonder* will determine the earnings from one penny invested for 2,000 years at 2% interest compounded yearly.**

Step two—Structure chart

2. The structure chart of Figure 11.1 shows a project comprising primarily tools classes. (No objects will be generated.)

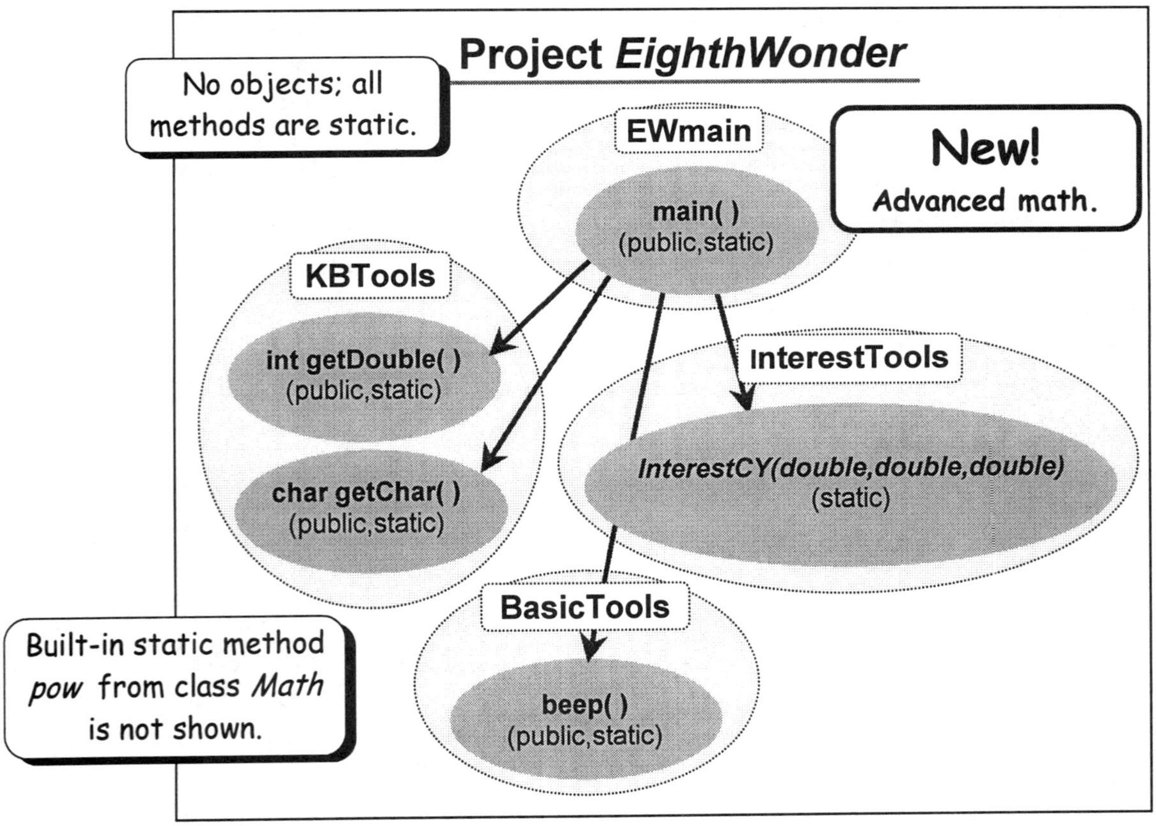

Figure 11.1
Project *EighthWonder* structure chart

- Class *InterestTools* holds static method *InterestCY* (interest compounded yearly), which receives parameters *principal*, *rate*, and *time* (*p*, *r*, and *t*) and returns the *earned income*.
- Class *EWmain* holds the *main* method—which inputs values from the keyboard and displays the results.

Step three—Write the program

3. Create project *EighthWonder* within solution *Chapter11* and add previous classes *KBTools* and *BasicTools*.

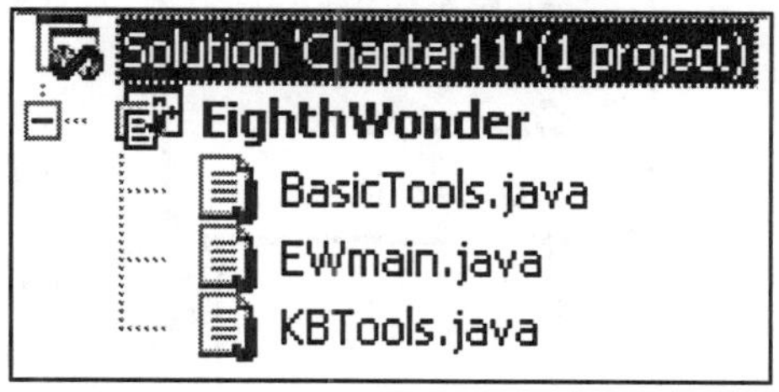

An analysis of the project suggests that we would find it most helpful to create methods *getDouble* and *getChar* to input numbers of type *double* and *char* from the keyboard.

- Method *getDouble* will allow us to use decimal point accuracy when we input *principal*, *rate*, and *time*.
- Method *getChar* will provide a convenient way of exiting a loop.

Why didn't we add these methods to class *KBTools* in Chapter 10? Quite simply, we didn't know at the time they would be needed. *The beauty of classes is the ability to add behaviors and attributes at any time as the need arises.*

4. As suggested above, add methods *getDouble* and *getChar* of Figure 11.2 to class *KBTools*.

5. Next, add and complete new class *InterestTools* of Figure 11.3.

   Looking to class *InterestTools*, a question comes to mind: Does it make sense for a class to hold only one small method? The answer is yes, because it allows for easy expansion with other related methods.

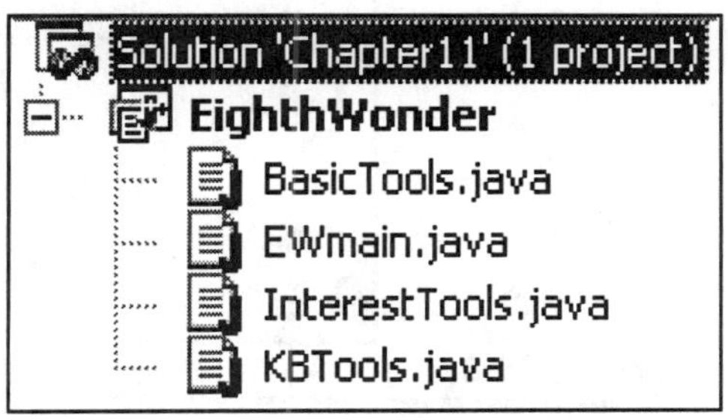

```
static double getDouble( ){
      int i;
      byte[ ] bArray = new byte[9];
      try{
            System.in.read(bArray);
      }
      catch(IOException error){
            System.out.println(error.toString( ));
      }
      for(i=0;bArray[i]!=13;i++)
            ;
      String s = new String(bArray,0,i);
      Double d = new Double(s);
      return d.doubleValue( );
}

static char getChar( ){
      int i;
      byte[ ] bArray = new byte[3];
      try{
            System.in.read(bArray);
      }
      catch(IOException error){
            System.out.println(error.toString( ));
      }
      return (char)bArray[0];
}
```

Type *double* = 64 bits.

New! *Character* and *Double* input.

Character plus carriage return (13) and line feed (10).

Return only the character.

Figure 11.2
Adding methods *getDouble* and *getChar*

```
// Method interestCY returns interest compounded yearly.
public class InterestTools
{
      static double interestCY(double p,double r,double t){
            return p*Math.pow(1+r,t);
      }
}
```

1+r raised to the t power.

New! Class *Math*.

Figure 11.3
Class *InterestTools*

ESPRESSO

Am I seeing Double?

Looking at the bottom of method *getDouble* of Figure 11.2 we see a most intriguing set of statements:

```
String s = new String(bArray,0,i);
Double d = new Double(s);
return(d.doubleValue( ));
```

The first two are standard genesis statements that also perform conversions. The first statement creates a *String* object from a byte array object, and the second uses a class wrapper to create a *Double* object from the *String* object.

However, what can be confusing is that identifier *d* is a reference to the integer object and not the variable itself. In other words, return *d* and you get the address of the variable. In order to extract the value of the variable, we call upon method *doubleValue*.

Just remember, there is a difference between class *Double* (capital D) whose object names are references, and intrinsic type *double* (small d) whose variable names hold the data itself.

6. Finally add main class *EWmain* of Figure 11.4 to project *EighthWonder*.

   - We input the three variables (*p*, *r*, and *t*) from the keyboard as type *double*, send them as parameters to method *interestCY*, and print the results.

   - The user then has the choice of entering any character but ESC and performing the calculation again, or pressing ESC and exiting the program.

```
public class EWmain
{
    public static void main (String[ ] args){
        double p,r,t;
        do{
            System.out.println("\nGive me the principal, rate, and time:");
            System.out.println("Such as: 1 cent=.01, 2%=.02, 2000 years=2000");
            System.out.println("Press ENTER after each:");
            p = KBTools.getDouble( );
            r = KBTools.getDouble( );
            t = KBTools.getDouble( );
            BasicTools.beep( );
            System.out.println("You earned: $"+InterestTools.interestCY(p,r,t));
            System.out.println("Press ENTER to continue.");
            System.out.println("Press ESC,ENTER to exit.");
        }while(KBTools.getChar( ) != 27);
    }
}
```

27 is the ASCII code for ESC.

Figure 11.4
Class *EWmain*

Step four—Execute the program

7. Execute the program (and be ready for a real surprise!).

In terms of trillions of dollars (10^9), enter below your earnings for one penny (.01) compounded at 2% (.02) per year for 2,000 (2000) years.

Earnings = ________________________ trillion!

8. Try other combinations of *p*, *r*, and *t*. For example, does increasing the interest rate from 2% to 3%, or decreasing the time from 2,000 to 1,000 years make much of a difference in our Red Sea case?

Yes **No**

9. Would you now agree that compound interest is the eighth wonder of the world?

Yes **No**

Vignette #2: Project *StripChart* will draw a sine wave to the screen whose amplitude is input from the keyboard.

10. Add project *StripChart* to solution *Chapter11* and include all necessary classes. (**CLICKR** on *solution Chapter11*, **Add Project**, etc.)

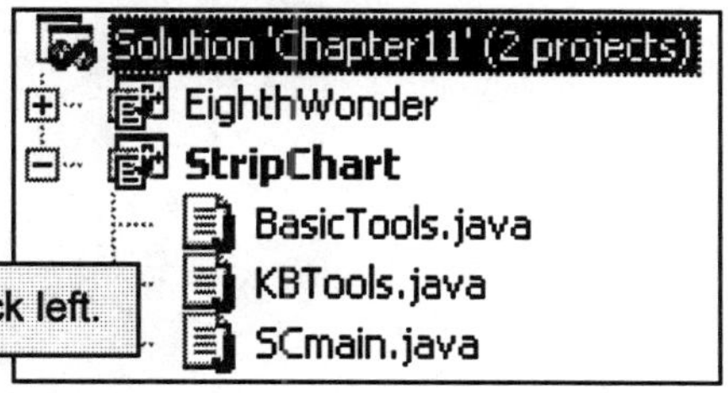

BOLD TYPE = click left.

11. If you can, develop project *StripChart* entirely on your own. If you need assistance, refer to the suggestions below.

Project *StripChart* suggestions

- The following program segment uses the *sin* method from class *Math* to create the strip-chart waveform of Figure 11.5.

```
int x,angle,amplitude = 25;
for(angle=0;angle<=360;angle+=20){
     x = (int)(35+amplitude*Math.sin(2.0D*Math.PI*angle/360));
     while(x-- >0)
          System.out.print(" ");
     System.out.println("*");
     BasicTools.msec(500);
}
```

PI (3.14) is a field in class *Math*.

New! Trigonometric operations.

- Place a modified version of the above code within method *sinWave*, in turn within class *SCmain*. Method *sinWave* receives an *amplitude* parameter from *main* (which in turn inputs the amplitude value from the keyboard).

12. Did your output resemble that of Figure 11.5 and were you able to change the amplitude from the keyboard?

    Yes   **No**

13. Change the offset (presently 35) and angle increment (presently 20) and note the changes.

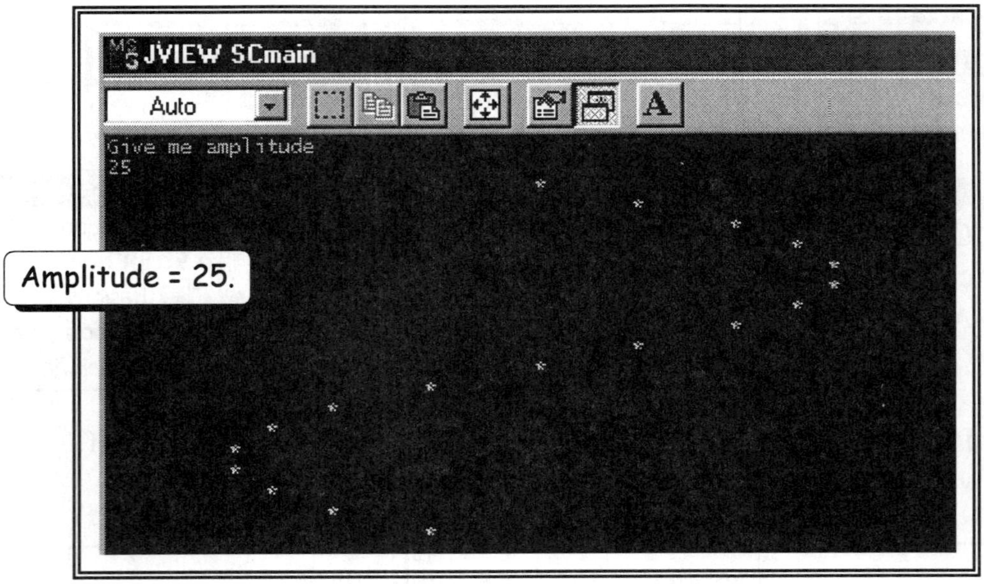

Figure 11.5

Project *StripChart* output

14. Modify the code to generate an FM (frequency modulated) wave that gradually increases in frequency. (Hint: The increase in *angle* is not a constant.)

Vignette #3: Project *DiodeCurve* will draw the *current* versus *voltage* profile of a silicon diode on the screen.

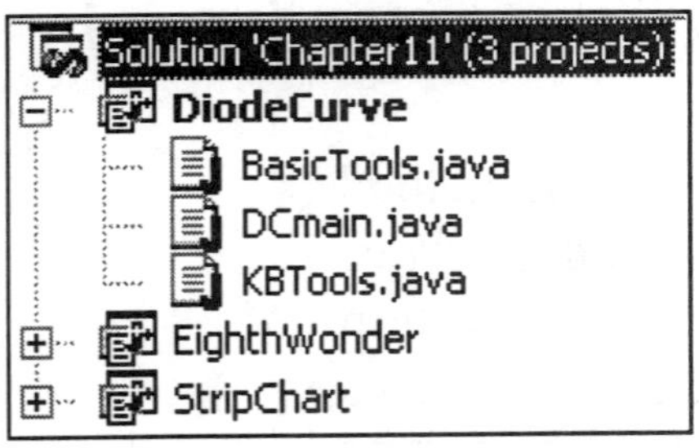

15. Add project *DiodeCurve* to solution *Chapter11*.

16. As before, try to complete the project entirely on your own, referring to the suggestions on the next page only as necessary.

17. Did your output resemble that of Figure 11.6?

    Yes **No**

18. Modify your project so the corresponding voltage/current values are printed beside each point. Were you successful?

    Yes **No**

Project DiodeCurve suggestions

- The following program segment uses the *exp* (exponential) method from class *Math* to generate the diode curve of Figure 11.6.

```
double i,voltage,current;
for(voltage=0;voltage <= .8;voltage+=.04){
    current = (int)(.15*Math.exp(8*voltage));
    for(i=0;i<current;i++)
        System.out.print(" ");
    System.out.println("*");
    BasicTools.msec(500);
}
```

New! Exponential operations.

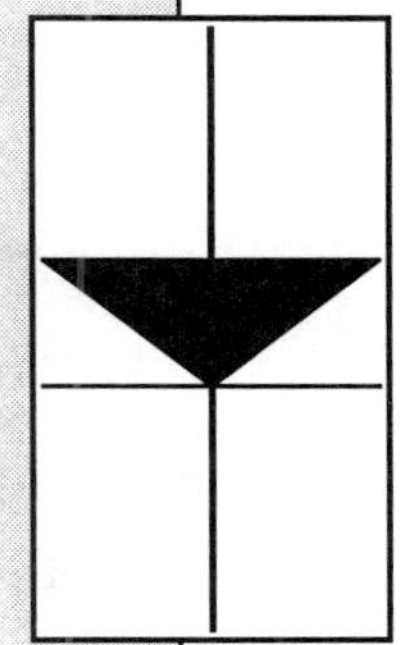

- As before, place a modified version of the code into method *diodeCurve*, within class *DCmain*.
- Modify the code to input key values of your choice (such as .15 or 8) from the keyboard.

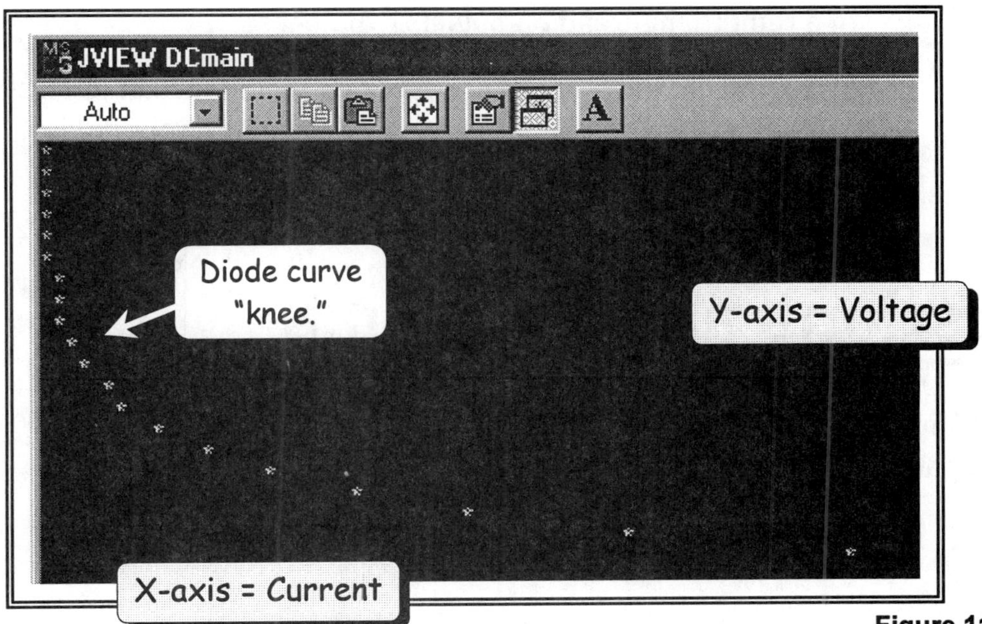

Figure 11.6
Project *DiodeCurve*

Exercises

a) The following equation shows the interest equation modified for variable (yearly, monthly, and daily) compounding.

$$E = P*(1 + R/C)^{T*C}$$

By inputting values for C from the keyboard, determine the interest for yearly, monthly, and daily compounding over various rate and time periods. (Hint: C = 1, 12, and 365 for yearly, monthly, and daily compounding.)

b) Generate a table of earnings for a principal of $1,000 at 4% for all time periods from 100 to 1000 years in increments of 100 years.

c) Using the *atan* (arctangent) and *sqrt* (square root) methods of class *Math*, write a program that inputs the real and imaginary components of a voltage vector, and displays its polar equivalents (*magnitude* and *phase angle*).

d) Using the *exp* method, plot a graph of an RC rise or decay curve.

e) Using the *sqrt* method, write a program that inputs the two sides of a right triangle and outputs its hypotenuse.

f) Using the *log* method, write a program that inputs an interest rate and outputs the time in years required to double your money.

Questions and Problems

1. At 3% interest, how long does it take to double your money? (Hint: $1.03^x = 2$, use logarithms to solve for *x*.)

2. Based on the results of question 1, what is the "rule of 72"?

3. Give three examples of floating point numbers.

4. Why are the methods of class *Math* static?

5. Why doesn't project *EighthWonder* require objects?

6. Based on the results of project *EighthWonder*, do you believe that a monetary system built on debt and interest (such as ours) must eventually fail?

7. Referring to Figure 11.2, *Double* is a class type and *double* is a variable type.

True **False**

8. Referring to method *getChar* of Figure 11.2, why do we create an array for three elements, but only return one (the 0th element)?

9. Modify method *main* of Figure 11.4 so your earnings are printed out in multiples of the national debt ($5 trillion). Summarize your modifications below.

10. For each statement below, explain in detail what is contained in variables *s*, *d*, and *x*.

```
String s = new String(bArray,0,i);
Double d = new Double(s);
x = d.doubleValue( );
```

11. In the statement below (from project *StripChart*), why is the "D" (which stands for *double*) not necessary?

```
x=(int)(35+amplitude*Math.sin(2.0D*Math.PI*angle/360));
```

CHAPTER

12

Project HighCard

Inheritance and Random Numbers

Objectives

- *To create a class that inherits a higher-level class*
- *To generate random numbers*
- *To play a simple card game*
- *To pass object parameters*

Discussion

Inheritance

Suppose we create a class called *Mammal*, which holds all the attributes and behaviors belonging to all mammals. At a later time, suppose we create class *Cat*. Because cats are also mammals, does it not follow that all the attributes and behaviors of class *Mammal* are automatically valid for class *Cat*?

Rather than repeat them, why not *inherit* them? That way, when writing class *Cat* we need only include those specific attributes and behaviors that are unique to cats. In other words, through class *Cat* we automatically have access to all the behaviors and attributes of class *Mammal*. Furthermore, if class *Mammal* in turn inherits properties from class *Kingdom*, we have access to those also.

As we go from *Kingdom* to *Mammal* to *Cat*, the properties at each level become less general and more specific. It follows that the number of animals belonging to each category narrows and their characteristics become more closely related. If it were not for inheritance, class *Cat* would have to include all the behavior of classes *Mammal* and *Kingdom*. The result would be classes of enormous size and redundant behavior.

Inheritance in action–polymorphism

Consider the program hierarchy of Figure 12.1, where class *Cat* inherits the behavior of class *Mammal*. The keyword is *extends*. That is, when class *Cat* extends class *Mammal* it means that class *Cat* inherits the behavior of class *Mammal*. In fact, since class *Cat* is presently empty, all of its behavior is inherited.

Now, the question is, what animal sounds will we hear when we execute method *main*?

This is called *upcasting*.

```
Cat myCat = new Cat( );
Mammal myMammal = new Cat( );
myCat.talk( );
myMammal.talk( );
```

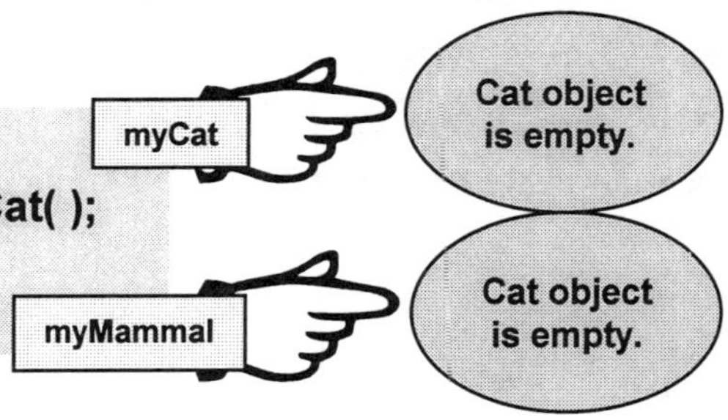

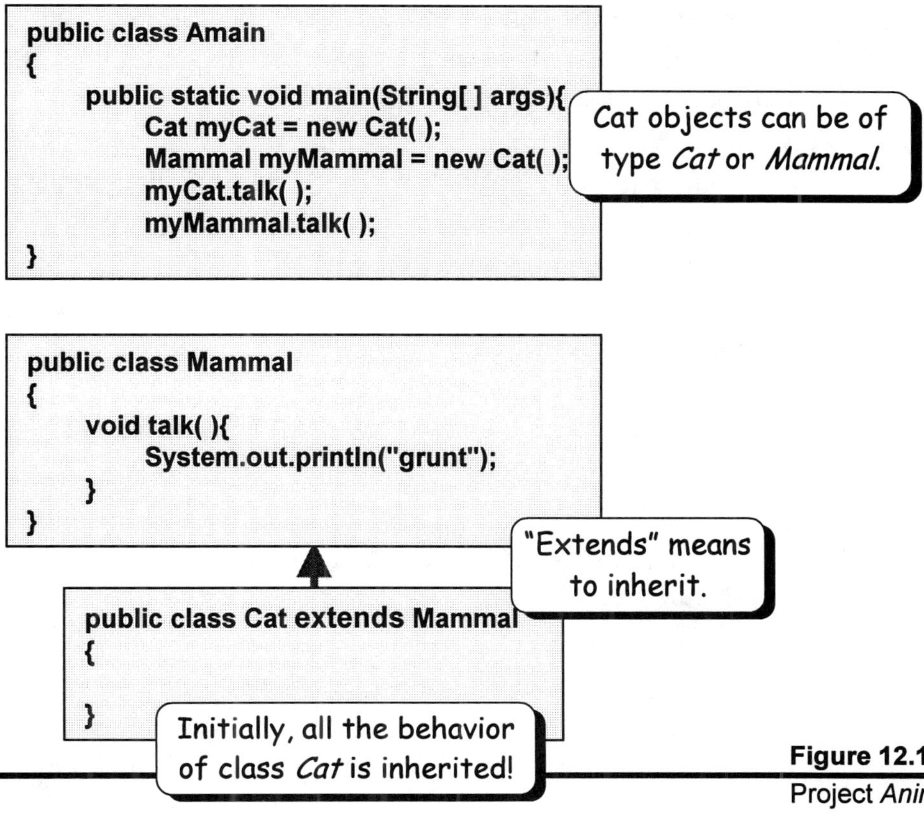

Figure 12.1
Project *Animal*

The answer is, we hear two mammal "grunts." What this tells us is that a cat object can be of two types (*Cat* and *Mammal*). It also tells us that class *Cat* inherited its talking behavior from class *Mammal*.

However, suppose we are not satisfied with the generalized "grunt"; we wish to have our *Cat* object say the more cat-like "meow" when asked to talk. To accomplish this, we simple add a more specialized *talk* method to class *Cat*.

```
public class Cat extends Mammal
{
    void talk( ){
        System.out.println("meow");
    }
}
```

Now, when we re-run method *main*, we hear two "meows". We have changed the behavior of our Cat objects!

The ability of the same object to have several types and to respond differently ("meow" versus "grunt") when sent the same message (*myCat.talk( )*) is known as *polymorphism*.

> Here is how it works: When method *talk* is called, the system first searches level *Cat* for the *talk* method. If it finds it, it uses it ("meow")—overriding method *talk* at the *Mammal* level. If it doesn't find the *talk* method at the *Cat* level, it goes up to the *Mammal* level ("grunt") and so on.

By the way, if we now wish to hear a grunt, we have to create a *Mammal* object and call its *talk* method (bypassing the *Cat* object).

```
Mammal herMammal = new Mammal( );
herMammal.talk( );
```

Because the system can not always determine ahead of time (at compile time) which form the object will take, it uses a technique called *late binding* (or *dynamic binding*) when calling certain methods.

The built-in classes

Because the projects of this text are limited in size, good examples of inheritance are found more readily within the built-in classes. In fact, the built-in classes of Java are one big multi-layer family tree, with all but the very highest class (class *Object*) inheriting properties from all those above. We have reserved the *Debug and modify* section for a study of inheritance within the built-in classes.

Although our user-defined classes have little need for inheritance, we will look at one example in this chapter. We will create a low-level class called *CardTools*, to hold several static methods for processing cards. Why not have low-level class *CardTools* inherit the methods of high-level class *BasicTools*? This is logical and reasonable because the methods of class *BasicTools* are more general and apply to nearly all projects.

> It is also correct to say that class *CardTools* is a *sub* or *child* class *derived* from *base*, *parent*, or *super* class *BasicTools.*

Random numbers

To enter the gambling business, J++ offers static method *random* from class *Math* (first introduced in Chapter 6), and non-static method *nextInt* from class *Random*. Because we require only one stream of random numbers, we choose static method *random* for this project.

Here is how it works. Method *random* returns a pseudo-random number of type *double* in the range of 0.0 to 1.0 each time it is called. To adjust the range from integer *a* to integer *b*, we use the following general formula:

```
ranValue = (int)(a + Math.random( )*(b – a + 1));
```

In our case, we need to shift this range of random values to a range of 13 integers from 2 to 14—representing 2 through 10, Jack, Queen, King, and Ace. Setting *a* to 2 and *b* to 14, the statement below solves the problem:

```
cardValue = (int)(2 + Math.random( )*13);
```

Objects anyone?

By now we know the story: If we play *High Card* alone (a rather dull and uninspiring activity), no objects will be needed. Since project *HighCard* pits two players against each other in a game of chance, user-defined objects are most certainly on the agenda.

Object parameters

To pass an array or string object as a parameter, we simply pass its reference (name). So, why can't we do the same with a user-defined object? We can, and it's just as simple!

Let's say that *cp1* references an object of class *CardPlayer*. The first statement on the following page calls method *aMethod* and passes *cp1*; the second receives the reference and places it in variable *player*. That's all there is to it.

```
aMethod(cp1);
```

```
aMethod(CardPlayer player){
}
```

The only question remaining is, why would we ever want to pass objects? Suppose we have a lot of code in our application class—too much to include in *main* alone (where the objects were created). We just modularize the code and pass object references to any new modules that need to access the objects. We've come a long way from passing simple integers.

High card

High card is about as simple a card game as you will find anywhere. A single card is dealt to each player, and the highest card wins a dollar. The accumulated winnings are displayed and play continues until either player exits the loop.

Hands-On Procedure

Step one—Project definition

1. This chapter introduces a simple card game.

> **Project *HighCard* will deal a single random card to each player. One dollar is awarded the player with the highest card. The total cumulative earnings of both players are displayed after each round of play.**

Step two—Structure chart

2. The structure chart of Figure 12.2 shows the usual three layers: The high-level *main* class, the mid-level *object-spawning* class, and three low-level *tools* classes. (Remember, for simplicity, we are no longer showing the built-in classes.)

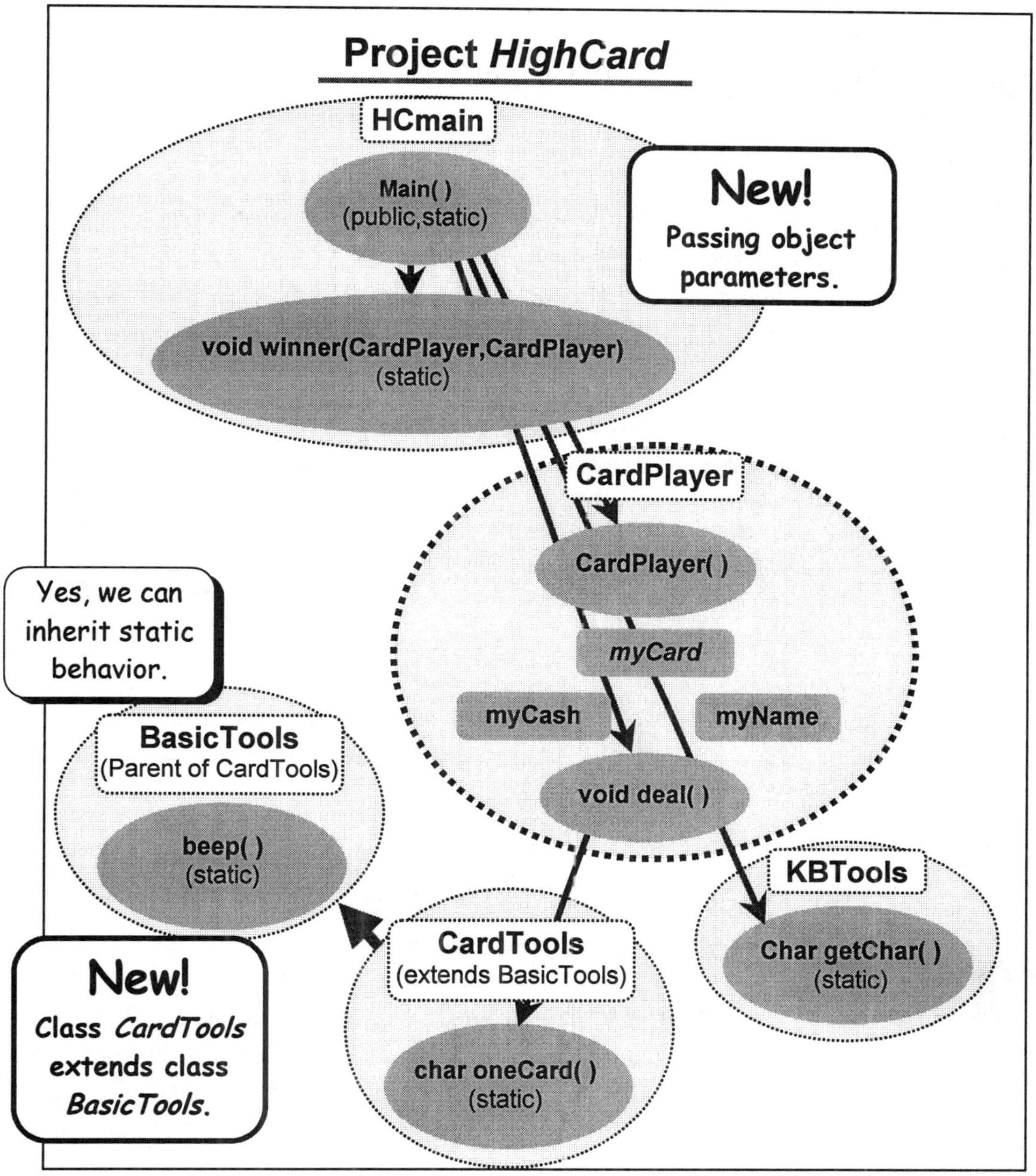

Figure 12.2

Project *HighCard* structure chart

Step three—Write the program

3. Create project *HighCard* within solution *Chapter12* and add the standard *BasicTools* and *KBTools* classes.

4. Add and complete new class *CardTools* of Figure 12.3.

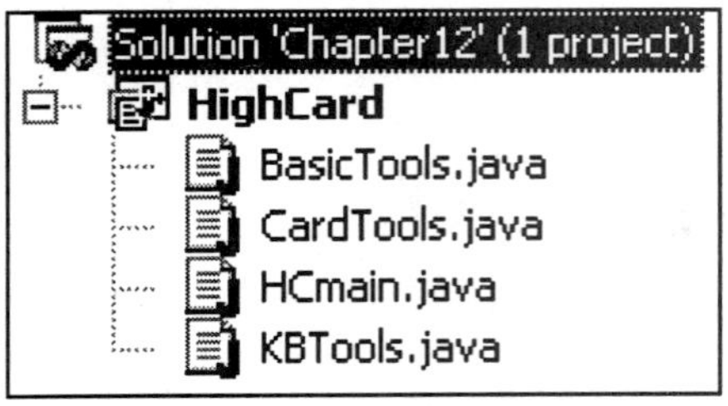

- Method *oneCard* returns a single random number from 2 to 14 each time it is called.
- By adding "extends *BasicTools*," method *CardTools* inherits the methods of superclass *BasicTools*, just as if all the methods of *BasicTools* were part of class *CardTools*. (Yes, we can inherit static methods.)

```
// Method oneCard "deals" a single random card
// each time it is called.
public class CardTools extends BasicTools
{
        static int oneCard( ){
                return (int)(2 + Math.random( )*13);
        }
}
```

New!
Inheritance.

Figure 12.3
Class *CardTools*

5. Next, add and complete new class *CardPlayer* of Figure 12.4.

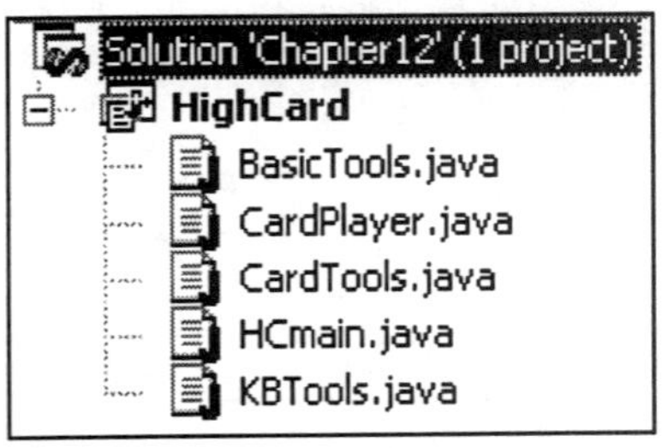

Class *CardPlayer* is the template blueprint for each gambler who wishes to enter the game. It has a constructor method to give each object a distinct and separate personality. As always, a number of useful methods surround and act upon the member variables.

How does method *deal* generate a random card? First, it calls method *oneCard*, which places a random integer from 2 to 14 into member variable *myCard*. For display purposes, the numbers from two through nine are converted to ASCII (add 48), and the numbers from 10 to 14 are converted to their ASCII card counterparts ('T,', 'J,' 'Q,', 'K,' and 'A') by the use of a switch statement.

```
// Class CardPlayer is a template class that
// will spin off player objects.
public class CardPlayer
{
    String myName;
    int myCard,myCash;

    CardPlayer(String name){
        myName = name;
    }

    void deal( ){
        char ASCIIcard = 0;
        myCard = CardTools.oneCard( );
        if(myCard < 10)
            ASCIIcard = (char)(myCard + 48);
        else
            switch(myCard){
                case 10: ASCIIcard = 'T';
                         break;
                case 11: ASCIIcard = 'J';
                         break;
                case 12: ASCIIcard = 'Q';
                         break;
                case 13: ASCIIcard = 'K';
                         break;
                case 14: ASCIIcard = 'A';
                         break;
            }
        System.out.println(myName+", your card is "+ASCIIcard);
    }
}
```

> As is usually the case, the behavior (methods) of this class directly support its "bulls-eye" (the member variables).

Figure 12.4
Class *CardPlayer*

6. Finally, create class *HCmain* of Figure 12.5.

> For the first time we have modularized *HCmain* with two methods: *main* and *winner*. The reason is always the same: to offload onto method *winner* the more specific and detailed code, leaving the more general and conceptual code for *main*.

```
// Method main calls and passes objects (object
// references) to method winner.
public class HCmain
{
      public static void main (String[ ] args){
            char ch;
            CardPlayer p1 = new CardPlayer("Mary");
            CardPlayer p2 = new CardPlayer("Sam");
            do{
                  p1.deal( );
                  CardTools.beep( );
                  p2.deal( );
                  CardTools.beep( );
                  winner(p1,p2);
                  System.out.println("\nPLAY AGAIN?");
                  ch = KBTools.getChar( );
            }while((ch == 'Y')||(ch == 'y'));
      }

      static void winner(CardPlayer p1,CardPlayer p2){
            if(p1.myCard > p2.myCard)
                  ++p1.myCash;
            if(p2.myCard > p1.myCard)
                  ++p2.myCash;
            System.out.println(p1.myName+" = "+p1.myCash);
            System.out.println(p2.myName+" = "+p2.myCash);
      }
}
```

New!
Class *CardTools* inherits class *BasicTools*.

New!
Passing objects.

Figure 12.5
Class *HCmain*

7. Looking to *HCmain* of Figure 12.5, there are two important new features:

   - First, note how method *beep* is now called:

```
CardTools.beep( );
```

This is possible because class *CardTools* extends (inherits) all the methods of class *BasicTools*.

- Second, method *winner* receives object references as parameters. This is simply the most convenient way for method *winner* to gain access to all the data members of each object.

> A complete analysis of project *HighCard* using singlestepping is a suggested exercise.

Step four—Execute the program

8. Execute project *HighCard* and note the possible screen output of Figure 12.6. Did the program function as expected?

   Yes **No**

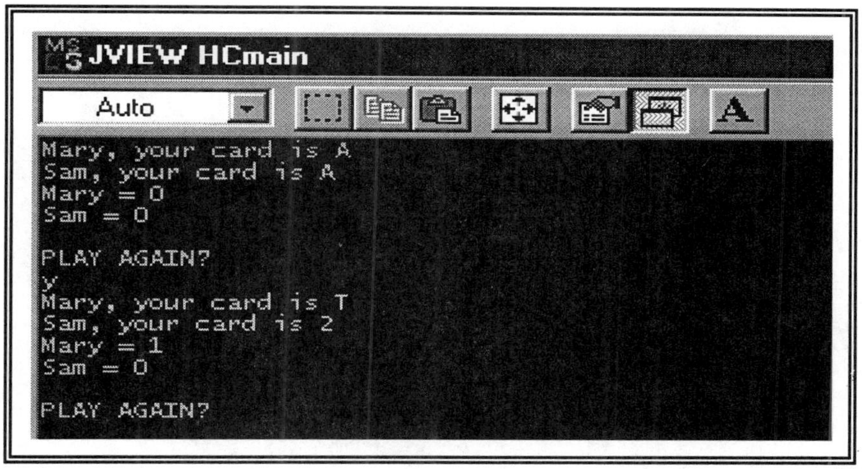

Figure 12.6
Project *HighCard* output

9. Run the program a number of times and tabulate the results.

   a) Do the cards seem to come up randomly?

   Yes **No**

   b) Does the winning percentage of any player tend towards 50%?

   Yes **No**

Step five—Debug and modify

> As promised in the discussion, we have reserved this section for a quick look at the inheritance hierarchy of the built-in classes. Remember, every class but the very highest-level class (*Object*) inherits properties from above.

10. If you have access to a *Java hierarchy chart*, locate package *java.lang*. An analysis of the chart reveals the hierarchical structure of several familiar classes. For example, Figure 12.7 shows the "family tree" that includes classes *Math*, *Number*, and *Exception*. In all cases, is it true that any given class directly inherits the properties of only one higher-level class?

    Yes **No**

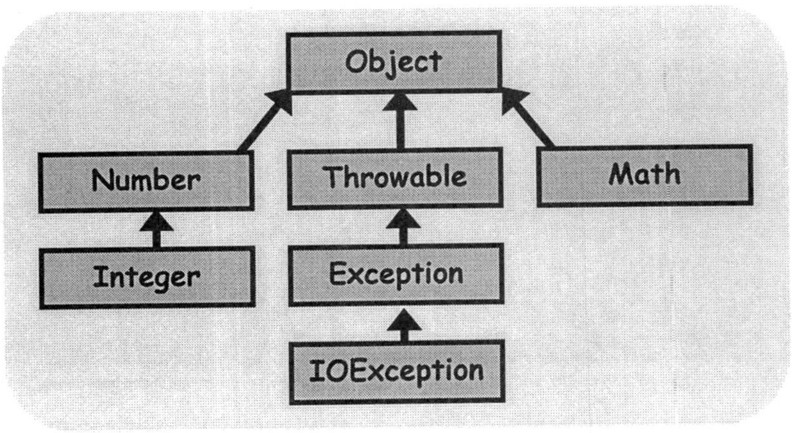

Figure 12.7
Class inheritance hierarchy example

11. By using the Help facilities (**Help, Contents, MSDN Library Visual Studio 6.0, Visual J++ Documentation, WFC and Java Reference, Java API**, etc.), locate and bring up any of the classes shown in Figure 12.7 (except *Object*). Does this class extend the class above it—and only the class above it?

    Yes **No**

ESPRESSO

What is an *abstract* method?

Consider the following class hierarchy:

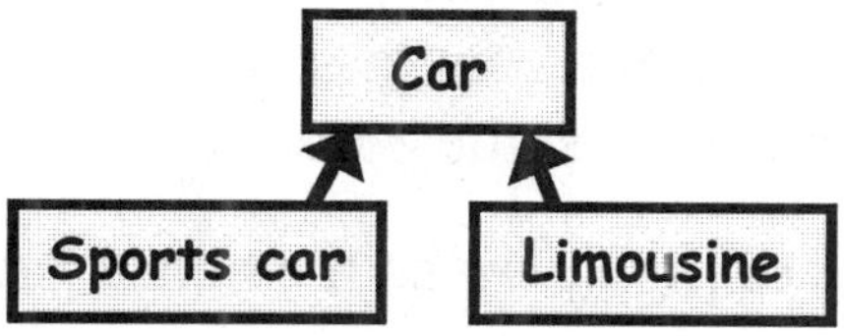

It certainly is reasonable that class *Car* should have a method called *shiftGear*, since that is a common behavior of all cars. The problem is, various car types do it in different ways (the *sports car* uses a stick shift; the *limousine* uses an automatic). So, at the *Car* level we can't implement (complete) the method by filling in the specific code. This can only be done within the lower-level classes *sports car* and *limousine*, when each writes its own *shiftGear* method that overrides that of class *Car*.

Therefore, to tell the compiler and programmer that method *shiftGear* within high-level class *Car* has not been implemented (completed), we tag both the method and the class *abstract*.

Let's test our theory with classes *Integer* and *Number*. Note that both classes contain a method called *doubleValue*. Within subclass *Integer*, it specifically states that this method will convert an *integer* to a double—and it contains the code to do so. However, within superclass *Number*, it simply states that a "numeric value" will be converted. Since it doesn't know what that numeric value is (integer? float?), it can't contain any specific code…and therefore is tagged *abstract*.

Then, why have a class called *Number* at all? The answer is, class *Number* is simply part of an inheritance chain—which collectively might contain attributes and behaviors of interest to class *Integer*. (Would method *talk* in Class *Mammal* become abstract if we only specified sounds at the *Species* level?)

Exercises

a) Singlestep through the program of this chapter until you understand the purpose and function of every statement.

b) Add an additional player object to your game of *high card.*

c) Create the game of *coin flip*, in which a player wins or loses a bet based on the outcome of a coin toss. (Are objects necessary if one player is competing against the house?)

d) Modify the game of *high card* so the house pays a bonus of $5 for every ace.

e) Modify the game so play stops when either player reaches $100.

f) To program *HighCard*, add the ability to input bets (using *getInt* from *KBTools*).

g) Write a statistical program that deals a thousand pairs of cards (as quickly as possible) and displays the ongoing, real-time percentage of time that each player wins. Also, show the percentage of time the players tie.

h) Add suit ranking (spades, hearts, diamonds, and clubs) to the game of *high card.* That is, an Ace of spades is higher than an Ace of hearts, etc.

i) Redesign program *HighCard* so *KBTools* also inherits from class *BasicTools*. (Is *KBTools.beep()* now legal?)

j) Based on Figure 12.1, what sounds are heard by the following *main* program segment?

Upcasting.

```
Mammal myMammal = new Cat( );
Cat myCat = new Cat( );
Mammal yourMammal = new Mammal( );
myMammal.talk( );
myCat.talk( );
yourMammal.talk( );
```

ESPRESSO

…and that's *final*!

Suppose we wish to set up a biological system in which all mammals can only talk in "grunts" (no "meows" allowed). In other words, we must prevent method *talk* in class *Cat* from overriding the same method in class *Mammal*. Simple, just tag method *talk* in superclass *Mammal* as final.

```
public class Mammal
{
    final void talk( );
        System.out.println("grunt");
    }
}
```

- Static methods are final be default.
- Static variables can also be tagged final. This prevents them from being changed. In other words, final variable = read-only variable.

Questions and Problems

1. Class *Car* might inherit behavior from what Superclass?

2. Refer to class *HCmain* of Figure 12.5. To access data member *myCash* as shown, why is it necessary that *myCash* of class *CardPlayer* (Figure 12.4), be tagged *friendly* or *public*?

3. Why are member variables also called *global* variables?

4. What is accomplished by the following class definition?

   class Gold extends Metal;

5. Referring to Figure 12.4, what is the purpose of the statement *ch+=48;*?

6. What special method gives an object its "personality"?

7. In the following statement, *t1* is an object reference. What is *Time*?

   Static void timeSpan(Time t1);

8. Why are the methods of most tools classes *static*?

9. Based on the *mammal/cat* analogy, which of the following classes is analogous to *mammal* and which is analogous to *cat*?

   Class *CardTools* is analogous to ______________

   Class *BasicTools* is analogous to ______________

10. Can user-defined classes *inherent* (extend) built-in classes?

11. Class *CardTools* of Figure 12.3 was used primarily to demonstrate the concept of inheritance. Nevertheless, is there any logic to having a class with just one small method? (Hint: Look to the future.)

ESPRESSO

A Java program lives II!

In the final ESPRESSO of Chapter 9 we looked upon a J++ program as a living entity. Now, with inheritance, we can modify our image as shown below. That is, all inherited (extended) attributes and behaviors also come alive after compilation and genesis execution.

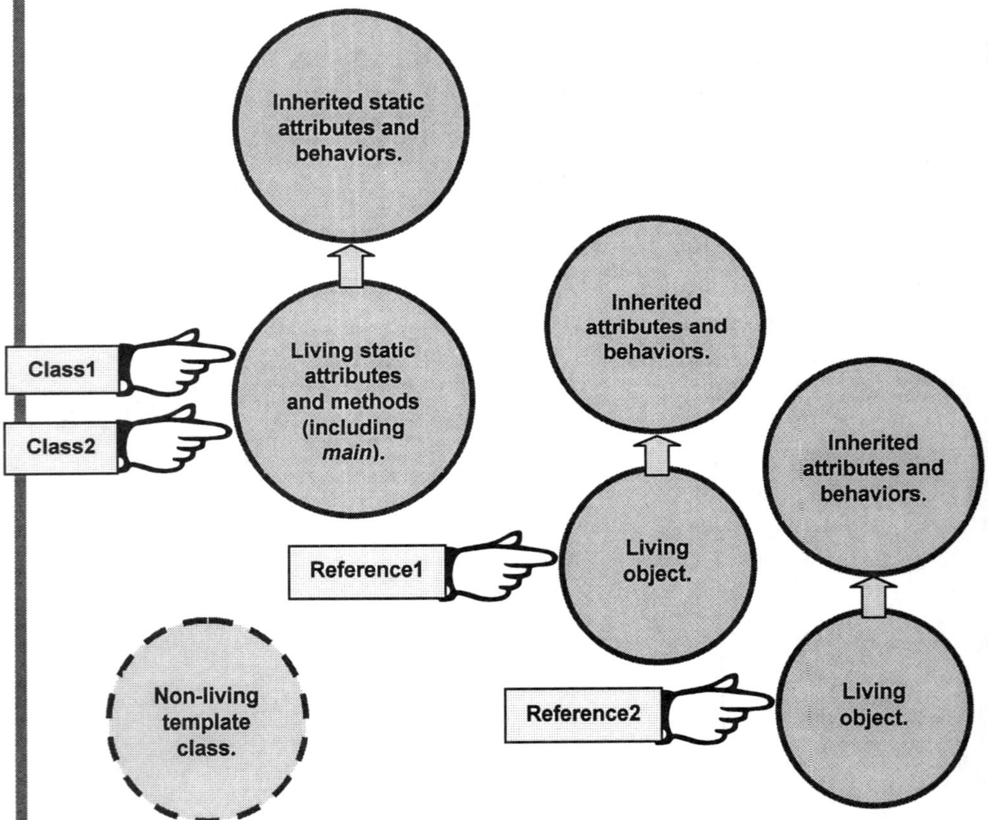

CHAPTER

13

Project Hollywood

File I/O

Objectives

- *To store and retrieve data on a hard disk file*
- *To process ASCII data for display*

Discussion

One very welcome advantage of a high-level language is that input and output from a floppy or hard disk file is no more difficult than input and output by way of the keyboard and screen.

The code listed below opens a file and inputs (reads) ASCII data from hard drive file *myInFile.TXT* and stores it in byte array *myArray* for processing. It is simple and compact.

```
byte[ ] myArray = new byte[500];
FileInputStream in = new FileInputStream("myInFile.TXT");
while(in.available( ) > 0)
     bytesRead = in.read(myArray);
```

Although not required for this chapter's primary project, the converse process is even simpler. The code below outputs (writes) ASCII data from byte array *myArray* and stores it to hard drive file *myOutFile.TXT*:

```
byte[ ] myArray = new byte[100];

FileOutputStream out = new FileOutputStream("myOutFile.TXT");
out.write(myArray,0,myArray.length);
```

Code placed here will initialize the array.

Offset into the byte array.

Lights, camera…execution

In this project, we turn into novice screenwriters. Our task is to enter a movie script into J++'s text editor, save it to the hard disk for safe-keeping, and then read it back out for real-time display on the screen.

However, it's not quite that easy. A real movie script also includes special action tags, in addition to the usual dialog. We want these special action items to also take place on the screen…in real time. In our case, the only special symbols required are those of Table 13.1.

Symbol	Action
*T	Tab
*D	Delay
*N	New Line
*7	Beep

Table 13.1
Special action tags

These tags are especially important for us, because we are writing a western called "The Man from Kansas." In movies of the old west, background sound is vital...and of course we are all painfully aware of the required time lag between the dialog of these solemn men of few words.

ESPRESSO

Aren't disks very slow devices?

Imagine fetching characters from a disk, one at a time. Each character on the spinning disk must rotate under the head and serial data must be read in, a bit at a time.

Given these facts of life, the only logical and reasonable way of reading data from a disk is a block at a time. That is precisely how the *read* method works.

```
while(in.available( ) > 0)
        bytesRead = in.read(myArray);
```

Blocks of data will be read in until method available (from class *FileInputStream*) returns a value that is no longer greater than zero.

Objects?

The old west, of course, is filled with wonderful and varied objects: Horses and stagecoaches and guns. But will we need objects for this chapter's project? The answer is no, because there simply is no need for multiple, unique, and individual instances of any user-defined class.

Hands-On Procedure

Step one—Project definition

1. This chapter's project involves some creative writing.

> **To carry out project *Hollywood*, we first write and store a script on disk. The system reads back the script and shows the action on the screen.**

Step two—Structure chart

2. The three levels of project *Hollywood* are shown on the structure chart of Figure 13.1.

> Why didn't we make class *Movie* a template class, ready to spin off movie objects?
>
> The answer is familiar: We are dealing with only a single movie, so multiple instances of class *Movie* are not needed. Instead, we have created class *Movie* purely for modularization reasons—to off-load lower level, more-detailed code from class *Hmain*.
>
> However, including class *Movie* in our project makes it easy to upgrade the project to handle multiple movie objects. You will have just such an opportunity as an exercise.

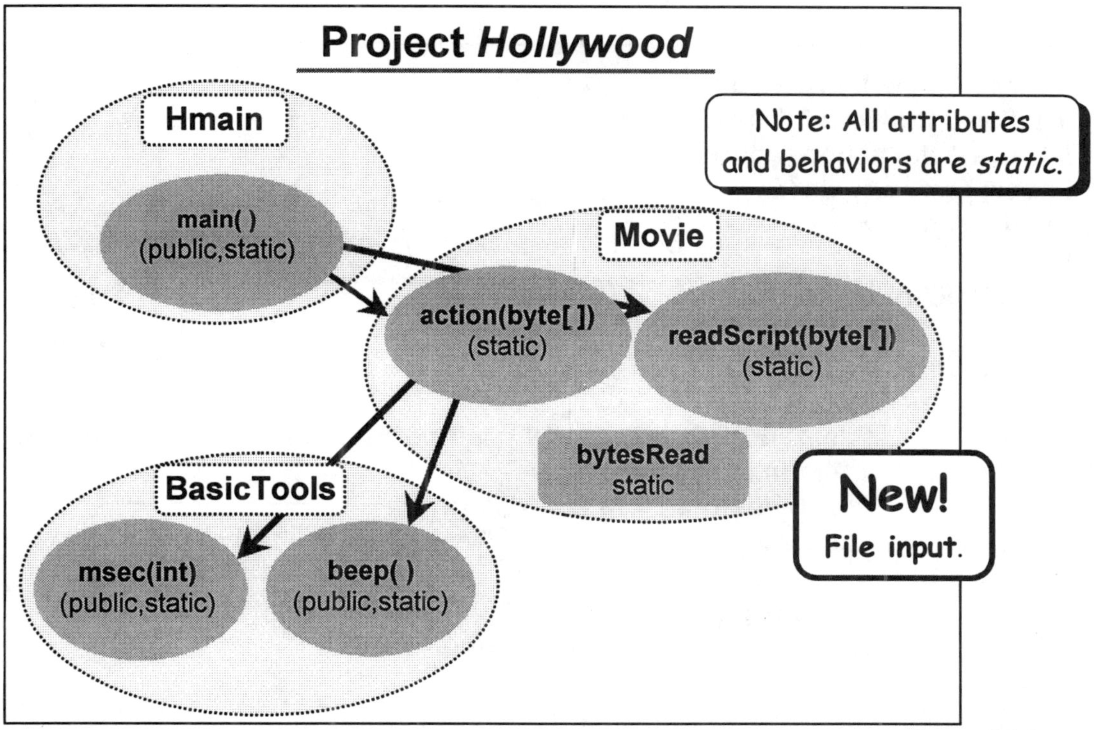

Figure 13.1
Project *Hollywood* structure chart

Step three—Write the program

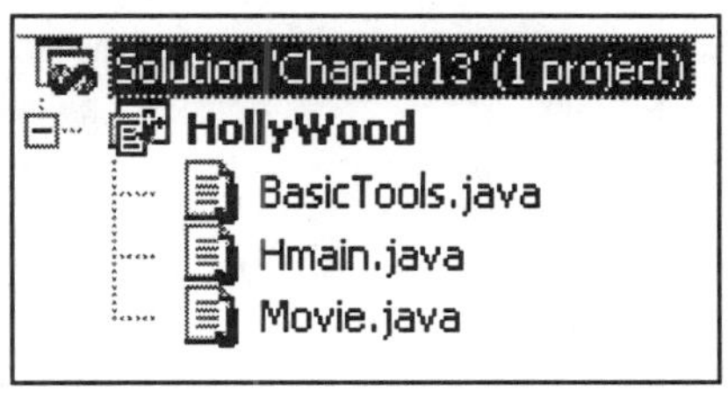

3. Create project *Hollywood* within solution *Chapter13* and add previous class *BasicTools*.

4. Add and complete new class *Movie* of Figure 13.2.

   - Method *readScript* receives a reference to a byte array, creates a *FileInputStream* object, and uses the reference (*in*) to access the *read* method—which reads all the characters of the move script from the disk into the byte array. Method *close()* closes the file and releases any system resources.

   - Method *action* receives the byte array of characters input from the disk and enters a loop. If the next character is not an asterisk ('*'), we print the character to the screen. If it is an asterisk, we check the following character (7, D, N, or T) and perform the required action (beep, delay, new line, or tab) by way of the *switch* statement.

```
// Class Movie holds two major methods:
// 1. Read the script  (readScript).
// 2. Start the action (action).
import java.io.*;
public class Movie
{
    static int bytesRead;

    static void readScript(byte[ ] bArray){
        try{
            FileInputStream in = new FileInputStream("Screenplay.TXT");
            while(in.available( ) > 0)
                bytesRead = in.read(bArray);
            in.close( );
        }
        catch(IOException ioe){
            System.out.println(ioe.toString( ));
        }
    }

    static void action(byte[ ] bArray){
        int i;
        for(i=0;i<bytesRead;i++){
            if((char)bArray[i] == '*'){
                switch((char)bArray[++i]){
                    case '7': BasicTools.beep( );
                              break;
                    case 'D': BasicTools.msec(2000);
                              break;
                    case 'T': System.out.print('\t');
                              break;
                    case 'N': System.out.println( );
                }
            }
            else
                System.out.print((char)bArray[i]);
        }
    }
}
```

Class *FileInputStream* belongs to package *java.io*.

New! File input.

Returns the number of bytes read.

Figure 13.2

Class *Movie*

5. Next enter class *Hmain* of Figure 13.3.

   Method *main* is a classic high-level design. The first line creates an array object, the second line reads the data from the hard disk, the third line displays the action, and the last line holds the script on the screen for several seconds.

```
// Class Movie reads the script and starts
// the action.
public class Hmain
{
      public static void main (String[ ] args){
            byte[ ] bArray = new byte[500];
            Movie.readScript(bArray);
            Movie.action(bArray);
            BasicTools.msec(4000);
      }
}
```

Get script from hard drive.

Figure 13.3
Main class *Hmain*

6. It's now time to write the script of our movie ("The Man from Kansas"). Figure 13.4 shows the result. The action tags (7, D, N, and T) can be placed anywhere in the text.

```
*N*TMy name is Marshall Dunkan. *DI'm from
Kansas.
*D*TThis town is too small for both of us!
*N*D*T*T*7 Yep!
*N*D*TAre you going to get out of town?
*N*D*T*T*7 Nope!
*N*D*TAre *Dyou *Dsure?
*N*D*T*T*7 Yep!
*N*D*T*T T*7H*7E*7 *DE*7N*7D*7!
```

Figure 13.4
Screenplay for "The Man from Kansas"

7. The next step is to enter the screenplay into file *Screenplay.TXT*. Fortunately, J++ has a text editor that is ready and waiting. Just follow these simple steps:

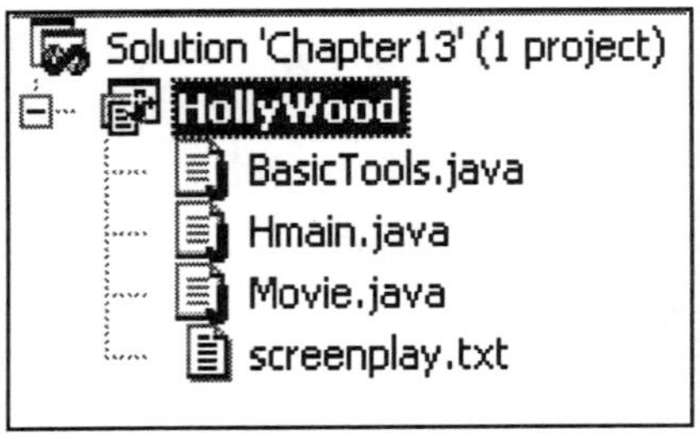

a) From the *file* menu, choose **New File** to bring up the *New File* dialog box, select the **New** tab, **Text File**, **Open**.

b) Enter the screenplay exactly as shown in Figure 13.4. When done, **File**, **Save Text File As**, enter File name *screenplay.txt*, **Save**.

c) **File**, **Close** to return to the Java files.

Step four—Execute the program

8. Execute the program and watch the action.

a) Was the dialog displayed as shown in Figure 13.5?

Yes **No**

b) Did beeps and delays occur at the expected places?

Yes **No**

Figure 13.5
Screenplay output

Step five—Debug the program

Breakpointing

> Singlestepping is a very powerful troubleshooting tool, yet it has its limitations. First of all, there are those pesky loops that one can become trapped in. Second, it's difficult to quickly move to a program location of particular interest.
>
> The solution is *breakpointing*. By setting a breakpoint, we can move to any program location at full speed. Then, perhaps, singlestep from the breakpoint. In other words, singlestepping and breakpointing combine to provide a most potent troubleshooting brew.
>
> We can set a temporary breakpoint using the cursor, or we can set any number of permanent breakpoints.

9. Using F10 and F11 as necessary, step inside method *action* of class *Movie* to the first statement (the *for* loop).

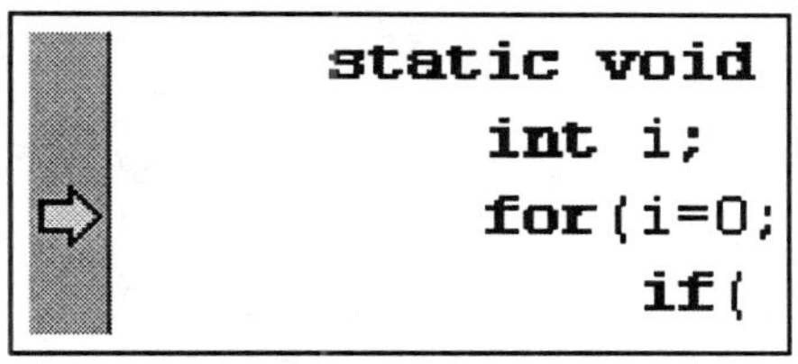

Cursor breakpoint

10. Position the cursor at the case '7': statement within the switch function. To execute full speed to this breakpoint Ctrl/F10 (or **Debug, Run to Cursor**). Did the "present position" (yellow) arrow move to the breakpoint?

    Yes **No**

11. Examine the output window (*jview.exe*). Based on the script of Figure 13.4, is this indeed the correct breakpoint location?

    Yes **No**

12. By pressing F10 (and F11 as needed), can we singlestep from the breakpoint location?

    Yes **No**

13. By moving the cursor, set another breakpoint of your choice and press Ctrl/F10. Did the system properly execute to the new breakpoint?

    Yes **No**

Permanent breakpoint

14. This time we will set a permanent breakpoint at the *case 'D'* position. To accomplish this, place the cursor anywhere within the *case 'D'* statement line, **CLICKR**, **Insert Breakpoint**. Did a small red circle appear at the corresponding line within the gray bar at the left of the screen?

    Yes **No**

15. Execute (*Start*) the program from the beginning. Did processing action properly stop at the permanent breakpoint location, and did the yellow (present location) arrow appear over the breakpoint?

    Yes **No**

16. Using the same technique, add two additional permanent breakpoints at locations of your choice. By clicking the Start button each time, do we properly move from breakpoint to breakpoint?

    Yes **No**

17. When done, remove all breakpoints. (Place cursor at breakpoint line, **CLICKR**, **Remove Breakpoint**. A disabled breakpoint turns white.)

Exercises

a) Modify the "D" symbol to include a time parameter. (Suggestion: Place the delay time after the D, as in D4 for four seconds.)

b) Finish the screenplay script of Figure 13.4 by adding in a gunfight at the end. Determine who won the gunfight by using the random number generator from class *Math*—but give the Marshall a three to one advantage. (Hint: Both contingencies must be written into the script, and a special symbol will cause the program to determine the path and jump to the proper array element.)

c) Write a short program that writes the alphabet to file alphabet.TXT. (Hint: Make a small addition to the "write" program in the discussion.)

d) Write a script for a secret agent in which all numbers in a file are replaced with *x*s. (Hint: Read the file, censor the numbers, and write the file back.)

e) Remove the *char* cast operator from the *print* statement (shown in **bold** below) and re-run the program. Explain the results.

*System.out.print(**(char)**bArray[i]);*

f) Redesign project *Hollywood* to include two or more movies. (Suggestion: Make class *Movie* a template class and include data member *myMovie* to hold the name of the movie.)

Questions and Problems

1. Given the statement below, what is *in*?

   FileInputStream in = new FileInputStream("herFile.TXT");

2. Referring to class *Movie* of Figure 13.2, why is variable *bytesRead* global?

3. Referring to the statement below (from Figure 13.2), why did we increment variable *i*? What is the purpose of the *char* cast operator?

```
switch((char)bArray[++i])
```

4. When *bArray* is sent as a parameter (as in Figure 13.3), exactly what is passed?

5. From what class did method *available* of Figure 13.2 (called from within method *readScript*) come from?

6. What does the following program segment accomplish?

```
int bytesRead;
byte[ ] myArray = new byte[7];
try{
     FileInputStream in = new FileInputStream("inFile.TXT");
     while(in.available( ) > 0)
          bytesRead = in.read(myArray);
    FileOutputStream out = new FileOutputStream("outFile.TXT");
    out.write(myArray,0,myArray.length);
    in.close( );
    out.close( );
}
catch(IOException ioe){
     System.out.println(ioe.toString( ));
}
```

7. What does it mean to *open* and *close* a file?

CHAPTER

14

Project IRS Agent

Vectors and Menus

Objectives

- *To create a vector of IRS objects*
- *To add a menu to our program design*

Discussion

If three people are playing cards, we need three objects. If 100 people have bank accounts, we create 100 objects. It's a pretty clear rule. But suppose you are in charge of the venerable Internal Revenue Service (IRS) with its 150 million "clients." Are you going to write a program with 150 million genesis statements?

Certainly not; that would be quite impossible. Because the array type can hold object references just as easily as integers, we could adopt the same solution we did way back in Chapter 7. However, when storing large numbers of related objects (object references), we have a better solution: The *Vector* class.

The *Vector* class

The *Vector* class defines a collection of elements of type *Object*. It offers two major advantages over the simple array. First, the vector is dynamically resizable. This means, as we add or remove new elements, the vector automatically expands or contracts. Second, being a full-fledged class, we have a number of very useful methods at our disposal.

With project *IRS Agent*, we use a vector to store 100 *TaxPayer* objects. The first step is to create a vector object.

```
Vector v = new Vector(25,10);
```

Using this version of three available constructors, we create an initial vector capacity of 25, and append an additional 10 elements dynamically each time the need arises.

The next step is to add taxpayer objects to the vector. As a case in point, the code below appends two *TaxPayer* objects to the end of the vector object—where ID holds an integer identification number.

```
v.addElement(new TaxPayer("John Q. Taxpayer",ID));
v.addElement(new TaxPayer("John Q. Taxpayer",ID));
```

To retrieve objects from the vector, we make use of the *elementAt* method from class *Vector*. (Since a vector can hold any number and combination of objects, we use the cast operator when retrieving objects.)

```
TaxPayer tRef = (TaxPayer)v.elementAt(ID);
```

As always, to fully appreciate the power and versatility of the vector, review the three constructors and 24 methods that make up the class. There are methods to search, load, retrieve, size, and manipulate the elements of a vector.

Menus

Menus are extensively used in programming for the same reason they are used in everyday life: To provide a convenient way for the user to select from among a number of choices. As we will see in this chapter, programmers like to implement menus with the *switch* statement.

Hands-On Procedure

Step one—Project definition

1. In this chapter, we process a large number of objects.

> **Project *IRSAgent* first creates and stores 100 *TaxPayer* objects in a vector. We select one taxpayer by way of an ID, and then display a menu of three choices: *1. Enter exemptions*, *2. Enter income*, and *3. Show taxes*. We make our selection, and follow the appropriate action.**

Step two—Structure chart

2. The top two levels of project *IRSAgent* are shown on the structure chart of Figure 14.1. (For simplicity, classes *BasicTools* and *KBTools* are not shown.)

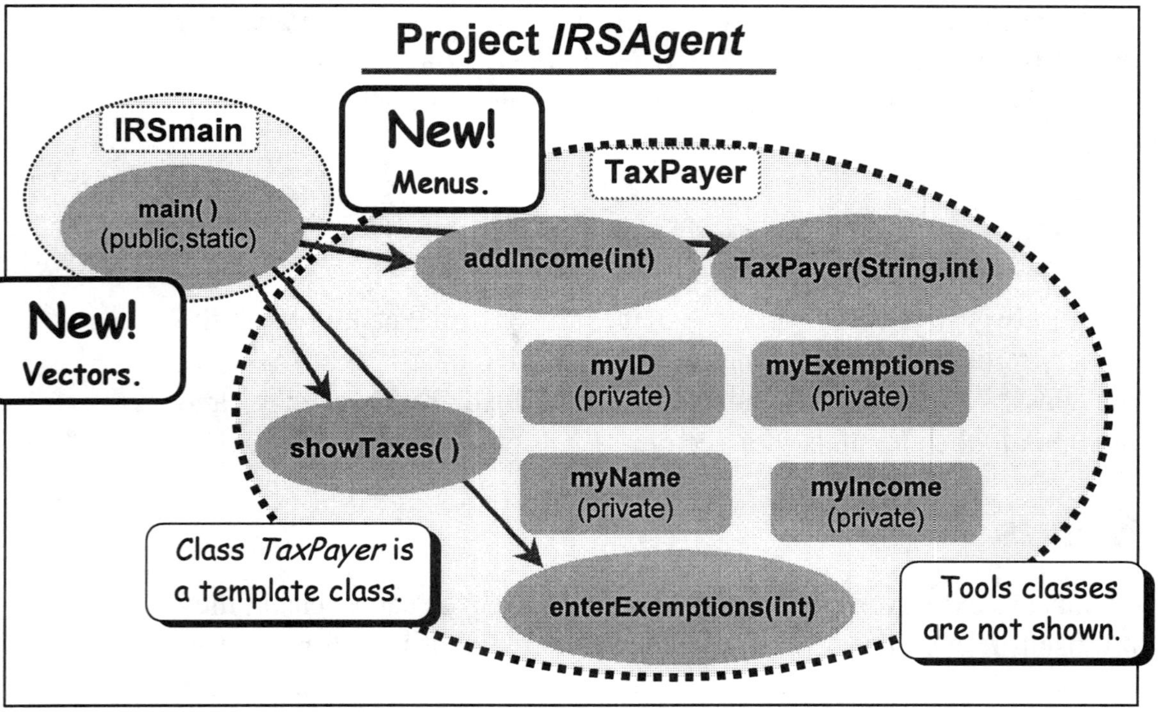

Figure 14.1

Project *IRSAgent* structure chart

Step three—Write the program

3. Create project *IRSAgent* within solution *Chapter14* and add the usual "tools" classes.

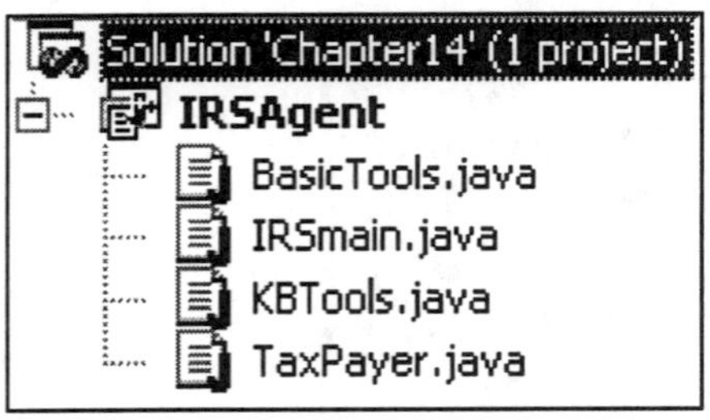

4. First, add and complete new class *TaxPayer* of Figure 14.2. The four methods and four data members are very straightforward.

   a) By examining method *showTaxes*, explain below how the taxes due are calculated.

   b) Why is it especially critical that all the attributes of class *TaxPayer* be private?

```
// Class TaxPayer is an object-producing template class.
public class TaxPayer
{
   private int myIncome,myID,myExemptions;
   private String myName;

   void enterExemptions(int exemptions){
      myExemptions+=exemptions;
      System.out.println("Total exemptions = "+myExemptions);
   }

   void addIncome(int income){
      myIncome+=income;
      System.out.println("Total income = "+myIncome);
   }

   void showTaxes( ){
      int taxes;
      taxes=40*(myIncome - myExemptions*1000)/100;
      System.out.println("$"+myIncome+" and "+myExemptions+" exemptions.");
      System.out.println(myName+" #"+myID+", you owe $"+taxes);
      BasicTools.beep( );
   }

   TaxPayer(String name,int id){
      myID = id;
      myName = name;
   }
}
```

Reminder: Think of the member variables as the bulls-eye, with methods surrounding and operating upon them.

Inputs to exemptions and income are changes to existing values.

If you wish, any of these can be made constants (final).

The constructor method assigns taxpayer IDs and names at the time of object creation.

Figure 14.2
Class *TaxPayer*

5. Next enter *main* class *IRSmain* of Figure 14.3.

   a) How many menu items are programmed?

   b) How many initial vector elements are created?

```
// Class IRSmain presents the menu and processes the data.
// Vectors are used to hold the TaxPayer objects.
import java.util.*;
public class IRSmain
{
   public static void main (String[ ] args){
      int i,ID;
      char choice,ch;
      Vector v = new Vector(25,10);
      for(i=0;i<100;i++)
         v.addElement(new TaxPayer("John Q. Taxpayer",i));
      do{
         System.out.println("What is your tax ID number?");
         ID = KBTools.getInt( );
         System.out.println("Hello taxpayer #"+ID);
         TaxPayer tRef = (TaxPayer)v.elementAt(ID);
         do{
            System.out.println("\n\tSelect 1,2,3, or 4");
            System.out.println("\tFollow all keyboard inputs with ENTER.");
            System.out.println("\t1. Increase/decrease exemptions");
            System.out.println("\t2. Enter additional income.");
            System.out.println("\t3. Show taxes due.");
            System.out.println("\t4. EXIT MENU.");
            choice = KBTools.getChar( );
            switch(choice){
               case '1': System.out.println("#"+ID+", enter exemption change:");
                         tRef.enterExemptions(KBTools.getInt( ));
                         break;
               case '2': System.out.println("#"+ID+", enter additional income.");
                         tRef.addIncome(KBTools.getInt( ));
                         break;
               case '3': tRef.showTaxes( );
            }
         }while(choice != '4');
         System.out.println("\nDO YOU WISH TO EXIT THE PROGRAM?");
         ch = KBTools.getChar( );
      }while((ch != 'Y')&&(ch != 'y'));
   }
}
```

New! A vector of objects.

Create a vector of 100 objects.

New! A menu.

Figure 14.3

Main class *IRSmain*

6. Briefly, here is how the code of class *IRSmain* progresses:

   - We create a vector object.

```
Vector v = new Vector(25,10);
```

   - We fill up the vector with 100 *TaxPayer* object references.

```
For(I=0;I<100;I++)
   v.addElement(new TaxPayer("John Q. Taxpayer",i));
```

   - We retrieve the *TaxPayer* reference at element "ID."

```
TaxPayer tRef = (TaxPayer)v.elementAt(ID);
```

   - Using *tRef*, we access the attributes of a *TaxPayer* object:

```
tRef.enterExemptions(KBTools.getInt( ));
```

```
tRef.addIncome(KBTools.getInt( ));
```

```
tRef.showTaxes( );
```

   - We are given an opportunity to exit the present taxpayer routine and also to exit the entire program.

```
      }while(choice != '4');
      ch = KBTools.getChar( );
}while((ch != 'Y')&&(ch != 'y'));
```

Step four—Execute the program

7. Execute the program and test project *IRSagent*. First, enter any taxpayer ID from 0 to 99. Then enter any combination of menu items "1," "2," and "3." When done, press "4." Did the program work as expected?

   Yes **No**

8. By going back and forth between various taxpayers (various ID numbers), add income and change exemptions in any way you wish.

By keeping track of taxes due, can we conclude that member variables are global variables (within each object) that store information permanently?

Yes **No**

Step five—Debug and modify

Conditional breakpointing

In previous chapters we covered *run-to-cursor* and *permanent* breakpoint techniques. In this chapter, we will complete our study with *conditional* breakpoints. They're conditional because the break depends on the state of the system.

9. The IRS suspects money laundering going on with taxpayer 50 or 51. Therefore, the IRS sets a conditional breakpoint that stops all processing whenever taxpayers 50 or 51 accumulates more than $1,000,000. In official breakpoint language this becomes:

```
(((myID==50)||(myID==51))&&(myIncome > 1000000))
```

Step 1: Set a permanent breakpoint right after *myIncome* is updated, as shown in Figure 14.4. (Set cursor, **CLICKR**.)

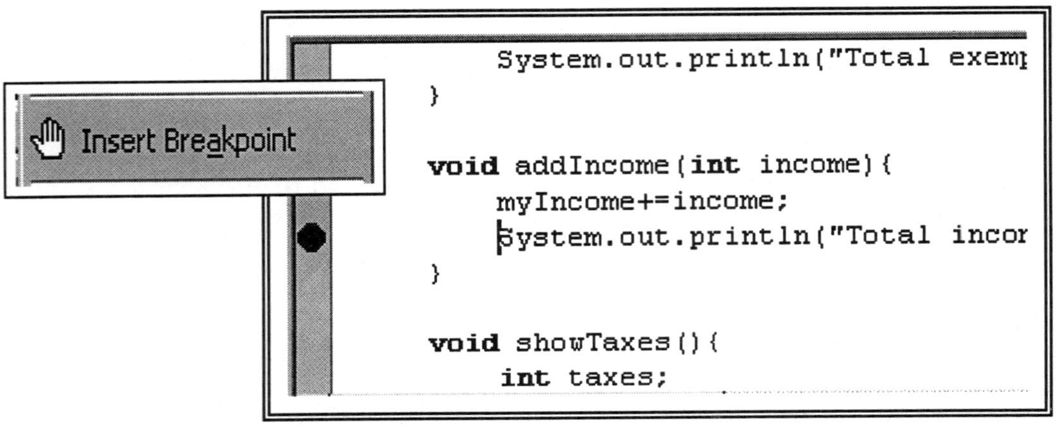

Figure 14.4
Breakpoints window

Step 2: **CLICKR** anywhere on the breakpoint line, **Breakpoint Properties** to bring up the *Java Breakpoint Properties* dialog box of Figure 14.5, fill in as shown, **OK**.

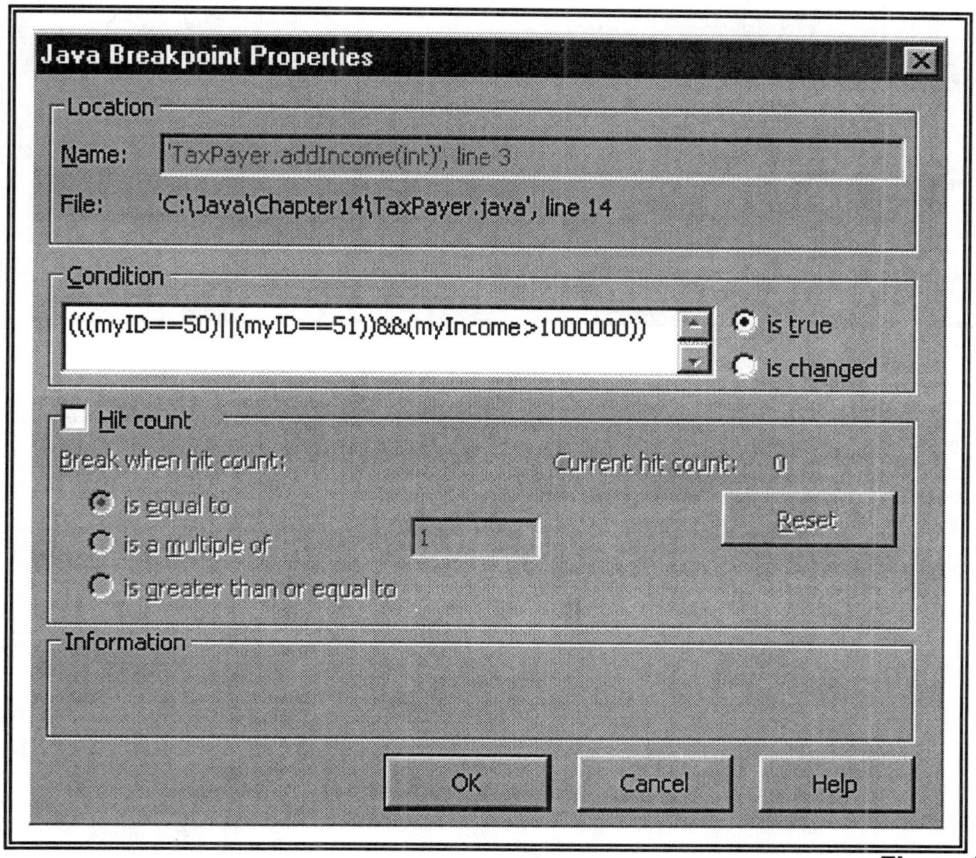

Figure 14.5
Java breakpoint properties dialog box

Step 3: Start the program and keep track of all income accumulated by taxpayers 50 and 51. When the figure exceeded $1,000,000 for either, did the system properly break?

Yes **No**

10. Figure 14.6 shows the special *Variables* window that automatically comes up whenever the break condition is reached. Does it give the state of the system at the breakpoint?

Yes **No**

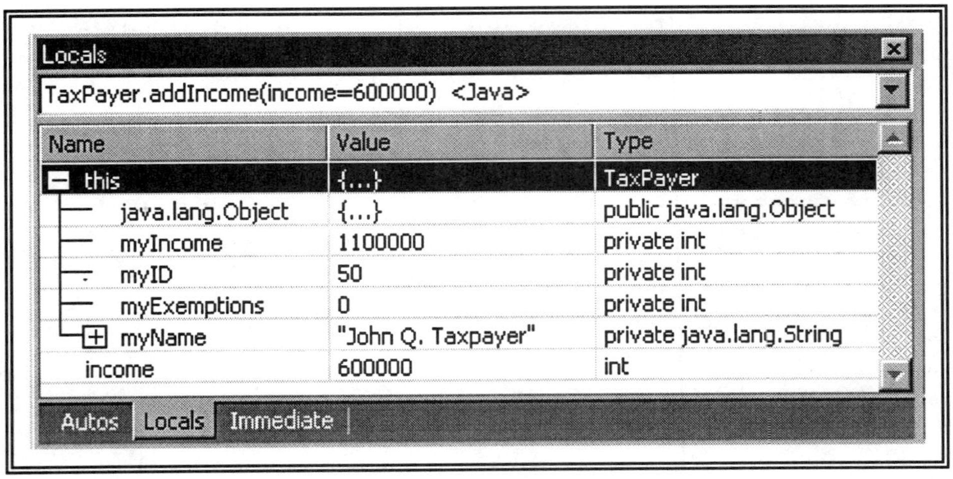

Figure 14.6
Variables window.

11. Referring back to Figure 14.5, set the *hit count* to 3 and re-execute the program. Did the system now break only after the condition was met for the third time?

    Yes **No**

12. If you wish, experiment further with conditional breakpoints until you are thoroughly familiar with the technique. (Suggestion: Set multiple conditional breakpoints.)

Exercises

a) To class *TaxPayer*, add a method and data member that handles deductions. Be sure to modify the formula within method *showTaxes* to account for these deductions.

b) To make the whole system more secure add code to require a password to enter any taxpayer's account.

c) Show how to use an array of names so the constructor method will initialize the names of the taxpayers at the time of object creation. (Hint: Reduce the list of taxpayers from 100 to 10.)

d) Create class *Student*, which holds methods *getName*, *setGrade*, and *showGrade*. From the *main* method, create a class of 30 students, give student number 8 the name of Sam Smith and a grade of B, and student number 27 (Tai Nguyen) a grade of A. Verify both grades.

e) Modify class *Student* of the previous project to hold arrays of grades. (Hint: When setting and showing grades, the element number will have to be sent as a parameter.)

f) As a research project, study class *Hashtable*, with an eye towards using real social security numbers for taxpayer IDs.

g) Add data member *myAge* and method *showAge* to class *Student*. Randomly assign each student an age of six, seven, or eight at the time of object creation. Then, process the array of objects to list all the students (by name or number) who are six years old.

Questions and Problems

1. Show how to create a vector object of 500 soldier objects and give each the rank of private. How would you access private 162?

2. The elements of a vector hold: (choose one)

   Objects **References to objects**

3. Why are *switch* statements and method calls often used with menus?

4. When object references are removed from a vector, does it automatically shrink in size?

5. Will our system, as presently designed, take ID numbers as large as present day social security numbers (nine digits)?

6. Referring to Figure 14.3, which statement performs each of the following:

   a) Creates 25 vector elements (to be increased 10 elements at a time).

   b) Creates 100 *TaxPayer* objects and loads their references into the vector.

   c) Extracts a *TaxPayer* reference from the vector.

   d) Accesses method *showTaxes* within a *TaxPayer* object.

Section II

GUI (Applet) Applications

When we pass through this Section II portal, we will enter the wondrous world of the GUI (*Graphical User Interface*). It's a very different world from the stand-alone environment we just left. It's the world of the window and the mouse. It's the world of the future!

Fortunately, we have a relatively painless way of entering this new GUI world: The celebrated *Internet applet*. As an added bonus, we will add HTML code and design a variety of Web browser pages.

Because the reader is by now well aware of the five project design steps used in Section I (from definition to testing), we will dispense with their use in Section II.

Part 4

Web Page Design Basics

The four chapters of Part 4 cover the basics of Web page design. We will write our first applet, add a few basic HTML tags to our repertoire, activate the *Explorer* Web browser, write color graphics routines, and include a variety of fonts and images.

CHAPTER

15

Project Hello World Applet

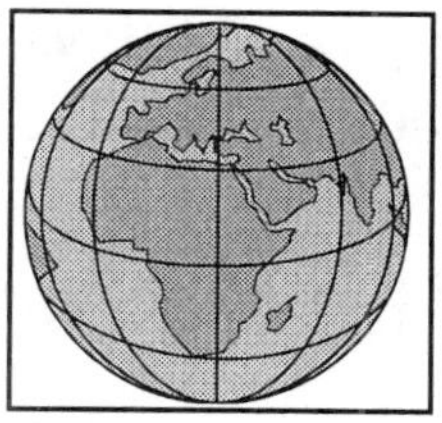

Internet Explorer

Objectives

- *To study the default HTML program*
- *To write a simple applet*
- *To activate the Explorer Web browser*

Discussion

Java achieved stardom because of its connection with the Internet. It was the right product at the right time, for it answered a long-standing need for an efficient and convenient method of transferring and executing programs on the Internet. The rest is history.

HTML and applets

By far the most popular component of the Internet is the *world wide Web* (WWW). Using hypertext techniques, users can move from one WWW page to the next—no matter where in the world these pages are—by simply clicking on *hotlinks.*

Each page in the WWW is a file written in HTML (*hypertext markup language*). The address of each page is called its URL (*uniform resource locator*). When the user clicks on a hotlink, the URL locates the page and transfers it to the user's computer. The browser executes the HTML program and displays the page. An applet is a Java program that is transferred along with the HTML code and is called by a special HTML tag.

The big three

What makes the study of Java applets so different, so intriguing, so challenging, so rewarding...*and so potentially puzzling*...is that three separate and distinct programs are directly involved. These "big three" programs are:

- The Web browser program
- The HTML program
- The Java applet program

To visualize these three programs, refer to the nested windows of Figure 15.1. The browser (Microsoft *Explorer 4.0/5.0*) starts things off by creating an outer window, complete with tool and scroll bars. Within this browser window is a nested window to display the HTML page, and further nested within the HTML window is one or more smaller windows to display the applets.

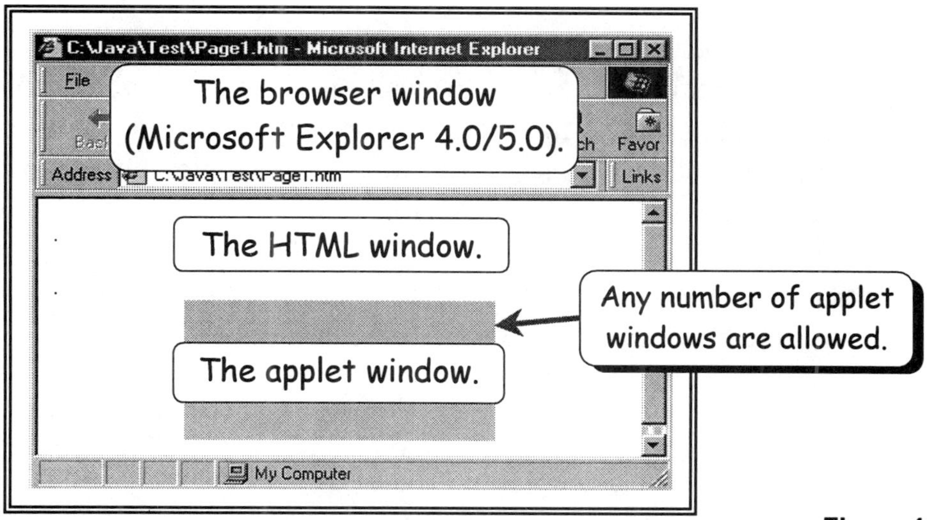

Figure 15.1
Applets involve nested windows

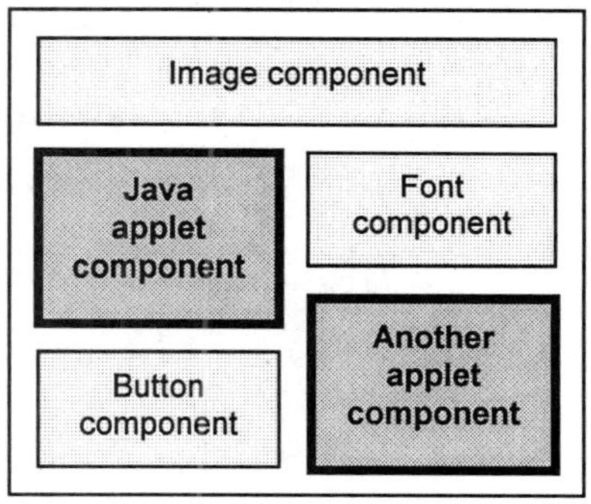

Think of an HTML program as consisting of various rectangular displayed *components* placed at desired locations about the HTML window. An applet is simply another component represented by a program segment written in Java. When an HTML Web page is transferred, the piggybacked Java applets go along for the ride. When the HTML program is executed, the applets are executed and displayed within the Web page.

However, an applet is also a GUI (graphical user interface), complete with windows and mouse interaction.

The challenge of the century

An applet is a Java program that we write. However, because an applet is also a GUI, it requires a master control program to be running in the background. After all, someone must be looking over our shoulder, ready to take appropriate action as we manipulate the mouse or strike a key. With applets written in J++, that someone is the *Explorer 4.0/5.0* Web browser. In other words, the browser program and our applet program must run "simultaneously." How do we coordinate the actions of these two programs? It was the programming challenge of the century.

The challenge of the century required the solution of the century (Figure 15.2). The key is to position our own custom applet class (*HelloWorldApplet*) to inherit behavior from several built-in classes (primarily class *Applet*). By way of example, let's assume that method *paint* is responsible for writing graphics and text to a window. At an appropriate time, the master program (the browser) automatically calls built-in method *paint* of class *Container*—but we wish the browser to call our custom *paint* instead.

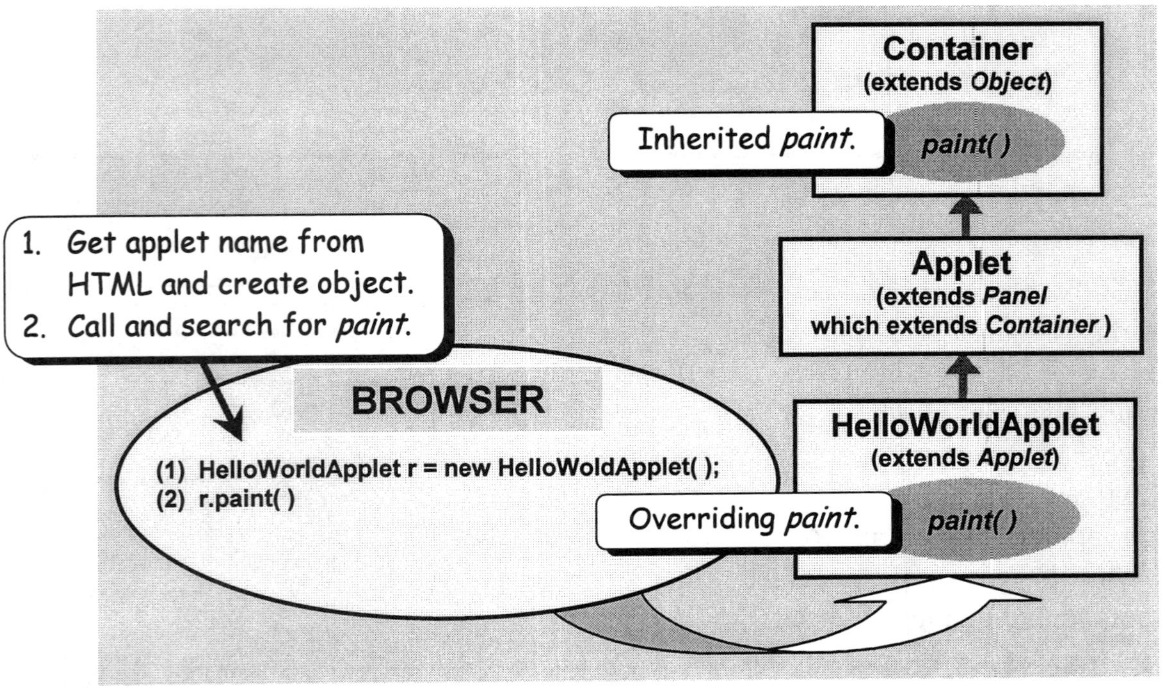

Figure 15.2
The key to applet programming

Here is how it's done: Using data from the Applet portion of the HTML code, the browser creates an object of class *HelloWorldApplet* and uses the reference (*r*) to call built-in method *paint* from inherited class *Container*. Following the rules of inheritance, the system starts at the bottom (*HelloWorldApplet*) and searches for method *paint* up through the inheritance hierarchy.

> The way we enter the picture is to "stand in the way" and override built-in method *paint* with our own custom version in class *HelloWorldApplet*.

A deeper look

Now that we have a bird's-eye view of the applet process, let's move in closer and delve a little deeper into each of the three programs (*browser*, *HTML*, and *applet*). First up, the greatly simplified and condensed, high-level Web browser program of Figure 15.3.

```
public class Browser
{
    public static void openBrowserWindow(URL HelloWorldApplet){
        (Create Explorer window)
        (Execute HelloWorldApplet.htm){
            (Process APPLET tag){
                (Create applet window)
                HelloWorldApplet r = new HelloWorldApplet( );
                Graphics g = r.getGraphics( );
                r.init( );
                r.start( );
                r.paint(g);
                while(web page active){
                    if(browser window changed)
                        r.paint(g);
                }
                r.stop( );
            }
            r.destroy( );
        }
        (Exit web page)
    }
    (Exit Explorer Window)
}
```

CLICKL on START

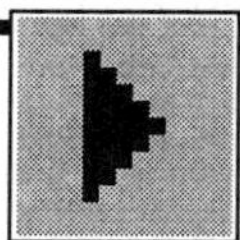

Reference name *r* is arbitrary.

Create applet and Graphics objects.

New!
Simplified browser code.

Figure 15.3
Simplified browser code

The Web browser program

We start with the Web browser program because it is the master program. It's the browser that starts the show, it's the browser that runs the show, and it's the browser that stops the show. However, keep in mind that we don't write or modify the browser program—it comes with the software.

Briefly, for now, this master browser program follows the sequence of nested windows: First, the nested *Explorer*, *HTML*, and *applet* windows are opened in succession. The system then creates applet and graphics objects, and calls a sequence of inherited methods—some of which we override.

The HTML program

Next in line, in order of execution, is the HTML program (*HelloWorldApplet.htm*). Each Internet Web page corresponds directly to one HTML program. When a Web page is selected, it is the HTML program that is transferred. When a Web page is displayed, it is the HTML program that is executed.

The baseline HTML program

Whenever we create a new applet solution, the VJ6 system automatically gives us the baseline HTML program of Figure 15.4.

New!
HTML tags.

```
<HTML>
<HEAD>
<META NAME="GENERATOR" Content="Microsoft Visual Studio 6.0">
</HEAD>
<BODY>
<P> </P>
<!-- Insert HTML here -->
<applet
   code=Applet1.class
   name=Applet1
   width=320 height=200
   VIEWASTEXT>
   <param name=label value="String passed from HTML host.">
   <param name=background value="008080">
   <param name=foreground value="FFFFFF">
</applet>
</BODY>
</HTML>
```

New!
Java *applet* call.

Figure 15.4
The baseline HTML program

Although these baseline programs might be of some use to an experienced programmer, they are of limited help to the beginner. Our course of action will be to wipe the slate clean and include only the code that pertains to the task at hand.

The HTML tags

An HTML program consists of text surrounded by special tags. Looking back at the baseline HTML program of Figure 15.4, the HTML tags are special commands that appear between the *less than* (<) and *greater than* (>) symbols. Most of the tags have an opening and closing version, with the closing version using an extra forward slash. All affected text is placed between these tags.

We will call the HTML tags shown in Table 15.1 the *default* tags. This is because they are automatically generated by the VJ6 system and most of them appear in every program. We can certainly expect to add to this list in future chapters. A complete list of all the tags used within this text is found in Appendix A.

Opening Tag	Closing Tag	Description
<applet>	</applet>	Holds the class name and window size of a Java applet.
<body>	</body>	Brackets all text and graphics.
<head>	</head>	Generally holds only the title.
<hr>	none	Horizontal rule.
<html>	</html>	Brackets html document
<meta>	none	Used for search engine identification and "slide shows."
<title>	</title>	Brackets title of document.

Note the applet tags.

All tags can be any combination of UPPER and lower case.

Table 15.1
The default HTML tags

Next, let's turn our attention to the last called and most deeply nested member of the "big three," the JAVA applet program.

The JAVA applet program

An *applet* is a program written in Java that is called from within the corresponding HTML program by way of the APPLET tags. The location and size of the applet window depends upon where the applet tag is placed and any attributes that may be included.

Class *Applet*

When the Java language was first applied to the Internet, it was altogether logical and natural that a special package be created to hold a variety of web supporting behavior. This package was called *applet* and its most significant class was called *Applet*. But where to place this new built-in class in the overall inheritance hierarchy?

Since each applet becomes a window within a Web page, the designers decided to position class *Applet* just below package *AWT* (abstract windows toolkit) at the end of the inheritance lineage shown by Figure 15.5. It was a natural move because class *Applet* was ideally positioned to inherit some very useful windows-based behaviors—especially the graphics, fonts, images, and external events of class *Component*.

Just as important, did you notice where our user-defined applet class (*HelloWorldApplet.java*) fits into the whole picture? It extends the new *Applet* class! In other words, we inherit all the behavior of class *Applet* and everything it inherits—all the way up the ladder. In fact, be forewarned that most of the behavior of our applet will be based on inherited behavior.

An applet program can comprise any number of classes—as long as one of them extends built-in class *Applet* and includes at least one inherited method (such as *paint*).

> The user-developed applet class must extend class *Applet* and must include at least one overriding inherited method that is automatically called by the browser.

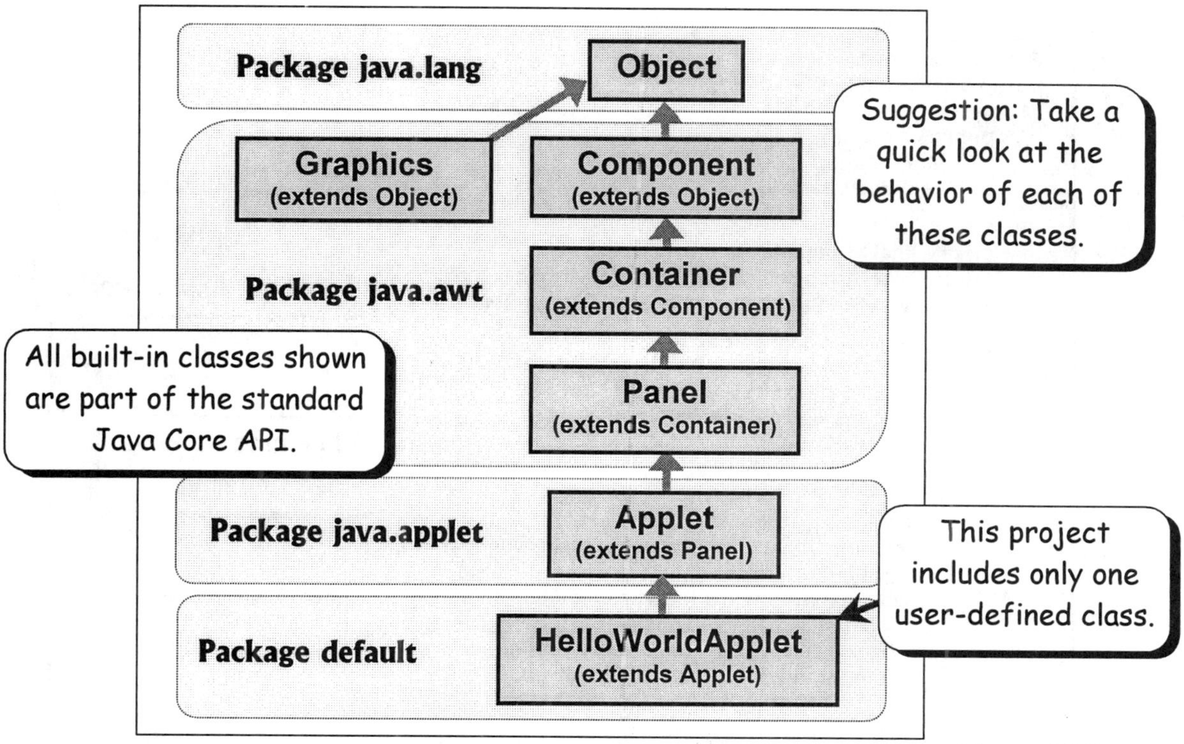

Figure 15.5
Class hierarchy for project *HelloWorldApplet*

The baseline applet program

Whenever we use the J++ *Visual Studio* to create a Web page, the system automatically creates the rather imposing baseline applet program of Figure 15.6. As with our baseline HTML program, most of the code is of limited use to a beginning programmer and will be deleted.

The big three combined

We have now taken a brief look at all of the big three programs involved in Web page processing. The next step is to combine them, and to put the whole ensemble into action. The result will be the creation of our very first full-fledged Web page—complete with applet. We'll wrap up the whole process with a careful step by step analysis.

```
import java.awt.*;
import java.applet.*;
public class Applet1 extends Applet
{
    public void init( ) {
        initForm( );
        usePageParams( );
    }
    private final String labelParam = "label";
    private final String backgroundParam = "background";
    private final String foregroundParam = "foreground";
    private void usePageParams( ){
        final String defaultLabel = "Default label";
        final String defaultBackground = "C0C0C0";
        final String defaultForeground = "000000";
        String labelValue;
        String backgroundValue;
        String foregroundValue;
        labelValue = getParameter(labelParam);
        backgroundValue = getParameter(backgroundParam);
        foregroundValue = getParameter(foregroundParam);
        if ((labelValue == null) || (backgroundValue == null) || (foregroundValue == null)){
            labelValue = defaultLabel;
            backgroundValue = defaultBackground;
            foregroundValue = defaultForeground;
        }
        label1.setText(labelValue);
        label1.setBackground(stringToColor(backgroundValue));
        label1.setForeground(stringToColor(foregroundValue));
        this.setBackground(stringToColor(backgroundValue));
        this.setForeground(stringToColor(foregroundValue));
    }
    private Color stringToColor(String paramValue){
        int red; int green; int blue;
        red = (Integer.decode("0x" + paramValue.substring(0,2))).intValue( );
        green = (Integer.decode("0x" + paramValue.substring(2,4))).intValue( );
        blue = (Integer.decode("0x" + paramValue.substring(4,6))).intValue( );
        return new Color(red,green,blue);
    }
    public String[ ][ ] getParameterInfo( ){
        String[ ] [ ] info = {
                { labelParam, "String", "Label string to be displayed" },
                { backgroundParam, "String", "Background color, format \"rrggbb\"" },
                { foregroundParam, "String", "Foreground color, format \"rrggbb\"" },
            };
            return info;
    }
    Label label1 = new Label( );
    void initForm(){
        this.setBackground(Color.lightGray);
        this.setForeground(Color.black);
        label1.setText("label1");
        this.setLayout(new BorderLayout( ));
        this.add("North",label1);
    }
}
```

Applet1 extends *Applet*.

New! Baseline Applet code.

All comments have been removed.

Figure 15.6

The baseline applet

ESPRESSO

Only one object?

In Chapter 6 we suggested that objects should be created only when the logic and nature of the project demands multiple instances of a template class. Well, our applet class (*HelloWorldApplet*) is a template class and the browser only generated a single instance.

The justification is simple: Object creation is the only way the browser can access the necessary non-static inherited methods (such as *paint*). By the way, we can (but seldom will) generate multiple instances of an applet class by simply listing multiple APPLET tags in the HTML program.

Hello World

To maintain long-standing tradition, our first Web browser project will be to write the very familiar greeting *"Hello World"* to the browser window.

When performing each of the projects of Section II, the reader must write two programs: The HTML program run by the Web browser, and the Java applet that is called by the HTML program.

Hands-On Procedure

1. We begin, as usual, with a project definition:

Project *HelloWorldApplet* writes *Hello World* to the applet window at location 20, 20.

2. The next step is to create the project workspace. We begin, as always, by bringing up the *New Project* dialog box of Figure 15.7.

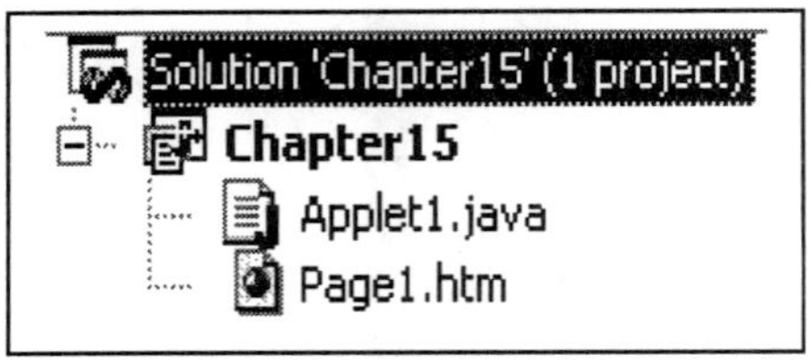

However, this time we select *Web Pages* and *Applet on HTML*, as shown. After filling in the solution name (*Chapter15*), **Open** to create the initial *Project Explorer* window.

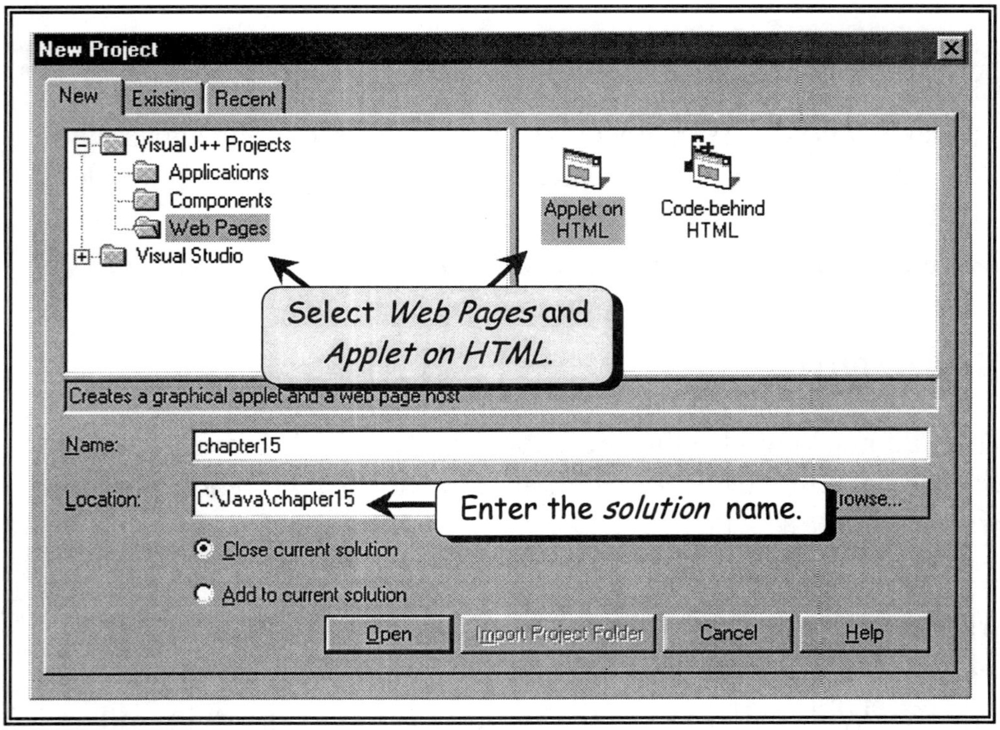

Figure 15.7
New Project dialog box

3. Note that *Applet1.java* (holding the default Java source program) and *Page1.htm* (holding the default HTML source program) were automatically created by the system and placed into default project *Chapter15*.

4. The next step is to change the default file names.

To rename *Page1.htm* and *Applet1.java*, **CLICKR**, **Rename**. (Unlike class *Class1* of *Section I*, we can rename *Applet1.java*.)

If you prefer, remove *Applet1.java* and add back a new file with a name of your choice using the techniques of Section I. However, we recommend the rename method.

Write the program

HelloWorldApplet.htm

5. **DCLICKL** on the *HelloWorldApplet.htm* icon to bring up the initial, default baseline program of Figure 15.4.

> When HTML programs are selected, three tabs appear in the *Text View* window. They will be put to good use in future chapters when our Web page designs take on more sophistication. For now, always select the *Source* tab.

6. Clearly, the most unusual feature of the HTML source code of Figure 15.8 is the box that appears where the applet code should be. This box gives us an opportunity to change the size of the applet and to view its content. Because this is best done through other means, we will always view the source text.

To bring up the applet source text, move the cursor anywhere inside the box and **CLICKR** to bring up the corresponding menu. **CLICKL** on *Always View As Text* to generate the HTML program of Figure 15.9.

Did applet code replace the box, and did attribute VIEWASTEXT appear within the opening applet tag?

Yes **No**

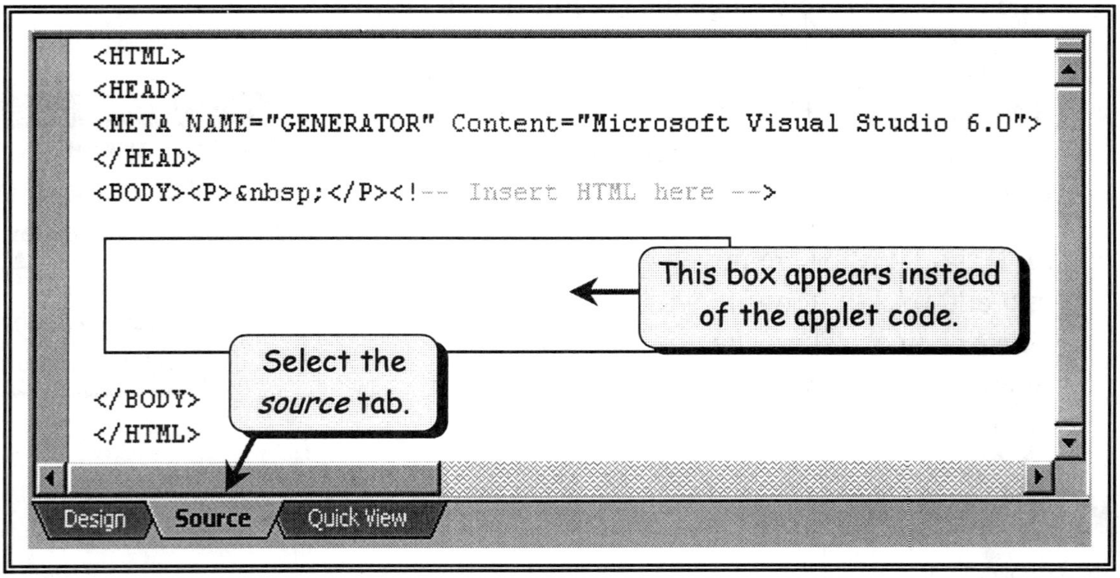

Figure 15.8
The initial HTML program
showing applet box

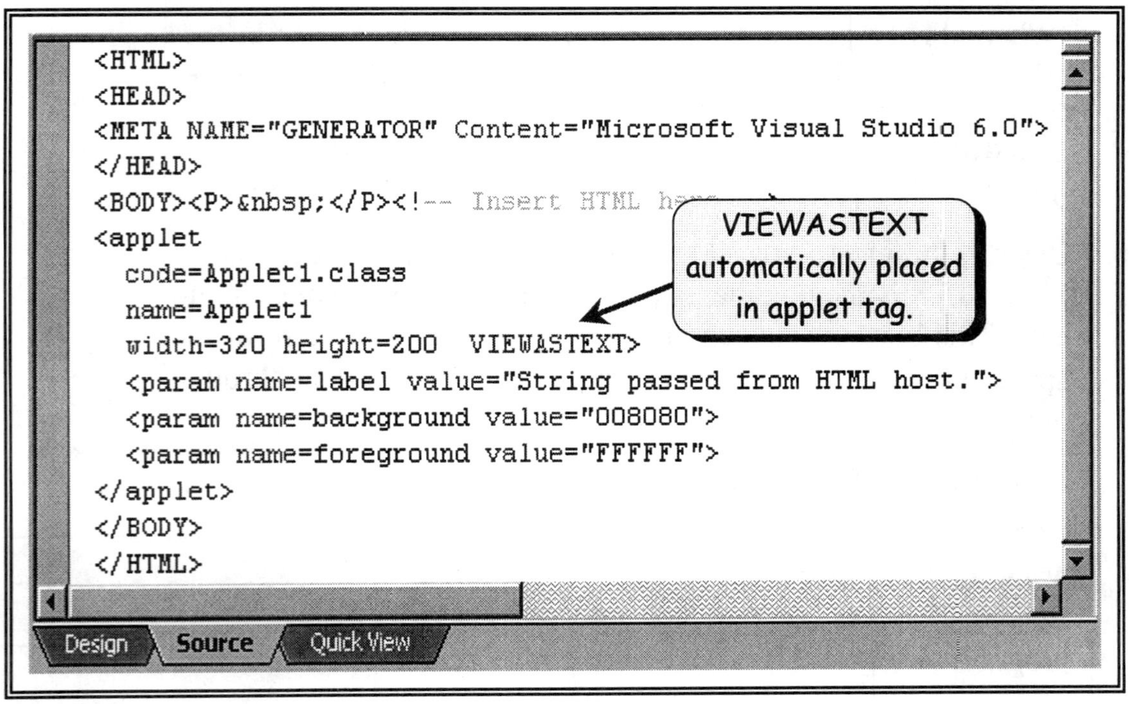

Figure 15.9
Box replaced by
Applet source code

7. By modifying and deleting code as necessary, generate the barebones HTML program of Figure 15.10 (*HelloWorldApplet.htm*). Note the three changes from the default baseline version:

- The META tags have been deleted. (They are there to aid search engines and to implement a special "slide show" mode.)
- The TITLE has been changed.
- The *height* and *width* have been reduced to 50 by 200 pixels.

Hello World Applet is our document title.

```
<HTML>
<HEAD>
<TITLE>Hello World Applet</TITLE>
</HEAD>
<BODY>
<applet
   code=HelloWorldApplet.class
   name=HelloWorldApplet
   width=200  height=50  VIEWASTEXT>
</applet>
</BODY>
</HTML>
```

New! User-modified HTML program.

Our HTML code will always include VIEWASTEXT.

Figure 15.10
The HTML program

HelloWorldApplet.java

8. **DCLICKL** on *HelloWorldApplet.java* to bring up the initial, default applet program previously listed (Figure 15.6).

9. By deleting most of the comments and code, and by making use of method *drawString* from class *Graphics*, generate applet program *HelloWorldApplet* of Figure 15.11.

Note: A complete analysis of *HelloWorldApplet* will come later in the chapter.

Don't forget to change the class name.

New! User-modified applet.

```
import java.awt.*;
import java.applet.*;
public class HelloWorldApplet extends Applet
{
    public void paint(Graphics g){
        g.drawString("Hello World",20,20);
    }
}
```

The "H" (in *Hello*) is 20 pixels to the right and 20 pixels down from the upper left of the applet window.

Figure 15.11
The Java applet

Looking to Figure 15.11, did you notice:

1. The lack of static? This means that class *HelloWorldApplet* is a template class, requiring the browser to use a genesis statement to create an instance (object) of this class, and to use the corresponding reference to access overriding or inherited methods.
2. The import statements? They are there to enable access to classes that lie in other packages. Looking back to Figure 15.5, *import java.awt* enables us to access method *drawString* of class *Graphics*, and *import java.applet* enables us to inherit the methods of class *Applet*.
3. The *extends Applet* tag? It means that class *HelloWorldApplet* inherits all the behavior of built-in class *Applet* (as well as every class up the chain of inheritance).

Execute the program

10. Build the project to check for syntax errors. (**Build**, **Build**.)

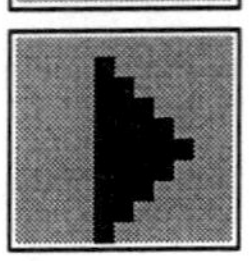

11. Start the program to enter the *Debug* mode. Because we changed the name of the HTML file, the system automatically brings up the *Properties* dialog box (*Launch* tab) of Figure 15.12. As before, it just wants to make sure that the file name and pathway are correct. Since they are, **OK** to continue execution.

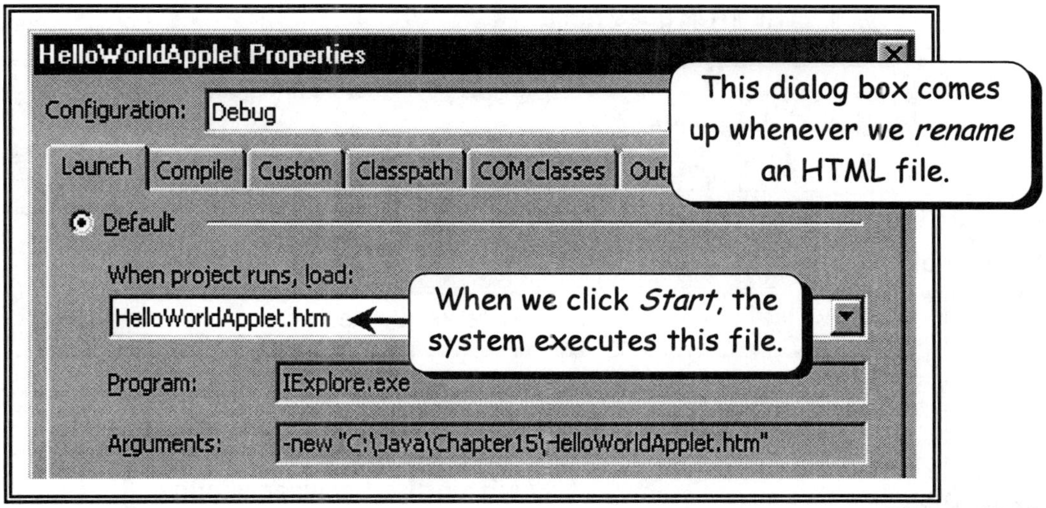

Figure 15.12
Properties dialog box

12. The following events take place as the system launches the Web page of Figure 15.13:

    - The *Explorer* browser window is opened.
    - The browser executes *HelloWorldApplet.htm*.
    - A 200 by 50 pixel applet window is created within the HTML window at the location determined by the <APPLET> tag.
    - The browser creates an object of class *HelloWorldApplet* and an object of class *Graphics* and calls several inherited methods. When overriding method *paint* is called, "Hello World" is written to the screen at the 20/20 location.

13. Referring to Figure 15.13, the contents of the "Address" box is the *URL* (uniform resource locator) of the present HTML file. Enter our applet's URL below:

    HWA URL = __________________________________.htm

14. To exit the browser window, click the "X" icon at the upper right of the screen.

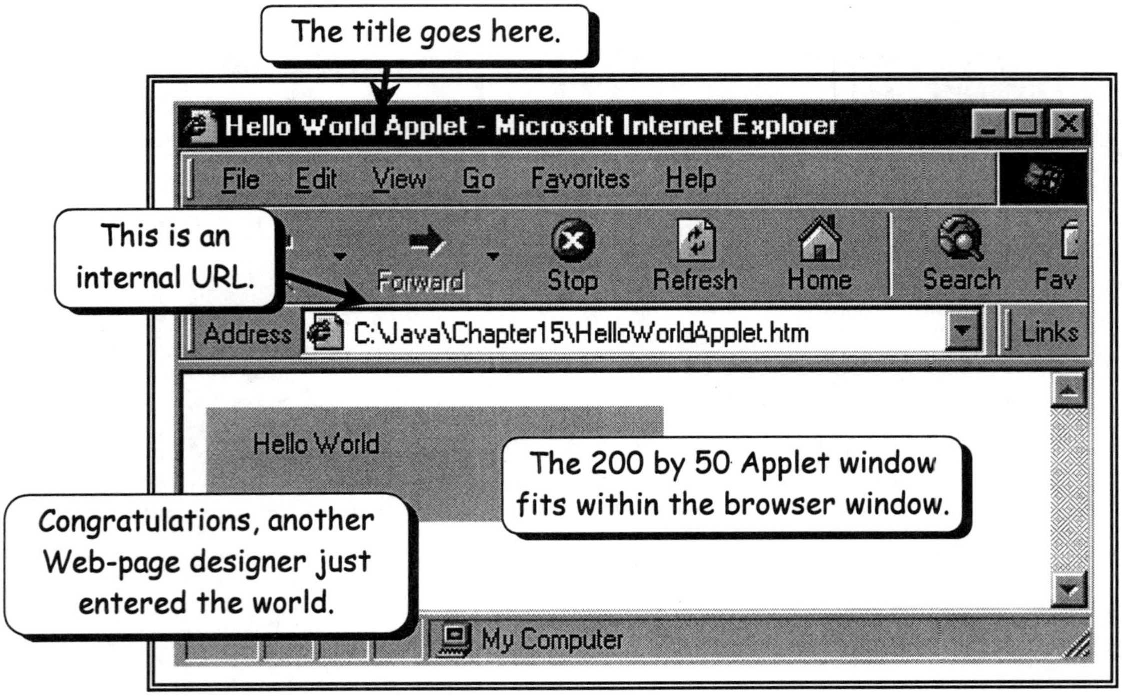

Figure 15.13
Internet Explorer output screen

Program analysis

15. We have seen the Web page displayed. Now it's time to go back and answer the "how" by following the action from beginning to end, step by step.

> During the process, be sure to refer to the big three programs (browser, HTML, and applet) as needed. But always remember: The browser code of Figure 15.3 is greatly simplified and generalized.
>
> Suggestion: Make copies of the big three programs and have them all in front of you (Figures 15.3, 15.10, and 15.11).

Step 1: We first turn to the browser program of Figure 15.3. It all begins when the user clicks START and commands the VJ6 Visual Studio to activate the browser system. Method *openBrowserWindow* is called and the Internet *Explorer* window is created.

Where's *main*?

Doesn't all code require an initial entry point? When we examine the browser program, method *main* is nowhere to be found. The fact is, we might as well go searching for the source of the Nile, for the entry point is buried deep in the VJ6 system code. What's important is that *main* does not appear within our applet code. It's the browser—not us—that always begins program action.

Step 2: The browser calls the HTML program of Figure 15.10 (*HelloWorldApplet.htm*) and begins execution. Title "Hello World Applet" is written to the color bar at the very top of the browser screen.

Step 3: When the <applet> tag is reached, a 200 by 50 pixel applet window is created at the top left (default location) of the browser screen.

Step 4: Within the browser program, genesis statements create an object of class *HelloWorldApplet* (referenced by *r*) and an object of class *Graphics* (referenced by *g*).

Step 5: The browser calls public methods *init* and *start* (all inherited from class *Applet*). Method *init* performs all required initialization and method *start* begins applet program action.

Because our new *HelloWorldApplet* object inherits (extends) class *Applet*, which in turn extends all the superclasses back to class *Object*, the browser has immediate access to all the methods of all the inherited superclasses by way of reference *r*.

Step 6: The browser calls method *paint* within object *HelloWorldApplet* (overriding the inherited version from class *Container*), and sends a graphics reference (*g*) as a parameter. Using reference *g*, method *drawString* within the *Graphics* object is called (Figure 15.11) and "Hello World" appears on the screen at the designated location (20 pixels over and 20 pixels down within the 200 by 50 pixel applet window).

Does the term *overriding* seem familiar? It was first encountered in Chapter 12 when we discussed *inheritance* and *polymorphism*. If the same method is defined at two inheritance levels, the lower-level method takes precedence.

The reason we are overriding the *paint* method of class *Container* is so we can add our own custom graphics instructions. (Does it not follow that we will nearly always override method *paint* for this reason?)

Step 7: The browser program enters and remains within a loop as long as the Web page is active. Whenever the browser window changes in any significant way (the window is shrunk to an icon and returned), the browser automatically re-calls overriding method *paint*.

Step 8: Should we leave the present Web page (perhaps to move to another), the browser exits the *while* loop, calls method *stop* (inherited from class *Applet*), and all applet processing action stops (until method *start* is again executed by the browser).

Step 9: When we exit the Web page, the browser executes the *destroy* method (from inherited class *Applet*) and all processing action related to the applet stops. (All the initialization performed by method *init* is undone.)

Debug and Modify

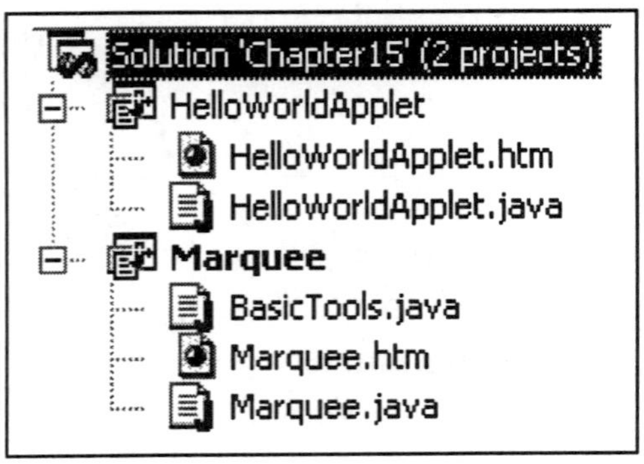

This chapter's debug and modify section will deal with motion and change. Our design goal is to simulate the scanning action of a theater marquee.

16. Add project *Marquee* to solution *Chapter 15*, add class *BasicTools*, make *Marquee* the present (**bold**) project, and rename the default files as shown.

17. Complete the HTML program (*Marquee.htm*) using the same code as *HelloWorldApplet.htm* of Figure 15.10—but be sure to appropriately change the code, name, and title values. (Suggestion: Use *copy/paste* techniques.)

18. Modify your applet according to Figure 15.14. Be sure to change the class name to *Marquee*.

```
import java.awt.*;
import java.applet.*;
public class Marquee extends Applet
{
    public void paint(Graphics g){
        int i;
        for(i=0;i<200;i++){
            g.drawString("Gone With the Wind”,i,20);
            BasicTools.msec(50);
            g.clearRect(i,10,100,10);
        }
    }
}
```

For motion:
1. Draw
2. Hold
3. Clear
4. Update

The *x* location increases.

The top of the clear rectangle (10) must be above the bottom of the printed text (20).

Figure 15.14
Marquee.java

As shown below, the *y* value for *drawString(String,x,y)* defines the bottom of the string, and the *y* value for *clearRect(x,y,width,height)* defines the top of the rectangle.

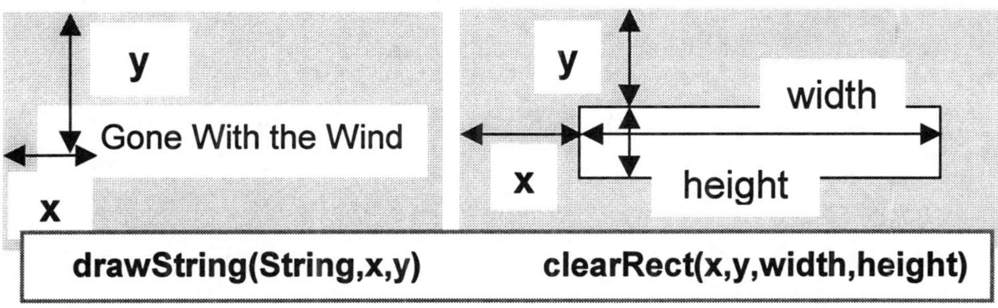

19. Execute the applet. Did “Gone With the Wind” move slowly across the screen?

Yes **No**

20. What two small changes, taken separately, will each approximately double the speed of motion? Try them!

21. Review the code line by line until you thoroughly understand how it works.

ESPRESSO

Why is class Graphics *abstract*?

Consider the following two genesis statements from the browser program shown in Figure 15.3.

```
HelloWorldApplet r = new HelloWorldApplet( );
Graphics g = r.getGraphics( );
```

Why doesn't the second one follow the classic "new" format? The answer is, class *Graphics* is *abstract*. This means we can't create graphics objects directly (using *new*). Why did the designers of Java do this?

Again, it's a matter of logic. An instance of class *Graphics* can not stand alone, but must be associated with a particular display surface. Think of the paint that an artist uses to complete a beautiful seascape. The paint has no meaning by itself; only when it is associated with the canvas.

By forcing us to use method *getGraphics* from class *Component*, we must pass a reference (*r*) into method *getGraphics* (where it is placed into *this*). Therefore, the graphics context created (*g*) is automatically associated with *this* component (*r*).

We will revisit abstract methods and classes in a future chapter when we come across the *interface*.

Exercises

Reminder: When you create additional projects related to this chapter's solution, you have two choices: Simply rewrite the code of an existing project, or add a new project to the present solution.

- To add a new project, **CLICKR** on the present solution, **Add Project**, etc. Be sure to **CLICKR, Set as StartUp Project** to select the desired project.
- Rename all files so the default (system-generated) *java* and *htm* files have the same name as the project.

a) Write project *blink*, which causes *Hello World* to blink on and off 10 times.

b) By making simple modifications to project *Marquee* of Figure 15.14, make "Gone with the Wind":

- Remain on the screen after the motion.
- Scan from left to right 10 times.
- Scan from top to bottom.
- Scan at a diagonal.
- Bounce back and forth between the edges of the applet window. Each time it hits the edge, a beep is sounded.

c) Write project *Numbers*, which prints out the numbers from 1 to 10 on a horizontal line. (Hint: Make use of the concatenation operator ("+"), as shown below.)

```
int i;
for(i=0;i<11;i++)
     g.drawString(i+",",i*10,30);
```

ESPRESSO

Scan forever?

Suppose we want "Gone With the Wind" (Figure 15.14) to continuously scan across the screen, as long as the Web page is open. It seems simple enough: Just place the code within a *while(true)* loop.

There is even a second possibility: the *repaint* method, which simply directs the browser to re-call *paint*. Just put *repaint* at the end of the code and we have an infinite (recursive) loop. We don't even need the *while(true)* anymore. The good news is, it's all so simple.

Now for the bad news. When we switch to another Web page or another window, both infinite loops continue to run. This we can not tolerate, as it may seriously degrade system performance. In fact, it might cause the browser to completely hang up.

Therefore, does this mean that we can't perform any action continuously within our applet? No it doesn't, because Java allows for a concept called *multithreading*—which solves the problem beautifully.

However, until we get there (Chapter 24), don't expect to find any infinite loops in our applets.

d) Similar to project *Numbers*, make use of the code below to write project *Alphabet,* which slowly prints out the letters of the alphabet. (Be sure to go into *Alphabet.htm* and increase the applet window width to 350.)

```
int i; char ch;
for(i=0,ch=65;i<26;i++,ch++)
      g.drawString(ch+“,”,i*12,30);
      BasicTools.msec(500);
```

e) Modify the previous project *Alphabet* so the letters are printed on a diagonal.

f) Write project *FreeFall*, which shows the word "rock" falling in real-time in simulated space. (Hints: $D = 16t^2$. For greater realism, use small increments for variable t by making it a floating point type.)

g) Modify project *FreeFall* so the rock falls in a trajectory pathway. (Hint: The rock has a constant x velocity component.)

h) Write program *HI*, which shows the word "HI" appearing at a random location within the applet window every half second for 10 seconds.

i) Write program *Pong*, which shows an asterisk bouncing around the inside of the applet window. (Hint: When the asterisk hits a side, the velocity component reverses for only the component perpendicular to the wall.)

j) Write program *StopWatch*, which uses an asterisk to simulate the second hand of a clock (for a time period of your choosing). (Hint: Make use of the trig methods from class *Math*.)

k) Within *HelloWorldApplet.htm*, make a second copy of the entire APPLET tag and run the program. Explain the results.

Questions and Problems

1. A Web page is an *html* file whose complete address is a URL.

   True **False**

2. If an applet contains no *main* method, how does method *paint* get called?

3. User-defined class *HelloWorldApplet* and built-in classes *Container* and *Component* contain method *paint*? Which one is called? Why?

4. What is the difference between opening and closing HTML tags?

5. What corner of a graphics window is at $x = 0$ and $y = 0$?

6. What does it mean to singlestep through a program?

7. Why is an applet program more "intelligent" than an HTML program? (Hint: Does an HTML program offer anything comparable to *repetition* and *selection*?)

8. When we access a graphics method from our applet, from where do we get the graphics reference?

9. What would happen if we listed the applet call tags twice within the HTML file?

10. Give several reasons why an applet (such as class *HelloWorldApplet*) must be a template class (requiring the browser to create objects).

11. A werewolf is a polymorphic form. Of what two types is a werewolf?

12. With the *console* projects of Section I, clicking *Start* caused the J++ system to search for and execute method *main*. With the *Applet on HTML* projects of this section, clicking *Start* causes the J++ system to search for and execute the HTML program.

    True **False**

CHAPTER

16

Project Modern Art

Color Graphics

Objectives

- *To create a work of modern art*
- *To include color graphics in our applets*
- *To create a program "flight recorder"*

Discussion

Can a simple blue square be a work of art? Of course it can. Modern art allows for a nearly limitless expression of form, color, and texture. However, when the computer is our canvas, we add yet another dimension: Our works of art can change with the passage of time.

For this chapter's project we will turn into practitioners of modern art. Our canvas will be the applet window, and our palette will be the endless variety of forms, colors, and movements that are created through the methods of class *Graphics*.

HTML update

Remember, Web pages are built out of both HTML code and nested Java applets. As we improve our Java abilities, we should also update our HTML skills. That is the purpose of these HTML update sections.

The new HTML tags introduced in this chapter are summarized by Table 16.1 (and are also found in Appendix A).

- The line break (BR) and paragraph (P) tags start a new line and can be placed anywhere. However, the paragraph tag also includes some white space.

- The center (CENTER) tag centers all items between its opening and closing tags.

- The header (*Hn*) tag prints a title to the screen whose size varies from $n = 1$ (large) to $n = 6$ (small).

For the header and paragraph tags, we have the option of adding the ALIGN=direction attribute, where direction is left, right, or center. For example, the following tag centers the given header.

```
<h2 ALIGN=center>Modern Art</h2>
```

Opening Tag	Closing Tag	Description
 	none	Line break
<CENTER>	</CENTER>	Center the items
<Hn>	</Hn>	Header level (n = 1–6)
<P>	none	New paragraph

Table 16.1
New HTML tags

Applet update

The class hierarchy of project *ModernArt* (Figure 16.1) is identical to that of the previous project (*HelloWorldApplet*).

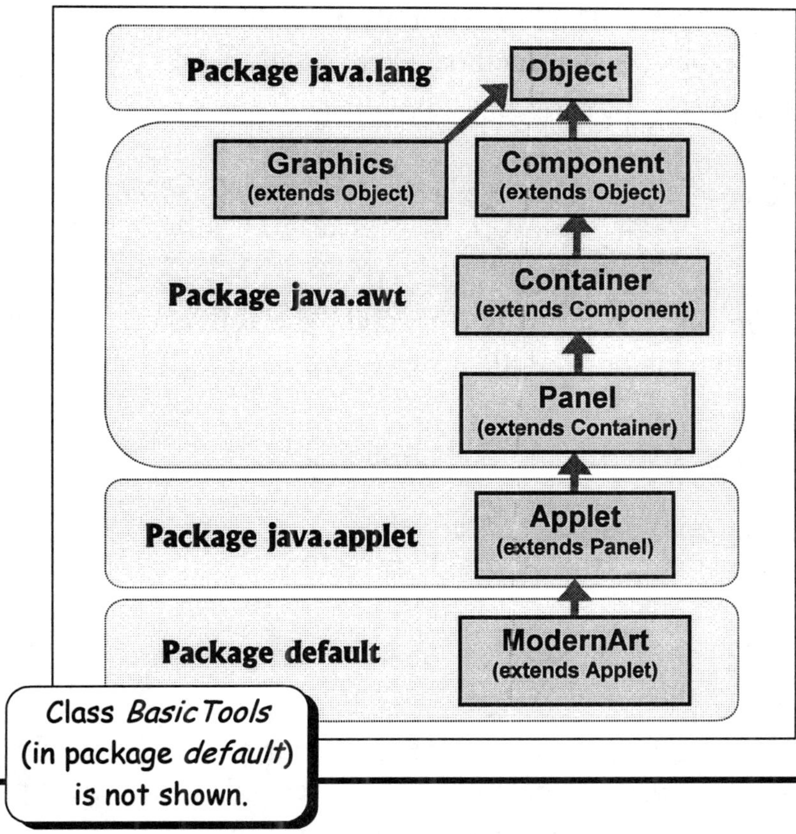

Figure 16.1
Project *ModernArt* class hierarchy

Class *Graphics*

Class *Graphics* is large and varied—as you would expect from a class given the responsibility of printing all manner of form and color to the screen. Table 16.2 is a partial listing of the available constructors and methods, and includes those most likely to be used in this and future projects. For a complete listing of all 43 constructors and methods, we can turn—as always—to the *Contents*, *Index*, or *Search* facilities of the *Help* menu.

Template?

Because a single applet can have any number of separate graphics objects, it should come as no surprise that none of the 43 constructors and methods of class *Graphics* are static. Therefore, class *Graphics* is a template class, requiring the creation of objects and references in order to access its methods.

One way our applet gets access to class *Graphics* was reviewed in the previous chapter: The browser runs a genesis statement to create a graphics object, calls method *paint*, and passes the graphics reference (*g*).

```
Graphics g = r.getGraphics( );
r.paint(g);
```

Reminder: Graphics (*g*) is associated with *this* applet (*r*).

Our overriding *paint* method receives the reference and obtains access to all the methods of the browser-created *Graphics* object.

```
public class ModernArt extends Applet
{
      public void paint(Graphics g){
            g. (any of the 42 Graphics methods)
      }
}
```

As an alternative, we are free to create our own graphics objects whenever we wish (automatically associated with *this* applet through inheritance.): **Graphics myg = getGraphics( );**

Constructors

Name	Description
Graphics( )	Constructs a new **Graphics** object.

Methods

Name	Description
clearRect(int, int, int, int)	Clears the specified rectangle.
create( )	Creates a new Graphics object.
Draw3DRect(int, int, int, int, bool)	Draws a 3-D highlighted outline of the specified rectangle.
drawArc(int, int, int, int, int, int)	Draws the outline of a circular or elliptical arc.
drawBytes(byte[ ], int, int, int, int)	Draws the text given by the specified byte array.
drawChars(char[ ], int, int, int, int)	Draws the text given by the specified character array.
drawImage(Image, int, int, Color, IO)	Draws as much of the specified image as is currently available.
drawLine(int, int, int, int)	Draws a line, using the current color, between the points (*x1*, *y1*) and (*x2*, *y2*).
drawOval(int, int, int, int)	Draws the outline of an oval.
drawPolygon(int[ ], int[ ], int)	Draws a closed polygon defined by arrays of *x* and *y* coordinates.
drawRect(int, int, int, int)	Draws the outline of the specified rectangle.
drawRoundRect(int, int, int, int, int, int)	Draws an outlined round-cornered rectangle using this graphics context's current color.
drawString(String, int, int)	Draws the text given by the specified string, using this graphics context's current font and color.
Fill3DRect(int, int, int, int, boolean)	Paints a 3-D highlighted rectangle.
fillArc(int, int, int, int, int, int)	Fills a circular or elliptical arc covering the specified rectangle.
fillOval(int, int, int, int)	Fills an oval bounded by the specified rectangle.
fillPolygon(int[ ], int[ ], int)	Fills a closed polygon defined by arrays of *x* and *y* coordinates.
fillRect(int, int, int, int)	Fills the specified rectangle.
fillRoundRect(int, int, int, int, int, int)	Fills the specified rounded corner rectangle.
setColor(Color)	Sets this graphics context's current color.
setFont(Font)	Sets this graphics context's font to the specified font.
toString( )	Returns a String object.
translate(int, int)	Translates the origin of the graphics context.

Table 16.2
Class *Graphics*

Color

To change the color of any Java graphics or text, we use the *setColor* method from class *Graphics*. Although our choice of color is not as extensive as with HTML, we can avail ourselves of the predefined choices of Table 16.3.

The Predefined Java Colors	
black	magenta
blue	orange
cyan	pink
darkGray	red
gray	white
green	yellow
lightGray	

Table 16.3
The 13 Java predefined colors

As a case in point, should you wish all graphics from a certain point on to be blue, then we enter the following:

```
g.setColor(Color blue);
```

Motion

A particularly striking use of graphics is the creation of change and motion. To accomplish this, we use the four-step algorithm introduced in project *HelloWorld*:

1. Write 2. Hold 3. Erase 4. Update

The sample program segment below causes a "ball" to drop in free-fall for four seconds under the influence of cyber-gravity.

```
for(t=0;t<400;t++){
    g.fillOval(50,16*t*t/10000,20,20);
    BasicTools.msec(10);
    g.clearRect(50,16*t*t/10000,25,25);
}
```

$d = 16t^2$, where 1 pixel = 1 foot, and *t* goes from 0 to 4s in 10ms increments.

Make the *clear* rectangle slightly larger than the *draw* rectangle.

Hands-On Procedure

1. This chapter's project turns us into modern artists.

> **Project *ModernArt* writes to the screen the mosaic shown in this chapter's title page—a square at a time.**

2. Create project *ModernArt* within solution *Chapter 16*, rename the applet and HTML files, and add class *BasicTools*—as shown.

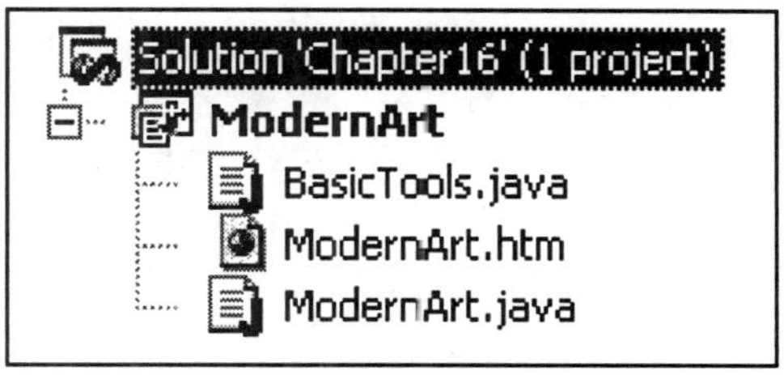

Write the program

The HTML file

3. By modifying the baseline code created by the system, develop the *ModernArt.htm* file of Figure 16.2. (Reminder: **DCLICKL** on *ModernArt.htm*, **Source** tab to bring up the source code.)

```
<HTML>
<HEAD>
<TITLE>Modern Art</TITLE>
</HEAD>
<BODY><CENTER>
<H2>Mosaic</H2>
This work of art symbolizes<BR>
the building of civilization.<P>
<APPLET
   code=ModernArt.class
   name=ModernArt
   height=185 width=185 VIEWASTEXT>
</APPLET>
</CENTER>
</BODY>
</HTML>
```

New! Adding text.

Be sure to change the default names for *code* and *name*.

We adjust the Applet window size to match the graphics.

Figure 16.2
ModernArt.htm

4. An analysis of the program centers on the new tags introduced by Table 16.1.

   - The center tag (<CENTER>) brackets the entire program, so all items will be centered.

   - The header level tags (<H2>) specify a second-level centered header.

   - The break tag (<BR>) begins a new line.

   - The paragraph tag (<P>) begins a new line and leaves some white space. The closing paragraph tag (</P>) is optional.

ModernArt.java

5. By modifying the baseline code created by the system, develop the *ModernArt.java* file of Figure 16.3. (Reminder: **DCLICKL** on *ModernArt.java* to bring up the source code.)

We import packages *awt* and *applet* to access classes *Graphics* and *Applet*.

```
import java.awt.*;
import java.applet.*;
// Method paint uses a nested loop
// to draw the mosaic.
public class ModernArt extends Applet
{
      public void paint(Graphics g){
            int i,j;
            g.setColor(Color.blue);
            for(i=0;i<6;i++)
                  for(j=0;j<(6-i);j++){
                        g.fillRect(j*30+30*i+5,i*30+5,25,25);
                        BasicTools.msec(500);
                  }
      }
}
```

Be sure to change the default class name.

New!
Graphics motion.

Figure 16.3
Applet *ModernArt*

6. The program code is quite straightforward, so the analysis will be brief.

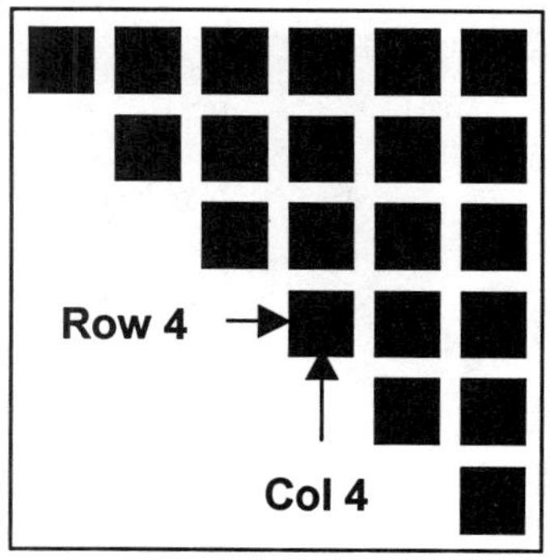

- The central feature of the program is a nested loop. The outer loop (*i*) controls the rows and the inner (*j*) loop controls the columns.
- The first program segment below reduces the square count by one for each successive row, and the second segment shifts the starting square for each successive row.

```
J < (6 – i)
```

```
J*30 + 30*i
```

Execute the program

Quick View

7. The Visual Studio offers a quick way of testing your Web page without opening the *Explorer* Web window. As shown by Figure 16.4, just **CLICKL** on the *Quick View* tab.

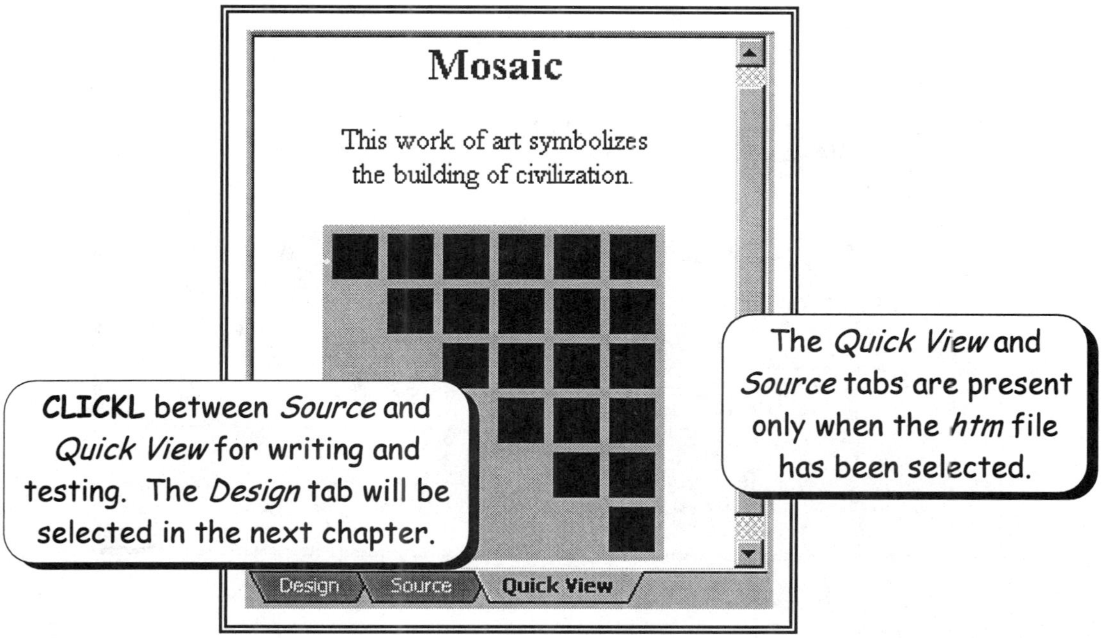

Figure 16.4
QuickView

Why is *Quick View* so quick?

Java's execution speed is slow because the JVM (Java virtual machine) must compile each line of byte code down to machine language as the program runs. This process is especially wasteful when our program contains loops, for the compilation of the same code must occur over and over.

However, suppose we compile this loop code down to machine code the first time and store it. Then, each additional time the loop is processed, we execute the compiled code rather than the byte code. Would that not greatly speed up the overall execution speed? This is exactly what takes place when we use *Quick View*.

Of course we can't do this with the full-fledged browser window because all timing must be standardized.

8. Start the program using the conventional (*Start*) method.

9. Because we again changed the name of our *htm* file, chances are the *Properties* window of Figure 16.5 will come up. If the new HTML path and name are correct (and they should be), **OK**.

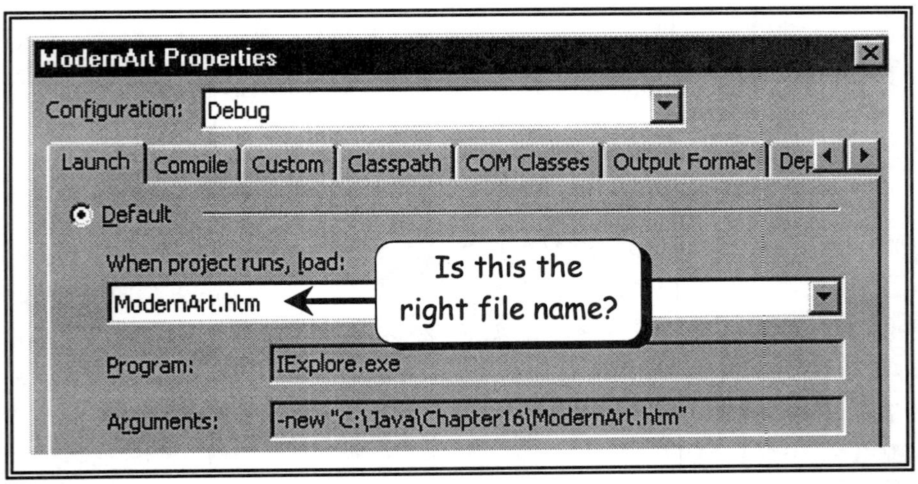

Figure 16.5
Properties window

10. Observe the browser window of Figure 16.6.

    a) Was a 185 by 185 pixel applet window properly displayed within the browser window?

       Yes **No**

    b) Did the center, header, paragraph, and break HTML tags properly position the text?

       Yes **No**

    c) Were the blue squares drawn slowly and correctly?

       Yes **No**

    d) Was the drawing speed much slower than when tested with *Quick View*?

       Yes **No**

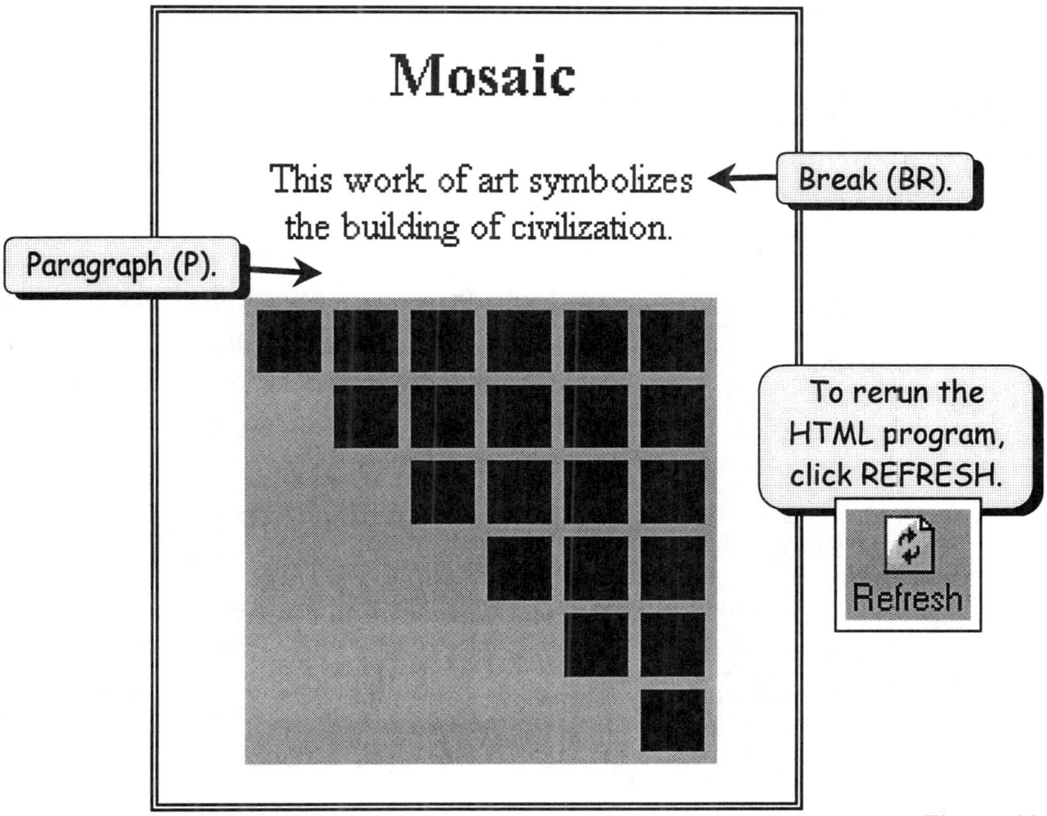

Figure 16.6
Project *ModernArt* output screen

Debug and modify

This chapter's debug and modify section is a little different. It's a study session. The question is, exactly how does the browser cycle through all those methods introduced in the previous chapter?

To answer this question with direct experimental data, we will create a "flight recorder" that will track our progress through the various methods. Each time we enter a method, it will send a special identifying character to array *history*. Each time we enter the *paint* method, the updated character array will be displayed.

11. We'll start our study with a close look at class *Applet* of Table 16.4. Arrows point to five methods of particular interest. When we add in method *paint* from class *Component*, we get the "magnificent six"—so named because they are always called by the browser during applet execution.

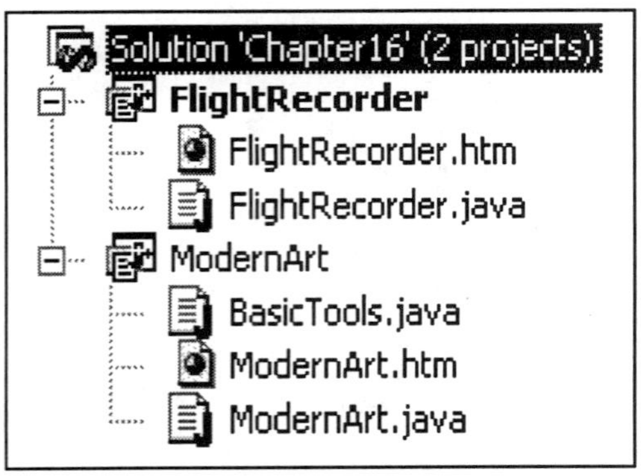

12. Create a new project called *FlightRecorder* within solution *Chapter16*. Add and rename files as necessary. Be sure to set *FlightRecorder* as the *StartUp Project*.

13. Bring up *FlightRecorder.htm*. Using *ModernArt.htm* of Figure 16.2 as a guide, complete the HTML program as desired. (Set *width = 200* and *height = 100*, and be sure to change the *code*, *name*, *title*, and *header* as necessary.)

14. Fill in *FlightRecorder.java* as shown in Figure 16.7.

Do you see how the program works? Whenever any of the magnificent six methods are called by the browser and executed, a code letter is added to array *history*. Whenever *paint* is executed, the updated array is displayed in red.

Can you predict which four methods will be called when the Web page is first opened, and can you predict their order?

Constructors

Name	Description
Applet( )	Standard constructor.

Methods

Name	Description
destroy( )	Called by the browser to reclaim the applet and destroy any allocated resources.
getAppletContext( )	Determines the applet's environment in which it runs.
getAppletInfo()	Returns information about this applet.
getAudioClip(URL)	Returns the AudioClip object specified by the URL argument.
getAudioClip(URL, String)	Returns the AudioClip object specified by the URL and name arguments.
getCodeBase( )	Gets the base URL.
getDocumentBase( )	Gets the document URL.
getImage(URL)	Returns an Image object that can then be painted on the screen.
getImage(URL, String)	Returns an Image object that can then be painted on the screen.
getLocale( )	Gets the locale for the applet.
getParameter(String)	Returns the value of the named parameter in the HTML tag.
getParameterInfo( )	Returns information about the parameters than are understood by this applet.
init()	Called by the browser to perform any needed initialization.
IsActive( )	Determines if this applet is active.
play(URL)	Plays the audio clip at the specified absolute URL.
play(URL, String)	Plays the audio clip given the URL and a specifier that is relative to it.
resize(Dimension)	Requests that this applet be resized.
resize(int, int)	Requests that this applet be resized.
setStub(AppletStub)	Sets this applet's stub.
showStatus(String)	Requests that the argument string be displayed in the status window.
start( )	Called by the browser to start applet's execution.
stop( )	Called by the browser to stop applet's execution.

Table 16.4
Class *Applet*

```
import java.awt.*;
import java.applet.*;
public class FlightRecorder extends Applet
{
        char[ ] history = new char[50];
        int i = 0;

        public FlightRecorder( ){
                history[i++] = 'C';
        }

        public void init( ){
                history[i++] = 'I';
        }

        public void destroy( ){
                history[i++] = 'D';
        }

        public void paint(Graphics g){
                history[i++] = 'P';
                g.setColor(Color.red);
                g.drawChars(history,0,i,10,30);
        }

        public void start( ){
                history[i++] = 'S';
        }

        public void stop( ){
                history[i++] = 'Q';
        }
}
```

These must be permanent and global.

Load the character, then increment *i*.

All of the magnificent six methods override their superclass counterparts.

Draws the character array from 0 to length *i* at location x = 10 and y = 30.

Figure 16.7

FlightRecorder.java

> All of the magnificent six methods override their inherited counterparts. If any one is deleted from our applet, then the system would automatically revert to its inherited counterpart.

15. Run the program and note the character array displayed. Did it show that the sequence of method execution was *Constructor*, *Initialization*, *Start*, and *Paint* (CISP)?

    Yes **No**

16. Change the size of the window any way you can, but always keep the applet displayed. Under these conditions, are any of the magnificent six again called?

    Yes **No**

17. Shrink the browser window down to an icon and bring it back. How many additional times was the *paint* method executed?

    Additional *paints* for each "bring back" = __________

18. Move the browser window behind the Visual Studio window and bring it back. How many additional times was the *paint* method executed?

    Additional *paints* for each "bring back" = __________

19. Throughout all these operations, is it true that the *Constructor*, *Initialization*, and *Start* methods were executed only once at the very beginning of window creation?

    Yes **No**

20. Was the *Stop* (*Quit*) method ever executed? (Did we ever go to another Web page?)

    Yes **No**

21. Since the *Destroy* method is executed after we exit the Web page, it can never be displayed by the *paint* method.

    True **False**

22. Do you believe that it's highly likely that the Microsoft Corporation will modify and change the way the browser calls these methods with each new J++ release?

    Yes **No**

Exercises

a) Cause a blue circle to move once across the screen. (Hint: Make use of methods *drawOval* and *clearRect*, and perform a draw, hold, erase, update sequence.)

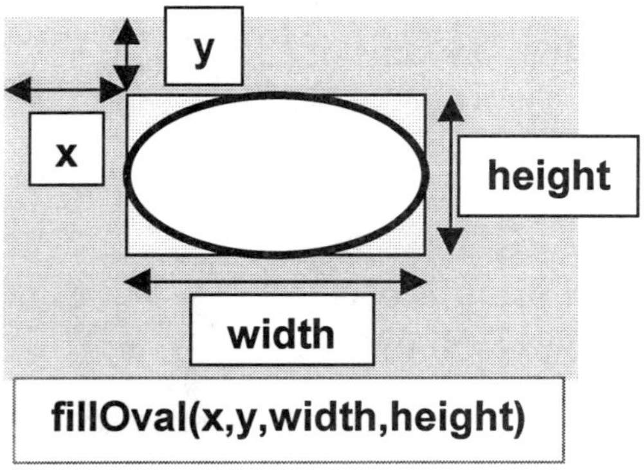

b) Modify the previous blue circle exercise so the blue circle bounces back and forth 10 times.

c) Further modify the blue circle exercise so the ball gradually speeds up.

d) Modify blue circle so the ball changes color upon each bounce.

e) Using method *drawChars*, print the alphabet to the screen on a diagonal. (Hint: It is possible to create an array with only a single element.)

f) Using a *for* loop and method *drawLine*, print 10 telephone poles (evenly-spaced vertical lines) to the screen.

g) Write a Java applet that tosses a coin (prints a single circle to the screen). There is a 50% chance it is heads (green) and a 50% chance it is tails (red). (Hint: Use *Math.random*.)

h) Modify program *CoinToss* to toss the coin 100 times at the rate of four per second. The percentage of times that the coin came up heads (green) is printed.

i) Further modify project *CoinToss* so the results appear in real time as a bar graph.

j) Modify method *paint* of this chapter so that each mosaic square is printed in random colors. (Suggestion: Create method *color*, which accepts *int* and *Graphics* (*g*) parameters and sets the corresponding color. Consider including method *color* in a tools class.)

k) Create a pulsing blue circle that grows and shrinks in size, without moving from its position.

l) Using the *fillArc* method, write project *MoonPhase*, in which an orange circle gradually opens until it is full. The parameters of *fillArc* are *x*, *y*, *width*, *height*, *startAngle*, and *arcAngle*. (Hint: Continuously redraw the arc in a loop, gradually increasing the *arcAngle*.)

m) Modify *MoonPhase* so the moon follows a trajectory across the sky as the phase changes.

n) Using the *drawPolygon* method, create a solid star.

o) Write a program that rolls a pair of dice 1000 times and uses a bar graph to display (in real time) the frequency of numbers (2 through 12) as the dice are rolled. (Hint: Make use of arrays and *Math.random*.)

p) Program *Fireworks* below shows a single rocket and display. By adding a loop and randomizing one or more constants, create a full-fledged multiple-rocket display.

```
import java.awt.*;
import java.applet.*;
public class Fireworks extends Applet
{
    public void paint(Graphics g){
        int t,x=0,y=0,angle,xEnd,yEnd;
        for(t=0;t<600;t++){
                x = 20*t/100;
                y = 16*t*t/10000 – 130*t/100 + 300;
                g.fillOval(x,y,10,10);
                BasicTools.msec(10);
                g.clearRect(x,y,12,12);
        }
        g.setColor(Color.orange);
        for(angle=0;angle<360;angle+=5){
                xEnd = x + (int)(100*Math.sin(6.28/360*angle));
                yEnd = y + (int)(100*Math.cos(6.28/360*angle));
                g.drawLine(x,y,xEnd,yEnd);
                BasicTools.msec(10);
        }
    }
}
```

Time (*t*) is measured in units of 10ms.

Set the applet window to width=300, height=500.

q) Write an applet that draws alternating bands of two colors.

r) Write project *TryYourLuck*, which first divides the screen into four vertical sections. Fifty small circles are printed to the screen at random locations at the rate of four per second. Each circle that lands in the left-most quadrant pays $3. At the end, your program prints "You bet $50, you win _____." (Hint: Make use of *Graphics* methods *drawLine* and *fillOval*.)

s) Write project *TargetShoot*, which first prints a small rectangular target to the right of the applet window. Fifty cyber-bullets are fired at the target at random *y*-axis positions at the rate of two per second. Each bullet that strikes the target briefly turns the target red.

t) Write an applet that prints 50 circles to the screen at random locations and of random color. Each orange circle pays $10. Two orange circles in a row win the jackpot of $500. Your total winnings are displayed. (Suggestion: Create class *GraphicsTools* that includes method *myColor*. Method *myColor* accepts a number from 1 to 13 and uses *switch* to set the corresponding color.)

> Method *translate* provides a means of moving all the elements of a given graphics context (everything referenced by *g*) in unison. For example, *g.translate(1,0)* moves the origin of the *g* graphics context to the right by one pixel position.

u) Create an American flag. Using method *translate*, show the flag being hoisted up a flagpole. (Hint: Use loops to create the stars and stripes.)

v) Using several graphics methods, create a dog likeness. Using method *translate*, take the dog for a walk. (Hint: Use method *clearRect*, and perform a draw, hold, erase, update sequence.)

w) Using a second graphics context (*Graphics h = getGraphics( )*), create a cat. Using individual *translate* methods, have the dog and cat simultaneously move in opposite directions.

x) Design a home page for a company that includes a moving graphics logo.

y) Be an artist! Design a modern art display of your own choosing.

z) Create two tree objects (*oak* and *walnut*), each initialized to five pixels. Both trees grow at random heights from one to ten pixels each day for a month. If each day is represented by one second, show the trees growing on the screen real time. (Hint: Suggested applet is shown below.)

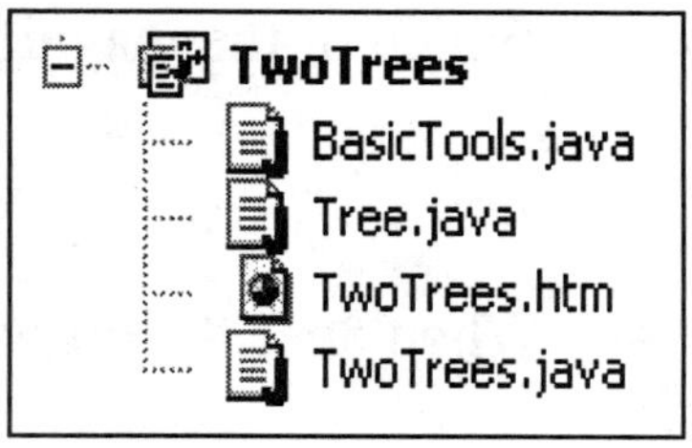


```
import java.applet.*;
public class TwoTrees extends Applet
{
    Tree oak, walnut;
    public void init( ){
        oak = new Tree(5);
        walnut = new Tree(5);
    }
    public void paint(Graphics g){
        int i;
        for(i=0;i<30;i++){
            oak.addHeight((int)(1+Math.random( )*10));
            walnut.addHeight((int)(1+Math.random( )*10));
            g.fillRect(30,300-oak.getHeight( ),20,oak.getHeight( ));
            g.fillRect(100,300-walnut.getHeight( ),20,walnut.getHeight( ));
            BasicTools.msec(300);
        }
    }
}
```

Class *Tree* includes the constructor, methods *getHeight* and *addHeight*, and private attribute *height*.

If you wish, add a green oval (leaves) to the top of each tree.

As with Exercise z), apply color graphics to any of the object-based exercises of previous chapters (especially Chapters 6 and 9).

Questions and Problems

1. From what class do most of the methods used by an applet come from?

2. The HTML compiler ignores *new line* (Enter) codes.

   True **False**

3. Which of the magnificent six methods is executed first?

4. When does the browser call method *stop*?

5. The following graphics instruction paints a square to the screen. Add a second instruction that puts a square of one quarter the area in the center of the first.

```
g.fillRect(100,100,100,100);
```

6. Why would we create two or more graphics objects within a single applet window? (Hint: See exercises *u*, *v*, and *w*.)

7. Within our applet, why is method *paint* an overriding method?

8. Why is the following genesis statement illegal?

```
Graphics g = new Graphics( );
```

9. Referring to Exercise z), do we have to use *Tree* objects? What advantage is there in using objects? (Hint: What if we expand the project to include 50 trees, each with 50 attributes?)

CHAPTER

17

Project City Desk

Fonts, Parameters, and HTML Design Aids

Objectives

- *To set font size, color, and style*
- *To incorporate parameters into our project*
- *To design a newspaper-like Web page*
- *To introduce the HTML design aids*

Discussion

It wasn't long after the daily newspaper became a popular form of communication that editors recognized the importance of text formatting. To announce the end of a great war, or the marriage of a beloved princess, only the most impressive font structure would do.

Publishing on today's Internet is no different. Text formatting and font structure go a long way toward upgrading a ho-hum, run-of-the-mill Web page to an impressive eye-catcher. However, unlike our city desk editor, we have some very special techniques at our disposal that can only be obtained through the power of Java programming.

As we learned in the two previous chapters, Web page design involves two separate programs: The HTML program and the Java applet program. The same is true with text formatting. When we are working with the HTML portion of our Web design, we choose from a number of text formatting tags. When we are working with the Java applet portion of our design, we select appropriate methods from classes *Font*, *FontMetrics*, and *Graphics*.

HTML text formatting

Based on our previous experience, we know that all formatting within an HTML document is done by way of special tags. Table 17.1 shows the tags that deal specifically with fonts.

As a case in point, the HTML tags shown below produce the headline that follows (yellow letters on blue backing).

```
<P><STRONG><FONT color=yellow face="Arial Black"
size=6 style="BACKGROUND-COLOR:blue">
LifeFound on Mars!</FONT></STRONG></P>
```

Life Found on Mars!

Opening Tag	Closing Tag	Description
<B>	</B>	Bold.
<BLOCKQUOTE>	</BLOCKQUOTE>	Setting a block of text.
<DIV ALIGN >	</DIV>	Divide a page into logical sections. Align left, right, or center.
<FONT SIZE="n" FACE=" " STYLE=" " COLOR="#N"> where n = 1 to 7 where N = 000000 to FFFFFF	</FONT>	Font size, type, style, and color.
<I>	</I>	Italics.
<pre>	</pre>	Preformat.
<U>	</U>	Underline.

Table 17.1
HTML text formatting tags

When it comes to HTML, variety is the name of the game. There are numerous formats, dozens of font names, seven sizes, special text enhancements, buttons, fields, and literally thousands of colors. It's overwhelming; we need HELP! And help is just a tab away.

The HTML design aids

What's the best way to design HTML pages? How about conjuring up a little old fashioned magic? Not real magic of course, but something almost as good. It all centers on that *Design* tab that automatically appears when the HTML file is selected. For a brief sampling of this "rapid development" magic, just turn to Appendix B now or at any time in the future.

Applet update

Instead of special tags to format text, Java uses the methods of classes *Font*, *FontMetrics*, and *Graphics*. As shown by Figure 17.1, none of the behavior of these three classes is inherited.

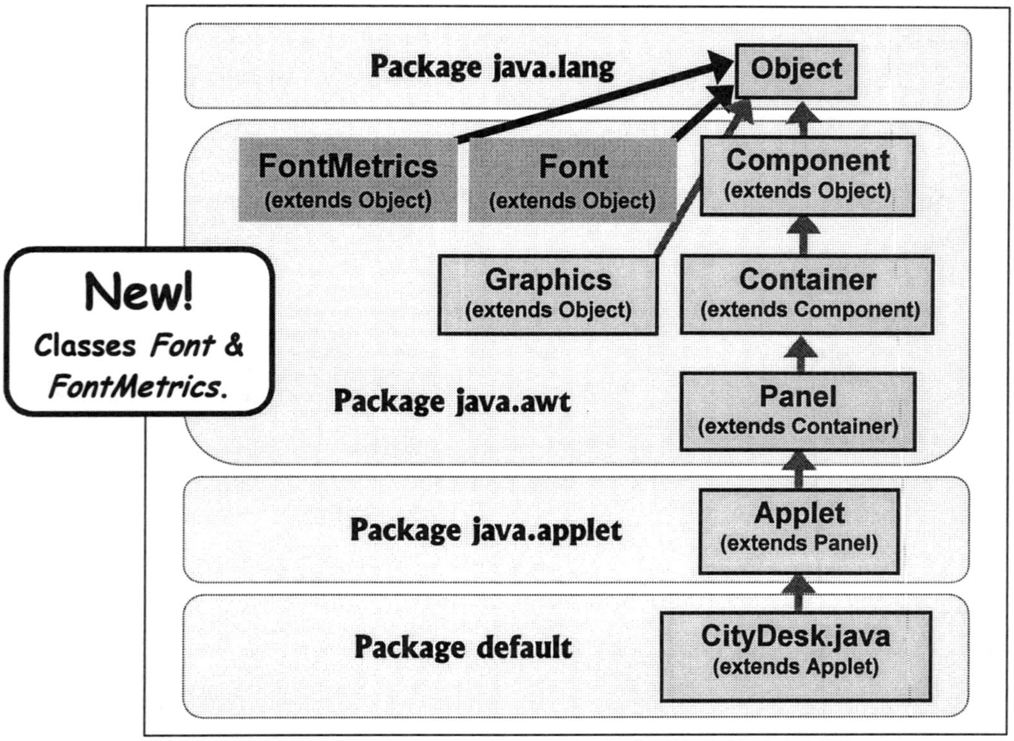

Figure 17.1

Project *CityDesk* class hierarchy

To create applet fonts, we adopt the same three steps used by the newspaper printers of colonial America: (1) Create one or more trays of fonts, (2) set the font type, and (3) print the page.

```
(1) Font myF = new Font("Courier",Font.BOLD,35);
(2) g.setFont(myF);
(3) g.drawString("Independence Declared",20,20);
```

The first is a genesis statement that uses the *Font* constructor to create a specific font object of face *courier*, style bold, and size 35 pixels. (A default value will be used for any characteristic not listed.) The second sets the font of our choice at a given position, and the third prints the characters.

An interesting effect is achieved by rapidly changing font characteristics within a loop. As a case in point, the code shown below gradually increases the size of string "Superman."

```
for(i=1;i<50;i++){
    Font myF = new Font("Arial",Font.BOLD,i);
    g.setFont(myF);
    g.clearRect(50,50-i,30*i,i);
    g.drawString("SUPERMAN",50,50);
    BasicTools.msec(10);
}
```

The size changes from 1 to 50 pixels.

As the size of string *Superman* increases, so does the size of the clear rectangle.

What's interesting about the above code is that fifty font objects are created, one for each font size, with a single *Font* reference (*myF*) updated to point to each newly created font object.

ESPRESSO

Who collects my garbage?

During our "Superman" example, we created 50 font objects. However, when we finished, the first 49 were left floating (had no references pointing to them). Will these 49 fonts then become useless *cyber-garbage*, with no means of referencing their position?

The answer is no, for Java has an automatic background process known as garbage collection. It keeps track of all references that are created to a given object. When the number reaches zero, the object becomes garbage and is routinely deleted.

Many things can trigger garbage collection: The amount of memory on the heap is small, or the system simply hasn't done a collection for quite some time.

Font Metrics

When we examine any word processor text, we note that thin letters such as *t* do not take up as much horizontal space as thick letters such as *M*. If we use Graphics method *drawString* to write whole strings to the screen, this is of no concern—the correct spacing takes place automatically.

However, if we use Graphics method *drawChars* to draw individual characters, then spacing is a problem and we must turn to the methods and constructors of class *FontMetrics*.

Looking to the example below, the first statement (a *get* genesis statement) creates a *FontMetrics* reference (*myFm*) from the *Font* reference (*myF*). The second uses a font metrics method to return the width of character *ch* in pixels. Making use of these *x* (width) values, we can properly space individual characters.

```
myFm = getFontMetrics(myF);
x = myFm.charWidth(ch);
```

A font metrics reference must be associated with a font reference.

Font color

To change the color of any Java text, we use the same *setColor* method introduced in the last chapter. As a suggestion, you may find it convenient to add the following method to any appropriate new or previous tools class (such as *BasicTools*).

```
public static void myColor(int num,Graphics g){
    switch(num){
        case 1: g.setColor(Color.black);
                break;
        case 2: g.setColor(Color.blue);
                break;
        case 3: g.setColor(Color.green);
                break;
    }
}
```

Be sure to add *import java.awt.*;* to any class containing this method.

Note: Pass the graphics reference.

List all 16 colors if you wish.

By way of method *myColor*, colors can be conveniently selected by number (integer). This technique is especially useful when generating random colors.

Parameters

To jazz up our Web browser newspaper, we will rely on some applet special effects. Since a new edition must be released every day, we certainly don't want to perform a daily rewrite of this applet.

The solution is to use *parameters*—to pass information from the body of the HTML document to the applet. As demonstrated below, we pass string "Mars Landing!" from the HMTL file by using the *param* tag, and we receive the parameter within the applet by way of the *getParameter* method.

```
<param name=title value ="Mars Landing!">
```

In HTML file.

```
myHeadline = getParameter("title");
```

In Java file.

Project *CityDesk*

Project *CityDesk* will give us an opportunity to design the front page of the daily edition of "The Web Chronicles." The purpose of the front page is to attract attention, and to entice the fickle Web surfer to stop and take note.

Our first applet design will be a high-impact headline zooming out of the page. As a modification, we'll slowly print out the headline one character at a time. Developing these headlines will give us a golden opportunity to review and compare arrays and strings.

Hands-On Procedure

1. This chapter's project uses fonts, colors, and motion.

After a conventional HTML newspaper header, our applet will show the bright red headline slowly zooming out of the page. The headline will be passed as a parameter from the corresponding HTML program.

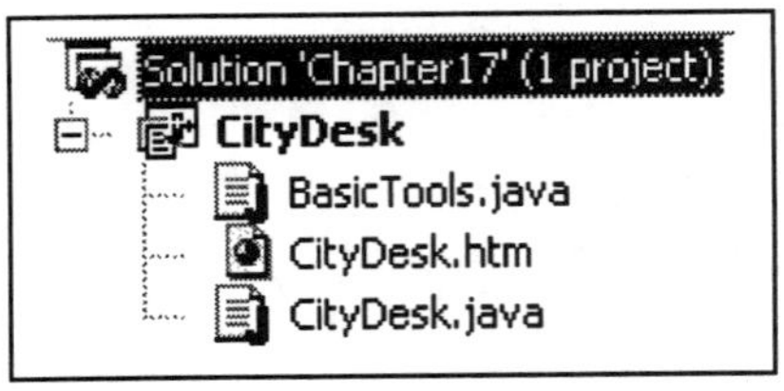

2. Create project *CityDesk* within solution *Chapter17*. Add and rename files as necessary.

Write the program

HTML update

3. By modifying the baseline code, develop *CityDesk.htm* of Figure 17.2.

Don't forget Appendix B.

```
<HTML>
<HEAD><TITLE>City Desk</TITLE></HEAD>
<BODY><CENTER><STRONG>
<FONT color=darkblue face="Book Antiqua" size=6
style="BACKGROUND-COLOR:orange">
The WebPage Chronicles</FONT>
<P><U><FONT color=blue size=3 face=Courier>
<PRE>Sunday April 1, 2025       Published Daily</PRE>
</FONT></U><HR>
<APPLET
  code=CityDesk.class name=CityDesk
  height=85 width=500 VIEWASTEXT>
  <PARAM NAME="headline" VALUE="Mars Landing!">
</APPLET><HR>
<FONT color=green face="Bookman Old Style" size=4>
Today a group of astronauts landed on Mars for<BR>
the first time.  No little green people in sight.
</FONT></STRONG></CENTER>
</BODY></HTML>
```

Pass parameter "Mars Landing!" using ID "headline".

New! Parameters.

New! Fonts and color.

Figure 17.2
CityDesk.htm

4. Note the use of the preformat (PRE) tag. All text between the tags appears on the screen exactly as it is written.

```
<PRE>Sunday April 1, 2025              Published Daily</PRE>
```

Applet update

The purpose of the applet is to accept today's headline from the HTML program and to gradually increase its size.

5. Write the corresponding applet (*CityDesk.java*) of Figure 17.3.

```
import java.awt.*;
import java.applet.*;
public class CityDesk extends Applet
{
   private String myHeadline;

   public void init( ){
      myHeadline = getParameter("Headline");
   }

   public void paint(Graphics g){
      int i;
      for(i=1;i<70;i++){
         Font myF = new Font("Arial",Font.BOLD,i);
         g.setFont(myF);
         g.setColor(Color.red);
         g.clearRect(0,0,500,85);
         g.drawString(myHeadline,225–3*i,40+i/3);
         BasicTools.msec(75);
      }
   }
}
```

This global variable is accessible to all methods within the class.

New! Overriding method *init*.

New! Receiving a parameter.

New! Fonts.

Figure 17.3
CityDesk.java

6. Note the following special features of *CityDesk.java*:

   a) Method *init* (initialization) is another overriding method that is inherited from class *Applet* and automatically called by the browser. It's a handy place to put all code that is to be executed only once before *paint* is called.

   b) As first described in the discussion, the zooming process follows six steps: Create the font object (with an ever increasing size parameter), set the font, set the color, clear the old string, draw the new enlarged string, and delay for 75ms.

c) To keep the headline centered, the string's *x*-axis is progressively moved to the left and the *y*-axis moved down. The same is true with the *y*-axis, width, and height of the clear rectangle.

d) Like any variable definition, a genesis statement can be split into two parts.

```
String myHeadline;
MyHeadline = getParameter("Headline");
```

The first statement is the definition, and the second is the assignment. Why do this? Figure 17.3 gives a prime reason: Reference *myF* must be defined globally so both methods *init* and *paint* can gain access.

7. Test the Web page by executing *cityDesk.java* and displaying the front page of Figure 17.4. Does the headline slowly zoom out of the page?

Yes **No**

Figure 17.4
CityDesk Web page

Debug and modify

> In this section we switch from a zooming string headline to one that slowly prints out the headline one character at a time.

8. Add class *CityDeskMetrics.java* of Figure 17.5 to project *CityDesk*.

9. Enter *CityDesk.htm* and update the APPLET tag to point to *CityDeskMetrics.htm* (instead of *CityDesk.htm*).

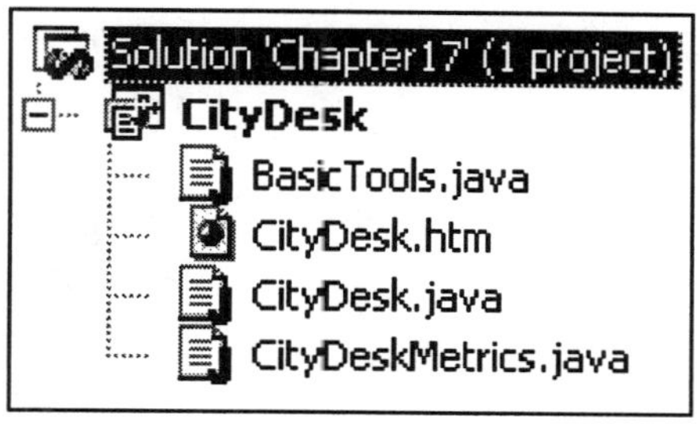


```
import java.awt.*;
import java.applet.*;
public class CityDeskMetrics extends Applet
{
        private String myHeadline;
        private char[ ] myCHeadline = new char[20];
        private FontMetrics myFm;
        private Font myF;

        public void init( ){
                myHeadline = getParameter("Headline");
                myCHeadline = myHeadline.toCharArray( );
                myF = new Font("Arial",Font.BOLD,70);
                myFm = getFontMetrics(myF);
        }

        public void paint(Graphics g){
                int i,x;
                g.setFont(myF);
                g.setColor(Color.red);
                for(i=0,x=0;i<myHeadline.length( );i++){
                        BasicTools.msec(500);
                        g.drawChars(myCHeadline,i,1,12+x,60);
                        x += myFm.charWidth(myCHeadline[i]);
                }
        }
}
```

New! Font metrics.

New! Drawing characters.

Figure 17.5
CityDeskMetrics.java

10. Applet *CityDesk.java* offers many new features. Concentrating on what's new, let's step through the program as it would be processed and executed.

    a) First, we define object references of classes *char[]*, *FontMetrics*, and *Font*.

    ```
    private char[ ] myCHeadline = new char[20];
    private FontMetrics myFm;
    private Font myF;
    ```

    b) Next, the browser calls method *init*. Using a method of class *String* (*toCharArray*) we convert the string to a char array. We create a *Font* object (reference by *myF*) and a *FontMetrics* object (referenced by *myFm*).

    ```
    myCHeadline = myHeadline.toCharArray( );
    myF = new Font("Arial",Font.BOLD,70);
    myFm = getFontMetrics(myF);
    ```

    c) Finally, the browser calls method *paint*. We print a character, then update the horizontal position variable (*x*) by successively adding that character's width.

    ```
    g.drawChars(m_cHeadline,i,1,20+x,60);
    x += myFm.charWidth(myCHeadline[i]);
    ```

11. Run the Web page and note the headline. Are the characters slowly printed one at a time, and are they properly spaced (Figure 17.6)?

    Yes **No**

12. What small change would we make to the program of Figure 17.5 so the characters were still evenly spaced, but slightly further apart? (Try it!)

Figure 17.6
CityDeskMetrics Web page

Exercises

a) Write an applet that prints your name to the screen in large blue letters. Five seconds later your name turns to green.

b) Write an applet that prints your name alternately, all in small letters and then all in large letters.

c) Modify the above applet so your name also switches between **bold** and *italic*. (Hint: You will need two font objects.)

d) Write an applet that causes your name in large red letters to move across the headline banner from left to right. Then, cause the process to repeat five times.

e) Show a blue ball moving slowing across the screen from left to right. Within the ball (and moving with it) the word *Earth* is written in orange.

f) Modify exercise e) so both the blue ball and the word *Earth* increase in size from left to right.

g) Modify the Superman code of the discussion so the word "SUPERMAN" zooms in and out ten times.

h) Modify g) so "SUPERMAN" changes color randomly each zoom cycle.

i) In Figure 17.3, replace *Font.BOLD* by variable *i* and explain the displayed result.

j) Print out the letters of the Mars headline on a slight diagonal. (Be sure to use vertical as well as horizontal font metrics for proper spacing.)

k) Print out the letters of the Mars headline in fisheye fashion. (*Fisheye* means that the letters start small, grow in size, and then get small again.)

l) Modify *CityDeskMetrics.java* to print out the characters of the headline in random colors.

m) Write a program that prints random letters (A through Z) to the screen at random locations. The process continues until two of the same letter are printed in succession.

n) The routine below prints *Hello* and *Dolly* in different font styles. Rewrite the code using a single *Font* genesis statement and an array of two strings.

```
public void paint(Graphics g){
    int i,size=4;
    for(i=0;i<10;i++){
        Font myF1 = new Font("Arial",i,size+=4);
        Font myF2 = new Font("Courier",i,size+=4);
        g.setFont(myF1);
        g.setColor(Color.blue);
        g.drawString("Hello",20,80);
        g.setFont(myF2);
        g.drawString("Dolly",20,140);
        BasicTools.msec(200);
        g.clearRect(20,0,300,200);
    }
}
```

o) By adding the code shown below to *blockbuster.htm* and *blockbuster.java*, send the size of the font as a parameter.

```
<param name=size value=50>
```

```
String param;
param = getParameter("size");
mySize = Integer.parseInt(param);
Font myf = new Font("Arial",Font.BOLD,mySize);
```

p) Create a home Web page for the company you are working for or the college you are attending that includes moving text and graphics.

Questions and Problems

1. In the assignment statement below, what type is variable *myTitle*?

   myTitle = getParameter("title");

2. What three parameters are part of the *Font* constructor?

3. Using font metrics, show how to return a character height.

4. Are all the numbers from #000000 to #FFFFFF a different HTML color?

5. How many parameters can we pass from an HTML file to an applet?

6. Show how to convert string "High Noon" to an array of characters.

7. Is *FontMetrics* a class?

   Yes **No**

8. Multiple references can point to a single object, but one reference can not point to multiple objects.

   True **False**

CHAPTER

18

Project Solar System

Images and Trigonometry

Objectives

- *To add images to our Web page designs*
- *To create circular motion using trig functions*

Discussion

To be really cool, a Web page must use real image graphics—such as the icons used throughout this text. You'll be surprised how easy it is to add such enhancements. As always, adding images falls into two camps: The HTML camp by way of special image tags, and the Java camp by way of special methods.

Two widely accepted image formats are *GIF* (*Graphics Interchange Format*) and JPEG (*Joint Photographic Experts Group*). We have adopted the GIF format because they are better suited for computer-generated images. Where can we get these GIF images? Just about anywhere. They can be downloaded from the Web or purchased on CD-ROM. The disk that comes with this text stores all the required *gif* files within each corresponding project directory. (Additional images are stored in the folder *TextImages*.)

HTML update

Images

Let's start with the HTML camp. The special tags normally associated with imaging are listed in Table 18.1.

To insert a *GIF* image anywhere in our HTML document, we use the *IMG* tag. As a case in point, the statement below will display an image of the earth. (We assume that the image and HTML files are in the same directory.)

```
<IMG SRC="earth.gif">
```

As shown by Table 18.1, there are a whole slew of attributes we can add to the basic image tag. The tag below prints an enlarged image of the earth at the right of the page, and aligns text to wrap around the image at its left.

```
<IMG SRC="earth.gif" align=right  width=100  height=100>
....enter text here....
```

Opening Tag	Closing Tag	Description
<BODY bgcolor=Color>	</BODY>	Background color
<IMG SRC="name.gif" align=Hdirection align=Vdirection border= "n" width="x" height="y" hspace="x" vspace="y">	none	Place image Left, right, or center Top, middle, or bottom Border thickness Horizontal width Vertical height Horizontal space Vertical space
<hr size="n" noshade width="n"%>	</hr>	Horizontal rule n = size in pixels noshade gives indented look n = % of page

Table 18.1
HTML image tags

Background color

As shown below, we can easily set the background color of the entire HTML document. (What if we could set the background color of the applet window to the same color?)

```
<body bgcolor=Silver>
```

It's convenient to use one of the 16 predefined colors.

Horizontal rule

To the basic horizontal rule tag (<hr>), we can add *Size*, *Shade*, and *Width* attributes. As a case in point, the tags shown below will generate the horizontal rules of Figure 18.1.

```
<hr SIZE=10>
<hr SIZE=20 NOSHADE>
<hr SIZE=40 WIDTH=75%>
```

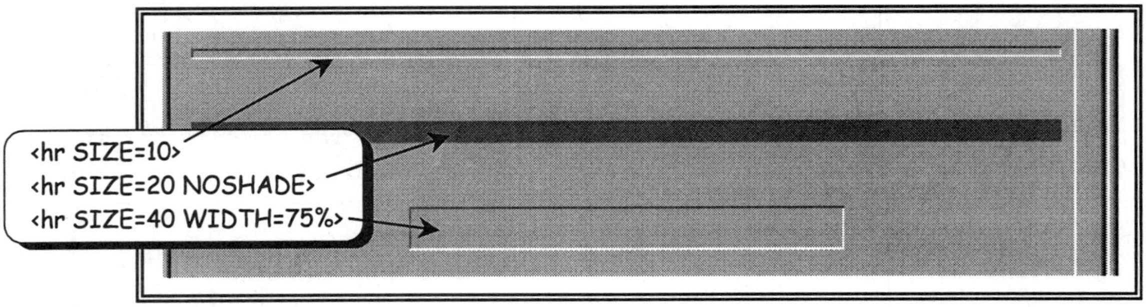

Figure 18.1
Horizontal rule examples

Applet update

The class hierarchy of Figure 18.2 shows that classes *Image* and *MediaTracker* are new.

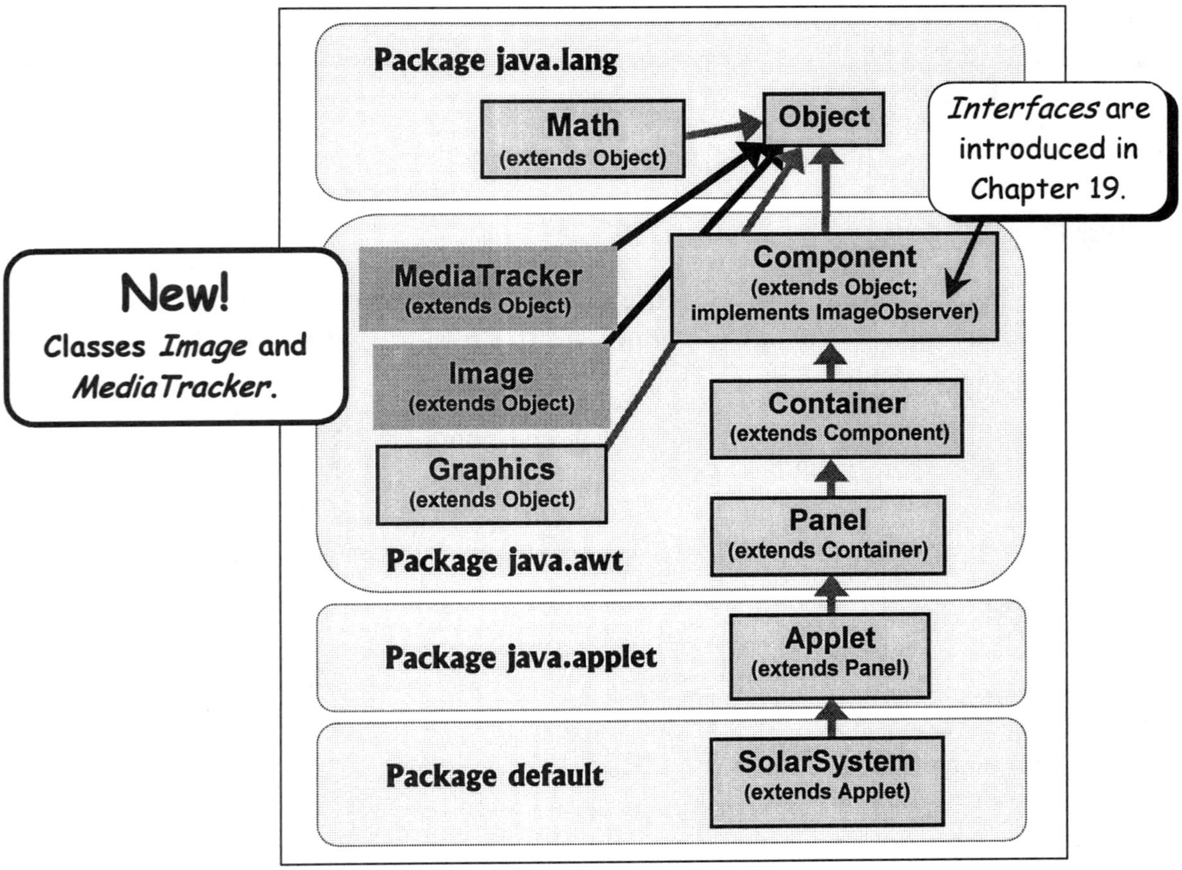

Figure 18.2
Project *SolarSystem* class hierarchy

An applet image is drawn in two steps.

(1) First, we use a get (*getImage*) genesis statement (inherited from class *Applet*) to create an image object and to associate the reference with the applet screen.

```
Image earth = getImage(getDocumentBase( ),"earth.gif");
```

Method *getDocumentBase* (also inherited from class *Applet*) returns the URL of the document that contains this applet.

(2) Second, we use the image reference to draw the image within the applet window.

```
g.drawImage(earth,x,y,width,height,this);
```

Method *drawImage* is from class *Graphics*. It accepts the image object, location, and size parameters. The *imageObserver* object (*this*) is the object to be notified as more of the image is converted.

Image downloading

When *getImage* is called, it issues a download request. Processing then continues as the image downloads in the background.

When method *drawImage* is called, it draws as much of the image as is currently available. As more of the image becomes available, the browser notifies the image observer—which in turn calls method *imageUpdate* (inherited from class *Component*) and the updated image is repainted. A simple (but unreliable) way of giving the image time to download is to use a time delay.

Background color

To achieve an interesting effect, we can set the applet window's background color to the same color as the HTML document window. This is accomplished by using inherited method *setBackground* from class *Component*.

```
setBackground(Color.lightGray);
```

Use any of the 16 named colors.

Elliptic motion

Project *SolarSystem* involves elliptic motion, as image earth orbits about image sun. Since all the methods of class *Graphics* are based on the rectangular coordinate system, we must make use of the trigonometric methods of class *Math* to generate circles and ellipses.

The following equations convert angles in degrees to x and y coordinates, where X_0 and Y_0 position the center of the ellipse and X_r and Y_r determine the radius of motion.

```
x = X0 + (int)(Xr*Math.sin(6.28*angle/360));
y = Y0 + (int)(Yr*Math.cos(6.28*angle/360));
```

Degrees are converted to radians.

True motion involves a *draw*, *hold*, *erase,* and *update* cycle. By way of review, the third step is performed with the *clearRect* method.

```
g.clearRect(x,y,width,height);
```

Hands-On Procedure

1. This chapter's project uses several space-related images.

An image of planet earth slowly revolves in an elliptic orbit about an image of the sun.

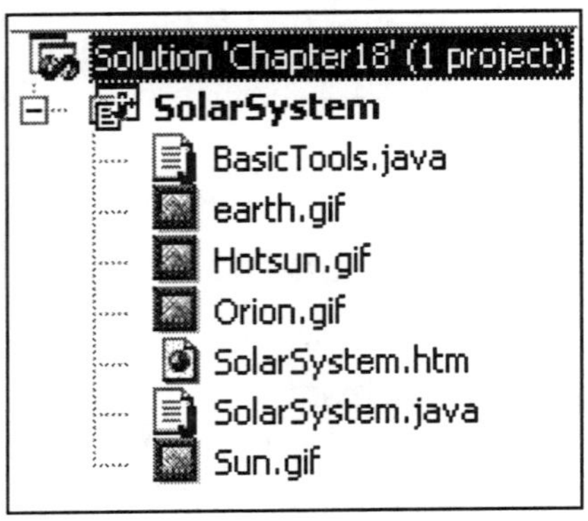

2. Create project *SolarSystem* within solution *Chapter18* and add all necessary files.

Copies of all *gif* files are in folder *TextImages*.

Write the program

3. Write the HTML program (*SolarSystem.htm*) of Figure 18.3. (If you wish, use the techniques of Appendix B.)

```
<HTML><HEAD>
<TITLE>Solar System</TITLE>
</HEAD>
<BODY bgColor=Silver><CENTER>
<IMG SRC="orion.gif" height=50 width=50 align=middle>
<FONT size=20 color=darkBlue>The Solar System</FONT>
<IMG SRC="orion.gif" height=50 width=50 align=middle><BR>
<HR size=3 width=80%>
<APPLET
   code=SolarSystem.class   name=SolarSystem
   height=140 width=300 VIEWASTEXT>
</APPLET>
<HR size=3 width=80%>
<IMG SRC="hotsun.gif">
<FONT size=5 color=MidnightBlue>The earth is in a slightly elliptic
orbit<BR> some 93,000,000 miles from the sun.</FONT><BR></CENTER>
</BODY></HTML>
```

New! Background color.

New! Images in HTML.

This HTML program uses images *orion*, and *hotsun*.

Figure 18.3
SolarSystem.htm

4. Write the corresponding applet (*SolarSystem.java*) of Figure 18.4. Note the two-step image-creation process:

   - One: Using method *getImage*, write a genesis statement to create an image object.
   - Two: Using method *drawImage*, place the image at the desired location and of the desired size.

Execute the program

5. Run the program and display the Web page of Figure 18.5.

   a) Were the images of the earth and sun fully formed? (If you encounter difficult with image formation, adjust the delay period.)

      Yes **No**

   b) Did the earth orbit the sun three times? (Remember, when the Web page was first displayed, the browser might have called *paint* more than once.)

      Yes **No**

```
import java.awt.*;
import java.applet.*;
public class SolarSystem extends Applet
{
     Image sun,earth;

     public void init( ){
          earth = getImage(getDocumentBase( ),"earth.gif");
          sun = getImage(getDocumentBase( ),"sun.gif");
          setBackground(Color.lightGray);
     }

     public void paint(Graphics g){
          int i,x,y,angle;
          for(angle=0;angle<(360*3);angle+=2){
               x=130+(int)(125*Math.sin(6.28*angle/360));
               y=50+(int)(45*Math.cos(6.28*angle/360));
               g.drawImage(earth,x,y,40,40,this);
               g.drawImage(sun,115,45,50,50,this);
               if(angle == 0)
                    BasicTools.msec(2000);
               BasicTools.msec(40);
               g.clearRect(x,y,40,40);
          }
     }
}
```

New! Background color.

Copies of all *gif* files are in folder *TextImages*.

LightGray is the same as HTML's silver.

New! Images.

Delay to allow images to fully form. (Adjust as needed.)

Adjust orbit speed.

Figure 18.4
SolarSystem.java

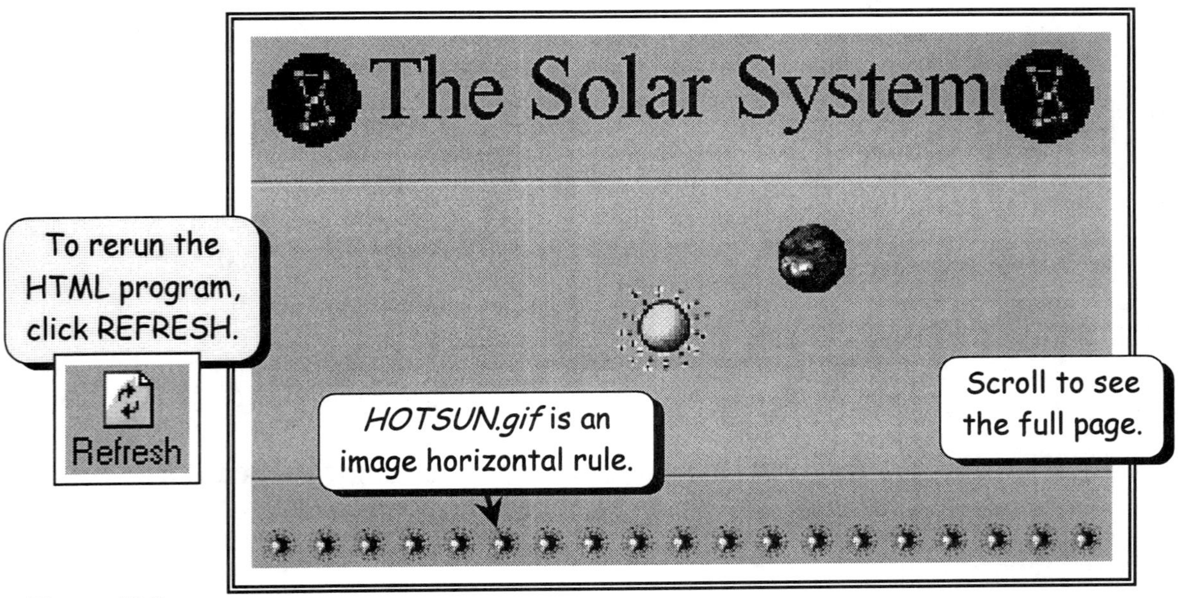

Figure 18.5
Project *SolarSystem* Web page.

Media tracking—a better way

Rather than drawing images as they are loaded, a better method is to use class *MediaTracker* to draw them after they have been loaded.

6. By adding the code shown in boxes (Figure 18.6) and deleting all "delay-related" code, modify *SolarSystem.java* so the earth and sun images will be fully loaded before they are drawn.

```
import java.awt.*;
import java.applet.*;
public class SolarSystem extends Applet
{
      Image sun,earth;
      MediaTracker  trackImage;                              [1]

      public void init( ){
            trackImage = new MediaTracker(this);             [1]
            earth = getImage(getDocumentBase( ),"earth.gif");
            sun = getImage(getDocumentBase( ),"sun.gif");
            trackImage.addImage(earth,0);                    [2]
            trackImage.addImage(sun,0);
            try{
                  trackImage.waitForAll( );                  [3]
            }
            catch(InterruptedException e){
            }
            setBackground(Color.lightGray);
      }

      public void paint(Graphics g){
            int i,x,y,angle;
            for(angle=0;angle<(360*3);angle+=2){
                  x=130+(int)(125*Math.sin(6.28*angle/360));
                  y=50+(int)(45*Math.cos(6.28*angle/360));
                  g.drawImage(earth,x,y,40,40,this);
                  g.drawImage(sun,115,45,50,50,this);
                  BasicTools.msec(40);
                  g.clearRect(x,y,40,40);
            }
      }
}
```

The split genesis statement is not necessary here (only *init* uses *trackImage*), but is more common.

New! MediaTracker.

Continuously redrawing the sun gives it an appealing flicker effect.

Figure 18.6
SolarSystem.java modified

7. Referring to Figure 18.6, the *MediaTracking* process takes place in three steps:

1 ▪ A split genesis statement creates a *MediaTracker* object and reference (*trackImage*).

2 ▪ Images earth and sun are added to the tracking system.

3 ▪ We enter a loop and wait for both images to be loaded.

> **Are we doing true animation?**
>
> No, we are not. True animation means that the image itself changes rapidly over time. All we are doing in project *SolarSystem* is moving a constant image about the screen. It's a crude form of animation, but its not true motion-picture type animation.
>
> Now if the earth rotated about its axis as it moved about the screen. Well, that would be a different story. Stay tuned.

Debug and modify

> HTML provides for automatic text wrap-around by way of the *align* attribute.

8. Add the following HTML code to the bottom of *SolarSystem.html* (just before </BODY>).

```
<P><img src="sun.gif" align=right width=100 height=100>
<FONT size=7 color=red>The sun will explode!</FONT><BR>
<FONT size=5 color=maroon>The sun is very, very hot--millions of
degrees! Someday the sun will run out of fuel and grow into a red giant.
Long before then, the human race will have headed for the stars looking
for a new home. Generations after generations will live on spaceships.
</FONT>
```

9. Re-run the applet. Did the text properly wrap around the image of the sun?

Yes **No**

Exercises

Additional icon images are found in directory *TextImages/Icons* on an enclosed disk. Each exercise below concentrates on the applet (Java) portion of the Web page. Add HTML code as desired.

a) By making two small changes to the applet program, have the earth rotate about the sun twice as many times and twice as fast, each time *paint* is called.

b) Display the day of the year (0 to 364) near the earth as it orbits the sun.

c) Using an array of strings, display the months of the year near image earth as it orbits the sun.

d) Add another planet (such as Mercury) to the solar system.

e) Show an image of the sun zooming straight out.

f) Using image *rock* (from folder *TextImages*), show an asteroid spiraling down into the sun.

g) Using image *baseball*, show an image of a baseball moving from left to right. For extra credit:

- The text "Home Run" is written when the baseball hits the right-hand side.
- The text "Home Run" is zoomed out from the screen.
- The baseball image starts at the lower left of the screen and grows in size as it moves to the upper right.
- Using kinematics equations ($D_y = 16t^2$, $D_x = V_o t$), show the baseball following a trajectory from left to right.

h) Show two images of anything moving towards each other. When they hit, both images stop.

i) Add an image of the moon orbiting the earth, as the earth orbits the sun. Hint: Make the *x* and *y* coordinates of the earth the new origin coordinates of the moon.

j) Using image *rock* from directory *gif*, write project *asteroids*, in which asteroids move from left to right at random vertical positions. When an asteroid hits the earth, the game is over. (The earth can be moving or resting.)

k) Modify project asteroids, so "CRASH" is written in large red letters when the earth is hit. (For extra effect, the word "CRASH" will zoom.)

l) Making use of image *Alien* (from directory *TextImages*), write a Web page that shows an alien vehicle coming in for a landing. (Hint: Distance = $3t^2$ for the moon; use units of t = 10ms for smoother motion.)

m) Making use of image *car* (from directory *TextImages*), write a Web page that shows a car moving towards us from the upper left to the lower right. (Hint: The image will increase in size as it moves. Method *drawLine* is a good way of making a road.)

n) Making maximum use of images, create a Web page of your own design.

Questions and Problems

1. What does *gif* stand for?

2. Using image *baseball.gif*, show how to place a large (100 by 100 pixel) baseball at the center of a 400 by 200 applet window.

3. Show the HTML instruction for placing a five-pixel wide horizontal rule across 80% of the screen.

4. When an image is used with text, what does **ALIGN=left** accomplish?

5. *bgcolor* is an attribute of what HTML tag?

6. What does method *getDocumentBase* return?

7. Does the rotating earth in this project obey Kepler's laws of motion? (Does the earth move faster when it is closer to the sun?)

8. How many radians are there in 270 degrees?

9. Show the trigonometric equations for drawing a perfect circle of asterisks of radius 25 at the center of a 100 by 100 pixel applet window.

10. What would the screen look like if we deleted the erase command (*clearRect*) from the program of Figure 18.4?

11. Referring to Figure 18.4, why did we declare both the *sun* and *earth* images to be member variables (global)?

```
image sun,earth;
```

12. Modify the program to show the pre-Copernican solar system. (Prior to Nicolaus Copernicus in 1543 it was believed that the sun revolved about the earth.)

13. In the *addImage* methods below, "0" is the image *id* (identification number).

```
trackImage.addImage(earth,0);
trackImage.addImage(sun,0);
```

Under these circumstances, why would the *waitForID* instruction below have the same result as *waitForAll*?

```
waitForID(0);
```

14. Based on question 13, we can choose which images we wait for.

True **False**

Part 5
External Events

We talk to our Web pages by way of the keyboard and the mouse. In the four chapters of Part 5 we'll learn how to handle these external events.

CHAPTER

19

Project Treasure Hunt

Events, Interfaces, and Class *Calendar*

Objectives

- *To include mouse events in our applets*
- *To use class Calendar to extract elapsed times*
- *To play the game of treasure hunt*

Discussion

Had computers been around at the turn of the century, Thomas Edison probably would have invented the mouse. It is simple, basic, and profound, and touches our modern lives as thoroughly as the light bulb and the movie camera. It would be hard to imagine using a Windows-based program without a mouse.

Applet update

To keep things simple in this first event-related chapter, let's focus totally on a single type of event: Whenever the mouse is moved, the browser sends the corresponding cursor location to our applet.

The basic action is very simple. When we move the mouse, the browser notices the move, automatically calls overriding method *mouseMoved*, and passes a reference to an object of class *MouseEvent*. Using the passed reference, we can access methods *getX* and *getY* to obtain the mouse coordinates for later use.

```
public void mouseMoved(MouseEvent e){
      Dx = e.getX( );
      Dy = e.getY( );
}
```

Nothing to it! Unfortunately, it's not quite that simple. To fully understand a *mouseMoved* event, we must delve into the interface and the listener.

The interface

Method *mouseMoved* handed the designers of Java a dilemma. Just as with methods *init* and *paint*, the browser automatically calls method *mouseMoved* at the appropriate time. So what's the problem; just inherit and override method *mouseMoved*—as always.

The problem is, method *mouseMoved* is not in our applet's inheritance lineage—and Java does not allow multiple inheritance. So, what did they do? They created the *interface*.

An interface is a lot like a class. For example, we can inherit and override the methods of an interface. To see the difference, let's look inside interface *MouseMotionListener*.

```
public abstract void mouseMoved(MouseEvent e){ };
public abstract void mouseDragged(MouseEvent e){ }
```

What we find are no member variables at all and only method signatures—so called because they are abstract definitions and contain no code. The reason for such harsh restrictions on the interface was to avoid ambiguities that may arise from member variables and methods with the same name inherited from two or more sources (i.e., from the extended class and the one or more interfaces).

To provide the inheritance linkage to method *mouseMoved*, we use the keyword *implements* (Figure 19.1) A class can extend only one class, but can implement any number of interfaces.

An interface is a collection of public abstract methods and constants. When a class implements an interface, it promises to override all of its abstract methods.

ESPRESSO

How do we create a duckbill platypus?

A duckbill platypus is both egg laying and a mammal. In other words, it inherits characteristics from two different parent classes. This is also true of the C++ language.

To avoid the confusion this brings to the source code, the founders of Java decided to limit direct inheritance to only one class. However, what do we do when our applet needs to inherit behavior from two classes and the rules say we can't? We implement the interface.

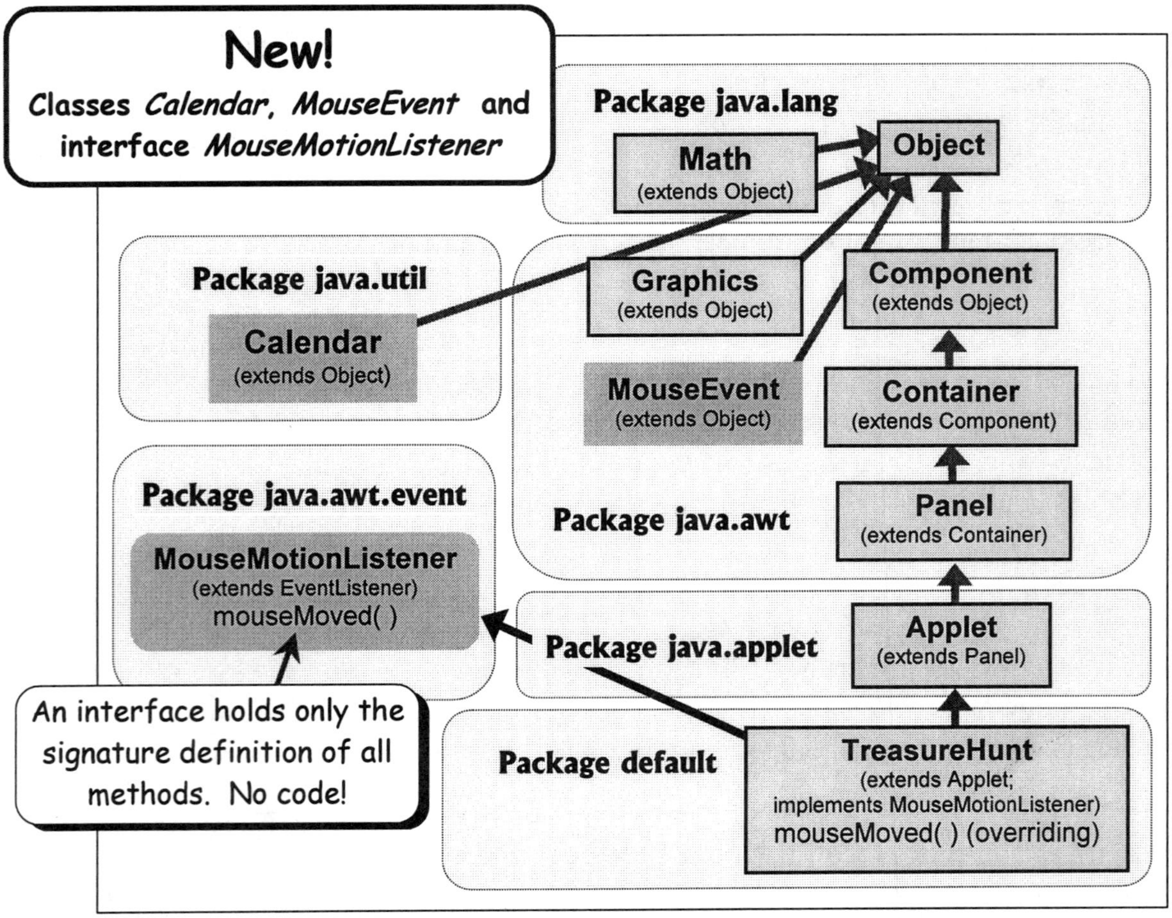

Figure 19.1

Project *TreasureHunt* class hierarchy

The listener

As we go about our daily lives, signals from all our five senses flood our minds with a constant barrage of external events. Without some means of screening and selecting events, and acting only upon those we wish, normal life would break down. We would be doing nothing but processing external events.

The same is true of computer systems. Every movement or click of the mouse, every keypress, every change in a window can contribute to a constant stream of external events. It would be quite time-consuming and overwhelming if the system were required to constantly check our applet for every possible overriding method.

Instead, why don't we tell the browser ahead of time which types of events our *TreasureHunt* applet is waiting for? That way it can call only those overriding methods it knows we are interested in. This we do by registering our applet as a *MouseMotionListener*.

```
addMouseMotionListener(this);
```

From class *Component*.

That is, we are notifying the system that our *TreasureHunt* Applet (*this*) is "listening" for mouse-motion type events, and we want the system to automatically call overriding method *mouseMoved* whenever the mouse is moved.

HTML update

Background image

In the last chapter, we changed the background color of our HTML screen. In this chapter, we'll add a background image. The browser performs this interesting feature by repeating a small image to fill an entire Web page. In this chapter we will use the *ground.gif* image to create a proper backdrop for our treasure hunt.

```
<BODY BACKGROUND="ground.gif">
```

The game of buried treasure

During applet initialization, buried *cyber*treasure is placed at a random location in the applet window. A blue circle appears that represents the treasure-locating device (metal detector). By way of the mouse, we can drag the detector to any part of the applet screen. The object of the game is to locate the buried treasure as quickly as possible. To help the treasure hunter, the blue circle turns orange when it gets close to the treasure (you're getting warm). When found, the circle turns red and the game is over.

In the *Debug and modify* section we'll add timing to the game so the winner can be accurately determined. Looking back to Figure 19.1, timing is handled by class *Calendar*.

Hands-On Procedure

1. This chapter's project requires the system to know the precise location of the mouse whenever it is moved.

Buried treasure is placed at a random location within the applet window. By moving the mouse, and by watching the color of the detector change from blue to orange to red, we locate the treasure as quickly as possible.

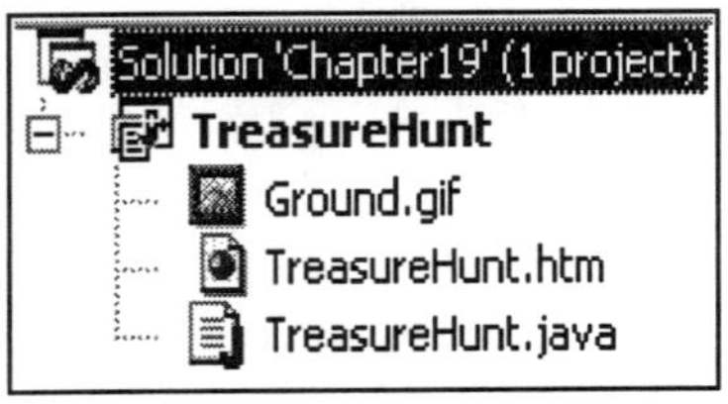

2. Create project *TreasureHunt* within solution *Chapter19.* Rename and add all necessary files.

3. Create Web file *TreasureHunt.html* of Figure 19.2.

```
<HTML>
<HEAD>
<TITLE>Treasure Hunt</TITLE>
</HEAD>
<BODY background=ground.gif><CENTER>
<FONT SIZE=30 COLOR=darkBlue>Treasure Hunt</FONT>
<HR>
<APPLET
   code=TreasureHunt.class
   name=TreasureHunt
   height=175 width=500 VIEWASTEXT>
</APPLET>
<HR>
</CENTER>
</BODY>
</HTML>
```

New!
Background image.

Figure 19.2
TreasureHunt.htm

4. Next, write applet *TreasureHunt.java* of Figure 19.3.

```
import java.awt.*;
import java.applet.*;
import java.awt.event.*;
public class TreasureHunt extends Applet
                              implements MouseMotionListener
{
     private int Dx,Dy,Tx,Ty,Cx,Cy;

     public void init( ){
          Tx = (int)(Math.rint(Math.random( )*450));
          Ty = (int)(Math.rint(Math.random( )*150));
          setBackground(Color.white);
          addMouseMotionListener(this);
     }

     public void paint(Graphics g){
          Cx = Math.abs(Dx – Tx);
          Cy = Math.abs(Dy – Ty);
          if((Cx<5)&&(Cy<5)){
               g.setColor(Color.red);
               g.drawString("YOU FOUND IT",Tx–35,Ty+35);
          }
          else if((Cx<25)&&(Cy<25))
                    g.setColor(Color.orange);
               else
                    g.setColor(Color.blue);
          g.fillOval(Dx–20,Dy–20,40,40);
     }

     public void mouseMoved(MouseEvent e){
          Dx = e.getX( );
          Dy = e.getY( );
          repaint( );
     }

     public void mouseDragged(MouseEvent e){
     }
}
```

New! Implementing an *interface*.

New! Registering a listener.

How close (C) is the detector (D) to the treasure (T)?

The browser calls method *mouseMoved* whenever the mouse is moved.

New! *MouseMoved* event.

Method *mouseDragged* must be included (even if no custom code is added) because it is part of the *MouseMotionListener* interface.

Figure 19.3
Completed applet

5. An analysis of *TreasureHunt.java* follows the order in which the browser calls overriding methods:

   a) Method *init* is called first. The treasure is placed at a random location (*Tx* and *Ty*), and we register our applet as a *MouseMotionListener* (so the browser will call our overriding *mouseMoved* whenever the mouse is moved).

   b) Method *paint* is called and the detector's position is initialized to the upper left-hand corner of the screen ($x = 0$, $y = 0$).

   c) When the mouse is moved, the browser creates an object of class *MouseEvent*, sends a reference (*e*), and calls method *mouseMoved*. The location of the detector (*D*) is returned and the screen is repainted.

   d) Within method *paint*, the distance from the treasure is determined and used to set the detector color to blue (far), orange (near) or red (found it).

6. By refreshing the Web page, play the treasure hunt game several times (Figure 19.4). Did it work as expected, and was the location of the treasure random?

   Yes **No**

Figure 19.4
TreasureHunt Web page

ESPRESSO

Repaint?

We learned previously that it was dangerous to use *repaint* because a recursive (forever) loop is created. Yet, here we are, using *repaint* in method *mouseMoved* (Figure 19.3).

The answer is, when used in this way, it's not recursive. The chain is broken because method *repaint* does not appear within method *paint*.

Using *repaint* is a handy way of refreshing our applet window whenever a *mouseMoved* event occurs. Because *paint* erases old graphics, no *clearRect* is required. As an option, we can use the following overloaded version of *repaint* to update any portion of the applet window.

```
repaint(int x, int y, int width, int height)
```

Adding the elapsed time

We will now modify the applet to give the elapsed time required to locate the treasure. The player with the shortest time is the champion treasure-hunter.

To keep track of time we make use of class *Calendar*. Each time a *Calendar* object is created, we take a snapshot of the date and time. We extract the seconds field, and use some interesting code to change clock time (0 to 59) into elapsed time.

7. Modify *TreasureHunt.java* as shown in Figure 19.5. The added code is shown in **bold**. (If you create a new project, be sure to change all class-name references.)

```
import java.awt.*;
import java.applet.*;
import java.awt.event.*;
import java.util.*;
public class TreasureHunt extends Applet implements MouseMotionListener
{
        private int Dx,Dy,Tx,Ty,Cx,Cy;
        Calendar myC;
        int present,past,time=0;

        public void init( ){
                Tx = (int)(Math.rint(Math.random( )*450));
                Ty = (int)(Math.rint(Math.random( )*150));
                setBackground(Color.white);
                addMouseMotionListener(this);
                myC = Calendar.getInstance( );
                past = myC.get(myC.SECOND);
                setFont(new Font("Areal",Font.BOLD,25));
        }

        public void paint(Graphics g){
                Cx = Math.abs(Dx – Tx);
                Cy = Math.abs(Dy – Ty);
                if((Cx<5)&&(Cy<5)){
                        g.setColor(Color.red);
                        g.drawString("It took you "+time+"s!",150,25);
                }
                else if((Cx<25)&&(Cy<25))
                                g.setColor(Color.orange);
                        else
                                g.setColor(Color.blue);
                g.fillOval(Dx–20,Dy–20,40,40);
                myC = Calendar.getInstance( );
                present = myC.get(myC.SECOND);
                if(present != past)
                        if(present > past)
                                time+=(present – past);
                        else
                                time+=((60-past)+present);
                g.drawString(Integer.toString(time),10,30);
                past=present;
        }

        public void mouseMoved(MouseEvent e){
                Dx = e.getX( );
                Dy = e.getY( );
                repaint( );
        }

        public void mouseDragged(MouseEvent e){ }
}
```

Type *Calendar* variable (reference) definition.

New!
Class *Calendar*.

Each assignment part of the *Calendar* genesis statement creates a new (updated) *Calendar* object.

Figure 19.5

Elapsed time
(added code is shown in **bold**)

8. Looking to Figure 19.5, we note the following:

   - *myC = Calendar.getInstance( )* creates a calendar object, complete with year, month, hour, minute, second, and millisecond data fields, each time it is called. *myC.get(myC.SECOND)* returns the value of the SECONDS field (0 to 59).

   - Variable *time* holds the total elapsed time since the game started. We wish to add to variable *time* the number of seconds elapsed since the last method call. This is done by adding the difference between present and past. However, if the present time is less than the past time, it means we crossed the 59 to 0 boundary and we must make appropriate adjustments (*(60–past)+present*).

9. Run the applet and find the buried treasure. At the end of the hunt, does the screen look like Figure 19.6?

   Yes **No**

Figure 19.6
Elapsed time

In the previous example, note that the time is updated only when the mouse is moved (and *paint* is called). To keep the clock updated continuously, you may want to come back after studying multithreading in Chapter 24.

Exercises

Additional background images are found in directory *TextImages/BackGround* on an enclosed disk.

a) As the mouse is moved about the screen, the product of its *x* and *y* coordinates is printed at the cursor location.

b) Modify a) so the product is written in large red numbers whenever it's an even multiple of 100. (Hint: Divide the product by 100 and look for no remainder.)

c) Repeat project *Treasure Hunt* using method *mouseDragged* instead of *mouseMoved*. (*mouseDragged* returns the *x* and *y* coordinates of the mouse only when the left button is down.)

d) Write an applet in which a circle is moved about the screen. When the circle is in the left-hand section of the window it is blue; when it crosses over to the right-hand side, it turns yellow.

e) A blue square 100 pixels high and 100 pixels wide is printed to the center of the applet screen. Whenever the cursor enters the square it turns orange.

f) Write an applet in which a circle is moved about the screen as the mouse is moved. The size of the circle is proportional to its *x* location.

g) Write an applet that prints two circles: red and blue. The blue circle moves as the mouse moves, and the red circle moves as the mouse moves with the left button down.

h) Write project *ForceField*, in which a blue circle is moved about the screen by the mouse. However, the circle won't penetrate into a 100 by 100 pixel square area in the center of the screen.

i) Using images *cat* and *mouse* (or simple circles if suitable images are not available), write an applet in which the mouse moves randomly away when the cat approaches. When the mouse leaves the applet screen, it has escaped; if it moves to within 5 pixels of the mouse, it is caught. (Ironically, the "mouse" moves the cat.)

j) Modify project *TreasureHunt* so the words "You found it!" appear above the red circle when the treasure is near the bottom of the screen.

k) Write project *dragObject*, in which a blue circle is dragged by the cursor only when both the left mouse button is down and the cursor is within the circle.

l) Modify project *drag* by first creating a menu of shapes. Using the drag technique, move the shapes about the screen to draw a picture. (Be sure to store the shape locations in an array.)

m) Design a game or display of your own choosing.

Questions and Problems

1. What is the difference between *mouseDragged* and *mouseMoved*?

2. An *event* is unexpected by the system.

   True **False**

3. How does the HTML system use a small image to fill in the entire background screen?

4. Carefully examining Figure 19.3, how close must the cursor get to the treasure in order for the detector to turn orange? Red?

5. Who creates an object of class *MouseEvent* and when is it created?

6. All abstract methods of an interface must be overridden. This eliminates possible name ambiguities between extended and implemented multiple inheritance pathways.

   True **False**

7. The browser only calls method *mouseMoved* if our applet has been registered as a *MouseMotionListener*.

   True **False**

8. In general terms, how would you modify the applet of Figure 19.3 so the metal detector no longer moves after the treasure has been found?

9. Referring to Figure 19.5, what does it mean when variable *past* is greater than variable *present*?

CHAPTER

20

Project HighCardApplet

Mouse Click Events, Lists, and Objects

Objectives

- *To include a mousePressed event in our applets*
- *To include user-defined objects*
- *To include lists in our HTML program*
- *To play the game of HighCardApplet*

Discussion

The computer mouse can move and drag graphic items across the screen—that we learned when hunting for treasure in the last chapter. In this chapter we will find that the versatile mouse can also select items. This most useful property is accomplished with the mouse button. Just move the mouse over the desired item on the screen, click left, and the item is selected.

Applet update

The class hierarchy chart of Figure 20.1 shows two major changes: Replace interface *MouseMotionListener* with interface *MouseListener* and include user-defined template class *Player*.

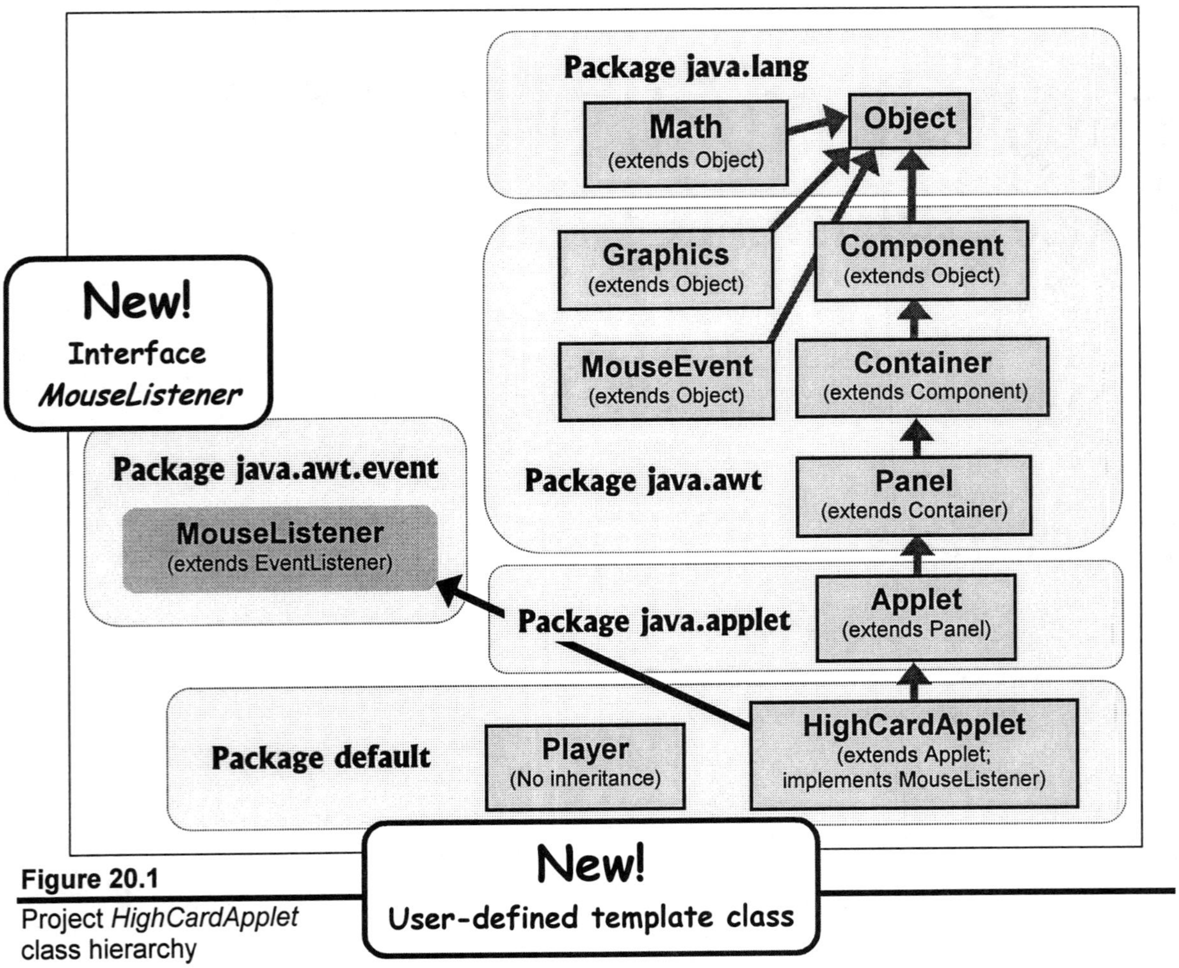

Figure 20.1
Project *HighCardApplet* class hierarchy

To select items with the mouse, we can choose from among the five abstract methods of interface *MouseListener*.

```
public void mousePressed(MouseEvent e){ } (left button down)
public void mouseReleased(MouseEvent e){ } (left button up)
public void mouseClicked(MouseEvent e){ } (left button down and up)
public void mouseEntered(MouseEvent e){ } (mouse enters component area)
public void mouseExited(MouseEvent e){ } (mouse exits component area)
```

> Reminder: All five abstract methods of interface *MouseListener* are definitions (signatures) only, and carry no internal code.

User-defined objects?

We've been so preoccupied with applets that perhaps you haven't even noticed: In Section II we have yet to include a user-defined template class (except the applet). All that will now change, for we have two players pitted against each other in a game of chance.

HTML update

Lists

Itemized lists are one of the most common techniques for organizing data. To set off each of the items in a list, we use bullets, numbers, or letters. Table 20.1 shows the two new HTML tags used in this chapter to generate lists.

Opening Tag	Closing Tag	Description
<OL type=X start=n> <LI>	</OL>	Ordered list A,a,I,i,1 Initial value Before each item
<UL type=shape> <LI>	</UL>	Unordered list Disk, circle, square Before each item

Table 20.1
HTML list tags

The first example below generates an ordered list from 7 through 10, and the second generates an unordered list using disk bullets.

```
<OL TYPE=1 START=7>
  <LI>John
  <LI>Mary
  <LI>Sam
  <LI>Tai
</OL>
```

7. John
8. Mary
9. Sam
10. Tai

```
<UL TYPE=disk>
  <LI>John
  <LI>Mary
  <LI>Sam
  <LI>Tai
</UL>
```

- John
- Mary
- Sam
- Tai

The HighCard game

In Chapter 12 we played the game of *high card*, with only the keyboard input and console output to control the action. In this chapter, we play the same game—except this time we bring with us all the input and display advantages of the applet. To be specific, we deal a card by simply clicking the card box, and we display all results using the power of applet fonts and graphics.

Hands-On Procedure

1. This chapter's project repeats the card game of Chapter 12.

By clicking each card box, we deal a card to each player. The player with the highest card wins $1, and the cumulative scores of both players are displayed.

2. Create project *HighCardApplet* within solution *Chapter20*. Be sure to add existing class *BasicTools.java*, and new class *Player.java*.

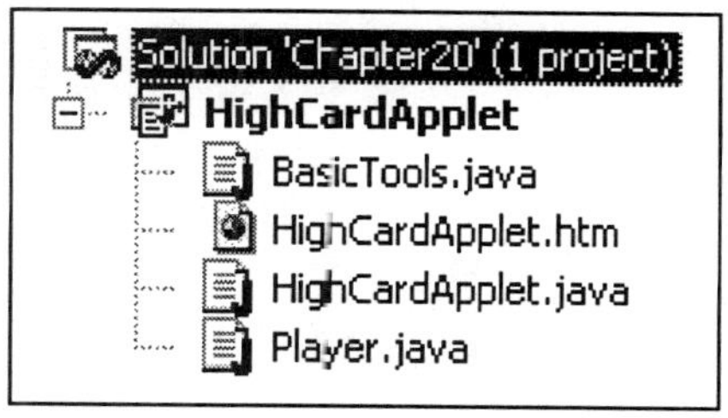

3. Create Web file *HighCardApplet.htm* of Figure 20.2. Is the list ordered or unordered?

   ordered **unordered**

```
<HTML>
<HEAD><TITLE>High Card Applet</TITLE></HEAD>
<BODY bgColor=white><CENTER><FONT color=maroon
face=Algerian size=8>
High card wins</FONT><BR>
<applet
    code=HighCardApplet.class
    name=HighCardApplet
    width=400
    height=120  VIEWASTEXT>
</applet><BR>
<FONT color = navy face="Kino MT" size=4>
<STRONG>
<OL>
  <Li>Click each card to deal.
  <Li>Which card is greater?
  <Li>Did the winner get $1?
</OL></STRONG></FONT>
</BODY>
</HTML>
```

New!
Ordered lists.

Figure 20.2
HighCardApplet.htm

4. Next, add class *Player.java* of Figure 20.3. This very small class will spin off objects that consist of only a single data member (the total cumulative cash winnings of each player) and a constructor to initialize each player's name.

5. Finally, complete applet *HighCardApplet.java* of Figure 20.4.

```
// This user-defined mini-class holds
// only a single method and a single
// member variable.
public class Player
{
        int myCash;
        String myName;

        Player(String name){
                myName = name;
        }
}
```

New!
User-defined template class.

Figure 20.3

Player.java

```
import java.awt.*;
import java.applet.*;
import java.awt.event.*;
public class HighCardApplet extends Applet
                                        implements MouseListener
{
        Player one,two;
        boolean P1,P2;
        int card1,card2,P;

        public void init( ){
                one = new Player("Sam");
                two = new Player("Mary");
                addMouseListener(this);
                Font myF = new Font("Arial",Font.BOLD,30);
                setFont(myF);
                setBackground(Color.white);
        }
```

1

This version of method *setFont* is inherited from class *Component*. It sets the font of this component.

Continued on the next page.

Figure 20.4

HighCardApplet.java (continued on the next page)

Continued from the previous page.

```
public void paint(Graphics g){
    if((P == 1)&&(P1==false)){
        card1 = (int)(1+Math.random( )*9);
        P1 = true;
    }
    if((P == 2)&&(P2==false)){
        card2 = (int)(1+Math.random( )*9);
        P2 = true;
    }
    g.drawRect(80,10,50,60);
    g.drawRect(280,10,50,60);
    g.drawString(card1+" ",97,50);
    g.drawString(card2+" ",297,50);
    if((P1==true)&&(P2==true)){
        if(card1>card2)
            ++one.myCash;
        else if(card2>card1)
            ++two.myCash;
        P1=false; P2=false; P=0;
    }
    g.drawString("Sam = $"+one.myCash,35,110);
    g.drawString("Mary = $"+two.myCash,240,110);
}

public void mousePressed(MouseEvent e){
    P = (e.getX( )<200)? 1:2;
    BasicTools.msec(400);
    repaint( );
}

public void mouseEntered(MouseEvent e){ }
public void mouseExited(MouseEvent e){ }
public void mouseClicked(MouseEvent e){ }
public void mouseReleased(MouseEvent e){ }
}
```

4

2

5

2

3

Slight delay to simulate dealing of card.

New!
MousePressed event.

Figure 20.4
HighCardApplet.java (continued from the previous page)

6. An analysis of *HighCardApplet.java* of Figure 20.4 reveals some interesting design logic.

> Each card can only be dealt once each round of play, no matter how many times the first is clicked. A round of play finishes when both cards have been clicked at least once and the winner determined.

One round of play progresses as follows:

1 a) The browser calls method *init*. The two user-defined player objects are created, and each is initialized with a specific name.

2 b) The browser calls method *paint*. Both cards and the total cash winnings are displayed. (All numbers are initialized to zero.)

3 c) A player clicks a card, and the browser calls method *mousePressed*. If the left-hand card (Sam) was clicked, variable *P* is set to 1; if the right-hand card (Mary) was clicked, *P* is set to 2. The screen is repainted.

4 d) Depending on the value of variable *P* (1 or 2), either *card1* or *card2* is dealt. Either *P1* or *P2* is set to *true*, which prevents that card from being dealt again (until *P1* or *P2* is reset to *false*).

5 2 e) When both cards have been dealt (*P1* and *P2* both *true*), the high card is determined, the corresponding cash account (*myCash*) increased by one, and the new winnings are displayed. (*P* is set to zero to prevent any cards from being dealt until they are clicked.)

7. Play the *HighCard* game several times. Does your Web browser screen resemble that of Figure 20.5, and did the game work as expected?

   Yes **No**

8. Can each card be dealt (clicked) only once each round of play?

   Yes **No**

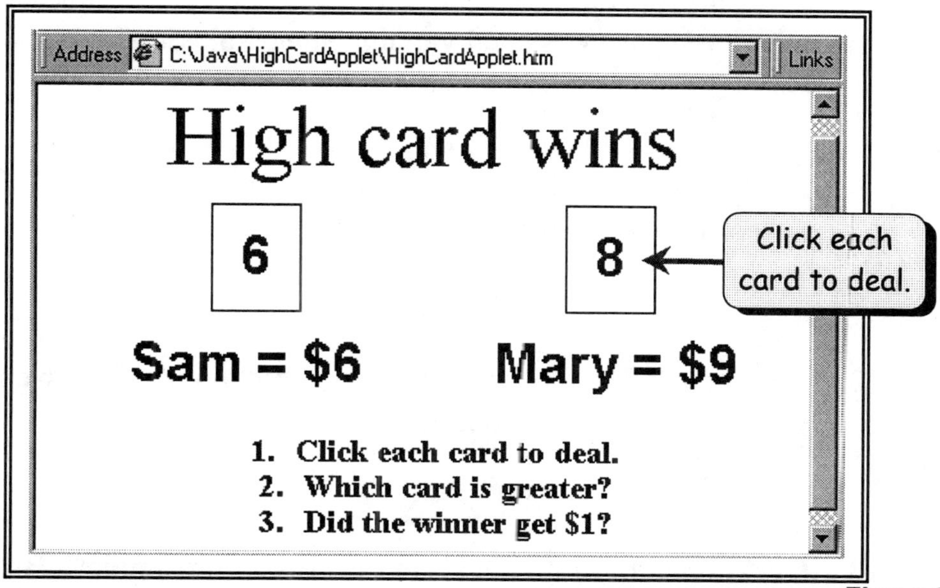

Figure 20.5
HighCardApplet screen output

Applets and breakpoints

Because the browser runs the show, can we ever hope to troubleshoot our applet by singlestepping? Yes, by setting breakpoints. But it has to be done very carefully.

- Do not attempt to singlestep into the browser code.
- Do not set a breakpoint between *draw* statements.

9. First, set permanent breakpoints at the locations shown below. (Position cursor at breakpoint, **CLICKR**, *Insert Breakpoint*.)

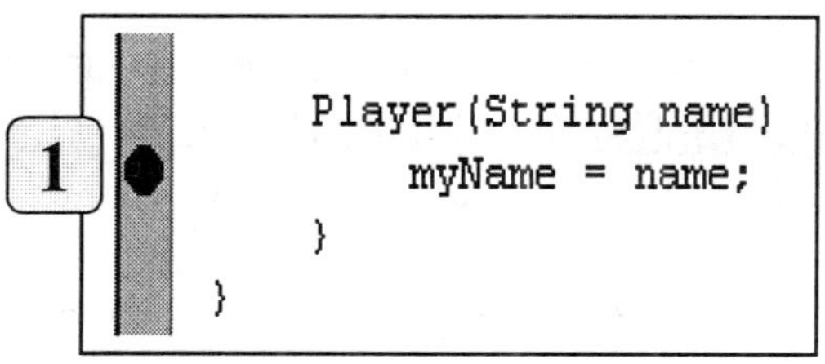

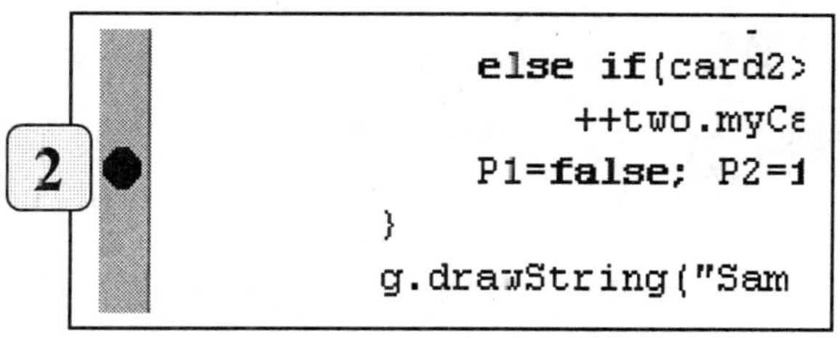

10. Click the *Start* toolbar button to begin execution. Did we break at point 1, and does local variable *name* hold *Sam*?

    Yes **No**

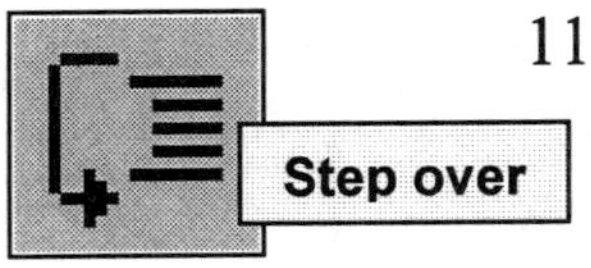

11. By pressing F10 (step over) twice, singlestep out of constructor *Player*. Did we return to method *init*?

    Yes **No**

12. Again click *Start* to run to the next breakpoint. Did we return to constructor *Player*, but this time with name = *Mary*?

    Yes **No**

13. Click *Start* to run to the second and final breakpoint. Bring up the *Explorer* window and play one round. Did we move to the second breakpoint and are all relevant variables (*P*, *P1*, *P2*, *card1*, and *card2*) holding expected values?

    Yes **No**

14. Click *Start* again. Did we play another round and return to the second breakpoint? (Why did we bypass the first breakpoint?)

    Yes **No**

15. Continue this study/troubleshooting process on your own using any variety of breakpoints. If you wish, switch to *Run to Cursor* type breakpoints. (Shift-F5 to exit the debugger.)

Exercises

a) Write an applet that paints a blue circle on the screen at the cursor location whenever the mouse is clicked down. (Hint: Make the *X* and *Y* values set by *mousePressed* global.)

b) Modify the above exercise so old circles remain as new ones are added. (Hint: Use an array to store the pairs of *X*,*Y* values and *repaint* each time.)

c) Each time the mouse button is clicked, an image of a dog (*dog.gif*) and the word "DOG" appear at a random location on the applet screen.

d) Each click of the mouse prints its *X* and *Y* coordinates in large numbers to the center of the screen.

e) Write program *CountUp*, in which a large integer at the center of the applet screen increases by one for each click of the mouse.

f) A square is drawn on the screen. Each click of the mouse causes it to increase slightly in size.

g) Modify f) so each click of the mouse anywhere within the square increases its size; any click outside the square decreases its size.

h) A blue circle is written to the center of the screen. When the left button is clicked, the circle turns red.

i) Modify h) so the circle cycles between blue and red as the mouse is clicked.

j) Write program *BigSmall*, in which "HelloWorld" increases in size when the cursor is moved into the applet area, and decreases in size when the cursor is moved outside the applet area. (Hint: Make use of methods *mouseEntered* and *mouseExited*.)

k) Modify program *BigSmall* so the color also changes. (Hint: Include a "flag" variable within the mouse methods that is tested by an *if* statement within *paint*.)

l) Write an applet that generates a polygon by using method *drawLine* to connect line segments at locations determined by mouse clicks. (Again, use an array to store *x,y* pairs.)

m) Write an applet that asks a multiple-choice question and offers three possible answers. Clicking on any of the answers causes "RIGHT" or "WRONG" to be printed.

n) Write an applet that displays a random number from 1 to 10 each time the mouse is clicked.

o) Modify n) so whenever the number is seven, you win $9; otherwise you lose $1. The cumulative winnings are displayed. The game is over when you win or loose $100.

p) Modify project *HighCard* of this chapter in any of the following ways:

- After both cards are dealt, the winning card turns red.
- Add a third player to the game.
- Using the techniques of Chapter 12, allow J, Q, K, and A to be displayed (in addition to two through nine).
- After each play, the cards are turned over (each card box filled with color). As each card is dealt (clicked), the fill color changes to white and the card value appears.
- The first player to reach $25 is the winner and the game quits.
- Make deuces (twos) wild.
- Show each card increasing in size as it is dealt.

q) When the mouse is clicked, a circle appears at that location on the screen. When the mouse is moved the circle also moves.

r) Write project *ShellGame*, in which two or more walnut shells (circles) appear on the screen. By clicking the mouse, the player is asked to guess which walnut holds the pea (small green circle). The pea appears and any winnings are paid. The pea disappears and play moves to the next round.

s) When the mouse is pressed, a blue circle appears. Holding the left button down causes the circle to be dragged anywhere on the screen. Releasing the button causes the circle to be permanently placed and turns the color of the circle to orange.

t) When the mouse button is pressed, a blue circle appears at a random location. When the button is released, the circle turns orange.

u) When the mouse cursor enters the applet screen, the entry point coordinates are printed to the center of the applet screen.

v) Write an original project that makes use of the *mousePressed*, *mouseEntered*, *mouseExited*, *mouseReleased*, or *mouseClicked* methods.

Questions and Problems

1. What is the difference between methods *mousePressed* and *mouseReleased*?

2. Show how to create an ordered list of four items beginning with the letter c.

3. Can methods *mousePressed* and *mouseMoved* be used in the same program?

4. Method *mouseDown* comes from class *Component*, which is a superclass of class *Applet*.

   True **False**

5. Who calls the *mousePressed* method?

6. In general terms, what changes would have to be made to the project if data member *myCash* of class *Player* were made private?

7. When does the browser call method *mouseEntered*?

8. Can a template class consist of only a single member variable?

   Yes **No**

9. Referring to Figure 20.4, why doesn't method *setFont(myF)* require a reference (and dot operator)?

10. Rewrite the following ternary operation (from Figure 20.4) using the standard long-hand format.

```
P = (e.getX( )<200)? 1:2;
```

11. Referring to Figure 20.4 (step 5), what action is taken when the two cards are the same value?

CHAPTER

21

Project Password

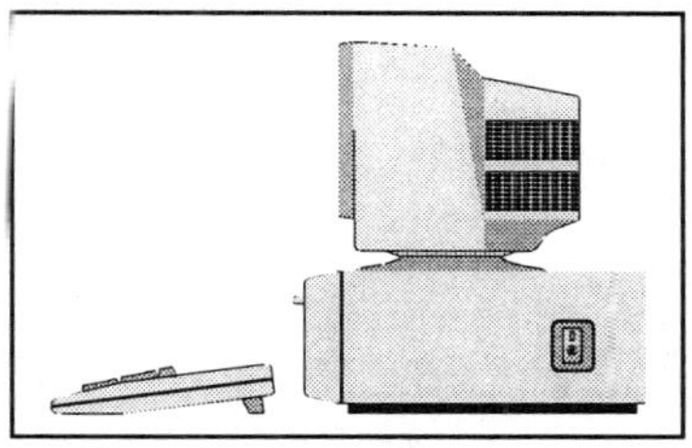

KeyPress Events

Objectives

- *To include the keypress event in our applets*
- *To design a password entry system*

Discussion

As we so clearly learned in the last two chapters, the mouse is an incredibly powerful and versatile device for inputting information from the user. However, there are times when only direct alphanumeric keyboard input will do. To handle this situation, Java gives us the very useful *keyboard event* methods.

Applet update

The class hierarchy for project *PassWord* (Figure 21.1) is very similar to the previous two chapters. Just add interface *KeyListener*, and we have the major change.

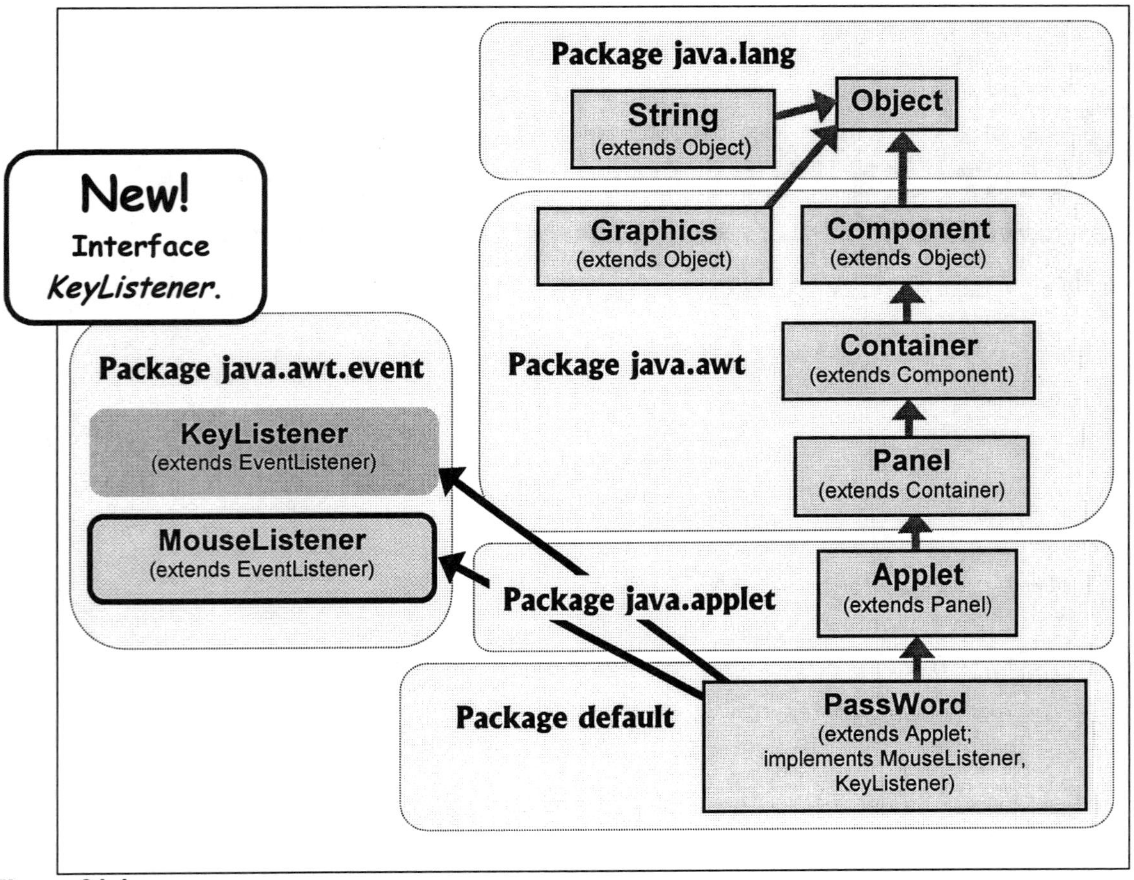

Figure 21.1

Project *PassWord* class hierarchy

Three method signatures belong to interface *KeyListener*.

```
public void keyPressed(KeyEvent e){ };
public void keyReleased(KeyEvent e){ };
public void keyTyped(KeyEvent e){ };
```

The *keyPressed* method is called when a key is pressed down, the *keyReleased* method is called when a key is released, and the *keyTyped* method is called when a key has been typed (pressed and released). Using the appropriate methods of class *KeyEvent* (such as *getKeyChar( )*), we can input individual characters—which are normally collected in an array for convenient display.

However, we must make sure that the characters entered have the right input focus (are associated with *this* applet). To accomplish this we can use the *requestFocus* method from class *Component*—or we can click the output screen at the display position.

HTML style update

Tables

Tables are very useful for displaying organized collections of data. Fortunately, HTML does it easily. The tags used by this chapter to generate tables are given in Table 21.1. The use of these tags can be tricky because they must be nested.

Opening Tag	Closing Tag	Description
<table border=n>	</table>	Table Size of border
<Caption align=direction>	</caption>	Caption top, middle, bottom
<TR align=direction>	</TR>	Table row Left, middle, right
<TH>	</TH>	Table header
<TD>	</TD>	Table data

Table 21.1
HTML table tags

In project *PassWord*, we will generate an HTML table that lists names and passwords.

The password process

The entry of a password is a standard feature of most software products. An entry box first appears on the screen. Characters are then entered from the keyboard until *Enter* is pressed. The resulting character array is converted to a string and compared to the stored password. If correct "You may enter" is printed; if not, "WRONG! Try again" is displayed.

Hands-On Procedure

1. This chapter's project involves keyboard entry.

> **The user enters a string password. The system indicates if the password is correct.**

2. Create project *PassWord* within solution *Chapter21*.

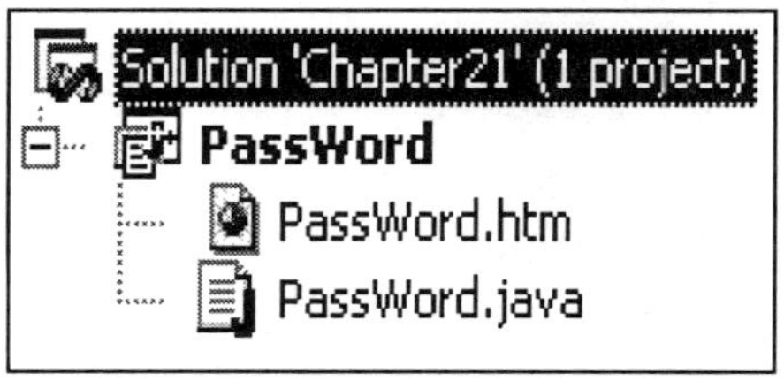

3. Complete HTML file *PassWord.htm* of Figure 21.2.

4. Look over the portion of the code that generates the table.

   a) Realizing that "R" stands for *row*, is it reasonable to conclude that "Name" and "Password" will be side-by-side in the same row?

   Yes **No**

   b) Does the <pre> tag allow us to place spaces between the word entries?

   Yes **No**

```
<HTML>
<HEAD><TITLE>PassWord</TITLE></HEAD>
<BODY><CENTER><FONT face="Book Antiqua" size=7>
It's time to log in</FONT><BR>
<FONT color=maroon face="Comic Sans MS">
Enter your password, press Enter.</FONT>
<APPLET code=PassWord.class
  height=90  name=PassWord  width=400
  VIEWASTEXT>
</APPLET>
<TABLE border=5>
<CAPTION align=top><FONT color=olive size=4>
Password list</FONT></CAPTION>
<TR align=middle>
  <TH><PRE>   Name   </PRE></TH>
  <TH><PRE>   Password   </PRE></TH></TR>
<TR align=middle>
  <TD><PRE> Sam </PRE></TD>
  <TD><PRE> Titanic </PRE></TD></TR>
<TR align=middle>
  <TD><PRE> Mary </PRE></TD>
  <TD><PRE> Titanic </PRE></TD></TR>
  </TABLE></CENTER>
</BODY>
</HTML>
```

New!
Tables.

Figure 21.2
PassWord.htm

5. Next, create applet *PassWord.java* of Figure 21.3.

a) Have we registered our applet as a *KeyListener*?

Yes **No**

b) Are all the abstract methods of the *KeyListener* interface included in the program?

Yes **No**

c) Is method *keyTyped* the only interface method that contains extra code?

Yes **No**

```
import java.awt.*;
import java.applet.*;
import java.awt.event.*;
public class PassWord extends Applet
                implements KeyListener                    1
{
    String pass = "Titanic";                              2
    char[ ] cEntry = new char[50];
    int i;  boolean flag;

    public void init( ){
        setBackground(Color.white);
        setFont(new Font("Arial",Font.BOLD,20));
        addKeyListener(this);                             3
        requestFocus( );
    }

    public void paint(Graphics g){
        g.drawRect(180,10,200,36);
        g.drawString("Enter password:",10,35);            4
        String sEntry = new String(cEntry,0,i);
        g.drawString(sEntry,190,35);
        if(flag == true){
            if(sEntry.equalsIgnoreCase(pass))
                g.drawString("YOU MAY ENTER",110,75);     6
            else
                g.drawString("Wrong! Try again",110,75);
            i=0;
        }
        flag = false;
    }

    public void keyTyped(KeyEvent e){
        cEntry[i++] = e.getKeyChar( );
        if(cEntry[i-1] == 10){
            i--;                                          5
            flag = true;
        }
        repaint( );
    }

    public void keyReleased(KeyEvent e){ }
    public void keyPressed(KeyEvent e){ }
}
```

New! Interface *KeyListener*.

New! *KeyTyped* event.

Figure 21.3

PassWord.java

6. Applet program *PassWord.java* of Figure 21.3 contains a wealth of interesting features. Let's cover them in the order of execution:

   - We implement interface *KeyListener* so its abstract methods can be inherited. 1

   - We set the password ("Titanic") in string *pass*, and we create a 50-element byte array to hold the input characters. 2

   - The browser calls method *init* and we register our applet as a *KeyListener* so the browser can properly call the corresponding event method. We also request that *this* component get the input focus. (The applet screen must be visible for this focus request to be granted.) 3

   - The browser calls *paint*, and the entry box, instructions, and input characters are displayed. Initially, string *sEntry* is empty (null). 4

   > The string genesis statement uses an overloaded constructor that converts a character array (*cEntry*) from element 0 and length *i* to a string.

   - For each key entry of an individual character, the browser calls *keyTyped*. Making use of method *getKeyChar* (from class *KeyEvent*), we enter each character into array *cEntry* and call *repaint*—thereby displaying the input string as it is typed. When done, we press *Enter* (ASCII 10), decrease the length (*i*) by one (to exclude the line feed from conversion), and set variable *flag* to true. 5

   - Using method *equalsIgnoreCase* (from class *String*), we check for the correct entry and respond accordingly. 6

7. Run the program and bring up the Web page of Figure 21.4. (If necessary, scroll to see the full table.)

Figure 21.4
Project *PassWord* Web page

8. Enter the correct password ("Titanic"). Did the system respond correctly (as shown in Figure 21.4)?

   Yes **No**

9. Repeat using an incorrect password. Did the system respond with "Wrong! Try again"?

   Yes **No**

10. Enter the correct password using various combinations of upper and lower case letters. Is the system case sensitive?

    Yes **No**

11. If necessary, scroll the Web page and view the table (Figure 21.4). By referring to *PassWord.htm* of Figure 21.2, determine how the table was created row by row.

> The key to understanding how HTML constructs tables is to concentrate on the rows. Starting at the top, each row is set off with the <TR> and </TR> tags. Within each row, we specify either header (TH) or data (TD) information.

Double entry

> Project *PassWord* includes only a single entry box. However, in a more typical case, the user's name would be entered in addition to the password. To handle such multiple entry boxes, the conventional technique is to require the user to first click the desired box before entering the corresponding data.
>
> Clicking the mouse on the input screen has another purpose: It gives the screen the input focus. This means that all input data will go to *this* applet screen (rather than another component or screen that may contain an input method).

10. Modify program *Password* as listed in Figure 21.5.

    a) Add code to generate two entry boxes (shown in Figure 21.6). 1

    b) Implement a *MouseListener* event and return the *Y*-axis click value from *mousePressed* (or *mouseTyped*). 2

    > The *requestFocus* command is needed only if you are using JDK's *appletViewer*.

    c) If Y < 50, characters entered from the keyboard go to the *name* array; otherwise characters entered go to the *password* array. The corresponding flag is set to *true*. 3

    d) Print the name or password as the characters are being entered. 4

    e) If both boxes have been clicked and data entered (both flags are true), we determine the entry condition. 5

```
import java.awt.*;
import java.applet.*;
import java.awt.event.*;
public class PassWordMultiple extends Applet
                              implements KeyListener,MouseListener
{
    String pass = "Titanic";
    String name = "Sam";
    char[ ] cEntryPass = new char[50];
    char[ ] cEntryName = new char[50];
    int i,j,Y;
    boolean passFlag,nameFlag;

    public void init( ){
        setBackground(Color.white);
        setFont(new Font("Arial",Font.BOLD,20));
        addKeyListener(this);
        addMouseListener(this);
    }

    public void paint(Graphics g){
        g.drawRect(180,10,200,36);
  1     g.drawString("Enter name:",10,35);
        g.drawRect(180,60,200,36);
        g.drawString("Enter password:",10,85);
        String sEntryName = new String(cEntryName,0,i);
  4     String sEntryPass = new String(cEntryPass,0,j);
        g.drawString(sEntryName,190,35);
        g.drawString(sEntryPass,190,85);
        if(passFlag && nameFlag){
            if((sEntryName.equalsIgnoreCase(name))&&
               (sEntryPass.equalsIgnoreCase(pass)))
                g.drawString("YOU MAY ENTER",110,125);
  5         else
                g.drawString("WRONG! Try again",110,125);
            i=0;
            j=0;
            nameFlag = false;
            passFlag = false;
        }
    }
```

Continued on the next page.

Figure 21.5

PassWord.java
(continued on the next page)

Continued from the previous page.

```
    public void keyTyped(KeyEvent e){
        if(Y < 50){
            cEntryName[i++] = e.getKeyChar( );
            if(cEntryName[i-1] == 10){
                i--;
                nameFlag = true;
            }
        }
        else{
            cEntryPass[j++] = e.getKeyChar( );
            if(cEntryPass[j-1] == 10){
                j--;
                passFlag = true;
            }
        }
        repaint( );
    }

    public void mousePressed(MouseEvent e){
        Y = e.getY( );
        // requestFocus( );
    }

    public void mouseClicked(MouseEvent e){ }
    public void mouseReleased(MouseEvent e){ }
    public void mouseEntered(MouseEvent e){ }
    public void mouseExited(MouseEvent e){ }
    public void keyReleased(KeyEvent e){ }
    public void keyPressed(KeyEvent e){ }
}
```

3

New! Clicking the mouse to give the input focus.

2

Only required for JDK's *AppletViewer*.

Figure 21.5
PassWord.java
(continued from the previous page)

11) Execute the program. Click each box and enter data, making sure to press *Enter* when done with each entry. As shown in Figure 21.6, are you allowed entry only after both the user name (Sam) and the password (Titanic) have been entered?

Yes **No**

Figure 21.6

Project *PassWordMultiple* correct entry sequence

Exercises

a) Write an applet in which simple keyboard entry is written to the screen location clicked by the mouse. (Hint: Override *mousePressed* as shown below and use *drawChars*.)

```
public void mousePressed(MouseEvent e){
      X = e.getX( );
      Y = e.getY( );
      repaint( );
}
```

b) As each key is pressed, the *single* corresponding character is printed to the center of the screen in large text.

c) Write project *ShoppingSpree*, which presents four or more images of items for sale arranged in a grid. You click on the item you want to purchase and enter the number of units desired. The system keeps track of and displays the total cumulative bill.

d) Write a program that shows two entry rectangles. By clicking each in succession, enter an integer into each. The product of the integers is displayed.

e) Modify program *PassWord* of this chapter in any or all of the following ways:

- Two or more passwords will allow entry.
- The password is case sensitive.
- A separate password for the manager and another for the user.
- Allow for several users, each with a unique user and password strings.
- When the entry box is clicked, an entry cursor (vertical line) shows the point of entry. Hint: Change the password to "|Titanic" and override *mousePressed* as shown below.

```
public void mousePressed(MouseEvent e){
      cEntry[l++] = '|';
      count++;
      repaint( );
}
```

- Three false entries and the system permanently locks you out (unless you enter the special manager's password.)

f) Write project *SailBoat*, which presents a graphical representation of a sailboat, complete with several sails. You click the sail and enter its name (main, spinnaker, jib, etc.). The system responds, "RIGHT" or "WRONG."

g) Write project *Jeopardy*, in which two or more answers are given. You click the desired answer and enter the question. The system responds with "correct" or "incorrect."

h) Modify project *HighCardApplet* of the previous chapter to allow entry of bets.

i) Write project *Censored*, which looks at the characters entered from the keyboard and replaces every number (0–9) with an *x*.

j) Modify i) so all four-letter words are blanked out.

k) Modify project *PassWordMultiple* so the name must be entered before the password.

l) Design a game or display of your own choosing.

Questions and Problems

1. What is the difference between methods *keyPressed* and *keyTyped*?

2. Regarding HTML tag TR, what does the "R" stand for?

3. Before the *keyTyped* method becomes active, it must be preceded by a mouse event or a *requestFocus* method.

   True **False**

4. Using a design of your choice, create a table that shows the high and low temperatures for every weekday (Monday–Friday) in a week.

5. What would happen to program execution if we failed to register our applet as a *KeyListener*?

6. Referring to Figure 21.3, why is *requestFocus* required for a *keyTyped* event, but not for a *mouseMoved* event?

7. When we press key "7," what is input by method *getKeyChar*?

8. Regarding project *PassWord* of Figure 21.3, would the user notice any difference if *keyReleased* or *keyPressed* were used (instead of *keyTyped*)?

9. After running the following program, what do you believe is accomplished by methods *getKeycode()* and *getKeyText(int)* (both from class *KeyEvent*)?

```
import java.awt.*;
import java.applet.*;
import java.awt.event.*;
public class TestApplet extends Applet implements KeyListener
{
    String keyString;

    public void init( ){
            addKeyListener(this);
            requestFocus( );
    }

    public void paint(Graphics g){
            g.drawString(keyString,20,20);
    }

    public void keyPressed(KeyEvent e){
            keyString = e.getKeyText(e.getKeyCode( ));
            repaint( );
    }
    public void keyReleased(KeyEvent e){}
    public void keyTyped(KeyEvent e){}
}
```

CHAPTER

22

Project Home Run

The Abstract Window Toolkit

Objectives

- *To overview the Abstract Window Toolkit*
- *To incorporate buttons and fields into our project*
- *To take a baseball quiz*

Discussion

When we use VJ6's *Visual Studio*, we are using a graphical user interface (GUI). A GUI takes full advantage of the human preference for gathering and disseminating information by visual means. Clearly, any viable language must give us a way of designing programs for windows.

The Abstract Window Toolkit (AWT)

To create windows programs with an object-oriented language, what could be more logical than to gather all the required classes and place them into a special package. That package is known as the *Abstract Window Toolkit* (AWT)—part of Java's Core API. We have made good use of several of its classes in previous projects.

Table 22.1 shows that package AWT includes a very large number of classes. When we consider that these classes are arranged in a hierarchy and that each class holds many methods, the task before us seems downright mindboggling.

The classes of package AWT		
BorderLayout	FileDialog	Menu
Button	FlowLayout	MenuBar
Canvas	Font	Panel
CardLayout	FontMetrics	Point
Checkbox	Frame	MenuComponent
CheckboxGroup	Graphics	MenuItem
CheckboxMenuItem	GridBagConstraints	Polygon
Choice	GridBagLayout	Rectangle
Color	GridLayout	Scrollbar
Component	Image	TextArea
Container	Insets	TextComponent
Dialog	Label	TextField
Dimension	List	Toolkit
Event	MediaTracker	Window

Table 22.1

The classes of package *AWT*

Components

To simplify and narrow our scope, the key word is *component*. Windows are made up of component objects arranged in a hierarchy: Frames, dialog boxes, buttons, menus, lists, choices, checkboxes, scrollbars, textboxes, other windows, etc. Is it any wonder that class *Component* of Figure 22.1 is the superclass of most of the classes involved in constructing windows?

In this chapter, we will limit ourselves to the shaded subclasses of superclass *Component*.

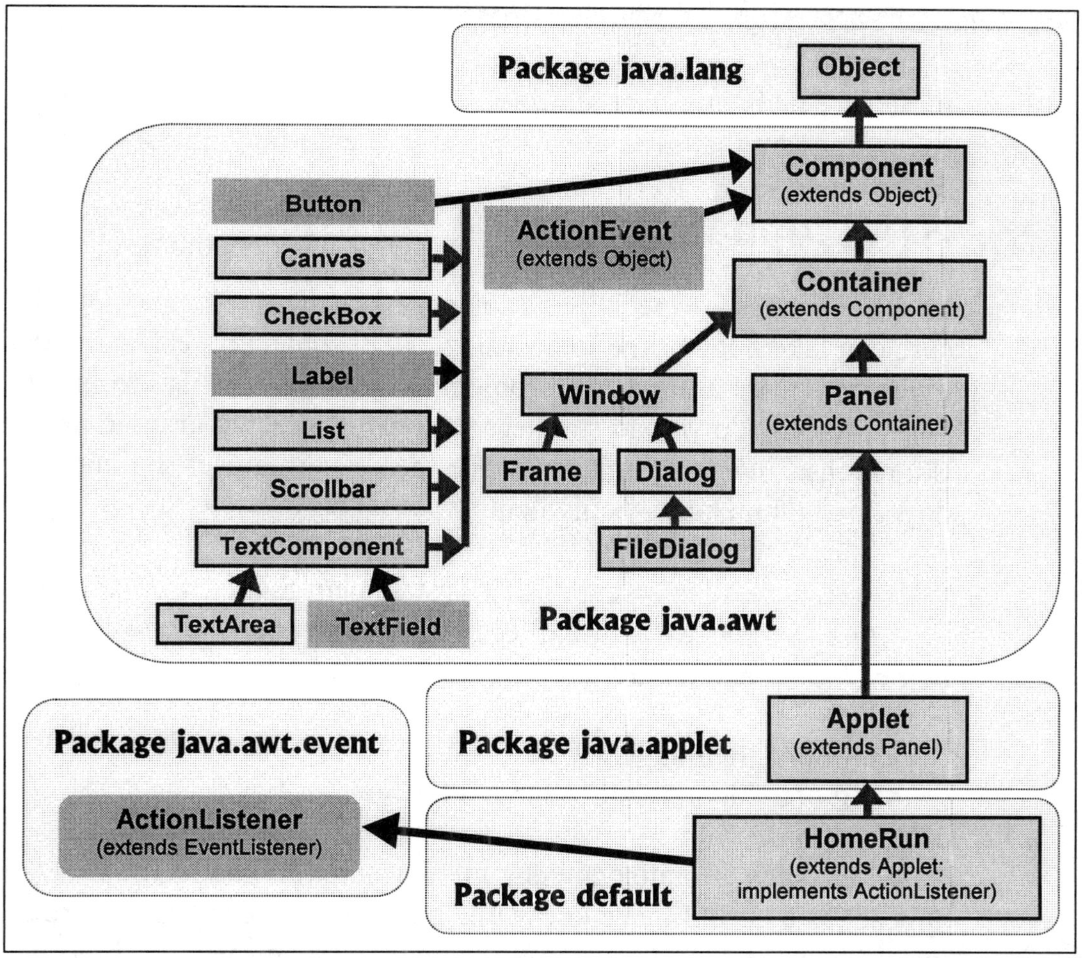

Figure 22.1
Project *HomeRun* class hierarchy

Loosely speaking, a car is a *container* holding a hierarchy of *components*. Some components are complex (such as the engine) and others are simple (such as the gearshift). The same can be said of window objects. The complex components are generally subclasses of *Container*, and the simple components are subclasses of *Component*. Ironically, a Container is also a Component.

With applets, it's the browser that creates the complex applet window container by default. Therefore, we will restrict ourselves in this chapter to filling it with the simple components of classes *buttons*, *labels*, and *text fields*.

- *Buttons* and labels are created from class *Button* and class *Label*, and are normally part of a toolbar. When we click on the button, some action is taken.
- Text Fields are created from class *TextField*. A text field is a component that gives the user a way of entering and editing text.

HTML update

Graphic images—especially large ones—are nice to look at, but they sure can take a long time to download. This chapter's HTML update gives us a way around the problem: When we download our Web page, we only download smaller versions of selected graphic images (known as *Thumbnail* images). We then give the user the option of downloading its larger equivalent.

It's all done with a single HTML statement that closely resembles a *hotlink*, a topic we will explore in the next chapter. (In the code below, "a" refers to *anchor*.)

```
<a href="LImage.gif">
<img src="SImage.gif" align = left>Click for full image.</a>
```

When such a statement is run, the smaller image (*Simage.gif*) appears as a hotlink. We know this because a border appears around the image, and "Click for full image" is turned to blue and underlined. If we click the hotlink, a new window is opened and the large image (*Limage.gif*) is fully displayed. Pressing "Back" returns the user to the original Web page.

Hands-On Procedure

This project is really two projects in one. The first deals with *buttons* and *labels*, and the second includes *text fields*.

1. Our first project involves a multiple-choice question about baseball.

> **Project 1: A component label asks the question, "How many home runs did Babe Ruth hit?" When the correct button is clicked, label "RIGHT" is written to the window.**

2. Create project *HomeRun* within solution *Chapter22*.

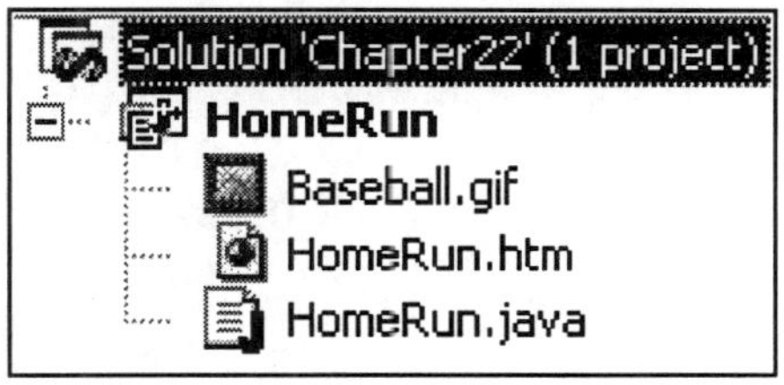

3. Create *HomeRun.htm* of Figure 22.2.

```
<HTML>
<head><title>HomeRun</title></head>
<BODY bgColor=white>
<CENTER><FONT size=7 color=navy>Home Run Quiz</FONT>
<HR>
 <APPLET
   code=HomeRun.class  name=HomeRun
   height=40  width=520  VIEWASTEXT>
</APPLET>
<HR>
<A href="Baseball.gif">
<IMG src="Baseball.gif">Click for full image.</A>
<FONT size=4 color=olive><P>
Babe Ruth hit his home runs<BR>in 8,399 times at bat.
</FONT></CENTER></P></BODY>
</HTML>
```

Thumbnail hotlink. For testing purposes, both images are the same.

New!
Thumbnail images.

Figure 22.2
Including a Thumbnail image

4. Create *HomeRun.java* of Figure 22.3.

```
import java.awt.*;
import java.applet.*;
import java.awt.event.*;
public class HomeRun extends Applet implements ActionListener
{
     String s = "How many home runs did Babe Ruth hit?";
     private Label Question = new Label(s);
     private Button Choice1 = new Button("688");
     private Button Choice2 = new Button("709");
     private Button Choice3 = new Button("740");
     private Label Response = new Label("                    ");

     public void init( ){
          Choice1.addActionListener(this);
          Choice2.addActionListener(this);
          Choice3.addActionListener(this);
          setBackground(Color.white);
          Font F=new Font("Arial",Font.BOLD,15);
          setFont(F);
          add(Question);
          add(Choice1);
          add(Choice2);
          add(Choice3);
          add(Response);
     }

     public void actionPerformed(ActionEvent e){
          Button buttonEvent = (Button)e.getSource( );
          String answer = buttonEvent.getLabel( );
          SetForeground(Color.red);
          if(answer.compareTo("740")==0)
               Response.setText("RIGHT!");
          else
               Response.setText("WRONG");
     }
}
```

1 — Make room for the text.

2

New! Button and Label components.

3 — All components are rectangles.

4

5

6

Interface *ActionListener* contains only a single abstract method (*actionPerformed*).

Figure 22.3
The button and label Applet

5. An analysis of the program follows four chronological stages: Create the components, register the components, add the components, and process the events.

   - First, two label and three button components are created by genesis statements. The button components are initialized with multiple choice selections. 1

   - Each button belonging to *this* applet is registered. (The labels are not action components and are not registered.) 2

Registering individual components makes it easier for the browser to efficiently respond to a specific action item.

   - Next, the labels and buttons are added to the browser window. (Placement is from left to right and top to down in the order listed.) 3

   - When a button is clicked, the browser checks for the proper registration, calls overriding method *actionPerformed* (from interface class *ActionListener*), and passes a reference to an object of class *ActionEvent*. 4

   - Using method *getSource* (inherited from class *EventObject*), we obtain the generic event object. Because we are sure that the generic actionEvent came from a button, we immediately cast it to type *Button*. Reference *buttonEvent* now points to the specific button that was clicked. 5

Two references now point to the one clicked button: *buttonEvent* and the chosen reference.

   - We use method *getLabel* (from class *Button*), to obtain the button's label as a string object. We compare this string object to "740," and make use of method *setText* (from class *Label*) to print "RIGHT" if the correct button was selected, and "WRONG" otherwise. 6

6. Run the program and note the screen output (Figure 22.4).

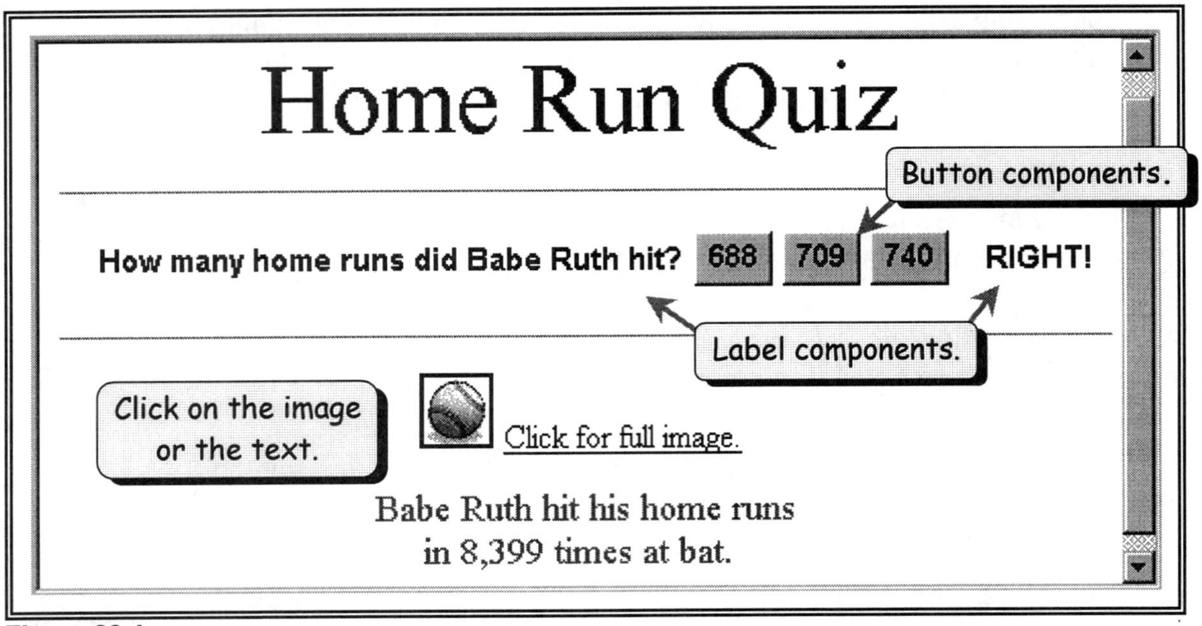

Figure 22.4
Home Run Web page

7. Click the three buttons. Is "RIGHT" displayed when "740" is clicked, and is "WRONG" displayed otherwise?

   Yes **No**

8. By dragging either side of the applet window, change its size. Were the components automatically rearranged from left to right and top to bottom?

   Yes **No**

9. Next we test the thumbnail image.

   a) Move the cursor over the text or the small baseball icon hotlink. Does a small hotlink "hand" appear?

      Yes **No**

   b) Click the hotlink. Do we jump to another full window and does the "larger" image (if we had one) appear?

      Yes **No**

   c) Click the *Back* arrow. Do we return to the Web page?

      Yes **No**

Project 2: In this second project, we switch to *TextField* components in order to input data from the keyboard. Specifically, we input our name and respond to another baseball question about home run hitting. (Watch for a way to lay out the components.)

10. Add project *HomeRun2* to solution *Chapter22*.

11. Create file *HomeRun2.htm* of Figure 22.5

> If you wish, include the thumbnail sketch of project *HomeRun* (Figure 22.2).

```
<HTML>
<HEAD><TITLE>Home Run Two</TITLE></HEAD>
<BODY bgColor=white>
<CENTER><FONT size=7 color=navy>Home Run Quiz II</FONT>
<HR><APPLET
   code=HomeRun2.class  name=HomeRun2
   height=55  width=520  VIEWASTEXT>
</APPLET><HR>
<FONT size=4 color=olive>
Press Enter after each entry. <BR>When answering the quiz
be sure to enter the full name.</FONT> </CENTER>
</BODY>
</HTML>
```

Figure 22.5
HomeRun2.htm

12. Next, create applet *HomeRun2.java* of Figure 22.6.

    How many of each of the following components were added to the applet window?

    Labels _______

    TextFields _______

```
import java.awt.*;
import java.applet.*;
import java.awt.event.*;
public class HomeRun2 extends Applet implements ActionListener
{
    String s1 = "What is your name?";
    private Label askName = new Label(s1);
    private TextField textName = new TextField(20);
    private Label respondName = new Label("            ");
    String s = "Who broke Babe's record?";
    private Label askBroke = new Label(s);
    private TextField textBroke = new TextField(20);
    private Label respondBroke = new Label("            ");

    public void init( ){
        textName.addActionListener(this);
        textBroke.addA ctionListener(this);
        setBackground(Color.white);
        Font F = new Font("Arial",Font.BOLD,13);
        setFont(F);
        setLayout(new GridLayout(2,3,5,5));
        add(askName) ;
        add(textName);
        add(respondName);
        add(askBroke);
        add(textBroke);
        add(respondBroke);
    }

    public void actionPerformed(ActionEvent e){
        String name, answer;
        SetForeground(Color.blue);
        TextField textEvent = (TextField)e.getSource( );
        if(textEvent == textName){
            name = textName.getText( );
            respondName.setText("Hello "+name);
        }
        if(textEvent == textBroke){
            answer = textBroke.getText( );
            if(answer.compareTo("Hank Aaron")==0)
                respondBroke.setText("RIGHT!");
            else
                respondBroke.setText("WRONG");
        }
    }
}
```

New! Text field components. (1)

(2)

New! Component layout. (3)

(4)

(5)

(6)

Figure 22.6

HomeRun2.java

13. The highlights of applet *HomeRun2* are as follows:

   - We create six component objects: Four labels and two text fields. Each text field is initialized to hold 20 characters. 1

   - We register the two text fields to the *ActionListener* system. (They are the only components that react to external events.) 2

   - Next we add a new twist: We call upon the layout manager to place the six components in a two-row by three-column grid, with five-pixel spacing between rows and columns. As shown, method *setLayout* (from class *Container*) receives an object of class *GridLayout* by way of constructor *GridLayout(2,3,5,5)*. 3

   - Next, we add the six new objects. As shown below, they are added to the grid in the order in which they are listed, left to right and top to bottom. 4

1	2	3
4	5	6

   - When an event occurs, we are sure it is a *TextField* event so we cast the incoming *ActionEvent* reference to a *textEvent* reference. 5

> Two references now point to the one active *TextField*: (1) *textEvent*; and (2) *textName* or *textBroke*.

   - If the *textEvent* is the name input (*textName*), we read the name with *Textfield* method *getText* into string *name*. Using *Label* method *setText*, we write "Hello ______" to label *respondName*. If the *textEvent* is the response input (*textBroke*), we read the input and compare to the correct answer (Hank Aaron). If correct, we print "RIGHT," otherwise we print "WRONG." 6

14. Run the program and note the screen output (Figure 22.7).

   a) Are the six components laid out in a two by three grid with five-pixel spacing?

      Yes **No**

b) After entering your name in the *name* field, does it respond with “Hello _________”?

Yes **No**

c) After entering various answers to the question (including the correct answer), does the system properly respond?

Yes **No**

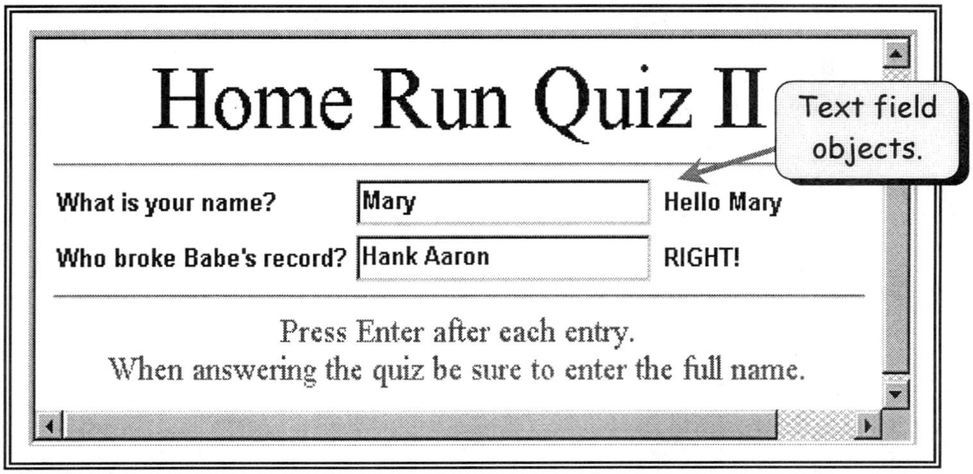

Figure 22.7
HomeRun2
Web page

Mixing buttons and textfields

So far, each of our two projects has involved all buttons and labels (phase 1) and all text fields and labels (phase 2). In other words, only one type of action event. In this section, it will be primarily your responsibility to create a project that combines both types of action events (buttons and text fields).

15. Project *Combination* will use a label to ask, “Man or woman?” The user will click either the *man* or *woman* button. A label will ask, “Your name?” A text field will get the name. Using another label the system responds “Hello Mr. __________” or “Hello Ms. __________”.

Hint

When an action event occurs within project *Combination*, we must first determine what type of action event it is (i.e., button or text field?). This we do using the *instanceof* operator. By adding the following code within your program, complete the project.

```
public void actionPerformed(ActionEvent e){
    Object  whatEvent = e.getSource( );
    If(whatEvent  instanceof  Button){
        Button buttonEvent = (Button)whatEvent;

        <additional Button code here>

    }
    if(whatEvent  instanceof  TextField){
        Textfield textEvent = (TextField)whatEvent;

        <additional TextField code here>

    }
```

whatEvent is upcast to type *Object* temporarily. (Just as <u>any</u> animal can be assigned to type "kingdom" temporarily.)

If *whatEvent* is also of type *TextField*, cast it accordingly.

ESPRESSO

Why didn't we create a container component to hold our button and text fields?

All components have a parent container. Since containers are really components that hold other components, class *Container* is derived from class *Component*.

We could have created our own container component, but we didn't have to because the Web page automatically generated its own when the applet was called.

Exercises

a) Add a fourth choice (such as 792) to the applet of Figure 22.3.

b) Create two buttons labeled "blue" and "yellow." Whenever the blue button is clicked, a circle below the buttons turns blue; whenever the yellow button is clicked, the circle turns yellow.

c) Create two buttons labeled "Sam" and "Mary" and a label. When each is clicked, "Hello Sam" or "Hello Mary" is displayed in the label.

d) Create a label that asks "What is the password?" If a text field inputs the correct word, "Access allowed" is printed; otherwise "Access denied" is printed.

e) Modify the above project so the user is allowed four tries before he or she is locked out.

f) Create two buttons (labeled "true" and "false"), a label, and a text field. One label states, "We landed on the moon in 1969." The reader clicks true or false and the system responds RIGHT or WRONG.

g) Create an applet of two labels and two text fields. However, the second pair only appears if the response to the first is correct. For example, ask for a name only if a password is correct.

h) Create an applet that offers a number of labeled buttons representing items to purchase over the Web. As each object is selected, its price is shown. When "done" is clicked, the total cost is displayed.

> Special note: The Microsoft *Windows Foundation Classes* (WFC) that come with VJ6 are generally considered to be an enhancement and replacement for the conventional AWT. Should they become a widely accepted standard, they would make an excellent advanced follow-on course of study after working with the simpler AWT of this text.

Questions and Problems

1. The AWT is a package.

   True **False**

2. Class *Graphics* is part of the AWT package.

   True **False**

3. Classes *Button* and *Label* extend what superclass?

4. Write "input" or "output" after each of the following:

   Button __________

   Label __________

   Text Field __________

5. Given the following HTML tag, circle the thumbnail image file.

```
<a href= "image1.gif"><img src= "image2.gif">Click for full image.</a>
```

6. A *hotlink* can be either text or image.

   True **False**

7. Can the keyboard input to a text field be edited (changed before it is accepted with *Enter*)?

   Yes **No**

8. How does the *instanceof* operator differ from the *equal to* (==) operator?

9. Although not often done, windows (frames) can be added to applets. Predict what the following code will perform and then confirm your predictions by running the code.

```
Frame myFrame = new Frame( );
Label myLabel = new Label("Hello, I am a window frame");

public void init( ){
    myFrame.setVisible(true);
    myFrame.setSize(200,100);
    myFrame.add(myLabel);
}
```

Part 6
Advanced Features

What sets a Web page apart is the use of exceptional features that make the presentation special.

In the five chapters of Part 6, we will look at *hotlinks*, *multiple applets*, *multithreading*, *animation*, *sound*, and *dynamic HTML*.

CHAPTER

23

Project Tourist

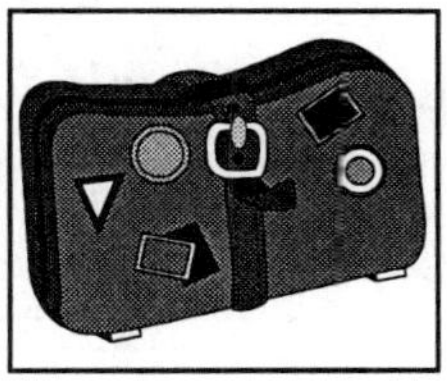

Hotlinks

Objectives

- *To write HTML programs that are associated by hotlinks*
- *To write an advertising page for foreign travel*

Discussion

In the last several chapters, we concentrated on making our Web pages more colorful, appealing, and attractive. This we did by liberally sprinkling them with style tags, and by including applets to provide motion and interaction.

Hotlinks and URLs

Now we turn our attention at long last to the real purpose of the Internet: The ability to jump to other Web pages—anywhere in the world! This is known as a *hotlink*. Hotlinks make the World Wide Web (WWW) appear to be a single computer, with all Web pages stored at one location.

Hotlinks are strictly an HTML service, and applets are not directly involved. Therefore, the class hierarchy of Figure 23.1 offers no new classes.

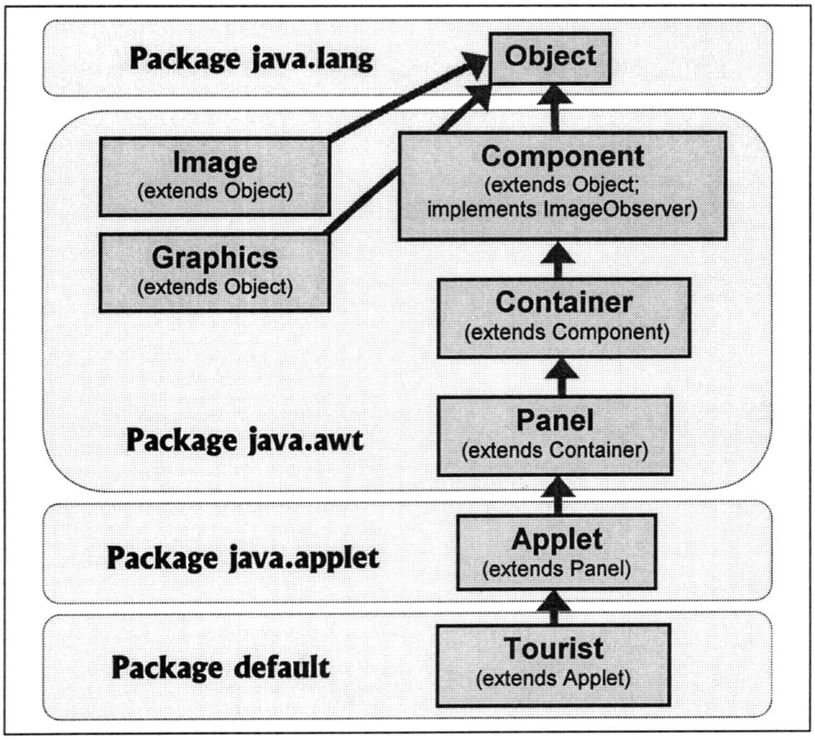

Figure 23.1
Project *Tourist* class hierarchy

There are two types of hotlinks: *text* and *image*. Both are established with the special tags of Table 23.1.

Opening Tag	Closing Tag	Description
<A HREF="file.html"> text OR <IMG SRC="file.gif">	</A>	Anchor/Hypertext reference hotlink text OR graphics hotlink

Table 23.1
HTML hotlink tags

The following generic hotlinks show how the tags are used. The first is a text hotlink and the second is an image (graphics) hotlink.

```
<A HREF= "http://www.myserver.com/myfile.htm">myhome</A>
```

```
<A HREF="http://www.myserver.com/myfile.htm"><IMG SRC="myhome.gif"></A>
```

When the browser executes the text hotlink, "myhome" appears in blue and is underlined. When we **CLICKL** anywhere on this hotlink, the WWW system searches for the proper page and brings it into our computer for execution and display.

When the image hotlink is executed, image *myhome.gif* appears on the Web page with a blue border. When we **CLICKL** anywhere on the image, we activate the hotlink. The process of jumping from one page to another using these hotlinks is known as *surfing*.

The URL

The string "http://www.myserver.com/myfile.htm" is the URL (Uniform Resource Locator) of the target page.

- *Http:* (*hypertext transport protocol*) specifies the service that will transfer the documents across the Web.

- *WWW.myserver.com* is the name of the host computer (or server) that holds the information. (The ending letters *com* signify a commercial site.)

- *myfile.htm* is the file name of the Web page. (If this file name is left out, the system searches for a default home page.)

> If a target HTML page is simply another file on your computer, and is not part of the formal WWW system, the URL is simply the directory/file pathway.

Hypertext and world travel

Hypertext is a hierarchical approach to linking documents. It provides a novel method of giving us information at just the right level of concept versus detail.

As a case in point, this chapter's project presents us with a high-level Web page on world traveling. During our reading of this page, we find hotlinks to France and Egypt. Each hotlink can be text or graphics or both.

> Any text or image can be a hotlink to another Web page.

The bottom line is that we are offered the option of surfing to another Web page to obtain more detail on France and its vineyards or Egypt and its pyramids (and perhaps returning to our Web page when done).

Do you see how hypertext works? As we drop down the hierarchy, clicking hotlinks as we go, the material gets more and more focused and detailed. As we return up to the higher levels, the pages become more and more broad and general. In other words, the reader chooses the level of detail desired at each place in any document.

File structure

When we surf to another Web page, the target file is generally on another computer—indeed, it may even be in another country. To simulate this real world case on a single computer, we will place the source and target Web pages in separate projects. (If you wish, place them in separate solutions.)

Flags anyone?

While pondering the subject of world travel, we get a bright idea: The flags of the world would make perfect graphics hotlinks for a Web page on international travel. And that's exactly what we do in this chapter.

We create a master Web page called *World*, complete with an eye-catching applet. Web page *World* offers two flag hotlinks to Web pages called *France* and *Egypt*—each with its own applet graphics. (Actually, only *France* is made hot; *Egypt* is left as an exercise.)

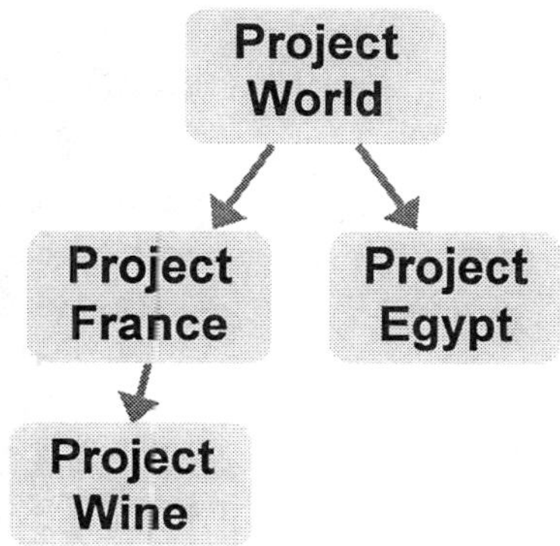

As an additional exercise, we can create Web page *Wine* and place a hypertext hotlink from page *France* to page *Wine*. Clearly, we could continue this process indefinitely (*Wine* to *Burgundy*?).

Hands-On Procedure

1. This chapter's project includes two Web pages.

> **A high-level Web page on world travel is hotlinked to a lower-level Web page on France. Both Web pages include eye-catching applets.**

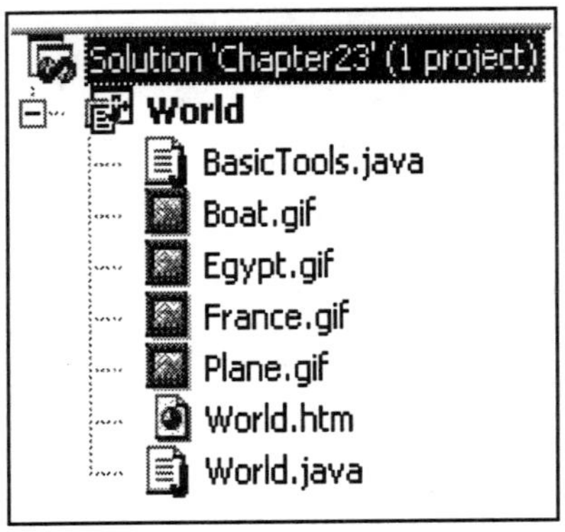

Web page *World*

2. Create project *World* within solution *Chapter23*. Be sure to add and rename all required files.

   - France.gif and Egypt.gif are used as hotlinks in the HTML file.

   - Boat.gif and Plane.gif are to be used for applet enhancement.

3. Complete HTML file *world.htm* of Figure 23.2.

```
<HTML><HEAD>
<TITLE>World Travel</TITLE>
</HEAD><BODY><CENTER>
<FONT size=8 color=olive>World Travel</FONT>
<HR SIZE=5>
<APPLET
   code=World.class
   name=World
   height=70  width=320  VIEWASTEXT>
</APPLET>
<HR SIZE=5>
<FONT size=4 color=navy>
You can get most anywhere by boat or by plane.
</CENTER><P>
<IMG SRC="Egypt.gif" align=left hspace=30>
Egypt is known for the great Nile river that<BR>
flows beside the Valley of the Kings.
<P><A href="C:\Java\France\France.htm">
<IMG SRC="France.gif" align=left hspace=30></A>
<A href="C:\java\France\France.htm">France</A> is
known for its wine country and for <BR>its great
cities. The skiing isn't bad either!</FONT>
</P>
</BODY>
</HTML>
```

This is the home page.

Be sure these pathways are correct.

Image hotlink.

Text hotlink.

New! Hotlinks.

Figure 23.2
World.htm

4. Reviewing *world.htm* of Figure 23.2:

   a) What is the URL of the target Web page (*France.htm*)?

   b) What is the text hotlink, that is, the word or phrase that will be blue and underlined?

   c) What is the graphics hotlink (the image that will have a blue border)?

5. Complete applet file *world.java* of Figure 23.3.

   a) What two gif images are used by the applet?

   b) Is the applet involved in any way in the hotlink process?

      Yes **No**

   c) Could we have used a *MediaTracker*?

      Yes **No**

   d) Why was the use of a *MediaTracker* unnecessary?

```
import java.awt.*;
import java.applet.*;
public class World extends Applet
{
      Image boat,plane;

      public void init( ){
            boat=getImage(getDocumentBase( ),"boat.gif");
            plane=getImage(getDocumentBase( ),"plane.gif");
            setBackground(Color.white);
      }

      public void paint(Graphics g){
            int i,j;
            for(i=0;i<4;i++){
                  for(j=0;j<8;j++){
                        g.drawImage(boat,160-20*j,0,10*j,10*j,this);
                        BasicTools.msec(150);
                        g.clearRect(160-20*j,0,10*j,10*j);
                  }
                  for(j=0;j<8;j++){
                        g.drawImage(plane,160+10*j,0,10*j,10*j,this);
                        BasicTools.msec(150);
                        g.clearRect(160+10*j,0,10*j,10*j);
                  }
            }
            g.drawImage(boat,20,0,80,70,this);
            g.drawImage(plane,230,0,80,70,this);
      }
}
```

New!
Zooming images.

Images will remain after zoom is done.

Figure 23.3
World.java

6. Execute *World.htm* and observe the Explorer window (Figure 23.4).

   a) Is the expected URL shown in the *Address* window?

      Yes **No**

b) When the cursor is moved over either the text or graphics hotlinks, does a "hand" appear and does the target URL appear at the lower-left of the Web explorer window?

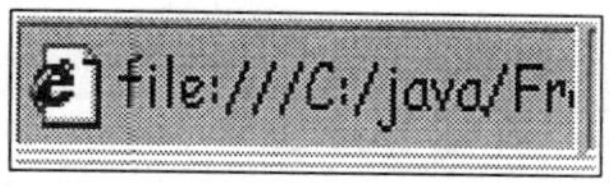

Yes **No**

c) Does the applet (*World.java*) show a zooming ship and plane?

Yes **No**

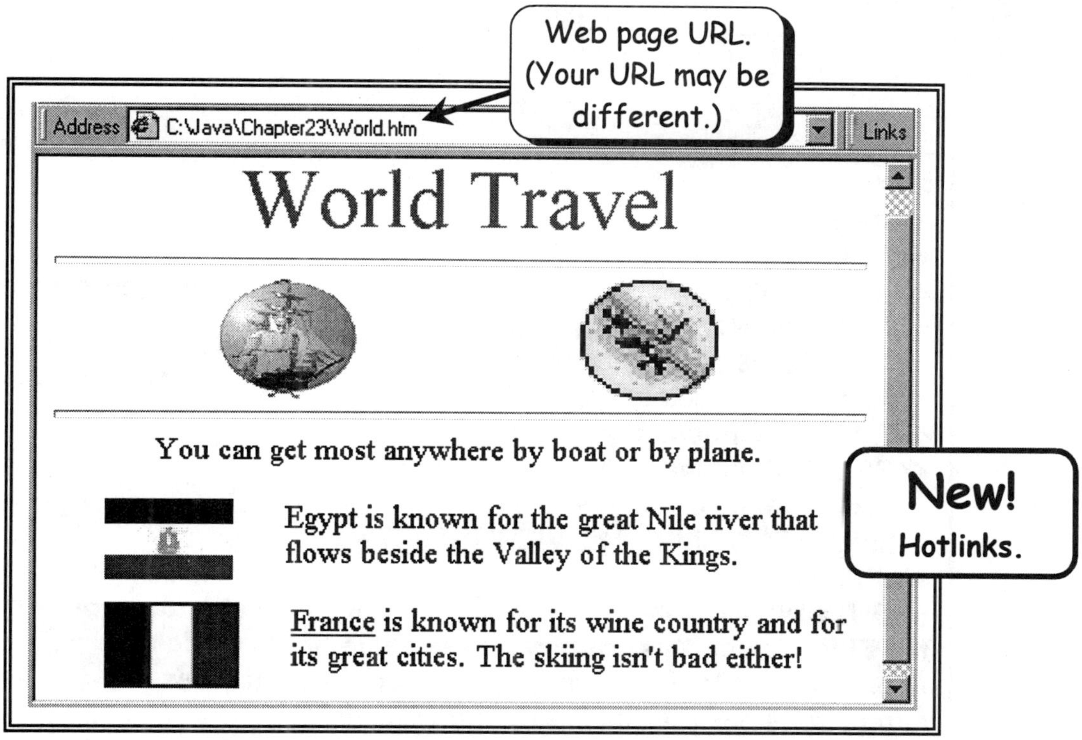

Figure 23.4
Web page *World*

7. If you wish, **CLICKL** on either hotlink (but remember that the target Web page has not yet been created). Did a message appear indicating that the target page was not found?

Yes **No**

8. Exit the Web page *World.htm* when done.

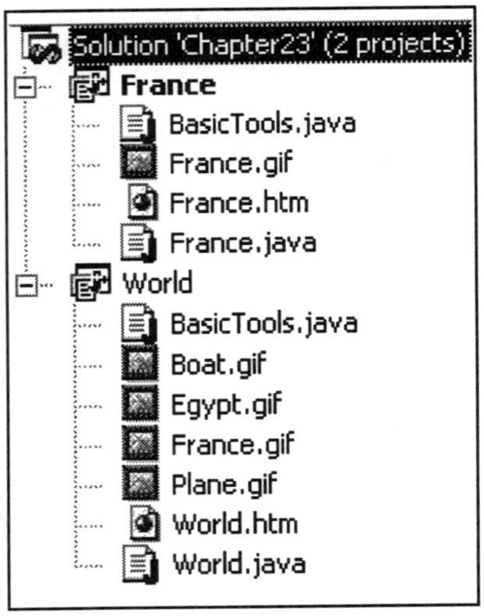

Web page *France*

9. Add project *France* to solution *Chapter23*. Add and rename all necessary files. Be sure to make project *France* the current (*StartUp*) project.

10. Complete file *France.htm* of Figure 23.5.

    a) What is the URL of this HTML page?

    b) What is the applet's (*France.java*'s) file pathway?

```
<HTML>
<HEAD>
<TITLE>France</TITLE>
</HEAD><BODY>
<CENTER><IMG src="France.gif">
<FONT size=8 color=olive>France</FONT>
<IMG src="France.gif"></CENTER>
<HR SIZE=10 noshade>
<APPLET align=left
   code=France.class  name=France
   height=200  width=140  VIEWASTEXT>
</APPLET>
<FONT size=4 color=navy>Although France is best known for
the Eiffel Tower, this country makes some of the world's
finest wines.<P> Paris is one of the world's great cities,
and is at its best during the springtime.</FONT>
<FONT size=6 color=maroon><P>See you there!</FONT> </P>
</BODY>
</HTML>
```

New!
Hotlink target.

Figure 23.5
France.htm

11. Complete applet *France.java* of Figure 23.6. What do each of the four parameters of method *drawLine* specify?

```
import java.awt.*;
import java.applet.*;
public class France extends Applet
{
	public void init( ){
		setBackground(Color.white);
	}

	public void paint(Graphics g){
		BasicTools.msec(1000);
		g.setColor(Color.blue);
		g.fillRect(15,160,70,15);
		g.setColor(Color.black);
		BasicTools.msec(1000);
		g.drawLine(25,160,30,150);
		BasicTools.msec(1000);
		g.drawLine(30,150,40,100);
		BasicTools.msec(1000);
		g.setColor(Color.blue);
		g.fillRect(25,80,50,20);
		BasicTools.msec(1000);
		g.setColor(Color.black);
		g.drawLine(45,80,50,10);
		BasicTools.msec(1000);
		g.drawLine(50,10,55,80);
		BasicTools.msec(1000);
		g.drawLine(60,100,70,150);
		BasicTools.msec(1000);
		g.drawLine(70,150,75,160);
		BasicTools.msec(1000);
	}
}
```

The Eiffel Tower is drawn each time *paint* is called.

Send *x,y* beginning and *x,y* end as parameters.

New!
Draw lines.

Figure 23.6
France.java

12. Execute Web page *France* and note the Explorer screen.

    a) Does the Web page resemble Figure 23.7?

    Yes **No**

    b) Was the Eiffel Tower drawn slowly?

    Yes **No**

Figure 23.7
Web page *France*

Surfing

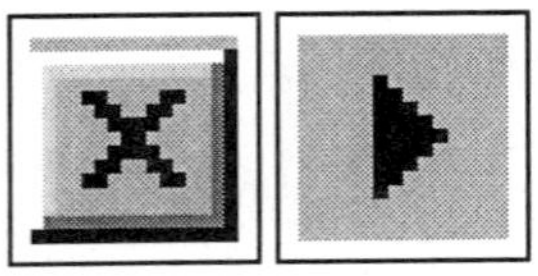

13. Exit Web page *France* and re-enter master Web page *World*.

14. Is the text hotlink blue and underlined, and is there a blue border around the image hotlink?

    Yes **No**

15. Move the cursor over either hotlink, but do not **CLICKL** yet.

    a) Did the cursor change into a small hand?

    Yes **No**

    b) Did the URL of the target page (*France.htm*) appear at the bottom of the Web page?

    Yes **No**

c) What is the URL of the target page?

16. **CLICKL** on either the text or the graphics hotlink. Did the system move to Web page *France* of Figure 23.7?

    Yes **No**

17. To return to the previous Web page (*World.htm*), **CLICKL** on the *Back* icon at the top of the Web page. Did we return to Web page *World*?

    Yes **No**

18. If you wish, now **CLICKL** on the *Forward* icon. Did we return to Web page *France*?

    Yes **No**

19. Suggestion: Go back and review the *html* and *java* programs for both Web pages until you thoroughly understand the function of every line of code.

Advanced hotlink features

> We can change the color of our hotlinks. We can even differentiate between "visited" (we have been there) and "unvisited" (we haven't been there yet) Web pages. However, be aware that the color of a visited link may not change until after it's been published on the Web.

20. Bring back *World.htm* and make the changes shown below to the BODY tag.

```
<body LINK=yellow VLINK=red>
```

21. Run Web page *World*. Is the text hotlink (**France**) now yellow in color, and is there a yellow border about the image hotlink?

    Yes **No**

22. After visiting Web page *France*, did the hotlink change color to red? (Remember, this may not happen until it is published.)

    Yes **No**

Exercises

> Additional flag images are found in directory *TextImages/Flags* on an enclosed floppy disk.

a) Using a design of your choice, create Web page *Egypt*. (Make it as colorful and attractive as you can.) Using both text and image hotlinks, go back to master Web page *World* and add text and image hotlinks to *Egypt*.

b) Create cross-hotlinks directly between Web pages *France* and *Egypt*. (That is, Web page *France* will have a hotlink directly to Web page *Egypt*, and vise-versa.)

c) Create Web page *Wine*, which gives a brief presentation of French wines. Create a hotlink from Web page *France* to this new web page. Using hotlinks and the *Back/Forward* icons, surf between pages *World*, *France*, and *Wine*.

d) Modify Web pages *France* and *Wine* (and also *Egypt*, if present), so each offers a hotlink back to *World* (as an alternative to pressing *Back*.)

e) Create a new master Web page (*Universe*?) that offers hotlinks to Web page *World*.

f) Create a set of hypertext Web pages that follow the living world hierarchy (kingdom, phylum, family, class, and species).

g) Create a Web page hierarchy for your favorite sport.

h) Add buttons, labels, and textfield components to any of your Web page designs to enable interaction between computer and user. (Hint: Have the user enter information, such as name and travel mode preference, etc.)

i) Write a Web page system (two or more Web pages) of your choice.

Questions and Problems

1. Create each of the following hotlinks.

   a) A text hotlink to Web page http://www.paramount.com using the word **movie**.

   b) An image hotlink to the same place using the image *film.gif*.

2. What happens when the cursor is moved over a hotlink?

3. Assuming the proper hotlinks are in place, can we jump from any Web page to any other Web page at any time?

   Yes **No**

4. What is a URL (Uniform Resource Locator)?

5. How might the following three topics be arranged in a hypertext format? (Which one would be at the highest level, and which at the lowest?)

   Tiger, mammal, cat.

6. Once we have been through a chain of Web pages, can we just use the *Back* and *Forward* icons from then on?

   Yes **No**

7. Why don't the URLs of this chapter require the http:// service designator?

8. How do we tell if a given image is also a hotlink?

CHAPTER

24

Project Eight Ball

Multithreading, Intralinks, and Multiple Applets

Objectives

- *To use multithreading to generate continuous motion*
- *To use intralinks to other page locations*
- *To write a Web page that uses two or more applets*

Discussion

As a display of their prowess, grandmaster chess champions will often play a number of opponents simultaneously. Of course they don't literally play all opponents at precisely the same time—that would be quite impossible. Instead, the champion quickly makes one move at a time at each board, playing in round robin fashion.

Applet update

Multithreading

In computer terms, the move-by-move progress of each individual chess game taken separately is called a *thread.* When multiple games are played simultaneously, it's called *multithreading*. All our user-defined programs so far have been single threaded, with the conventional applet code acting as that single thread.

With project *EightBall*, the problem before us is to keep a billiard ball bouncing continuously—at long as the Web page is open. When we pondered this problem before, we found that the easy solutions shown below would not work.

Forever loop

```
while(true){
    draw( );
    hold( );
    erase( );
    update( );
}
```

Recursion

```
paint(Graphics g){
    draw( );
    hold( );
    update( );
    repaint( );
}
```

The problem is, both of these forever loops just keep going, even when the Web page is not active. This we can't have. When we move to another Web page, these loops must stop.

Is there a way that we can keep action going as long as the Web page is active, but stop when we exit the page? (Is there a way we can have our cake and eat it too?) There is, and it is called *multithreading*.

The *run* thread

To generate continuous motion in a Web browser environment, we need two programming threads, as if there were two separate microprocessors running in parallel. One thread (processing the conventional applet code) already exists. What we need is a second thread to keep our eight ball bouncing continuously.

To accomplish this, the Java system provides for a special *run* thread that executes in parallel with the conventional thread. By continuously switching back and forth between the two threads, they will appear to be executing simultaneously. Furthermore, the conventional thread has a way of turning the *run* thread on and off as required.

Start and *run*

Adding two overriding methods to our applet carries out multitasking: *Start* and *run*. Method *start* has been used all along and is inherited from class *Applet*. Method *run* is new, and is defined in interface *Runnable*.

Briefly, here is how multithreading works:

The browser calls inherited method *start*—which in turn starts the new *run* thread. Within the *run* thread we place a special *while* statement that loops continuously as long as the web page is active. The system automatically switches back and forth between the conventional thread and this new run thread, thereby simulating two programs running continuously in parallel. When we exit the present Web browser page or move to another, the browser automatically calls method *stop*, which in turn also stops the *run* thread.

Do you see the beauty of the system? When the conventional thread is started, the *run* thread is also started. And, when the conventional thread is stopped, the *run* thread is also stopped.

After we have completed the program and tested the system, we will return with a more detailed analysis.

Class hierarchy

To carry out project *EightBall*, we must access the behavior of class *Thread* and interface *Runnable* (Figure 24.1).

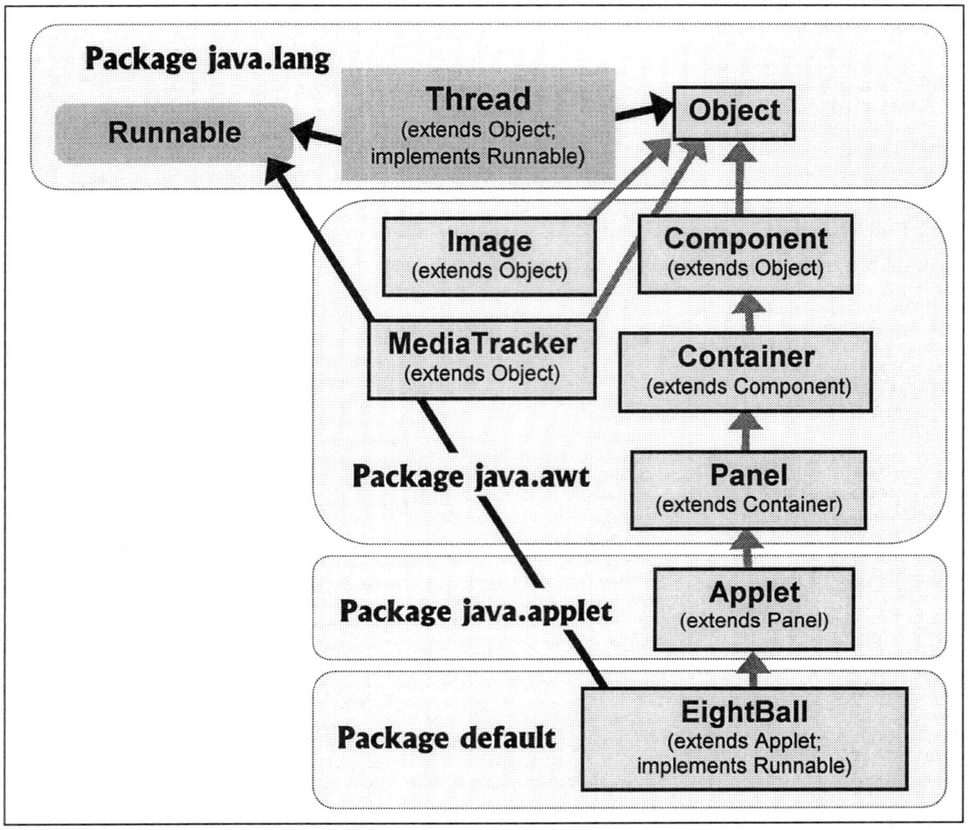

Figure 24.1
Project *EightBall* class hierarchy

HTML update

The previous chapter showed us how to create a global hotlink to another Web document. Did you know that we can also create a local hotlink to another location within the same Web page?

This is especially useful for very large and complex Web pages. The process is very similar to global hotlinks.

First we place an anchor at the source location: (The "#" means this is a local hotlink.)

```
<A HREF = "#keyword">Hotlink statement</A>
```

At the target location, we place a similar tag:

```
<A name = "#keyword">Hotlink statement</A>
```

A good way to use local hotlinks is with a menu format, with each menu item a local hotlink. We can also use local hotlinks to return to the original location. (Another way to return to a previous location is by way of the *Back* and *Forward* icons.)

Hands-On Procedure

1. This project will create a separate *run* thread that calls method *paint* from within an infinite loop.

> **Project *EightBall* will create a Web page based on the game of pool. It will show the image of a billiard ball continuously bouncing from side to side. Local hotlinks are listed as menu items.**

2. Create project *EightBall* within solution *Chapter24*, adding and renaming files as necessary.

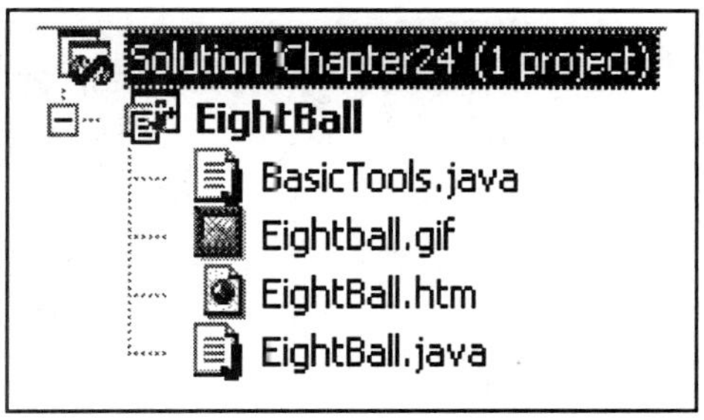

3. Complete file *EightBall.htm* of Figure 24.2. How many internal hotlinks does the program use? Circle your answer.

   a) 1 b) 2 c) 3 d) 4

```
<HTML>
<HEAD>
<TITLE>Eight Ball</TITLE>
</HEAD>
<BODY><CENTER>
<FONT size=8 color=maroon>Playing Pool</FONT>
</CENTER><P><FONT size=6 color=olive>
<PRE><B>   Menu</B></PRE></FONT>
<UL><FONT size=4>
<LI><A href="#play">How to play pool</A>
<LI><A href="#equipment">Equipment needed</A> </LI>
</UL></FONT>
<HR size=3 noshade><CENTER>
<APPLET
   code=EightBall.class
   name=EightBall
   height=60   width=500  VIEWASTEXT>
</APPLET>
</CENTER>
<HR size=3 noshade>
<P><IMG SRC="EightBall.gif" height=80 width=80 align=left hspace=10>
<FONT size=5 color=navy><A name=Play>How to play
pool</A></FONT><BR>
<FONT size=4>The stick must hit the cue ball, which in turn
strikes one or more of the other balls. If any ball but
the cue ball falls into the pocket, you can continue. Otherwise,
it's your opponent's turn. The Eight ball must be the last one in.
<P><HR><P><HR><P><HR><P><HR><P><HR><P>
<IMG SRC="EightBall.gif" height=80 width=80 align=left hspace=10>
<FONT size=5 color=navy><A name=equipment>Equipment
needed</A></FONT>
<BR><FONT size=4>You need a stick, a cue ball, and eight other balls,
numbered from one to eight.  It's also very helpful to have chalk to
remove the moisture from the cue stick tip.
</FONT> </P></FONT></CENTER>
</BODY>
</HTML>
```

New!
Internal hotlinks.

Spacers added for testing purposes.

Figure 24.2
EightBall.htm

4. Complete applet *EightBall.java* of Figure 24.3.

```
import java.awt.*;
import java.applet.*;
public class EightBall extends Applet
                        implements Runnable
{
    private Thread T8Ball;
    runFlag = true;
    boolean bounceFlag = false;
    int X=200,Y=5;
    Image E8Ball;
    MediaTracker trackImage;

    public void init( ){
        trackImage = new MediaTracker(this);
        E8Ball = getImage(getDocumentBase( ),"EightBall.gif");
        trackImage.addImage(E8Ball,0);
        try{
            trackImage.waitForAll( );
        }
        catch(InterruptedException e){ }
        setBackground(Color.white);
    }

    public void paint(Graphics g){
        g.drawImage(E8Ball,X,Y,50,50,null);
    }

    public void start( ){
        T8Ball = new Thread(this);
        T8Ball.start( );
    }

    public void stop( ){
        runFlag = false;
    }
```

New! Multithreading.

Create thread *T8Ball.*

1

4

The upper start is from class *Applet,* the lower from class *Thread.*

3

New JDK 1.2 method of stopping threads.

Continued on the next page.

Figure 24.3
EightBall.java (continued on the next page)

Continued from the previous page.

```
    public void run( ){
        while (runFlag){
            repaint(X–5,Y–5,65,65);
            try{
                Thread.sleep(30);
            }
            catch (InterruptedException e){
                runFlag = false;
            }
            if(X>400)
                bounceFlag = true;
            else if(X<50)
                bounceFlag = false;
            if(bounceFlag == true)
                X– =4;
            else
                X+=4;
        }
    }
}
```

Shorthand for *runFlag* == true.

2

Figure 24.3
EightBall.java (continued from the previous page)

5. To appreciate how multithreading takes place, let's follow its progress from beginning to end—as it would actually be executed.

1

a) The browser invokes the *start* method when the window is displayed. An object of class *Thread* is created globally and named *T8Ball*. Finally, method *T8Ball.start* is called and the new *run* thread from *this* object begins execution.

2

b) The system now executes the *run* thread in parallel with the *conventional* thread. Within the *while(runFlag)* loop of the *run* thread, we continuously perform the required *erase*, *draw*, *hold*, *update* motion algorithm.

Each time method *Thread.sleep(30)* is processed, the *run* thread ceases execution for 30ms.

Note that *Thread.sleep(30)* throws an exception.

c) When any event requires the applet thread to stop, the browser calls method *stop*. Member variable *runFlag* is set to *false*, we drop out of the *while* loop and exit method *run*. 3

d) If and when we reenter the window, the system calls *start* again, which in turn calls *T8Ball.start* to reactivate the *run* method. 4

6. Run the program and note the screen output of Figure 24.4. Does a ball bounce back and forth continuously across the screen?

Yes **No**

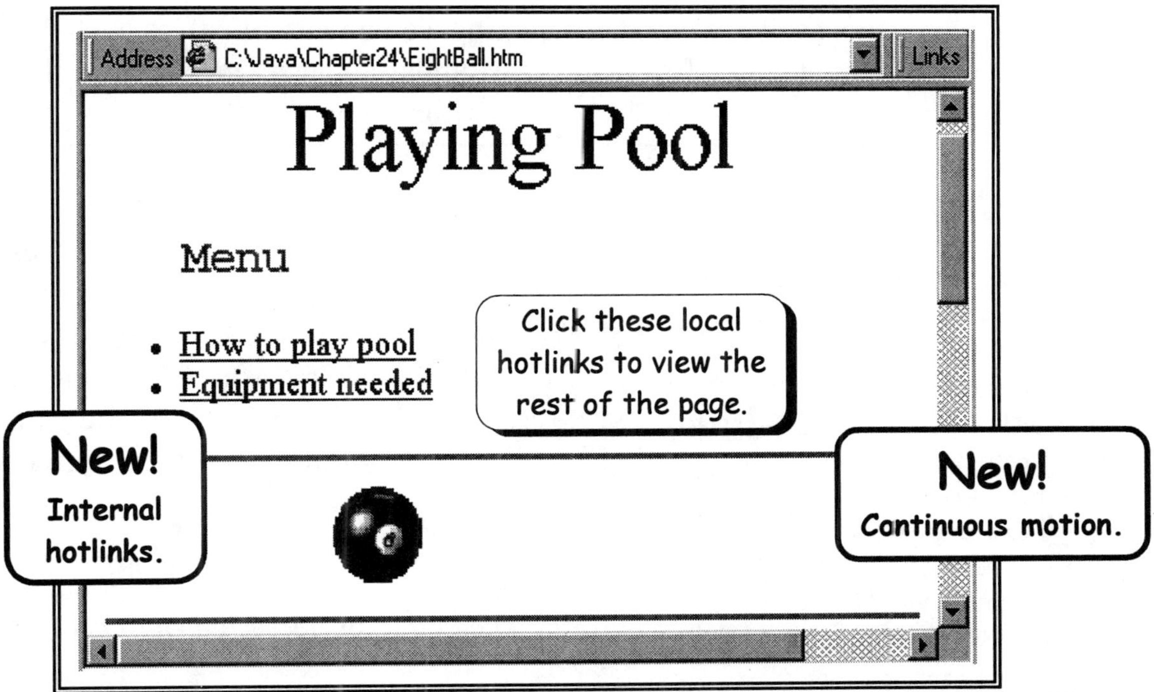

Figure 24.4
Project *EightBall* screen output

7. When we hide and bring back the Explorer window, is the ball still bouncing?

   Yes **No**

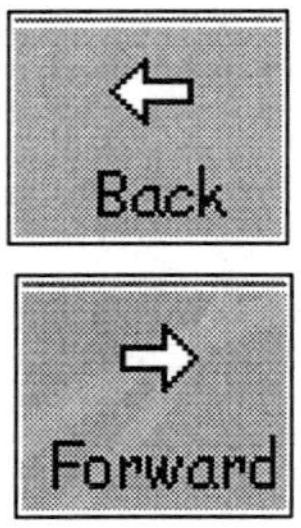

8. Click on the intra-hotlinks (the menu items). In each case does the Web page automatically shift to the proper location? Do the *Back* and *Forward* buttons properly retrace the sequence?

   Yes **No**

Multiple applets

> Can an HTML page have more than one applet? The answer is a resounding yes! A single Web page can have any number of applets spaced wherever we wish.
>
> Does this also pertain to multithreaded applets? Yes indeed. This is especially cool because we would see continuous motion all over our Web page.
>
> Suppose we advertise gambling equipment (dice) as well as pool equipment. How about two similar applets: One showing the moving eight ball and the other showing moving dice?

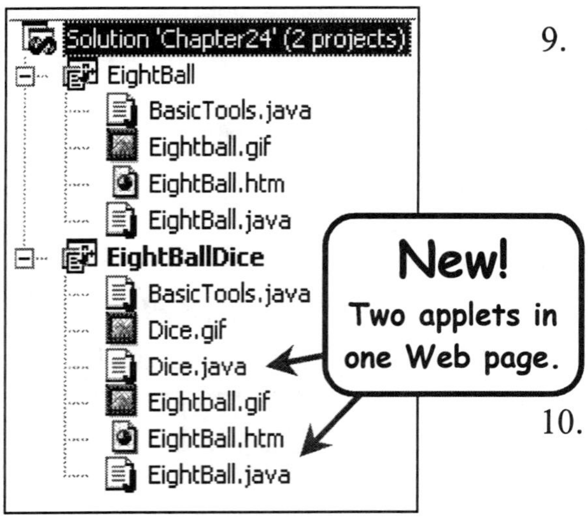

9. Create new project *EightBallDice* to solution *Chapter24*. Add all four files from project *EightBall* to project *EightBallDice*. (**CLICKR** on project *EightBallDice*, **Add**, **Add Class**, locate desired files, **DCLICKL**, etc.) Be sure to make *EightBallDice* the current project.

10. Add applet class *Dice.java* and graphics file *Dice.gif* to project *EightBallDice*.

11. Using copy/paste, copy all the code from *EightBall.java* to *Dice.java*.

12. Within *Dice.java*, modify the *getImage* statement as follows: (Be sure to change *E8Ball* to *TwoDice* throughout the program.)

```
TwoDice = getImage(getDocumentBase( ),"Dice.gif");
```

13. Create a separate thread for the dice.

```
private Thread TDice;

public void start( ){
        TDice = new Thread(this);
        TDice.start( );
}

public void stop( ){
        runFlag = false;
}
```

14. Decrease by half the speed that the dice move back and forth by substituting a "2" for the "4" in method *run*.

```
if(bounceFlag == true)
        X– =2;
else
        X+=2;
```

15. Next, modify *EightBall.htm* as shown below.

```
<APPLET
  code=EightBall.class
  name=EightBall
  height=60  width=500  VIEWASTEXT>
</APPLET>
<HR size=3 noshade>
<APPLET
  code=Dice.class
  name=Dice
  height=60  width=500  VIEWASTEXT>
</APPLET>
```

New!
Multiple applets.

16. Finally, change the dimensions of image *Dice.gif* from 50,50 to 80,50. (The dice image is a rectangle, and the eight ball image is a square.)

17. Execute the program.

    a) Did the screen resemble Figure 24.6 and did the two images move independently?

       Yes **No**

    b) Did the eight ball move more quickly than the dice?

       Yes **No**

    c) Could we have added a third multithreaded applet?

       Yes **No**

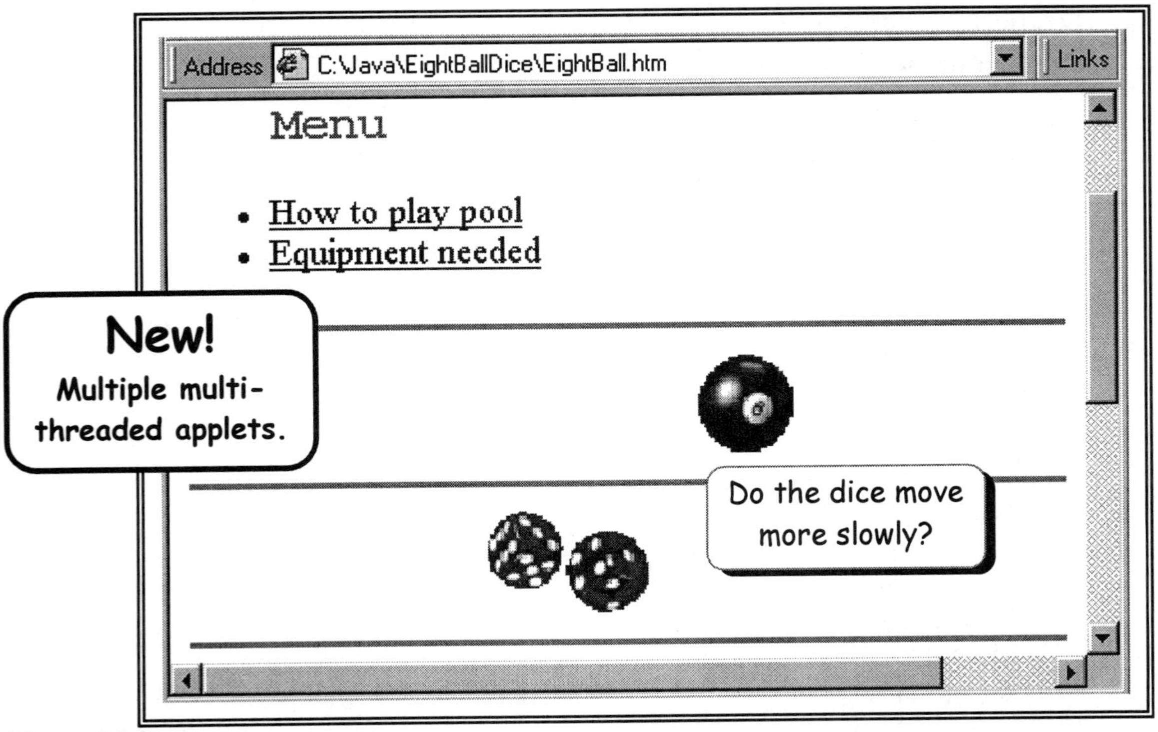

Figure 24.6
Two different multithreaded applets

Exercises

a) Using a *run* thread, cause *HelloWorld* to continuously blink on and off.

b) Using a *run* thread, modify any of the previous projects (*SolarSystem*, *CityDesk*, etc.) to generate continuous action.

c) Increase the size of the applet window to the shape of a pool table and program the eight ball to bounce off the sides. (Remember: angle of incident = angle of reflection.)

d) Add a second billiard ball to the pool table.

e) Create a panning marquee. (A word or phrase that continuously scans across the screen like that of a theater marquee.)

f) Create a Web page of three applets, each using a *run* thread.

g) Place the eight ball and dice applets side by side.

h) Include the following *run* method (and other *start/stop* code as needed) to project *TreasureHunt* of Chapter 19 so the clock time is updated continuously.

```
public void run( ){
    while(runFlag){
        repaint(0,0,60,50);  <-- Repaint just the time.
        try{
            Thread.sleep(300);
        }
        catch(InterruptedException e){
        }
    }
}
```

i) Create a multithreaded applet of your choice.

ESPRESSO

Why is *runnable* an interface?

Method *run* must be:

- inherited and overridden (but it is not in the *applet* inheritance lineage).
- completed by the programmer.

To satisfy these requirements, we implement interface *Runnable* in order to override abstract method *run*.

Questions and Problems

1. Why can't we place a forever structure (*while(true)*) within a paint method?

2. What is a *thread*?

3. Does *Thread.sleep()* throw an exception?

   Yes **No**

4. Both the *conventional* and *run* threads are started and stopped at very nearly the same time.

   True **False**

5. How does the HTML compiler tell the difference between a *global* and a *local* hotlink?

6. Referring to program *EightBall.html* of Figure 24.2, what HTML tag tells the system to wrap text around image *EightBall.gif*?

7. Do global and local hotlinks use different default colors?

   Yes **No**

8. What is the difference between an *Interface* and a *Class*?

9. How does the order in which applet tags are listed in the HTML file relate to their position on the Web page?

10. The old method of stopping a *run* thread was by way of a special *stop* method (*T8Ball.stop( )*). Why was this special *stop* method deprecated (removed) by JDK 1.2? (Hint: Does the old method have any control of exactly when we exit the run method?)

11. Referring to Figure 24.3, why do we use the following overloaded version of repaint?

```
repaint(X-5,Y-5,65,65);
```

12. Which of the following most closely describes the action of method *Thread.sleep(30)*?

    a) All processing action stalls within the *run* method (similar to the action of method *msec*).

    b) The system moves to other threads and continues processing there, returning to method *run* every 30ms.

CHAPTER

25

Project Good Earth

Animation

Objectives

- *To incorporate true animation into our Web pages*
- *To introduce the GIF89a image standard*

Discussion

True animation dates back to the Renaissance—where image sequences came alive when viewed through a slot on a spinning wheel. Next came Thomas Edison, who placed the images on moving cellophane. Today, we achieve animation by rapidly pulling images from computer memory and printing them to the screen.

Applet update

Animation

Animation is the rapid changing of still pictures, each one slightly different, to simulate continuous motion. With this in mind, the task before us seems simple enough: just create a *run* thread, store a sequence of graphics images in an array, and write them to the screen in continuous cycles. It's as simple as 1, 2, 3:

One, create a *run* thread.

```
Thread world = new Thread(this);
```

Two, load images into an array.

```
public void init( ){
    for(i=1;i<= NUM_IMAGES;i++){
        myImages[i-1] = getImage(getDocumentBase( ),strImage);
    }
}
```

Three, draw the images by continuously calling *paint* and updating index variable *myCurrImage* (my current image).

```
public void paint(Graphics g){
        g.drawImage(myImages[myCurrImage],x,y,50,50,this);
    }
}
```

In practice, however, it's not quite so simple. There are many supporting activities that must take place. To name the most demanding, we must make sure that all images are loaded before we begin the animation. For this, we will bring back the *mediaTracker* code first introduced in Chapter 18.

Class hierarchy

To generate computer animation, we combine a number of now-familiar classes with the *Runnable* interface. These are diagrammed in Figure 25.1.

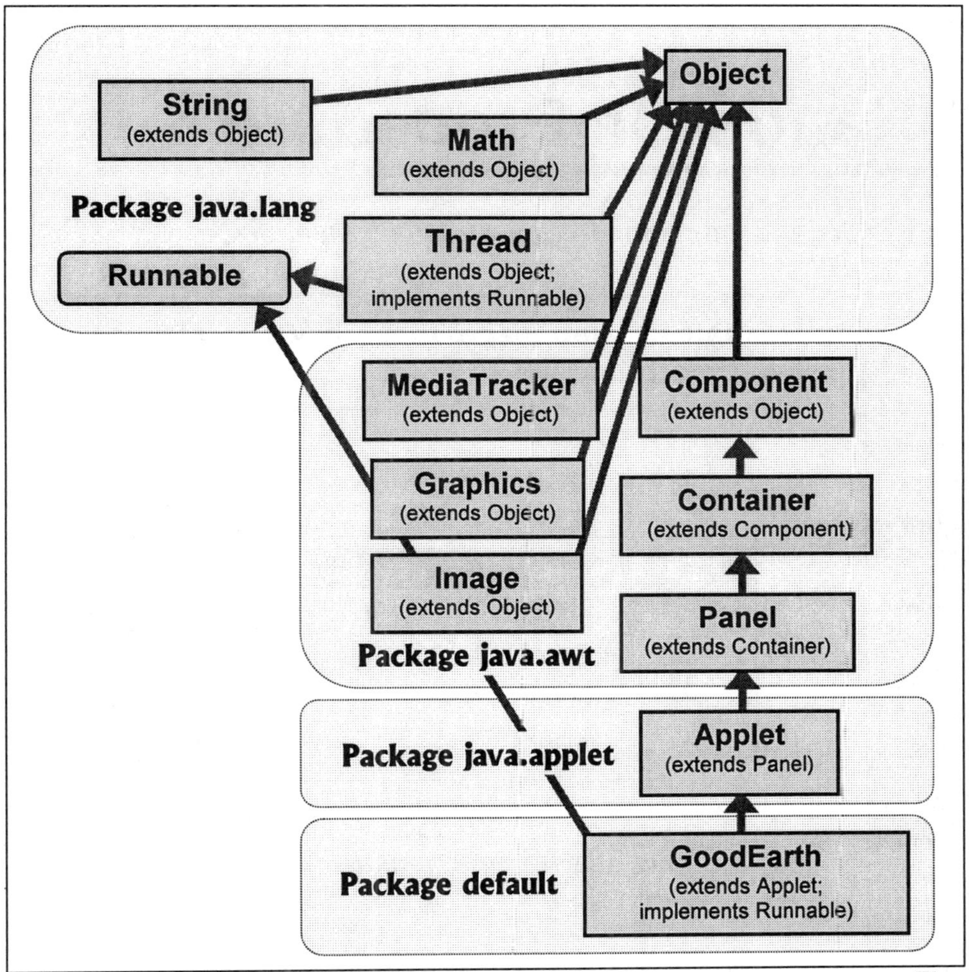

Figure 25.1
Project *GoodEarth* class hierarchy

HTML update

The latest piece of magic from the folks who design Web browsers and HTML software is called the *GIF89a* format. If you are lucky enough to own a browser that supports this format (and we do!), just place the image in the usual manner within any HTML program and watch the browser display multiple images in sequence. The result: Simple animation without tears!

Where can we get images in the GIF89a format? Just about anywhere. The GIF89a images used in this chapter were obtained from an inexpensive CD-ROM purchased at a computer store.

Hands-On Procedure

1. We add animation to project *SolarSystem* of Chapter 18.

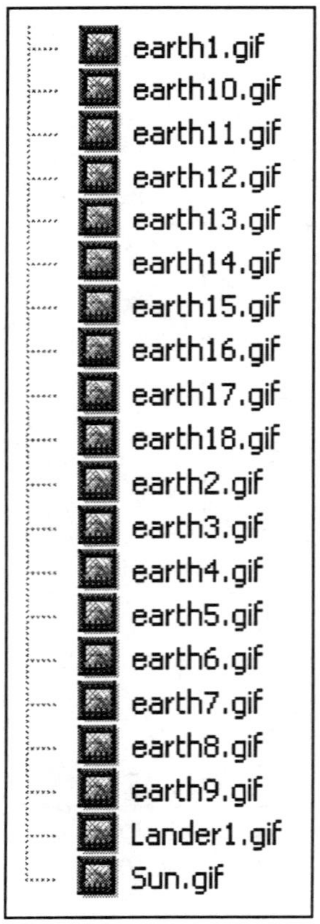

Create a Web page that shows a rotating planet earth orbiting the sun.

2. Create project *GoodEarth* within solution *Chapter25*.

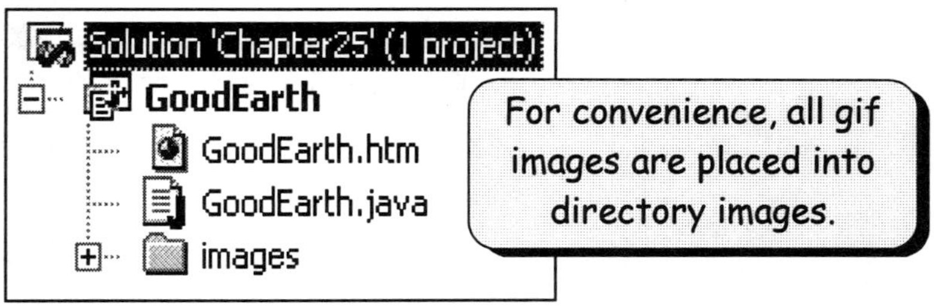

3. Be sure that directory *images* holds all necessary gif files.

4. Complete file *GoodEarth.htm* of Figure 25.2.

```
<HTML>
<HEAD>
<TITLE>GoodEarth</TITLE>
</HEAD>
<BODY>
<CENTER>
<FONT size=6 color=navy>SolarSystem II</FONT>
<HR SIZE=3>
<APPLET
    code=GoodEarth.class
    name=GoodEarth
    height=140  width=350  VIEWASTEXT>
</APPLET>
</CENTER>
<HR SIZE=3>
<IMG SRC="Images/lander1.gif" align=left hspace=10>
<FONT size=4 color=olive>The Lunar Lander</FONT>
<P><FONT size=3 color=maroon>Someday
we will travel about the solar system in solar taxis.
And we may even visit other worlds and other
races of people.
</FONT></P>
</BODY>
</HTML>
```

New!
GIF89a images.

Figure 25.2
GoodEarth.htm

5. Looking over *GoodEarth.htm*:

   a) Is the code very similar to *SolarSystem.htm* of Chapter 18?

      Yes **No**

   b) Is a GIF89a image handled the same as any other image?

      Yes **No**

6. Next, create applet file *GoodEarth.java* of Figure 25.3. (The code in boxes is required for animation.)

```
// This project combines multithreading and animation.
import java.awt.*;
import java.applet.*;
public class GoodEarth extends Applet
                                implements Runnable
{
     private Thread  world = null;
     private Image   myImages[ ],sun;
     private int         myCurrImage;
     private MediaTracker trackImage;
     private final int NUM_IMAGES = 18;
     private int x=200,y=140;
     private boolean runFlag = true;

     public void start( ){
          world = new Thread(this);
          world.start( );
     }

     public void stop( ){
          runFlag = false;
     }

     public void init( ){
          setBackground(Color.white);
          myImages   = new Image[NUM_IMAGES];
          MediaTracker trackImage = new MediaTracker(this);
          String strImage;
          for (int i = 1; i <= NUM_IMAGES; i++){
               strImage = "images/earth" +  i + ".gif";
               myImages[i-1] = getImage(getDocumentBase( ), strImage);
               trackImage.addImage(myImages[i-1],0);
          }
          sun = getImage(getDocumentBase( ),"images/Sun.gif");
          trackImage.addImage(sun,0);
          try{
               trackImage.waitForAll( );
          }
          catch(InterruptedException e){
          }
     }
```

1

2

New!
Animation.

Continued on the next page.

Figure 25.3

GoodEarth.java (continued on the next page)

Continued from the previous page.

```
public void paint(Graphics g){
    g.drawImage(sun,140,45,50,50,this);
    g.drawImage(myImages[myCurrImage],x,y,50,50,this);   [3]
}

public void run( ){
    int angle=0;
    while (runFlag){
        repaint(x-5,y-5,65,65);
        try{
            Thread.sleep(50);
        }
        catch(InterruptedException e){
        }
        x=125 + (int)(125*Math.sin(6.28*angle/360));
        y=45 + (int)(40*Math.cos(6.28*angle/360));
        angle++;
        myCurrImage++;                                    [4]
        if (myCurrImage == NUM_IMAGES)
            myCurrImage = 0;
    }
  }
}
```

Figure 25.3
GoodEarth.java
(Continued from previous page)

7. Applet *GoodEarth* of Figure 25.3 exhibits a number of interesting features. Since much of the code is identical to project *SolarSystem* of Chapter 18, we will concentrate on what's new: The animation code.

   - First we define an array of type *Image*—the key to the whole operation. **1**
   - Next, we enter a loop to create a sequence of *Image* objects and load their references into the array. Finally we register each image object with the *MediaTracker* system. **2**
   - From the *run* loop, we draw (repaint) each image. **3**
   - We move to the next image. If it's the last image, we return to the first. **4**

8. Run the program and note the screen output.

   a) Does it resemble Figure 25.4?

      Yes **No**

   b) Does the earth continuously rotate about the sun?

      Yes **No**

   c) Does the earth spin on its axis?

      Yes **No**

   d) Are all the images completely formed when they appear?

      Yes **No**

   e) Does the Lunar Lander spin?

      Yes **No**

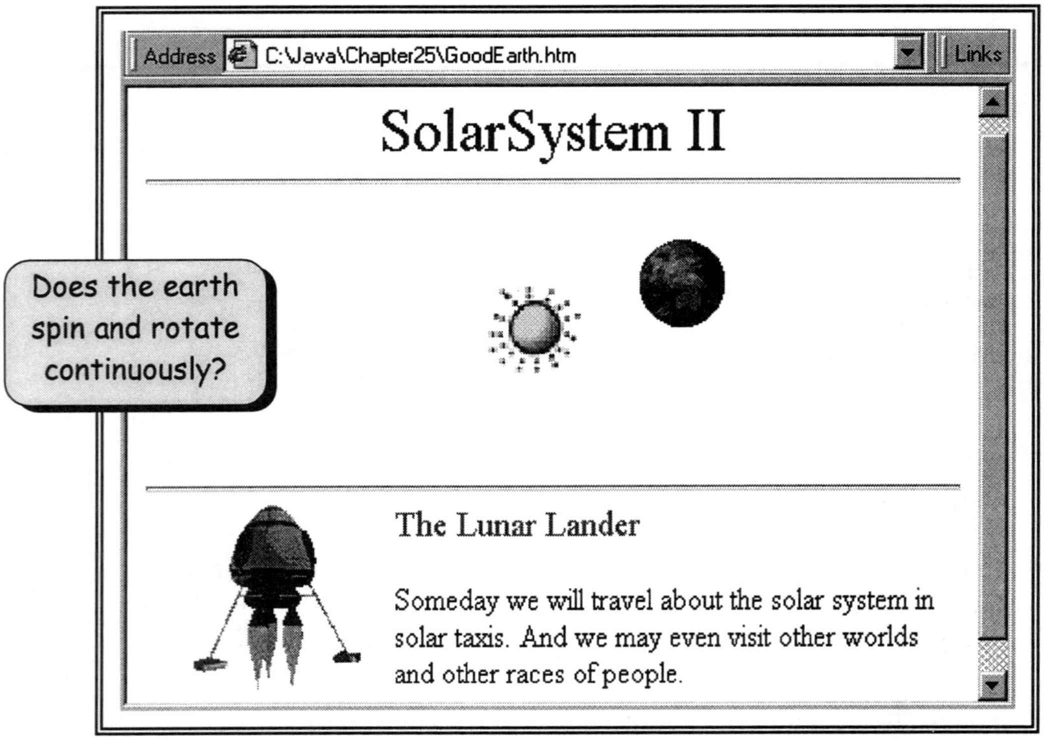

Figure 25.4

Project *GoodEarth* screen output

Reducing flicker

> Unfortunately, animation images are prone to flicker. It happens when all the pixels of an image are not displayed at once. One solution is to first draw the image off screen (memory), then simply transfer it to the visible screen. This is known as *double buffering*.

9. Modify *GoodEarth.java* for double buffering by adding (or changing) the boxed code shown in Figure 25.5.

```
private int X=200,Y=140;
private Graphics offScreenGraphics;
private Image offScreenImage;

public void init( ){
    offScreenImage = createImage(50,50);                      [1]
    offScreenGraphics = offScreenImage.getGraphics( );
    offScreenGraphics.setColor(Color.white);
    offScreenGraphics.fillRect(0,0,50,50);
    setBackground(Color.white);

public void paint(Graphics g){
    g.drawImage(sun,140,45,50,50,this);
[2] g.drawImage(offScreenImage,X,Y,50,50,this);
    offScreenGraphics.fillRect(0,0,50,50);
    offScreenGraphics.drawImage(myImages[myCurrImage],0,0,50,50,this);
}
```

Figure 25.5
Adding double buffering

10. Briefly, the two-step process is as follows.

    a) Using two genesis-like statements, we create an *Image/Graphics* object pair (known as the *buffer*). **1**

    b) Whenever paint is called, the buffer contents is drawn to the screen, the buffer is cleared, the next earth image is written to the buffer. **2**

11. Complete and execute the new double-buffered project. Did you notice any reduced flicker?

    Yes **No**

> Because the images of the earth are so simple, it's possible that you observed very little reduction in flicker. As an exercise, you may wish to try the technique on a larger, more complex image.

Exercises

> Additional GIF89a images are found in directory *TextImages/GIF89a* on an enclosed disk.

a) Folder *AnimationImages* (on the enclosed disk) offers three sets of animation files:

   Morph **(1–17) shows the face of a woman morphing into a cat.**

   Tumble **(1–17) shows a cartoon-like character tumbling.**

   Using any of these (or any other sets you may obtain), create an animation Web design of your own choosing. (Suggestion: Use the *Morph* set to show the image increasing in size as it morphs.)

b) Modify the orbit of the earth so it passes in front of the sun. The sun should be visible when the earth passes behind the sun, but not when the earth passes in front of it.

c) Modify *GoodEarth.java* so the earth changes direction each click of the mouse.

d) Add a rotating image of the moon revolving about the earth.

e) Reduce the number of images used in the earth animation from 18 to 9 and note the difference in the displayed image.

Questions and Problems

1. A static image that moves about the screen is true motion picture animation.

   True **False**

2. The GIF89a image format contains built-in means for animation.

   True **False**

3. What is accomplished by the following statement when $i = 4$? When $i = 12$?

```
strImage = "images/earth" + i + ".gif";
```

4. What is the difference between the following two overloaded methods?

```
g.drawImage(myImages[myCurrImage],x,y,null);
g.drawImage(myImages[myCurrImage],x,y,50,50,null);
```

5. The *run* thread executes in parallel with the browser thread.

   True **False**

CHAPTER

26

Project Sound Gallery

Interface *AudioClip*

Objectives

- *To incorporate sound into our Web pages*
- *To create a sound effects gallery*

Discussion

It is hard to imagine the excitement and wonder that must have prevailed when sound was finally added to movies back in the golden age of invention. We are now about to take the same step with our Web browser designs.

At the present time, the most widely used sound format is *au*, developed by *Sun Microsystems*. Because of this, adding sound to our Web pages is quite easy…once a sound card and speakers have been added to the system, that is. Sound snippets based on the *au* standard are found everywhere. Those used within this chapter (and contained on the enclosed disk) came from an inexpensive CD-ROM purchased at a local computer store.

With this brief chapter, we will set up a sound effects studio, with the intent of encouraging you to add sound to any of the previous Section II projects. As usual, sound can be added by way of the HTML program or the Java applet.

HTML update

Sound is added to an HTML program in hotlink format. As with conventional hotlinks to other Web pages, the trigger can be text, image, or both.

Assuming that files *speaker.gif* and *speaker.au* are contained in the present directory, all three options are listed below.

```
<A HREF="speaker.au">speaker</A>

<A HREF="speaker.au"><IMG SRC="speaker.gif"></A>

<A HREF="speaker.au"><IMG SRC="speaker.gif">speaker</A>
```

To allow the user to decide if it's worth downloading the sound file, the size and format of the file are often given as the text hotlink.

```
< A HREF="speaker.au">14K Sound @ 22.3kHz</A>
```

At the present time, HTML-generated sound is best done from the outside. That is, when the audio hotlink is activated, the browser downloads the sound and launches a helper application. The next thing you know, a special sound-player window appears (Figure 26.1). By clicking *Start* and *Stop*, we control the sound.

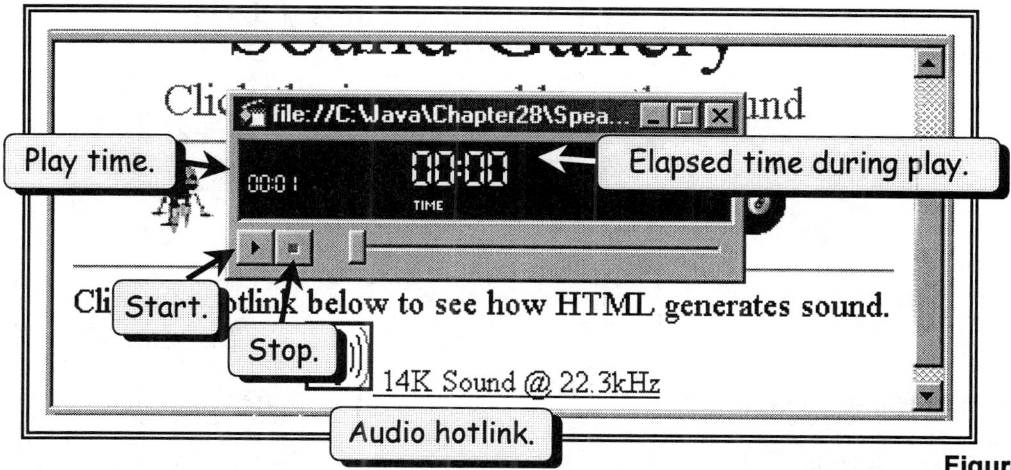

Figure 26.1
HTML sound generation

The small number at the lower left tells us how long this sound will play, and the larger number shows the elapsed time as the sound is generated.

For us, this method of sound generation is rather clumsy. For this reason, most of our sound work in this chapter will be accomplished via applets.

However, one useful sound feature we can take full advantage of is *background sound.* Just add the code below anywhere in your HTML program and *speaker.au* will be sounded every time you enter the page.

```
<BGSOUND SRC=speaker.au>
```

Applet update

To allow our applets to generate sound, we add interface *AudioClip* to a familiar collection of classes (see Figure 26.2).

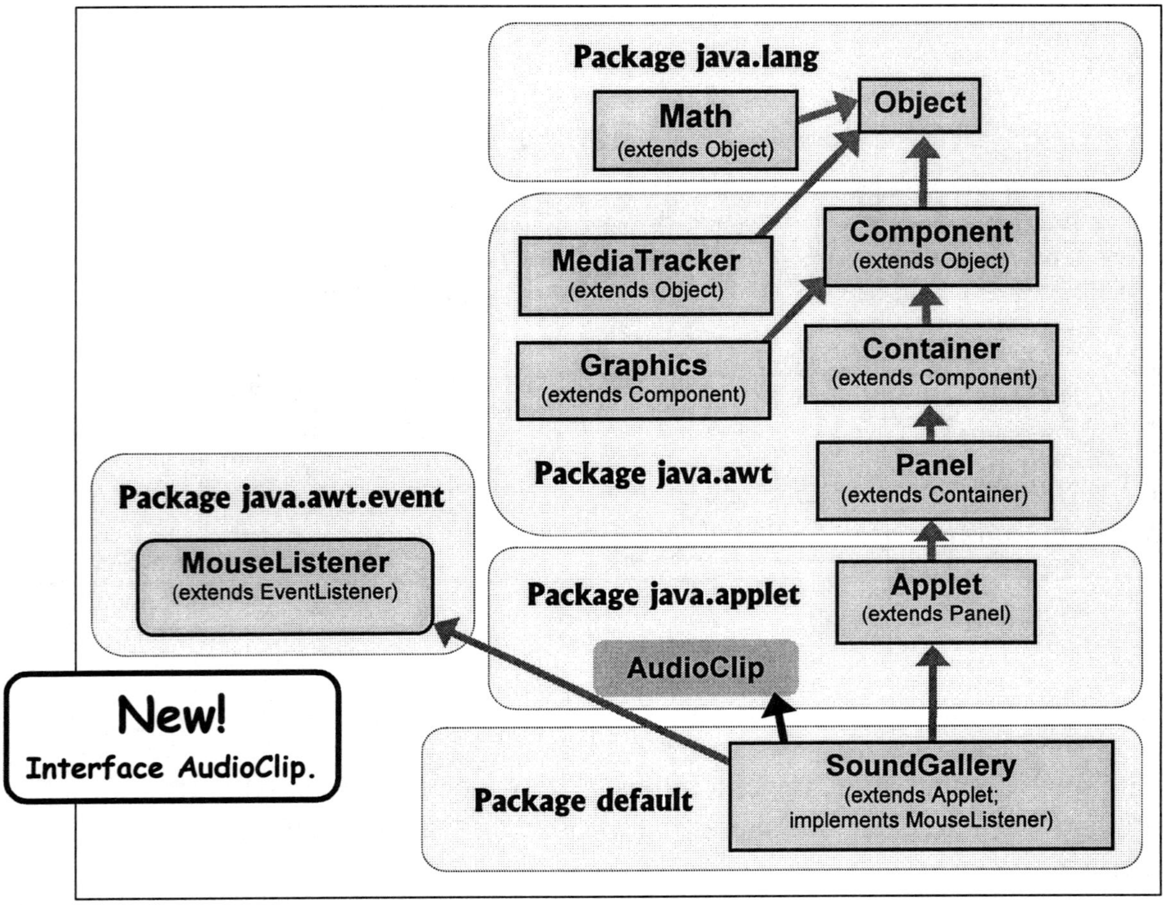

Figure 26.2

Project *SoundGallery* class hierarchy

The behavior of Interface *AudioClip*

Interface *AudioClip* offers the three abstract methods listed below.

- **Play( )** plays the audio clip one time from the beginning.
- **Loop( )** plays the audio clip over and over in a loop.
- **Stop( )** stops playing the audio clip.

Assuming that file *alien.au* is located in the present directory, the following are all the major options offered.

We play the alien sound snippet one time.

```
AudioClip ac = getAudioClip(getCodeBase( ),"alien.au");
ac.play( );
```

We play two sounds simultaneously.

```
AudioClip ac1 = getAudioClip(getCodeBase( ),"alien.au");
AudioClip ac2 = getAudioClip(getCodeBase( ),"plane.au");
ac1.play( );
ac2.play( );
```

We play one or more sounds continuously.

```
AudioClip ac1 = getAudioClip(getCodeBase( ),"alien.au");
AudioClip ac2 = getAudioClip(getCodeBase( ),"plane.au");
ac1.loop( );
ac2.loop( );
```

We play one or more sounds continuously for 10 seconds.

```
AudioClip ac1 = getAudioClip(getCodeBase( ),"alien.au");
AudioClip ac2 = getAudioClip(getCodeBase( ),"plane.au");
ac1.loop( );
ac2.loop( );
BasicTools.msec(10000);
ac1.stop( );
ac2.stop( );
```

Hands-On Procedure

1. In this chapter, we will create a sound effects gallery.

This project will display four images. When an image is clicked, the corresponding sound is heard.

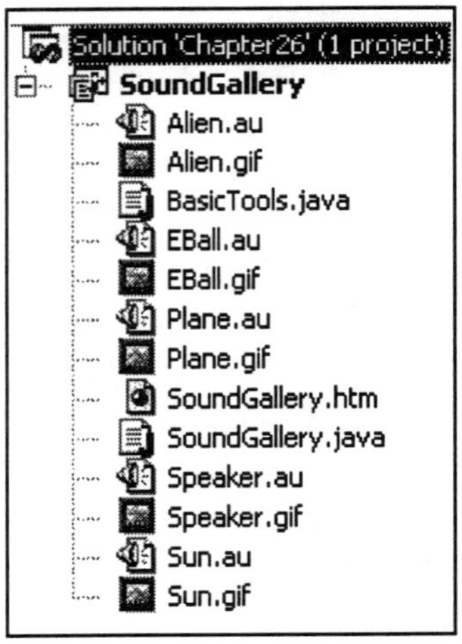

2. Create project *SoundGallery* within solution *Chapter26*. Be sure to load all necessary classes, images, and sound clips.

3. Next, create *SoundGallery.htm* of Figure 26.3.

New! Background sound.

```
<html><head>
<title>Sound Gallery</title>
</head>
<BODY><BGSOUND src="speaker.au">
<CENTER>
<FONT SIZE=10 COLOR=navy>Sound Gallery</FONT>
<BR>
<FONT SIZE=5 COLOR=olive>
Click the image and hear the sound</FONT>
<HR>
<APPLET
   code=SoundGallery.class  name=SoundGallery
   height=50  width=350  VIEWASTEXT>
</APPLET>
<HR>
<FONT SIZE=4 COLOR=maroon>
Click the hotlink below to see
how HTML generates sound.</FONT><BR>
<A href="speaker.au"><IMG src="speaker.gif">
14K Sound @ 22.3kHz</A>
</CENTER></BODY>
</html>
```

New! HTML-generated sound.

Figure 26.3
SoundGallery.htm

4. Finally, create applet *SoundGallery.java* of Figure 26.4. It's a fairly large program, but most of it deals with images and is therefore old hat. In fact, the only algorithm related to sound generation is shown below. We create an object of class *AudioClip* for each sound file, and call its *play* method.

```
AudioClip ac1 = getAudioClip(getCodeBase( ),"EBall.au");
ac1.play( );
```

5. Based on the code of *SoundGallery.java* (Figure 26.4), when an image is clicked, the sound will play:

   once **continuously**

   (How would your answer change if we substituted *loop* for *play*?)

```
import java.applet.*;
import java.awt.*;
import java.awt.event.*;
public class SoundGallery extends Applet
                                    implements MouseListener
{
      Image orion,alien,plane,sun,EBall;
      int x;
      MediaTracker trackImage;

      public void init( ){
            setBackground(Color.white);
            trackImage = new MediaTracker(this);
            alien = getImage(getDocumentBase( ),"alien.gif");
            plane = getImage(getDocumentBase( ),"plane.gif");
            sun = getImage(getDocumentBase( ),"sun.gif");
            EBall = getImage(getDocumentBase( ),"EBall.gif");
            trackImage.addImage(alien,0);
            trackImage.addImage(plane,0);
            trackImage.addImage(sun,0);
            trackImage.addImage(EBall,0);
            addMouseListener(this);
            try{
                  trackImage.waitForAll( );
            }
            catch(InterruptedException e){
            }
      }
```

Continued on the next page.

Figure 26.4
SoundGallery.java (continued on the next page)

Continued from the previous page.

```
public void paint(Graphics g){
      g.drawImage(alien,0,0,40,40,this);
      g.drawImage(plane,100,0,40,40,this);
      g.drawImage(sun,200,0,40,40,this);
      g.drawImage(EBall,300,0,40,40,this);
      if(x > 275){
            AudioClip ac1 = getAudioClip(getCodeBase( ),"EBall.au");
            ac1.play( );
      }
      else if(x > 175){
            AudioClip ac2 = getAudioClip(getCodeBase( ),"sun.au");
            ac2.play( );
      }
      else if(x > 75){
            AudioClip ac3 = getAudioClip(getCodeBase( ),"plane.au");
            ac3.play( );
      }
      else{
            AudioClip ac4 = getAudioClip(getCodeBase( ),"alien.au");
            ac4.play( );
      }
}

public void mousePressed(MouseEvent e){
      x = e.getX( );
      repaint( );
}

public void mouseEntered(MouseEvent e){ }
public void mouseExited(MouseEvent e){ }
public void mouseClicked(MouseEvent e){ }
public void mouseReleased(MouseEvent e){ }
}
```

New! Applet sound.

x determines which image was clicked.

Reminder: All the methods of an interface must be overridden.

Figure 26.4

SoundGallery.java (continued from the previous page)

6. Run the program and note the screen output of Figure 26.5. (Be sure all the appropriate *au* and *gif* files are in the present directory.)

   a) Click each of the four applet images. Do you hear the corresponding sound snippet played one time?

      Yes **No**

   b) Click the HTML sound hotlink. (If the *File Download* window comes up, **Open this file from its current location, OK**.) Does the display resemble Figure 26.1?

      Yes **No**

   c) Play the sound several times. Is this the same sound you heard when the window was first opened (the background sound)? Exit when done.

      Yes **No**

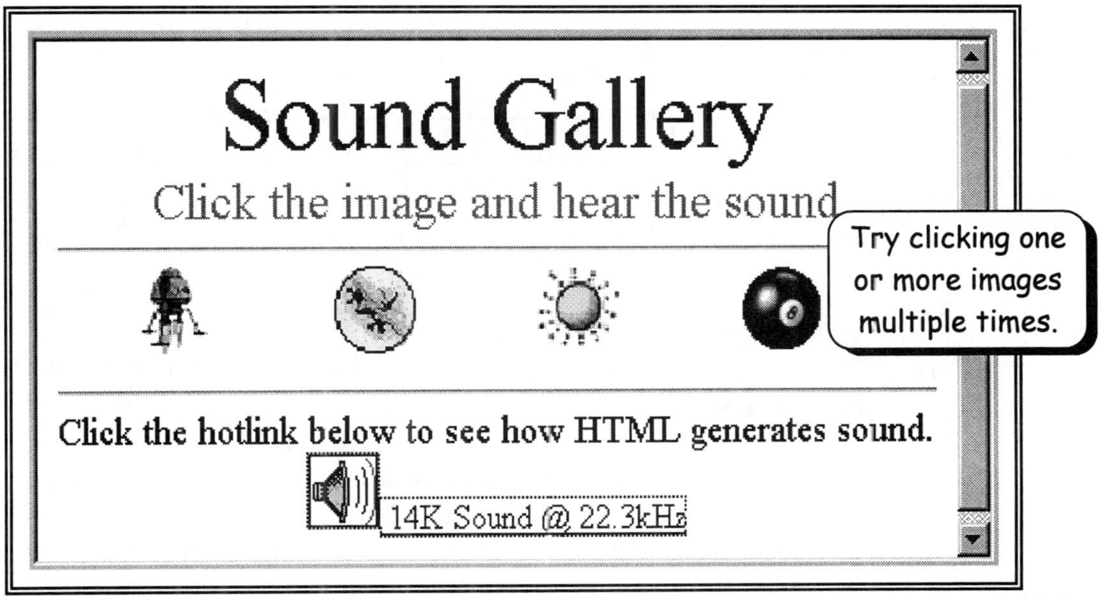

Figure 26.5
Project *SoundGallery.java* screen output

Things to try

7. Using the *loop* method, modify the program so each sound plays continuously once it's activated by a click.

8. Further modify the program so each sound plays continuously for 10 seconds.

9. Finally, modify the program so each sound is turned on and off by each mouse click.

10. Add image *note.gif* to the project at a location of your choice. Modify the program so all five sounds play simultaneously when image *note* is clicked. The sound stops when image *note* is clicked again.

11. Modify the program so image *note* (see 10.) is placed on a second row. (Hint: Use *getY( )* as well as *getX( )* to determine which image was clicked.)

Exercises

The exercises below all suggest adding sound to previous projects. The exact implementation is up to the reader. Additional sound effects are found in directory *TextImages/Audio* on an enclosed disk.

a) Add combinations of sounds to project *City Desk* to simulate the sounds of a busy street.

b) Add alien or sun sounds to projects *SolarSystem* or *GoodEarth*.

c) Add Eight Ball sounds to project *EightBall*. (For example, a sound each time the ball hits the side wall.)

d) Add plane sounds to project *Tourist*.

e) Add "win" sounds to projects *Treasure Hunt* or *HomeRun*. (In all cases, the sound occurs when the user is successful.)

f) Show how to play the four sounds of this project in "Bolero" fashion. That is, we start with one sound, and then add in another sound each five seconds until all four are playing.

ESPRESSO

Where is the code?

Back in Chapter 19 we learned that an *interface* is a collection of abstract signature method definitions that contain no code and must be overridden by the user's applet.

For interface *MouseListener*, no problem. We did exactly that within *SoundGallery.java* of Figure 26.4. But what about interface *AudioClip*? Where is the overriding code?

The answer is, the designers of J–+ put the code within inherited class *Applet*. They simply did us a favor, since the code for methods *play*, *loop*, and *stop* are quite standard and most likely will not have to be overridden with custom code from the user.

Questions and Problems

1. Using *car.au* and *car.gif*, show how to create a car-oriented sound hotlink.

2. What is the difference between methods *play* and *loop*?

3. Why is *AudioClip* an interface?

4. With a sound card, several sounds can be played simultaneously.

   True **False**

5. Write a typical genesis statement for creating a sound object. (See Figure 26.4.)

CHAPTER

27

Project Come Alive

Dynamic HTML (DHTML)

Objectives

- *To change an HTML page from static to dynamic*
- *To program in DHTML*

Discussion

Look back at any of our Web projects. The applet portions of our pages are full of motion, activity, and life. Now compare this to the HTML portions of the Web pages. Except for the GIF89a images, they are static, still, and dead. So, to solve the problem, why not simply expand the use of applets? This is not an attractive solution because Java applets are difficult to learn and they execute slowly.

The need to bring HTML alive was so great that it was not long before the ever-active folks at Microsoft and Netscape set out to remedy the situation. The result is *Dynamic HTML* (DHTML).

DHTML

Stated simply, DHTML gives the Web page designer real-time interactive control of the placement and appearance of all HTML elements. The key was the creation of new *scripting languages*, and a new way of looking at Web pages known as the *document object model.*

A scripting language is a simple, scaled-down programming language that gives our HTML documents a limited degree of intelligence. To be sure, a scripting language is anything but a full-fledged programming language. A motivated student can learn a scripting language in a week—a feat not possible with Java (as you are now painfully aware). Leading the list of popular scripting languages are *JavaScript* (Netscape) and *JScript* (Microsoft).

The document object model (DOM) refers to all the pieces that make up a Web page arranged in a top-down hierarchy. By using a sequence of dot operators that follow the top-down hierarchy, we can reference any HTML tag in the document and change any of its attributes—in real time!

In other words, using DHTML, we can disassemble a document into its various components (headers, images, paragraphs, applets, tables, etc.) and put them back together in any way we wish.

Writing DHTML

In simple outline form, here is the approach we will take with all DHTML projects developed in this chapter:

1. Write the code in ordinary HTML.
2. Add DHTML code in three steps.
   a) Assign an ID to each tag we wish to change.
   b) Write one or more functions to operate upon the tag.
   c) Call the function from somewhere within the program.

Hello World, DHTML style

Let's demonstrate the writing of a DHTML program with a very simple rendition of "Hello World". Our goal is to use a large size header to write "Hello World" to the screen in black letters, and then use DHTML code to immediately change the color to blue.

First, we write the program in ordinary HTML.

```
<HTML>
<HEAD>
</HEAD>
<BODY>
<H1>Hello World</H1>
</BODY>
</HTML>
```

Next, we add the DHTML code in three steps.

- Step one is to assign tag H1 an ID (identification).

```
<HTML>
<HEAD>
</HEAD>
<BODY>
<H1 ID=myHeader>Hello World</H1>
</BODY>
</HTML>
```

- Step two is to add a function that turns the header blue.

> *myHeader.style.color="Blue"* follows the *Document Object Model* (DOM). It says, go to object *myHeader*, find sub-object *style*, and finally sub-sub-object *color*—and turn it blue.

```
<HTML>
<HEAD>
</HEAD>
<BODY>
<H1 ID=myHeader>Hello World</H1>
<SCRIPT LANGUAGE="JavaScript">
   function ToBlue( ){
      myHeader.style.color="Blue";
   }
</SCRIPT>
</BODY>
</HTML>
```

This is written as a hierarchy, with *myHeader* containing *style*, which in turn contains *color*.

- Step three is to call the function.

```
<HTML>
<HEAD>
</HEAD>
<BODY>
<H1 ID=myHeader>Hello World</H1>
<SCRIPT LANGUAGE="JavaScript">
   function ToBlue( ){
      myHeader.style.color="Blue";
   }
ToBlue( );
</SCRIPT>
</BODY>
</HTML>
```

Call function *ToBlue( )*.

When the code is executed, "Hello World" will be written to the screen in default black letters. Function *ToBlue( )* will be called immediately from within the script block, and the color attribute will be dynamically changed to blue.

There you have it. It's as easy as one, two, three. Of course, you can well imagine that the clever folks who bring us this magic have expanded the process far beyond anything we can now imagine.

DHTML represents a truly revolutionary step forward in Web page design. The only reason it is played down in this text is because it does not directly involve the Java language—and Java is the primary subject of this text.

What then can we hope to accomplish with just a single chapter of a few pages? The answer is, we can do little more than give the reader a light taste of DHTML—a plate of appetizers rather than a full-course meal. Hopefully this will whet your appetite for more.

So, using our familiar vignette style, let's take a look at a few examples of just what DHTML can really do. Get ready to be amazed!

Hands-On Procedure

Vignette *HelloWorld*

1. Our first vignette will be a modification of "Hello World."

> **Write a DHTML program that continuously changes the color of header *Hello World* between green and blue.**

2. We begin as always with creation of the solution and project. Create project *HelloWorldDHTML* within solution *Chapter27*, and rename all files as shown.

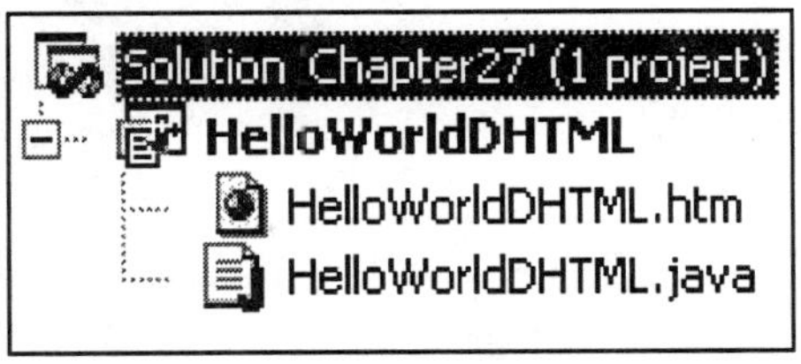

3. Because we won't be calling an applet for this project, we maintain only the shell shown below to satisfy the compiler. (As an alternative, we are always free to simply remove the APPLET tags.)

```
import java.awt.*;
import java.applet.*;
public class HelloWorldDHTML extends Applet
{ }
```

4. First, begin with the standard HTML program of Figure 27.1.

```
<HTML>
<HEAD>
</HEAD>
<BODY>
<H1>Hello World</H1>
</BODY>
</HTML>
```

Figure 27.1

Baseline HTML program

5. Execute the baseline program. Is "Hello World" printed in black?

   Yes **No**

6. Next, add the DHTML ID, function, and function call to generate the final program of Figure 27.2.

```
<HTML>
<HEAD>
<TITLE>Changing color</TITLE>
</HEAD>
<BODY>
<H1 ID = myHeader>Hello World</H1>
<SCRIPT>Language = "JavaScript">
   function ToBlue( ){
      myHeader.style.color="Blue";
      setTimeout("ToGreen( )",1000);
   }
   function ToGreen( ){
      myHeader.style.color="Green";
      setTimeout("ToBlue( )",1000);
   }
ToBlue( );
</SCRIPT>
</BODY>
</HTML>
```

Delay one second, then call the other function.

New! DHTML.

Figure 27.2

HelloWorld, DHTML style

Program action follows a straightforward recursive loop. First, "HelloWorld" is briefly printed to the page in default black. We call function *ToBlue( )*, which changes the color to blue and calls built-in function *setTimeout*. After a one second delay, function *ToGreen()* is called, and the process continues.

7. Run the program and note the Web page output of Figure 27.3. Did the output color alternate between blue and green as expected?

Yes **No**

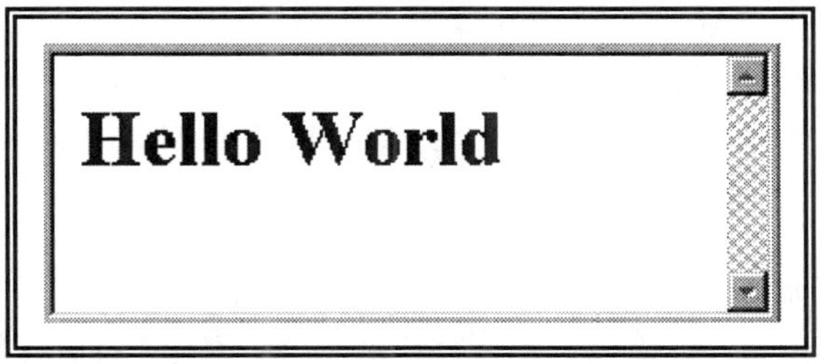

Figure 27.3
Project *HelloWorldDHTML* page output

Vignette *EarthMove*

8. Our second vignette will involve image motion.

> **Write a DHTML program that continuously zooms an image of planet earth back and forth on the page.**

9. Add project *EarthMove* to solution *Chapter27*. Add *earth.gif* (from Chapter 18), rename the files as usual, and be sure to condense the applet code.

10. Enter and execute the baseline HTML program of Figure 27.4. Does it display a static 100 by 100 pixel image of the earth at the center of the page?

Yes **No**

```
<HTML>
<HEAD>
<TITLE>The Moving Earth</TITLE>
</HEAD>
<BODY>
<CENTER>
<H2>This page shows a 100 by 100
<BR>centered image of the earth</H2>
<IMG SRC="Earth.gif" height=100 width=100>
</BODY>
</HTML>
```

Figure 27.4
Baseline HTML program *EarthMove*

11. When we add the DHTML code of Figure 27.5, we see a recursive action similar to the previous project.

```
<HTML><HEAD>
<TITLE>The Moving Earth</TITLE>
</HEAD><BODY><CENTER><P>
<H2 ID=myHeader>This page shows planet earth
<BR>continuously cycling towards us</H2>
<IMG SRC="Earth.gif" ID=Earth STYLE="position:absolute" >
<SCRIPT Langauge="JavaScript">
  function MoveLeft( ){
    Earth.style.top=20;
    Earth.style.left=100;
    Earth.style.height=25;
    Earth.style.width=25;
    myHeader.style.color="blue";
    setTimeout("MoveRight( )",500);
  }
  function MoveRight( ){
    Earth.style.top=50;
    Earth.style.left=300;
    Earth.style.height=100;
    Earth.style.width=100;
    myHeader.style.color="green";
    setTimeout("MoveLeft( )",500);
  }
  MoveLeft( );
</SCRIPT>
</BODY></HTML>
```

All commands follow the *Document Object Model* (DOM).

Object *top* is within object *style*, within object *Earth*.

New! Zooming DHTML objects.

Figure 27.5
DHTML *EarthMove*

There are several noteworthy items in DHTML program *EarthMove*:

- Using the *position:absolute* attribute, we have set up image *earth* for absolute positioning. This means its location on the Web page has no relation to any other tags (such as CENTER), and we can place and move the earth image anywhere on the page. We can even overlap image *earth* with any other object on the page.
- All script code instructions follow the DOM. For example, *earth.style.left=100* means that object *left* within object *style* within object *earth* is to be set to 100.
- We have borrowed code from the previous project to cause the header to change color.

12. Run the program and note the Web page output of Figure 27.6.

    a) Did image *earth* zoom in and out at the expected rate?

    Yes **No**

    b) Did the earth image overlap the header text, and did the header text change color?

    Yes **No**

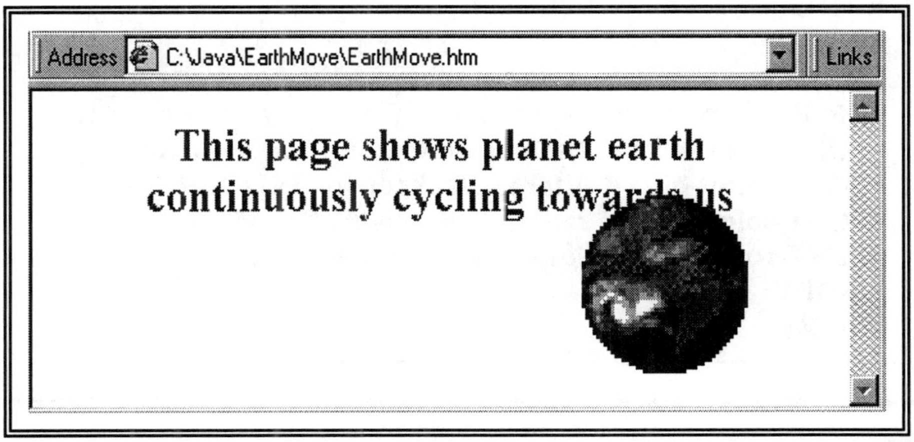

Figure 27.6
Project *EarthMove* page output

Vignette *MultipleChoice*

13. Our third and final vignette will involve an external event.

> **Write DHTML program *MultipleChoice*, that asks a question and lists four possible answers. When the cursor is moved over the correct answer, it changes color to red, increases in size, and an image appears.**

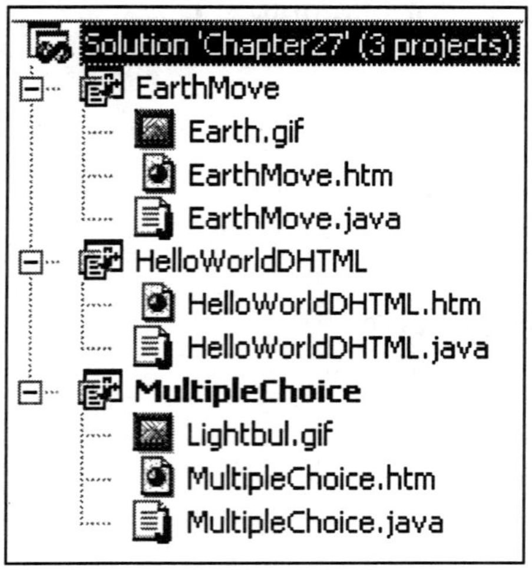

14. Add project *MultipleChoice* to solution *Chapter27*. Add GIF89a image file *Lightbul.gif*, rename the files as usual, and be sure to condense the applet code.

15. Enter and execute the baseline HTML program of Figure 27.7. Are the questions and answers presented in a very static (lifeless) manner?

Yes **No**

```
<HTML>
<HEAD>
<TITLE>Multiple Choice
</TITLE>
</HEAD>
<BODY>
<H2>Who was the fifth president of the United States?</H2>
<FONT color=blue>* Thomas Jefferson</FONT><BR>
<FONT color=blue>* Andrew Jackson</FONT><BR>
<FONT color=blue>* James Monroe</FONT><BR>
<FONT color=blue>* John Quincy Adams</FONT>
</BODY>
</HTML>
```

Figure 27.7
Baseline HTML program *MultipleChoice*

16. Add the DHTML code of Figure 27.8 and bring life (change and interaction) to the program.

```
<HTML>
<HEAD>
<TITLE>Multiple Choice</TITLE>
</HEAD>
<STYLE>
FONT.style1 {color:blue}
FONT.style2 {color:red}
</STYLE>
<BODY>
<IMG SRC="lightbul.gif" ID=LightBulb
STYLE="position:absolute" height=0 width=0>
<H3>Who was the fifth president of the United States?</H3>
<FONT color=blue size=4>* Thomas Jefferson</FONT><BR>
<FONT color=blue size=4>* Andrew Jackson</FONT><BR>
<FONT ID=Answer color=blue size=4 onmouseover="HighLight( )"
onmouseout="HighLight( )">* James Monroe</FONT><BR>
<FONT color=blue size=4>* John Quincy Adams</FONT><BR>
<SCRIPT language = "JavaScript">
  function HighLight( ){
    if(Answer.className=="style2"){
      Answer.className="style1";
      Answer.size=4;
      LightBulb.style.height=0;
      LightBulb.style.width=0;
    }
    else{
      Answer.className="style2";
      Answer.size=5;
      LightBulb.style.top=70;
      LightBulb.style.left=160;
      LightBulb.style.height=75;
      LightBulb.style.width=50;
    }
  }
</SCRIPT>
</BODY>
</HTML>
```

New! Style sheet.

className holds either style1 or style2.

New! External events.

Figure 27.8
DHTML program *MultipleChoice*

17. There are two major improvements in DHTML program *MultipleChoice*:

    - We have added style sheets to our program. Style sheets are named collections of attributes that can be designed ahead of time and listed within the style object. When we call a function to change a tag, the function can simply refer to the style name rather than numerous individual attribute names. The use of the style sheets is optional.

    - We have added external event control. Specifically, note the *onmouseover* and *onmouseout* commands added to the FONT tag that represents the answer. Whenever the cursor is moved on or off this answer, function *HighLight* is called. When the cursor is first moved over the answer, function *HighLight* checks to see if it's red. Since it is not, it sets the font to style2 (red), increases the size to five, and displays the image. When leaving the answer, the opposite happens.

18. Run the program and note the Web page output of Figure 27.9. When the cursor was moved over the correct answer (James Monroe), did it turn red and increase in size, and did the lightbulb image appear? When the cursor was moved off the answer, did it go back to its original state?

    Yes **No**

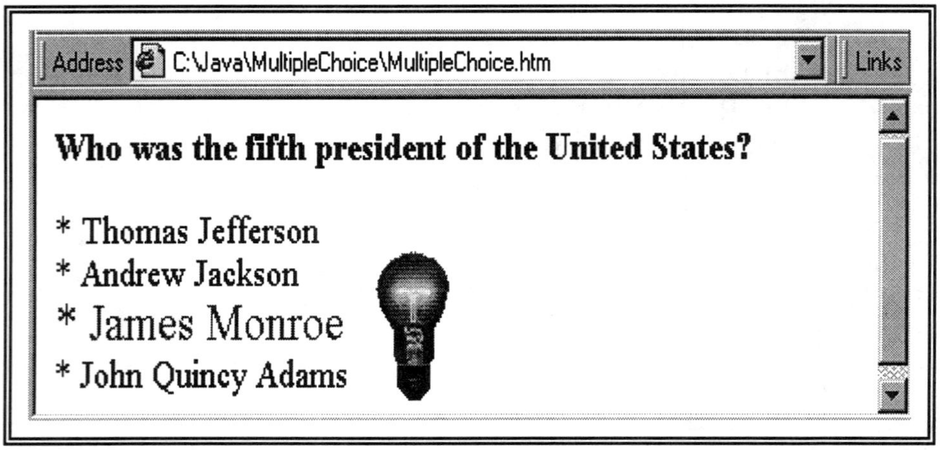

Figure 27.9
Project *MultipleChoice* page output

Exercises

Now that you have reached the final chapter, this group of exercises will break from tradition and simply list a few additional features of DHTML you may wish to try. *In most cases, additional research is required.*

Additional images and sound effects are found in directory *TextImages* on an enclosed disk.

a) Add *layers*: When several objects occupy the same position, the layers feature let's us specify which goes on top of which.

b) Add *click events*: Rather than functions called when the mouse moves over the item, functions are called when the mouse is clicked.

c) Add *marquee* behavior: Use the special MARQUEE BEHAVIOR tag to simulate a theater marquee.

d) Add *keypress events*: Functions are called when keys are pressed. Data can be entered from the keyboard.

e) Add *drag* and *drag-and-drop* features: Use the mouse to move various objects about the Web page.

f) Add dynamic applet control and sound control to a Web page.

Questions and Problems

1. Using HTML, it's possible to change the color of a font while it's displayed.

   True **False**

2. What DHTML attribute is used to identify a tag?

3. Write a function that continuously changes a font text style between "Times New Roman" and "Arial."

4. How would you modify DHTML program *HelloWorld* of Figure 27.2 to cycle between three colors?

5. How does the following show that the object model is a hierarchy?

Header.style.color

6. What image attribute allows the programmer to place the image at any location?

7. Given the attribute shown below, what is *TakeAction*?

Onmouseover = "TakeAction( )"

8. Why are style sheets optional?

Appendix A

HTML Tags

Opening Tag	Closing Tag	Description
<a HREF = "file.html" text OR <IMG SCR = "file.gif">	</a>	Anchor Hypertext reference Hotlink text OR Graphics hotlink
<applet>	</applet>	Holds the class name and window size of a Java applet.
<b>	</b>	Bold.
<blink>	</blink>	Blink.
<body background="image.gif" bgcolor="color">	</body>	Brackets all text and graphics. Places background image. Sets background color.
 	none	Line break.
<center>	</center>	Center.
<font size="n" face="style" color="#N">	</font>	Font size, style, and color.
<head>	</head>	Generally holds only the title.
<Hn>	</Hn>	Header level (n = 1–6, where 1 is the largest).
<html>	</html>	Brackets html document.
<hr size="n" noshade width="n"%>	</hr>	Horizontal rule. n = size in pixels. noshade gives indented look. n = % of page.

Opening Tag	Closing Tag	Description
<I>	</I>	Italics.
<IMG SRC="name.gif" align=Hdirection align=Vdirection border="n" width="x" height="y" hspace="x" vspace="y">	none	Place image. Left, right, or center. Top, middle, or bottom. Border thickness. Horizontal width. Vertical height. Horizontal space. Vertical space.
<META Name = " " Content= " " HTTP-EQUIV = " ">	None	Used to create an automatic slide show, and for identification during browser searches.
<OL type=X start=n> <LI>	</OL>	Ordered list. A,A,I,i,1. Initial value. Before each item.
<UL type = shape> <LI>	</UL>	Unordered list. Disk, circle, square. Before each item.
<pre>	</pre>	Preformat. (Maintain line breaks and spacing.)
<P>	none	New paragraph. (Optional: align=direction.)
<table border = n> <Caption align = direction> <TR align = direction> <TH> <TD>	</table> </caption> </TR> </TH> </TD>	Table. Size of border. Caption. Top, middle, bottom. Table row. Left, middle, right. Table header. Table date.
<title>	</title>	Brackets title of document.
<U>	</U>	Underline.

Opening Tag	Closing Tag	Description
<applet>	</applet>	Holds the class name and window size of a Java applet.
<body>	</body>	Brackets all text and graphics.
 	none	Line break.
<head>	</head>	Generally holds only the title.
<Hn>	</Hn>	Header level (n = 1–6, where 1 is the largest.)
<html>	</html>	Brackets html document.
<P>	none	New paragraph.
<title>	</title>	Brackets title of document.

Appendix B

The HTML Design Aids

How would you like to design a dazzling Web page, and then with a magical snap of your finger, turn it into an HTML program? All with little or no knowledge of the HTML language! If this seems like an appealing option then read on.

When using these powerful design aids, in essence we work backwards. That is, we first design the finished product, then we turn it into an HTML program.

> Be aware that the techniques given here are completely optional since you are always free to write an HTML program directly.

- Design the Web page. Using pencil and paper, make a sketch of your Web page design.
- Create a solution. Using standard techniques, create a solution/project of your choice. (For demonstration purposes, we choose solution *ChapterX*, project *ProjectX*.)

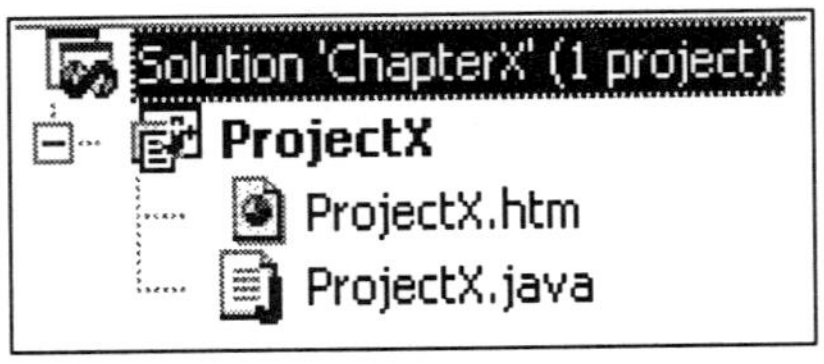

- Enter the *Source* mode. Bring up the HTML program and select the *Source* tab. Simplify the HTML code as listed below.

```
<HTML>
<HEAD>
<TITLE>ProjectX</TITLE>
</HEAD>
<BODY>
<APPLET
  code=ProjectX.class   name=ProjectX
  width=200 height=50 VIEWASTEXT>
</APPLET>
</BODY>
</HTML>
```

- Enter the *Design* mode. Select the *Design* tab. (The Design window will be clear.) **CLICKL** on the *View* menu and bring up the *Toobox* window. Your Developer Studio window should resemble Figure B.1.

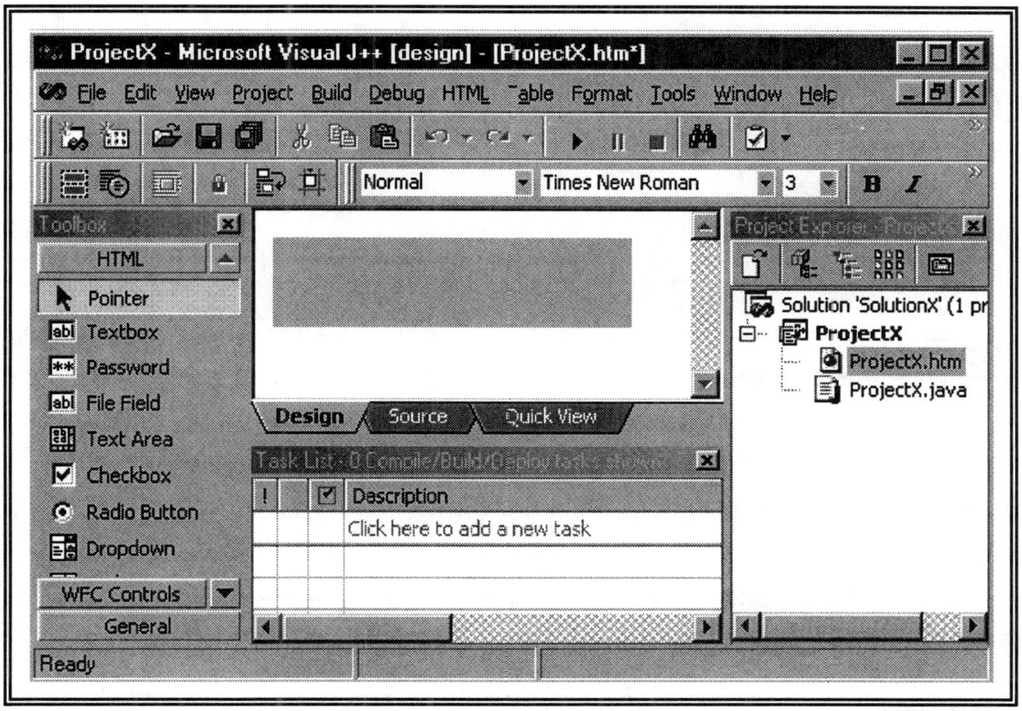

Figure B.1
Window/Toolbar menu

- Enter the first design element. Place the cursor to the left of the applet window and enter text *My Web Page* as the first element.

- Enter a line break (BR). The line break is required so the text will go above the applet window. With the cursor still positioned at the end of the text, **DCLICKL** (double-click-left) on the *Line Break* (BR) toolbox selection. (If you wish, you can select and drag any of the toolbar items to the text window.)

- Modify the text properties. Select the text title (*My Web Page*) and perform all of the following:

  a) Increase the font size to seven.
  b) Press the center toolbar button.
  c) Select any desired foreground and background colors.

  When done, your design should resemble Figure B.2.

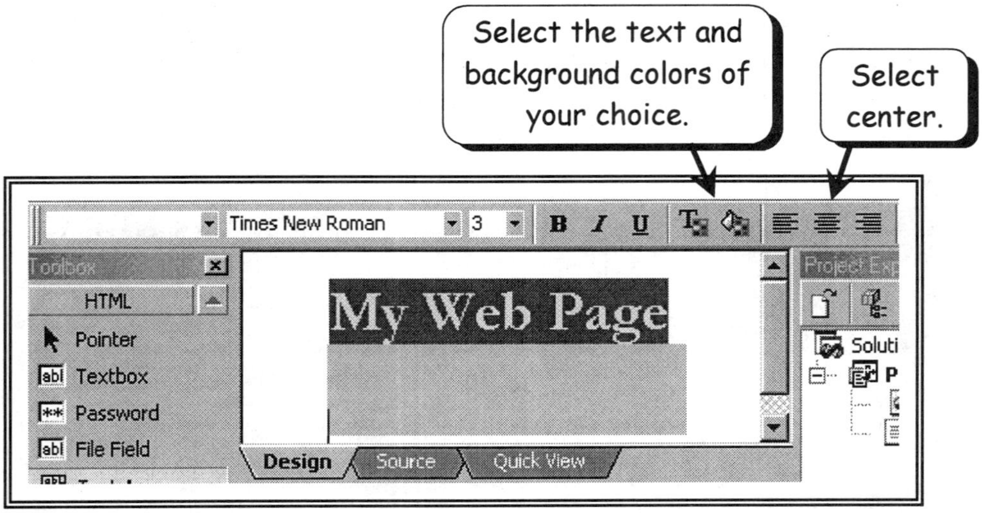

Figure B.2
Using the HTML toolbar

- Check the source code and perform a Quick View. At any time during the design process, you may wish to check the source code or view the window output. To do so, simply select the corresponding tab. Does the code match your design?

```
<DIV align=center><FONT face="" size=3
style="BACKGROUND-COLOR: #ffffff"><STRONG>
<FONT color=yellow face=Garamond size=6
style="BACKGROUND-COLOR: blueviolet">My Web Page</FONT>
</STRONG></FONT><BR> 
```

> Human beings usually can write code that is more compact and efficient than that generated by any machine. Therefore, at regular intervals during the design process, you may wish to return to the *Source* code to clean it up.

- Add a horizontal rule. Using the keyboard, add a single space between the text and the applet. Select horizontal rule within the Tool Box and drag it to just beneath the text. Widen as desired.

- Add other items of your choice. Continuing in like manner, add more text and toolbox selections until your design is complete.

- Enter the Edit HTML mode. At any time, we may switch to the *Edit* mode to modify and refine our design. Open the *View* menu, Other Windows, Document Outline and bring up the configuration of Figure B.3.

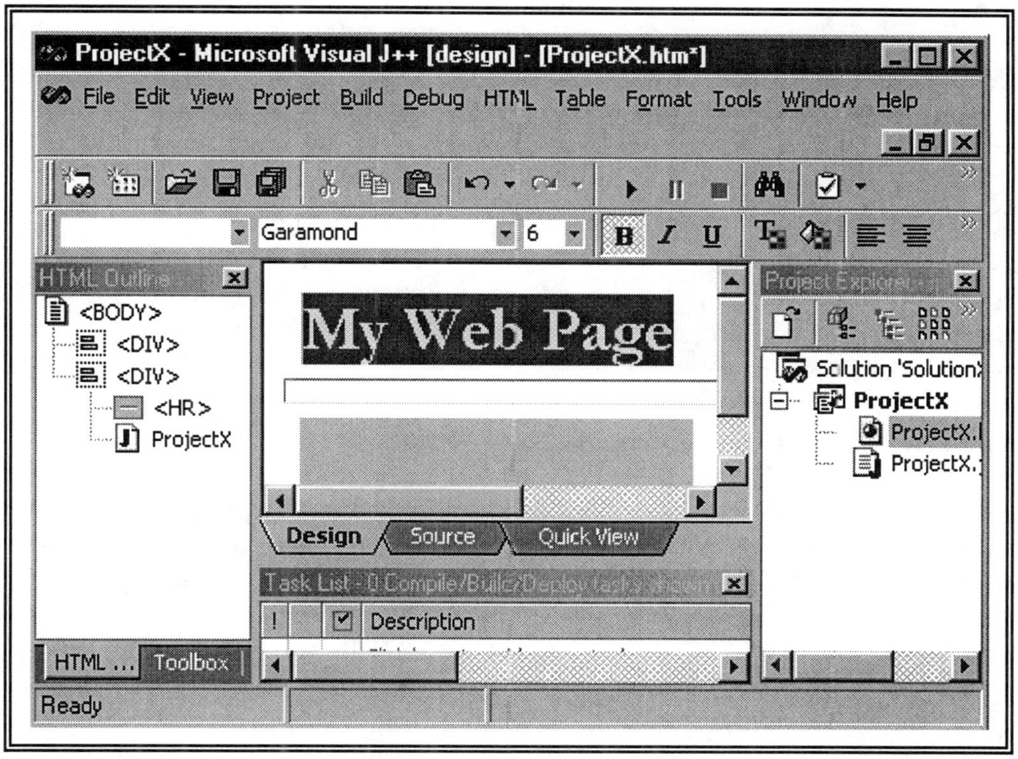

Figure B.3

The *Edit HTML* mode

- Modify any HTML element. Within the HTML Outline window, click various items and note that each is highlighted in the Design window. Make any desired changes to any of the items. (You may also click to select the desired item directly within the Design window.)

- You are on your own. These few steps are designed to get you started. In no way do we pretend to suggest that every nuance and feature of the HTML Rapid Development design system have been covered.

Index